WEBSTER'S 21ST CENTURY™

CONCISE CHRONOLOGY
of
WORLD
HISTORY

WEBSTER'S 21ST CENTURY™

CONCISE CHRONOLOGY

of

WORLD

HISTORY

3000 BC - 1993

David Rubel

NELSON REGENCY

A Division of Thomas Nelson, Inc.

Design: Tilman Reitzle
Editor: Sarah Weir
Contributing Editors: Mark Hoff, Noel Alicea, Julia
Banks, Ben Davis, Lisa Collins, Peter Baer

We would like to thank the following people for their
expertise and kind assistance in reviewing portions of this
chronology: Professor Paula Rubel, Professor Howard
Schless, Professor Alan Segal, Ted Storey, and Jay Tobler.

First published in 1993 by Thomas Nelson Publishers,
Nashville, TN.

Library of Congress Cataloging in-Publication Data

Webster's 21st Century Concise Chronology of World History.
p. cm.
ISBN 0-8407-6879-6 (MM)
ISBN 0-7852-8119-3 (TR)
1. Chronology, Historical   I. Thomas Nelson Publishers.
II. Title: Webster's twenty-first century concise
chronology/world history.
D11.W39   1993
902 ' .02--dc20

Printed in the United States of America

93 94 95 96 97 — 5 4 3 2 1

For my parents,
who taught me

As we found out in compiling this book, a lot happened during the last five thousand years. The Egyptians came and went. So did the Romans. So did Henry D. Perky, who developed the first ready-to-eat breakfast cereal. Shredded Wheat, however, is still with us.

What our editorial team has attempted to do is present a digest of these five millennia. For the most part, we've winnowed out the pebbles of history so that only the boulders remain. But we've also made an effort to produce more than a compendium of dates. Each event listed is also discussed, albeit briefly, so that the reader might gain some sense of context. We've tried to suggest why each event was notable enough for us to consider including it here.

Because history is more than politics, we've paid particular attention to events in the arts, sciences, religion, and philosophy. And to provide a fuller, more intimate chronicle of the average person's life, we've collected a number of tidbits in the Daily Life band. That's where you'll find Henry D. Perky along with his colleagues, the Kellogg brothers, of corn flakes fame.

This is not simply a list of when all the great books were published or when the kings and queens of England reigned. Instead, what you have in your hands is a story—or rather, a history, presented as narrative. The dates by themselves are meaningless. It usually doesn't matter whether something that happened in 1512 happened on a Monday or a Tuesday. What does matter is that the Missouri Compromise of 1820 and the Kansas-Nebraska Act of 1854 led directly to the Civil War in 1861.

This chronology is a road map to the human adventure since 3000 B.C. It lets you see everything at once, so that you can tell which roads lead where. It's compact, of course. After all, a map wouldn't be very useful if its scale were 1:1. We've had to leave a few things out here and there. But not Henry D. Perky.

D.R.

WEBSTER'S 21ST CENTURY™
CONCISE CHRONOLOGY
of
WORLD
HISTORY

3000 BC–476 AD

The Body Politic

c.3000 Menes, king of Upper Egypt, conquers the lower Nile Delta, unifying Egypt and founding the first of 30 dynasties, which rule until 332 BC.

c.2300 The Akkadians in the north, led by Sargon, conquer the Sumerians to the south, uniting Mesopotamia between the Tigris and Euphrates rivers and founding the world's first empire.

c.2100 Theban princes of the Seventh Dynasty reunite Egypt and inaugurate the Middle Kingdom.

c.1800 The Amorite king Hammurabi establishes the first uniform code of laws regulating contracts and private property rights. Criminal law is guided by the principle of "an eye for an eye, a tooth for a tooth."

c.1700-1400 Minoan civilization (named for King Minos) enjoys its golden age on the island of Crete in the Aegean Sea. Minoan society is eventually destroyed by a volcanic eruption.

c.1674 Nomadic Semites from the north conquer Egypt with the help of chariots and domesticated horses, founding the Hyksos Dynasty (until c. 1567 BC).

c.1650 The Hebrews move into areas controlled by Egypt, possibly under the rule of the Semitic Hyksos pharaohs.

Arts & Architecture

c.2800 Pharaoh Zoser and architect Imhotep build the earliest pyramid, the Step Pyramid at Saqqara.

c.2600 The Egyptians construct three pyramids at Giza, including the Great Pyramid of Cheops, and carve the Sphinx.

c.2100 Sumerian king Ur-Nammu builds the Ziggurat of Ur, a spiral tower after which many temples are later modeled.

c.2000 The Cretan palace of King Minos at Knossus introduces interior bathrooms with a water supply.

Religion & Philosophy

c.3000 The Sumerians, the first literate civilization, are using cuneiform, which employs symbols to represent syllables.

c.2700 The earliest references to the Babylonian hero Gilgamesh, revered in epic poetry, date from this time.

Science & Technology

c.3000 Weights and measures are standardized in Mesopotamia and Egypt.

c.3000 The Babylonians predict eclipses.

c.2600 The Chinese use the shadow cast by a vertical pole to estimate time.

c.2400 Sargon of Akkad produces maps of Mesopotamia for the purpose of land taxation.

c.1900 Mesopotamian mathematicians discover what later becomes known as the Pythagorean theorem.

Daily Life

c.3000 Oil-burning lamps come into use.

c.2700 The horse is domesticated in the steppe of Asia and in the Ukraine.

c.2600 Silk production begins in China under the deified Princess Si-Ling Chi.

c.2600 Ink is developed independently in Egypt and China using lampblack.

c.2600 Egyptian queen Hetepheres, mother of Pharaoh Cheops, becomes the first person to be embalmed. Only her internal organs have survived.

c.1500 Reign of Queen Hatshepsut of Egypt, the first recorded female ruler of a country.

c.1400 Achaean warriors invade modern-day Greece from the north, bringing with them iron and establishing the cult of Zeus. Mycenaean civilization develops.

c.1350 Assyria begins its supremacy in Mesopotamia. The Assyrian Empire, based at Nineveh, will eventually reach from the eastern coast of the Mediterranean to the Persian Gulf.

c.1350 Reign of the boy pharaoh Tutankhamen, whose elaborate tomb was discovered by Howard Carter in 1922.

c.1250 The Hebrews leave Egypt in the biblical Exodus, probably during the reign of Pharaoh Ramses II, and establish a religious state in Canaan (modern-day Israel).

c.1200 The Achaeans under King Agamemnon capture Troy after a ten-year siege, as described in Homer's *Iliad*. The key stratagem is a huge wooden horse, presented to the Trojans as a gift, but hiding Greek soldiers within.

c.1200 Shortly after the Trojan War, Dorians from the north begin occupying Achaean lands in Mycenae (southern Greece). Then, taking to the sea, the Dorians invade Crete and Rhodes.

Tutankhamen

---

c.1700 Huge stone circles are erected at Stonehenge and Avebury, possibly by sun-worshiping Druids.

c.1500 Bronze casting develops along the Yellow River in China. Popular subjects are tigers and dragons.

c.1300 Considered the greatest building of its time, the Citadel of Mycenae contains the earliest known European architectural sculpture.

c.1300 Musical notation appears on clay tablets in Syria.

---

c.2200 Hieroglyphic writing (unrelated to Egyptian hieroglyphics) appears in China during the Shang Dynasty.

c.1700 The Phoenicians develop their own alphabet consisting entirely of consonants.

c.1375 Pharaoh Akhnaten and Queen Nefertiti establish monotheistic worship of the sun god Aten in Egypt.

c.1200 Written in Sanskrit, the *Rigveda* hymns are the first of four Vedic texts that comprise the canon of orthodox Hinduism.

---

c.1800 Star catalogs are compiled in Babylonia under Hammurabi.

c.1800 Multiplication tables appear in Mesopotamia.

c.1450 Egyptians build water clocks.

c.1400 The first accurate plan of a city, Nippur in Mesopotamia, is made.

c.1350 Decimals are used in China.

c.1250 The Egyptians build a canal from the Nile to the Red Sea.

---

c.2600 The Egyptians begin writing on papyrus.

c.2500 Glass is first made in Egypt and Mesopotamia.

c.1500 Spun cotton appears in India.

c.1500 The cat is domesticated in Egypt.

c.1400 Iron smelting and weapons become common along the Mediterranean.

c.1150 The game of chess first appears in India.

3000 BC–1001 BC

The Body Politic	**c.961** Solomon becomes king of the Hebrews. He builds a temple in Jerusalem to house the ark of the Covenant. **c.922** Following Solomon's death (circa 933), his sons divide the Hebrew lands into the kingdoms of Israel and Judah. **c.850** Ahab of Israel marries Jezebel, the daughter of Phoenician royalty, consolidating the two kingdoms. **c.822** On the North African coast, Phoenicians found Carthage, later the seat of their Mediterranean trading empire. **c.753** The traditional date of the founding of Rome by Romulus and Remus.	**c.733** Corinthian Greeks establish Syracuse on the island of Sicily. **c.731** The Assyrians conquer Babylon. **c.721** The Assyrians conquer Israel and disperse the ten northern tribes, which become the Lost Tribes of Israel. **686** Athens begins its annual list of archons, ending the monarchy there. **c.660** Jimmu Tenno, the first emperor of Japan, makes his capital south of Kyoto. **621** Draco of Athens issues a harsh code of laws assigning death as punishment for nearly every offense.
Arts & Architecture	**c.850** Homer composes his two epic poems, the *Iliad* and the *Odyssey*. **c.800** The Olmecs build pyramids near modern-day Tabasco, Mexico. **c.750** Hesiod, a Greek poet, flourishes.	**605-563** Nebuchadnezzar rebuilds Babylon. The hanging gardens there are one of the Seven Wonders of the Ancient World. **c.600** The blind slave Aesop writes fables based indirectly on Egyptian and Hindu sources.
Religion & Philosophy	**c.1000** The Torah, encompasssing the five books of Moses that embody Jewish law and teaching, is first set into writing. **c.850** The prophet Elijah opposes the worship of idols. Queen Jezebel, who worships Baal, tries to have him killed.	**c.700-c.500** The *Upanishads* are set into writing. These philosophical works show recent mystic influences on Hinduism. **c.605-520** Life of Lao Ze [Lao Tsu], the founder of Taoism, whose principles are compiled in the *Tao Te Ching*.
Science & Technology	**876** The earliest known written symbol for zero appears in India. **585** Thales of Miletus correctly predicts a solar eclipse on May 28. He later proves several geometrical propositions that become the basis of Euclid's work.	**c.530** The Greek philosopher Anaximenes of Miletus suggests that air is the primary substance and that it can be changed into other forms and substances either by thinning (so that it becomes fire) or by thickening (so that it becomes clouds, earth, and rock).
Daily Life	**c.850** Assyrian boat builders invent the bireme, a galley with two banks of oars. **c.800** Ship building begins in Greece. **c.776** Teams from all over Greece gather for the first recorded Olympic Games.	

612 The Chaldeans take Nineveh, ending the Assyrian Empire and founding a new empire at Babylon (Second Babylonian).

c.594 Athens elects Solon to introduce economic and legal reforms.

586 After a revolt led by Zedekiah, Nebuchadnezzar II occupies Jerusalem. His troops destroy Solomon's Temple and deport the captive Jews to Babylon.

c.550 Sparta founds the Peloponnesian League in southern Greece. Athens and her allies form the rival Delian League.

547 Cyrus the Great of Persia defeats Lydia and Ionia, uniting Asia Minor.

538 Cyrus defeats Babylonia and ends the Babylonian Captivity of the Jews.

525 Cyrus's son Cambyses conquers Egypt, making the Persian Empire the largest in the world to this date.

516 Solomon's Temple is rebuilt in Jerusalem.

c.510 When Sparta attacks Athens, the Athenian tyrant Hippias flees, and Athens is reconstituted as a democracy.

c.509 Rome becomes a republic.

c.506 Athens decisively defeats Sparta at Eleusis.

Confucius

---

c.600 With Sappho, Greek literature begins to display personal expression.

534 Pesistratus of Athens introduces a contest in tragedy. A play by Thespis includes the first actor. Previously, all lines had been spoken by the chorus.

525-456 Life of Aeschylus, considered the father of Greek tragedy. The author of the *Oresteia* and *Seven Against Thebes,* Aeschylus uses two actors on stage along with the chorus, permitting more complicated plots as well as direct confrontation between the characters.

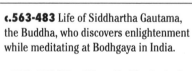

c.563-483 Life of Siddhartha Gautama, the Buddha, who discovers enlightenment while meditating at Bodhgaya in India.

c.551-479 Life of Kong Ze [Confucius], the legendary Chinese philosopher and author of the *Analects.*

---

c.530 Theodorus of Samos is credited with the invention of ore smelting, the bubble level, locks and keys, the carpenter's square, and the lathe.

c.530 The Greek mathematician and philosopher Pythagoras founds a school at

Croton in southern Italy, leading to the formation of the Pythagorean Brotherhood, which later makes striking discoveries in mathematics.

c.520 Anaximander introduces the sundial to Greece.

---

c.600 Tarquin the Younger builds the Circus Maximus for chariot races. Though men and women are usually separated in Roman society, they are not here.

c.600 Romans construct the first large-scale city sewer, the Cloaca Maxima.

c.600 Babylon under Nebuchadnezzar II becomes the largest city in the world with an area of 25,000 acres.

c.560 King Croesus of Lydia mints his own coinage, introducing a monetary economy to replace the barter system.

The Body Politic

c.500 At the height of its influence, with a population of one million people, Carthage has an active gold and ivory trade with West Africa. During a notable voyage, Hanno leads a fleet of 60 ships along the African coast to establish colonies and protect Carthaginian trade routes as far south as Gambia.

499 The Ionian Greeks revolt, but Darius of Persia puts down the rebellion (by 494). Darius then resolves to punish the mainland Greeks who aided the Ionians, beginning the Persian-Greek wars.

490 Ten thousand Greeks under Miltiades of Athens defeat an invading Persian army at Marathon. A messenger carrying news of the victory runs the entire twenty-six miles from Marathon to Athens, where he collapses and dies.

480 Darius's son, Xerxes, returns to Greece with an overwhelming army. He meets little resistance, except at the narrow pass of Thermopylae, where an overmatched force of Greeks under Leonidas fights to the last man. The Persians soon occupy Athens, but when Xerxes attempts to complete his conquest of Greece by forcing the Corinthian isthmus, the Athenian fleet destroys the Persian fleet at Salamis.

479 The Spartans smash the Persian army of occupation at Plataea.

Arts & Architecture

c.495-406 Life of Sophocles, the Greek dramatist and author of *Oedipus Rex* and *Antigone*. He introduces a third actor, reduces the choral odes to interludes, and uses painted sets. He also wins 20 prizes at the annual Dionysian festivals at which all tragedies make their debut.

Religion & Philosophy

c.490 The Greek thinker Gorgias promotes his philosophy of nihilism: that nothing exists, and that if something did, one could not know it.

c.480 Claiming that sense perceptions are all that exist, Protagoras concludes that reality may differ from person to person. Meanwhile, Heracleitus teaches that change is the essence of all things and that fire is the primary substance.

468-457 The Temple of Zeus at Olympia is constructed.

Science & Technology

c.500 The Pythagoreans teach that the earth is a sphere and not a flat disk.

c.500 Pythagorean physician Alcmaeon is the first to dissect human cadavers for scientific purposes. He recognizes the brain as the seat of the intellect.

c.500 The first observatory is erected in Babylon atop the temple of Belus, possibly by the astronomer Naburiannu.

480 Xerxes uses the first floating bridge to enable his army to cross the Hellespont in seven days and nights.

Daily Life

c.490 Darius of Persia has a thousand animals slaughtered each day for the royal table at his capital, Persepolis.

c.486 According to the writings of Confucius, construction begins on the Yun He [Grand Canal] in China.

Repaired and enlarged in the third and sixth centuries, the canal reaches an eventual length of 850 miles.

c.475 Ironworking appears in China a thousand years after becoming commonplace in the Near East.

457-451 Isolationist Sparta defeats Athens in the first of four wars between the two dominant city-states, brought on by Athenian encroachment into the Spartan sphere of influence.

448-429 Pericles rules Athens. The Age of Pericles is characterized by political stability, during which time the arts and philosophy flourish.

c.438 The sculptor Phidias and the architects Actinus and Callicrates complete the Parthenon atop the Acropolis in Athens, where the most important municipal and religious buildings are located. The Parthenon features Doric columns reminiscent of Egyptian and Assyrian styles.

431-404 During the second and third wars between Athens and Sparta, known collectively as the Peloponnesian War, Sparta allies with Corinth to once again defeat the Athenians.

431 Athens withstands a Spartan siege, but suffers a plague from 430-428.

411 The oligarchical Council of 400 replaces the Athenian assembly.

410 Democracy is restored in Athens.

404 With the defeat of Athens ending the Peloponnesian War, the oligarchical Thirty Tyrants temporarily take control of Athens.

Pericles

c.484-429 Life of Herodotus, whose *History* of the Persian wars is the first narrative, but not objective, history.

480-406 Life of Euripides, the Greek tragedian who writes *Medea*, *Iphigenia in Aulis*, and *The Trojan Women*.

470-404 Life of Thucydides, the first "scientific" historian, who writes *The Peloponnesian War*.

c.445-385 Life of Aristophanes, the comic dramatist who writes *The Clouds, The Birds, The Frogs*, and *Lysistrata*.

c.468-399 Life of Socrates, inventor of the Socratic method of question and answer and teacher of Plato.

458 The Temple of Delphi is destroyed by fire. At its height, the Oracle of Delphi was the principal shrine to Apollo.

c.427-347 Life of Plato, student of Socrates and founder of the Academy, where he taught Aristotle. His greatest work, the *Republic*, is thought to have been influenced by his experiences in Syracuse, where he served as an adviser to the tyrant Dionysius.

c.450 Empedocles of Acragas concludes that air, earth, fire, and water are the elemental substances. According to legend, Empedocles dies jumping into the volcano at Mount Etna when the gods fail to take him into the heavens, as he had predicted they would.

c.440 Leucippus of Miletus introduces the idea of the atom as an indivisible unit of matter. He teaches that every natural event has a natural cause.

406 Dionysius the Elder of Syracuse develops the forerunner of the catapult.

c.450 Carrier pigeons are used for long-distance communication in Greece.

c.450 The population of Greece is estimated at four million. The population of Athens is thought to be about one hundred thousand.

500 BC-401 BC

c. 585 BC   Thales of Miletus (a colony in Asia Minor) is the first Greek to develop a
rational, rather than mythological, philosophy. According to Thales, all
things are reducible to a first principle, which is water. Thales himself
becomes wealthy when he corners the market on olive-oil presses.

c. 550 BC   Anaximander of Miletus develops the work of Thales, concluding that the
first principle of all things is *apeiron* [indeterminacy] rather than a specific
form of matter, such as water. His young colleague Anaximenes of Miletus
suggests (circa 530 BC) that air is the fundamental substance and that
other elements are derived from its condensation or rarefaction.

c. 530 BC   Pythagoras of Samos migrates to the Greek colony of Croton in southern
Italy, where he develops a philosophy both mystical and scientific. Pythagoras's discovery that musical intervals can be expressed as ratios of whole
numbers leads him to believe that mathematics might contain the key to
understanding the universe.

c. 500 BC   A refugee from Cyrus the Great's conquest of Ionia (547 BC), Xenophanes of
Colophon resettles in Elea (southern Italy), where he attacks the anthropo-
morphism of the Homeric gods. If horses had hands, Xenophanes writes,
they would draw their gods in forms that resemble horses.

c. 475 BC   Parmenides of Elea develops Xenophanes's argument into a more general
philosophy of being, concluding that nothing new can be created nor anything destroyed. If something is, Parmenides argues, it could not have
arisen out of nothing, nor could it become nothing. Meanwhile, Heracleitus
of Ephesus expounds the idea that all things are constantly in flux, even
the mountains (albeit very slowly). Parmenides's pupil Zeno of Elea develops a set of famous paradoxes designed to discredit those who argue for
the existence of plurality and motion.

c. 450 BC   Living in a world shaped by the thought of Parmenides, Empedocles of
Acragas attempts to reconcile the Parmenidean doctrine that nothing can
be created with the human experience that things change. He concludes
that two forces (love and hate) bring the material elements (fire, air, earth,
and water) together and separate them. Anaxagoras of Clazomenae also

believes in a multiplicity of things, but the generating principle, according to Anaxagoras, is not indeterminate love and hate, but a purposeful *nous* [intelligence].

About this time, the Sophists (named after the Greek *sophizesthai* [the profession of being inventive and clever]) become influential. These teachers, who charge fees for their instruction, oppose the distinction, made by their predecessors, between the "real" world of absolutes and the phenomenal world in which people live. Attributed to Protagoras of Meno is the famous dictum that "Man is the measure of all things, of those which are that they are and of those which are not that they are not."

c.440 BC Leucippus of Miletus, the first of the atomists, disagrees with the Parmenidean proposition that nothing cannot exist. Rather, he argues that it exists as empty space. In Leucippus's view, the physical world is divided into empty space and space that is filled with absolutely indivisible atoms, the building blocks of matter. His young colleague Democritus of Abdera develops a universal system based on Leucippus's ideas, which later appears in Lucretius's *De rerum natura* (57 BC) and serves as a subject for the Ph.D. dissertation of Karl Marx.

c.468 BC
−399 BC The life of Socrates, who is considered a Sophist by many of his contemporaries (because of his tricky arguments), but who actually opposes the Sophists' arrogant use of their forensic skills to make the worse argument appear the better. Socrates's habit of making his points by asking leading questions becomes enshrined as the "Socratic method."

c.427 BC
−347 BC The life of Plato, who writes dialogues, including the *Republic,* which often feature Socrates as the principal character. Plato's absolutist philosophy, most famously expressed in his myth of the cave (from the *Politeia*), focuses on the world of perfect Ideas, of which worldly objects are merely imperfect representations.

c.384 BC
−322 BC The life of Aristotle, a student at the Academy founded by Plato, who eventually founds a rival school in Athens (the Lyceum). Reacting against Plato, who insists upon the importance of absolutes, Aristotle relies instead upon empirical observation and a sense of moderation and balance.

The Body Politic

c.400 The beginnings of the Mayan civilization in the Mexican Yucatan.

c.400 Egypt revolts successfully against Persian rule.

392 After a series of expeditions intended to punish the expansionist Syracusans, Carthage agrees to a peace treaty that restores prewar frontiers and resurrects Syracuse as the protector of the western Greeks.

c.380 The declining Persian Empire loses control of its provinces in India.

359 Philip II becomes king of Macedon (until 336) and begins building the great-est army in the region using the wealth he has obtained from newly discovered gold deposits.

338 Philip II smashes a combined army of Thebans and Athenians at Chaeronea, uniting Greece under his complete control. Then Philip announces a crusade against Persia.

336 With the assassination of Philip II, possibly arranged by the Persians, Philip's 20-year-old son, Alexander, inherits Philip's army and the ever-expanding Macedonian empire.

334 Crossing the Hellespont, Alexander defeats a Persian army on the banks of

Arts & Architecture

356 The Temple of Artemis at Ephesus, one of the Seven Wonders of the Ancient World, is burned by a man named Herostratus seeking immortality.

354 A tomb for King Mausolus of Caria is built at Halicarnassus. This first "mau-soleum" is one of the Seven Wonders of the Ancient World.

351 Demosthenes, the greatest of all Greek orators, delivers a series of bitter *Philippics* condemning King Philip II of Macedon.

Religion & Philosophy

399 Socrates is condemned to death for allegedly corrupting the morals of the youth of Athens. Refusing to flee the city, he chooses instead to drink a draught of hemlock and die rather than break the social contract he has made with the state.

c.390 Plato founds his school, the Academy, in a grove on the outskirts of Athens. It continues as a place of learning until 529 AD.

c.384-322 Life of Aristotle, author of the *Rhetoric*, the *Poetics*, the *Metaphysics*,

Science & Technology

c.400 Hippocrates establishes the profession of physician when he separates medicine from both religion and superstition. He also develops the Hippocratic oath, still taken by physicians today, and founds the first medical school on the island of Cos.

Daily Life

c.400 The semi-legendary Chinese artisan Lu Pan makes the first known kite.

c.350 The poor of Athens subsist mainly on beans, greens, beechnuts, turnips, wild pears, dried figs, barley paste, and sometimes grasshoppers.

350 References first appear in Greek writings to wheat imported from Egypt that is suitable for breadmaking.

334 Upon his return from Macedon, Aristotle founds the Lyceum in Athens, named after and dedicated to Apollo

the Granicus, which wins Anatolia for him and leads to the capture of Ionia.

333 Alexander defeats a huge Persian army under Darius III at Issus before continuing his march down the coast.

332 Alexander enters Egypt, where he founds Alexandria as a cosmopolitan center of learning that soon attracts many Greeks and Jews.

331 At the battle of Arbela, Alexander defeats the last Persian army under Darius III.

326 Alexander invades present-day Afghanistan, then marches through the

Khyber Pass into India, where he defeats an army supported by elephants. Alexander's troops refuse to continue when he orders a march to the Ganges.

323 Alexander the Great dies of a fever at the age of 33. Though central rule is maintained for a short time, the empire is ultimately divided among five generals: Antigonus (Anatolia and Syria), Cassander (Macedon), Lysimachus (Thrace), Ptolemy (Egypt), and Seleucus (the former Persian Empire).

301 Antigonus tries to reunite Alexander's empire, but he is defeated by the armies of Cassander, Lysimachus, and Seleucus at the battle of Ipsus.

Alexander the Great

---

323 Ptolemy, along with Alexander a student of Aristotle, founds the Museum at Alexandria and staffs it with professors whose salaries are paid by the state.

312 Appius Claudius Caecus begins construction of a thoroughfare, the Via Appia,

from Rome to Alba Longa. It is later extended to Capua and Brindisi. In the same year, Appius Claudius Caecus also orders the construction of the first Roman aqueduct, the Aqua Appia. This aqueduct will carry fresh water to Rome from springs ten miles away.

---

and the *Politics*. Along with his teacher Plato, Aristotle remains one of the two most influential Greek philosophers.

c.372-289 Life of Meng Ze [Mencius], a Chinese philosopher who teaches that human nature is inherently good.

342 Aristotle travels to Macedon at the invitation of Philip II to tutor the king's 14-year-old son, Alexander.

c.302 Zeno founds the Stoic school in Athens, which advocates living according to nature and the natural law.

---

c.380 Plato reportedly invents a water clock with an alarm.

c.370 Aristotle discovers that free fall is a form of accelerated motion, but he mistakenly believes that heavier objects fall faster than lighter ones.

352 Chinese observers record the earliest known sighting of a supernova.

c.350 Dinostratus squares the circle.

c.320 The lost *Conics* of Aristaeus dates from this time.

Lyceus, the god of shepherds. It houses a museum of natural history, a zoo, and a library.

c.330 Archestratus writes the humorous cookbook *Heduphagetica* about his travels in search of foreign delicacies.

327 Campaigning in India, Alexander the Great's soldiers discover the banana and sugar cane.

c.301 The Chinese build an irrigation network to control flooding in the Red Basin of Szechuan.

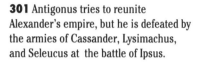

400 BC – 301 BC

The Body Politic

298 Demetrius, the son of Antigonus, takes Macedon after the death of Cassander, but he is soon forced out by Lysimachus, and after a campaign in Anatolia, he becomes a prisoner of Seleucus.

281 The army of King Pyrrhus of Epirus arrives in Italy at the invitation of the western Greeks of Tarentum. Threatened by the Romans, the Tarentines turn to Pyrrhus as a champion of the Hellenistic cause. Pyrrhus wins many battles, but he cannot secure the country.

280 At the battle of Heraclea, Pyrrhus wins the field completely, but loses so many men that his army is nearly broken, hence the term *pyrrhic victory*.

280 At Corupedium in Ionia, Seleucus defeats Lysimachus, who is killed during the battle. Seleucus then crosses to Macedon, possibly to begin the reconstitution of Alexander's empire, but he is assassinated as he steps off the boat.

279 Gauls begin to encroach on Macedon and Greece. When Demetrius's son, Antigonus II, forces them from Macedon, three tribes cross the Hellespont and establish Galatia in the Anatolian interior.

264-241 Rome and Carthage fight the first Punic War over Sicily. Syracuse allies with Carthage, but then switches to Rome, which gradually wins control with the aid of its newly formed navy .

Arts & Architecture

283 Sostratus of Cnibus builds a lighthouse at Pharos, an island in the harbor of Alexandria. Among the Seven Wonders of the Ancient World, the lighthouse rises to a height of 550 feet. Always lit, it is visible for a distance of more than 40 miles out to sea.

c.280 The sculptor Chares builds the Colossus of Rhodes, an immense bronze figure of the sun god Helios. Another of the Seven Wonders of the Ancient World, the statue takes 12 years to complete and stands approximately 70 cubits high (over 100 feet). Legends from the 16th century,

Religion & Philosophy

c.300 The Chinese develop the concept of *yin* and *yang*. These paired opposites represent the two forces thought to be acting in the universe.

232 Death of King Ashoka, widely known as the "Buddhist Constantine" for his role in converting much of northern India to Buddhism.

213 Emperor Shi Huang Di orders the burning of all Confucian texts, except for a single copy of each to be kept in the Chinese State Library.

Science & Technology

c.300 Euclid writes his *Elements* at Alexandria, summarizing the knowledge of geometry in what becomes a classic work.

287-212 Life of Archimedes, the Alexandrian mathematician who develops the principle of the lever and those of other simple machines. He demonstrates the effectiveness of the lever by pulling a large ship onto land by himself.

c.270 Aristarchus of Samos asserts that the sun is the center of the universe and that the earth revolves around it.

Daily Life

c.300 Carthage builds an economic empire in the Mediterranean, trading Egyptian linen, African ivory, Arabian incense, and many other exotic items.

c.300 Carthage produces the finest ships in the world, quinquiremes, with five banks of oars rowed by government-owned galley slaves.

c.300 The Chinese invent cast iron.

c.300 The Greek navigator Pytheas leads an expedition past Gibraltar, around the

c.256 China is unified under the Qin Dynasty. Confucianism is suppressed.

c.230 The state of Qi develops the system of federal bureaucracy that will manage China for the next two millenia.

227 Relieved of Carthaginian rule, Sicily, Sardinia, and Corsica are made provinces of Rome.

219-201 The second Punic War develops out of a conflict between Rome and Carthage over Saguntum in Spain. Following Rome's declaration of war, Carthage's proconsul in Spain, Hannibal, crosses the Alps with a train of elephants and invades the Po Valley.

216 Hannibal defeats four legions of Romans (about 20,000 men) at Cannae. For the next decade, while Hannibal's army roams the countryside, the Romans avoid major engagements and restrict themselves to a strategy of harassment.

c.215 The Great Wall of China is built to keep out Hun invaders from the north.

204 Scipio lands a Roman army in North Africa and twice beats Carthage's army.

202 Hannibal is recalled to defend Carthage, but he is defeated at Zama.

201 Carthage surrenders to Rome all its Mediterranean colonies, including Spain.

Hannibal

---

however, credit the Colossus with a height of 700 cubits, so tall that ships were able to pass between its legs, which stood astride the harbor. An earthquake destroyed the Colossus in 224 BC, and it lay in pieces for a thousand years before a Jew, sent by the Saracens, bought the

pieces so that they could be recast into instruments of war.

206 The Qin Dynasty ends with the death of Emperor Shi Huang Di. His tomb is later found to hold 8,000 life-size ceramic figures, each with a unique face.

---

c.260 The *Mo Ching*, written by the followers of Chinese philosopher Mo Ze, contains a statement of what will become Newton's first law of motion.

c.240 Eratosthenes uses a simple geometric formula to calculate the circumfer-

ence of the earth. His method involves measuring the height of the sun at two points of known latitude (Alexandria and Syene) simultaneously.

c.220 Apollonius of Perga discovers the ellipse and the hyperbola.

British Isles, and possibly as far north as Iceland and Norway.

268 The Roman denarius, a silver coin, is minted for the first time. With the ascendancy of Rome, its use becomes common throughout the Western world.

c.265 Gladiatorial combat becomes an increasingly popular spectacle in Rome.

c.250 Rome builds its first prison.

c.210 In Pergamum, parchment is developed from the processed skin of animals.

The Body Politic

197 Fearing a military alliance between Macedon and the Seleucid Kingdom, the Roman Senate sends two legions against Philip V of Macedon. Sophisticated Roman troops crush Philip's phalanx at Cynoscephalae in Thessaly, marking the end of hoplite warfare, which had dominated Greek military strategy since the ascendance of Sparta.

192 In response to a Roman declaration of war, the Seleucid king Antiochus III forms an alliance with the Aetolians and sends an army to Greece.

191 At Thermopylae, the Romans defeat Antiochus's army using the same maneuver Xerxes did in 480 BC.

190 The Romans destroy the Seleucid army at Magnesia in Asia Minor—and with it the means by which Antiochus's empire is maintained. The kingdom quickly breaks apart, leaving only Syria, Palestine, Mesopotamia, and Cilicia under the control of the Seleucids.

167 Anticipating a revolt in Judaea, the Seleucid king Antiochus IV sacks Jerusalem and pillages the Temple there. He leaves behind him an army of occupation, which suppresses all Jewish religious rites in favor of Hellenism and gives the Temple over to the worship of Zeus Olympius. These actions provoke the Maccabean revolt, led by the Jewish priest Mattathias of Modein.

Arts & Architecture

196 The Rosetta Stone honoring Ptolemy V Epiphanes is engraved in hieroglyphic and demotic Egyptian as well as in Greek. Unearthed in 1799, it will provide the key that permits Jean Champollion to decipher the inscriptions on the ancient monuments in Egypt.

Religion & Philosophy

c.200 The Indian epics *Ramayana* and *Mahabharata* are written. The *Ramayana* tells the story of Prince Rama, while the *Mahabharata*, which includes the *Bhagavad Gita*, takes the form of a dialogue between Prince Arjuna and his charioteer Krishna.

c.200 The first written version of the *I-Ching* appears. The oldest Chinese text, it is commonly ascribed to Wen, founder of the Zhou Dynasty (circa 1122 BC).

167-164 The Maccabees break with Jewish tradition by violating the Sabbath

Science & Technology

c.200 Concrete is first used in the Roman town of Palestrina.

c.180 The 360-degree circle is introduced into Greek mathematics, probably by Hypsicles in his *De ascensionibus*, a book on astronomy. Hypsicles also writes a

manuscript later printed as Book XIV of Euclid's *Elements*.

c.170 Rome boasts the first paved streets in the world. They are easier to clean and passable in all weather, but much noisier than unpaved roads.

Daily Life

c.200 The population of Alexandria is estimated at 500,000 people.

c.170 The first commercial bakers appear in Rome, although most households continue to grind their own flour and bake their own bread.

168 Female Macedonians captured by Rome at the battle of Pydna are sold into slavery for prices as much as 50 times higher than those brought by males.

c.140 The Chinese begin to make paper. They use it as a packing material, for

164 Mattathias's son, Judas Maccabaeus, recaptures Jerusalem and rededicates the Temple. The festival of Hanukkah is the annual commemoration of this event. Legend has it that upon retaking the Temple, the Maccabees found only enough oil to keep a light burning for one day, yet it miraculously lasted for eight.

153 Rome officially shifts the beginning of its civil calendar from March 15 to January 1, creating the present New Year's Day.

149-146 The third Punic War is dominated by the Roman siege of Carthage, which ends finally with the razing of the city and the plowing under of its ashes.

146 Weary of Greek factionalism, the Romans place the entire peninsula under direct Senatorial rule.

142 The Syrians grant autonomy to the Jews, now led by Judas Maccabaeus's brother, Simon.

141 The Parthians take Mesopotamia from the Seleucids.

138 Han emperor Wu Di sends Zhang Qian to the West in the hope of forming a military alliance against the Xiongnu [Huns]. Zhang reaches Bactria in present-day Afghanistan, but he does not realize that Bactria is merely the eastern fringe of the Hellenistic world.

Marcus Tullius Cicero

---

179 The Romans build the first stone bridge, the Pons Aemilius over the Tiber.

c.140 The Venus de Milo, a classic work of Greek sculpture, dates from this time. It will be rediscovered in 1820 among the ruins of a theater.

106-43 Life of Marcus Tullius Cicero, a man of modest origins whose eloquence won him a prominent place in the Roman Senate. The orations for which Cicero is remembered champion the high ideals of the Roman republic against the impending imperial monarchy.

---

to the extent that they resist attacks launched by those Hellenized Jews whom Antiochus has left in control of Jerusalem.

149 Hu Shin produces a Chinese dictionary of some 10,000 characters.

141-87 Reign of Han emperor Wu Di, who reluctantly supports an updated version of Confucianism as the basis for imperial government. The new state cult is implemented through the imperial university as well as through the examination system used to select public officials.

---

165 Astronomers in China record the earliest known sightings of what become known as sunspots.

c.140 Han Ying makes the first known references to the hexagonal shape of snowflakes.

c.130 Hipparchus of Nicaea, considered the most important astronomer of his time, uses parallax calculations made during a total eclipse of the sun to estimate accurately the distance from the earth to the moon as well as the size of the moon itself.

---

clothing, and for personal hygiene, but not for writing.

138 Caravans accompanying Zhang Qian on his extraordinary diplomatic mission bring the first peaches and apricots (called "Chinese fruit") to the West. Upon

his return to China, Zhang Qian brings back with him wine grapes, pomegranates, and walnuts.

110 Romans begin to cultivate oysters near present-day Naples, becoming the first Westerners to domesticate seafood.

c.100 An average of one caravan a month travels along the Silk Road, established by Han emperor Wu Di to export Chinese woven silks across Persia to the West.

73 Spartacus escapes from a gladiatorial school at Capua. With an army of 70,000 fellow runaway slaves and peasants, he begins the Slave War, defeating the legions sent against him and threatening Rome until his defeat in 71 by Crassus.

60 Pompey, Crassus, and Julius Caesar form the First Triumvirate to rule Rome.

56 Cicero tries to revive constitutional government. Pompey, Crassus, and Caesar meet at Luca to renew their coalition.

54 Riots and anarchy threaten Rome. The Senate turns to Pompey for protection.

53 The Parthians defeat and kill Crassus at Carrhae, leaving Pompey and Caesar to compete for leadership in Rome.

49 With his command due to expire, Caesar decides to stand for consul. The Senate, looking for a confrontation, insists that he first disband his legions. Caesar refuses, and when his last compromise is rejected, he crosses the Rubicon and invades Italy. "*Alea iacta est* [The die is cast]," he says.

48 Caesar defeats Pompey at Pharsalus in Thessaly. Pompey flees to Egypt and is

Arts & Architecture

c.100 At the Mexican religious center of Teotihuacán, construction begins on giant earth pyramids that will later be used by the Toltecs and the Aztecs.

65-8 Life of Horace, the Roman lyric poet and critic who is well known for his *Odes*.

63 Cicero delivers his first speech against the conspirator Catiline to the Roman Senate.

59-17AD Life of Livy, the Roman historian and most important prose writer of the Augustan age.

Religion & Philosophy

97 The Roman Senate forbids the practice of human sacrifice.

57 With *De rerum natura*, Titus Lucretius Caro revives Epicurean philosophy. He discusses the atomic nature of matter suggested by Democritus and insists that

fate is controlled not by inscrutable gods, but by the laws of nature.

47 Julius Caesar sets fire to the Egyptian fleet in the harbor at Alexandria, but the fire accidentally spreads to the Brucheum quarter and destroys the great library

Science & Technology

c.100 Negative numbers appear in Chinese mathematics.

c.80 The Greek physician Asclepiades is the first to distinguish between acute and chronic disease. Among his patients are Crassus, Cicero, and Antony.

c.80 Engineers in Greece invent the differential gear, allowing wheels on the same axle to turn independently.

52 Chinese astronomer Gen Shou Zhang builds an armillary ring, which he uses to observe the stars.

Daily Life

c.80 Gaius Sergius Orata develops a method for using the hollow spaces under floors (hypocausts) to heat Roman baths and houses using a central furnace.

63 Marcus Tullius Tiro, once a slave of Cicero, invents a method of shorthand.

54 Campaigning in Britain, Julius Caesar discovers the local Cheshire cheese.

c.50 The Syrians introduce glass blowing.

c.50 The Romans use sharpened goose quills for pens.

killed there. Caesar follows Pompey to Egypt, where he begins an affair with Cleopatra, the last of the Ptolemies.

47 Campaigning near Zela in Asia Minor, Caesar defeats Pharnaces III of Pontus. "*Veni, vidi, vici* [I came, I saw, I conquered]," Caesar declares.

45 Caesar bests Pompey's sons at Munda, confirming himself as ruler of the Roman world. He adopts his great-nephew Octavius (later Octavian) as his heir.

44 A month after being named dictator for life, Caesar is assassinated in the Senate on the ides of March (MAR 15) by republicans led by Brutus and Cassius.

42 Marcus Antonius [Mark Antony] and Octavian defeat Brutus and Cassius at the battle of Philippi, destroying the last hopes of the republican party.

41 Antony meets and adores Cleopatra.

31 Octavian's general Agrippa defeats the forces of Antony and Cleopatra at the naval battle of Actium. The couple escapes, but commits suicide a year later.

27 The Senate grants Octavian the title Augustus, denoting his primacy among Rome's magistrates. With the dictatorial powers also granted him, Augustus founds the Roman Empire and, taking the name Caesar, becomes its first emperor.

Julius Caesar

---

56 Famous for his lyrics, Catullus pens *Ave atque vale*, an elegy for his brother.

c.50 Vitruvius writes a book on Roman architecture and construction methods that will later become the primary Renaissance source for classicism.

38 In Rhodes, Agesander, Polydorus, and Athenodorus sculpt the *Laocoön*.

19 Virgil writes the greatest of Roman epics, the *Aeneid*. Based on the Homeric legends, it tells of the wanderings of Aeneas and the founding of Rome.

---

there. The smaller library in the Serapeum survives.

40 To replace the manuscripts lost in the Brucheum fire, Antony builds a new library and fills it with 200,000 scrolls from the library at Pergamum.

---

c.50 The *Ayurveda* is written, forming the basis of Hindu medical knowledge.

c.50 Andronikos of Kyrrhestes builds the Tower of Winds in Athens, a combination water-solar clock that is the most famous timekeeping device in Greece.

46 Acting on the advice of Sosigenes of Alexandria, a Greek mathematician and astronomer, Julius Caesar institutes the Julian calendar of 365.25-day years. January 1 remains the first day of the year. To realign the seasons, the year 46 has 445 days.

---

c.50 Canal locks are in use in China.

29 Octavian reopens ancient trade routes between Egypt and India.

27 Agrippa builds the first large public baths in Rome.

19 Agrippa builds the Aqua Virgo aqueduct to supply public baths in Rome.

c.10 Herod the Great, king of Judaea, constructs the first open-sea harbor at Caesarea Palestinae, using concrete poured into huge wooden forms.

The Body Politic	**6** Ten years after the death of Herod the Great, who ruled Palestine from 37-4 BC, Judaea becomes a province of Rome. **14** Augustus dies and, despite republican laws prohibiting a dynastic succession, his stepson Tiberius becomes emperor. **23** A famine triggers peasant revolts in China. The usurper Wang Mang, whose reforms benefited the poor, is killed. **25** The Han Dynasty in China is restored, becoming the Eastern (or Later) Han. **26** Pontius Pilate is named procurator of Judaea (until 36). As such, he sanctions the crucifixion of Jesus of Nazareth.	**37** Upon his death, Tiberius Caesar is succeeded by his murderous, profligate, and possibly insane nephew, Caligula. **41** Caligula's personal Praetorian Guard assassinates him and installs as emperor his infirm uncle Claudius, believed to be weak and incompetent. The Senate's acquiescence proves the subordination of republican traditions to the imperial. **43-47** Showing surprisingly capable leadership, Claudius conquers and proceeds to Romanize southern Britain. **49** Claudius marries his niece Agrippina, who convinces him to bypass his own son and name her son Nero as heir.
Arts & Architecture	**c.1** The Chinese use cast iron to build suspension bridges that are strong enough for vehicles to cross. **8** Having already banned Ovid's work, Augustus now exiles the poet of the *Metamorphoses* and the scandalous *Ars*	*amatoria* [*The art of love*] to Tomis on the Black Sea. **46-120** Life of Plutarch, the Greek biographer whose most celebrated work is *Parallel Lives*. His miscellaneous essays are collected in the *Opera moralia*.
Religion & Philosophy	**c.30** John the Baptist is beheaded. **c.33** Jesus of Nazareth is crucified at Golgotha between two thieves. **c.36** On the road to Damascus, intending to persecute the Christians there, the	rabbi Saul of Tarsus has a vision and converts to Christianity. After his conversion, he takes the name Paul. **c.49** Paul writes his *Epistle to the Thessalonians*, the earliest New Testament document.
Science & Technology	**c.25** For his *Geography*, Strabo collects all the geographical information known to his time. The dimensions he gives for the earth are substantially correct. **30** Aulus Cornelius Celsus collects Greek medical writing in his *De res medicos*.	**31** The Chinese develop a water-powered bellows for working with cast iron. **c.50** Pliny the Elder writes the *Historia naturalis*, a 37-volume encyclopedia summarizing contemporary knowledge of astronomy, geography, geology, botany,
Daily Life	**c.1** Estimates place the world's population at 250 million, up from 100 million circa 3000 BC. The Roman imperial population is between 70 and 100 million. With about one million Jews in Egypt, Alexandria is now considered the population center of world Jewry.	**c.1** The earliest ironworking found in Zambia dates from this period. **c.25** The Roman epicure Apicius invents a number of cakes and sauces and writes about cooking, perhaps even compiling a cookbook.

54 Agrippina has Claudius poisoned so that she can rule Rome through Nero, who is accepted as the new emperor.

59 Nero has his mother Agrippina killed.

64 A fire started at the Circus Maximus razes two-thirds of Rome. Nero probably did not fiddle as the city burned.

66 Jewish revolutionary Zealots ignite a popular uprising in Jerusalem that soon spreads through Judaea and Galilee. Nero names Vespasian to restore Roman rule.

68 Having been condemned to death by the Senate, Nero commits suicide, ending the Julio-Claudian line of emperors.

69 With the triumph of his allies in the civil war among Rome's armies, Vespasian becomes the first Flavian emperor.

70 Vespasian's son Titus retakes Jerusalem and burns the Temple. A surviving wall becomes the famous "Wailing Wall."

73 Jewish Zealots holding out at Masada kill themselves rather than submit.

96 With the murder of the last Flavian emperor, Domitian, the Senate names the former consul Nerva as his successor.

97 Nerva adopts as his heir the popular general Trajan, who becomes emperor upon Nerva's death in 98.

Nero

58-138 Life of Juvenal, the Roman satirist whose poems will influence nearly all European satire to follow.

64 The rebuilding of Solomon's Temple, begun by Herod the Great in 20 BC, is completed. This is the Third Temple.

71 The first public lavatory opens in Rome. It has urinals and flush toilets.

75-82 The Colosseum is built in Rome. Dedicated in 80 by the emperor Titus with three months of celebration, it seats 50,000 people.

---

49 Claudius expels the Jews from Rome.

c.62 The Romans execute Paul, the most important missionary of the early Church.

64 The first persecution of Christians begins in Rome under Nero.

c.65 *The Gospel According to St. Mark*, first of the four gospels, is written.

65 During the reign of Han emperor Ming Di, a mission of 18 Chinese journey to Khotan in eastern Turkestan to inquire into the teachings of Buddhism.

---

and zoology. His information comes entirely from secondary sources.

79 After watching the eruption of Mount Vesuvius with his uncle, who is killed, Pliny the Younger writes the first detailed report of a volcano's eruption.

84 Fu An and Jia Gui improve the armillary ring used for locating stars by adding a second ring that shows the movement of the sun through the sky.

c.90 Chinese mathematicians develop magic squares 300 years before the West.

---

43 Romans found Londinium (London).

c.50 Soap, a Gallic invention, is introduced to Rome by the Germans.

79 Mount Vesuvius erupts, destroying Pompeii and Herculaneum.

AD 1-99

The Body Politic

106 Massing ten legions along a troublesome northern border, Trajan overwhelms Dacia and makes it Rome's first and only province north of the Danube.

114-116 Campaigning in the style of Alexander, Trajan reduces Armenia, Assyria, and Mesopotamia to provincial status and invades the Parthian Empire.

117 Stricken with an incurable illness, Trajan dies a few days after adopting his nephew Hadrian as his imperial heir. Hadrian's rule will be characterized by a sense of limits. Almost immediately, he surrenders Trajan's newly won provinces and consolidates the Roman Empire within rational and defensible borders.

121-126 Hadrian visits the frontiers of his empire, traveling to Africa, Britain, the Rhine, the Danube, Anatolia, Greece, Arabia, and Egypt.

122-127 Hadrian's Wall, another defensible border, is built between Scotland and England to keep out the Picts and Caledonians.

132 Hadrian's founding of a new Roman city (Aelia Capitolina) at Jerusalem, his dedication of a temple to Jupiter there, and his prohibition of circumcision combine to trigger a Jewish revolt led by Simon Bar Kokhba. Believing Simon to be a messiah, the rebels take Jerusalem and attempt to rebuild the Temple.

Arts & Architecture

106 The 125-foot-high Column of Trajan is built with reliefs depicting the emperor's conquest of the Dacians.

c.115 Tacitus writes the *Annales* and the *Historia*, concise biographies of Roman emperors from Tiberius to Domitian.

Religion & Philosophy

130 Under the direction of Hadrian, work is completed on the Temple of Olympian Zeus in Athens, the largest temple in Greece.

c.150 Alexandria becomes a center for the study of Christian theology.

c.176 Marcus Aurelius resumes the persecutions of Christians. The last persecutions were carried out under Domitian. Since then, Christians have been protected by Trajan and Hadrian and tolerated by Antoninus. To continue practicing their religion, many Christians secretly take

Science & Technology

132 Zhang Heng invents a seismograph. His device uses a ball that drops from the mouth of a bronze dragon into the mouth of a bronze frog.

c.140 Ptolemy writes his *Megale syntaxis tes astronomias* [*Great astronomical com-*

position]. Later renamed the *Almagest* by Arabs, it becomes the most important astronomical text of the Middle Ages.

146 Galen of Pergamum begins the study of medicine, eventually becoming the most celebrated physician of his day.

Daily Life

110 The oldest surviving piece of paper used for writing dates from this time in China, where the eunuch Zai Lun is widely known for his papermaking skill.

118 Rome, the world's most populous city, swells to over one million people.

125 The poet Juvenal writes of "bread and circuses" and their use as palliatives to pacify the Roman masses.

125 An outbreak of the plague decimates entire villages throughout North Africa and Italy.

135 Hadrian's legions drive the Jewish nationalists from Jerusalem. Henceforth, Jews are forbidden to enter Jerusalem on pain of death.

138 Hadrian dies, but continuing the tradition of "adoptive" emperors begun by Nerva, he passes on the imperial purple to Antoninus Pius, who has been chosen for his fitness to rule.

161 Marcus Aurelius becomes emperor of Rome, succeeding Antoninus Pius whose reign has been marked by economic prosperity and public works construction.

180 Marcus Aurelius ignores the practice of adopting a capable successor and instead, on his death, leaves the empire to his son Commodus.

192 Commodus is assassinated at the instigation of his concubine and his favorite servant. The struggle to succeed him begins a civil war similar to that following the death of Nero.

193 The Praetorian Guard assassinates Publius Helfius Pertinax, the Senate's first choice to succeed Commodus. Then Didius Julianus attempts to use his wealth to buy the throne, despite warnings from the provincial legions. Finally, Septimius Severus, commander of the Danubian legions, marches on Rome, has Julianus killed, and seizes power.

Hadrian

---

118 Work is completed on the Roman Forum, henceforth the administrative and religious center of the empire.

120 The Pantheon, featuring the largest dome in the ancient world, is completed in Rome.

121 Suetonius writes *The Lives of the Caesars*, a gossipy chronicle of the lives of the Roman emperors.

c.150 Apuleius writes *The Golden Ass*, a collection of comic and romantic stories including that of Cupid and Psyche.

---

refuge in underground catacombs on the outskirts of Rome.

c.180 Irenaeus, the bishop of Lyons, writes *Against the heresies*, in which he describes and criticizes a number of heretical sects. Although poorly written, it is one of the first systematic expositions of the Catholic faith.

180 Marcus Aurelius leaves behind on his death his *Meditations*, a classic work of Stoic philosophy written in fragments during respites from public business.

---

c.150 Ptolemy's *Geographia* includes an atlas of the known world based on the reports of traveling Roman legions.

c.180 The Roman physician Galen compiles all current medical knowledge, much of it erroneous, into a single systematic treatment that will be widely used until the end of the Middle Ages.

c.180 The first writings on alchemy appear in Egypt.

c.190 Liu Hui calculates π to 3.14159.

---

165 Soldiers returning from the Parthian Empire carry a plague with them that sweeps across the rest of the Empire.

185 Emperor Commodus drains the Roman imperial treasury in order to stage spectacular gladiatorial matches.

The Body Politic

211 The Roman emperor Septimius Severus dies and is succeeded by his son, Caracalla, who murders his brother to insure sole authority for himself.

212 The Edict of Caracalla extends Roman citizenship to all freeborn subjects.

216 Seizing the opportunity created by a civil war, Caracalla invades Parthia in imitation of his idol Alexander.

217 Repulsed by Artabanus IV, the last Parthian king, Caracalla retires to Carrhae, where he is murdered. Macrinus succeeds Caracalla as emperor but is defeated at Nisibis and forced to sue for peace on Parthian terms.

220 The Han Dynasty, rulers of China since 206 BC (with the brief interruption of Wang Mang), disintegrates. A number of competing families fill the vacuum, but none can reestablish imperial authority throughout China.

226 Ardashir, who rules the district around the ruins of Persepolis, defeats Artabanus IV, replacing the Arsacid Dynasty with his own Sassanid Empire in Persia.

247 The Goths cross the Danube and raid Rome's Balkan provinces.

251 Fighting in Moesia and Thrace, the Goths slay the Roman emperor Decius and his son in present-day Serbia.

Arts & Architecture

c.200 At Amaravati in Madras, craftsmen begin work on elaborately carved stone stupas, or shrines, used to house Buddhist relics.

217 Caracalla builds an enormous, 20-acre complex of public baths containing

Religion & Philosophy

204-270 Life of Plotinus, the most important Neoplatonist philosopher. The Neoplatonists believe in an ultimate, indivisible being from whom all life derives and with whom the human soul strives to be reunited through contemplation and ecstatic revelation.

226 Ardashir embraces Zoroastrianism as the official religion of his new Sassanid Empire.

c.249 Attempting to restore Rome's ancient pagan religion, Decius decrees that worship of the gods be mandatory.

Science & Technology

c.200 The Chinese develop an improved harness device called the whippletree, which allows a team of two oxen to pull a single cart simultaneously.

c.250 Diophantus writes his *Arithmetica*, the earliest surviving work on algebra.

Some of his equations produce negative numbers as solutions, but he rejects these as "absurd."

c.275 The Chinese develop the first crude compass, which they use for "finding the south."

Daily Life

c.200 The first mention of a stirrup appears in writings by the Chinese.

c.200 Middle-class Romans typically own up to a dozen of the 400,000 slaves who perform the menial work of the empire. Wealthy Romans may own 1,000 slaves.

c.200 The roads in the Roman Empire are so well paved that travelers can sometimes average 100 miles per day.

204 In order to ease a recession in his native Leptis Magna (in North Africa), the emperor Septimius Severus purchases all

259 Postumus establishes a subempire in Britain, Spain, and Gaul. Repulsing the raiding barbarians, he restores peace and security to the region.

260 The Sassanid Persians under Shapur I capture and flay alive the Roman emperor Valerian, ending a struggle between the two empires over Mesopotamia and Syria.

262 Odaenathus of Palmyra defeats the Persians and restores Rome's lost eastern lands. With his wife Zenobia, he rules an autonomous kingdom within the Roman Empire until his murder in 266.

270-275 Reign of the Roman emperor Aurelian, who restores unity to the

empire. He sacks Palmyra (273), which had ceased to recognize Roman supremacy, and recovers Gaul (274).

282 Emperor Carus recovers Armenia and Mesopotamia from the Persians and restores the frontiers of Severus.

286 Two years into his reign, Diocletian divides the empire, retaining the east and placing Maximian in charge of the west.

293 Diocletian appoints Constantius and Galerius as lesser emperors, called *Caesares*. Control of the military and political bureaucracies is shared, but Diocletian retains imperial authority and becomes much more autocratic.

Caracalla

1,600 marble seats as well as reading rooms, auditoriums, and gardens.

220 The poet Kalidasa raises Sanskrit drama to its highest level with his play *Shakuntala* that recasts a popular, early Indian myth.

273 According to some accounts, the main Alexandrian library in the Brucheum is ordered destroyed by Aurelian.

290 Construction begins in Verona on what will become one of the finest early amphitheaters in Italy.

Some Christians comply, but others defy the emperor and face persecution.

254 The early Christian theologian Origen dies after a long and torturous imprisonment, having written extensively on the Old Testament in the *Hexapla*.

276 The Persian prophet Mani is killed, but his teachings survive and form the basis for Manichaeism, which combines elements of Christianity and Buddhism with Persian mysticism. Mani saw himself as the last prophet in the line of Abraham, Zoroaster, and Buddha.

---

the country's olive oil and distributes it free in Rome.

248 Rome celebrates its 1,000th birthday.

c.270 The silver content of the Roman denarius falls from 50 percent at the turn

of the century (under Septimius Severus) to 0.02 percent. Silver content has not been higher than 90 percent since the reign of Trajan (98-117).

c.280 The first mention of sugar appears in Chinese writings.

200-299

The Body Politic

c.300 Mayan civilization flourishes in the Yucatan (Mexico) until circa 1500.

303 Armenia is the first state to adopt Christianity as its official religion.

303 Diocletian orders the destruction of Christian churches and the reduction of Christians to slave status. An edict one year later imposes the death penalty.

305 Diocletian and Maximian abdicate. Caesares Constantius and Galerius take over in a peaceful transfer of power.

306 Constantius dies during a campaign in Britain and is succeeded as emperor by his son, Constantine.

312 Constantine defeats Maxentius, son of former emperor Maximian, at the battle of Milvian Bridge. With this victory, he becomes the absolute ruler of the western Roman Empire.

313 With the Edict of Milan, co-emperors Constantine and Licinius (of the eastern empire) return Christian property seized by Diocletian and grant Christians the freedom to worship publicly.

317 Tartars invade China, ending the Jin Dynasty and partitioning the country into north and south (until 587).

323 At Adrianople and Chrysopolis, the forces of Constantine defeat those of

Arts & Architecture

302 The emperor Diocletian presides over the opening of vast public baths in Rome. Larger even than those of Caracalla (opened in 217), the baths of Diocletian feature continuous streams of water pouring into basins through the wide mouths of lions cast from silver.

Religion & Philosophy

325 Constantine convenes the First Ecumenical Council at Nicaea, which is attended by bishops from Europe, Africa, and Asia. The council firmly rejects Arianism and establishes the Nicene Creed. Constantine banishes those few bishops who refuse to sign the creed.

335 The Church of the Holy Sepulchre is consecrated in Jerusalem on the site of Jesus's tomb at Golgotha.

381 The Second Ecumenical Council at Constantinople definitively proclaims the doctrine of the Holy Trinity.

Science & Technology

c.300 The Maya adopt a new calendar, combining the 365-day year of the Olmecs with the *tzolkin*, a sacred calendar composed of 20 weeks of 13 days each.

c.300 Chinese artisans begin to use coal, instead of firewood, as the primary source of fuel for the energy required in ironworking.

304 In his *Record of plants and trees of the southern regions*, Xi Han describes how some farmers use particular species of ants to protect their mandarin orange

Daily Life

c.315 The most important of the early monastic organizers, Pachomius, founds the first of nine communities (with several hundred monks each). To join a monastery, a monk must give up all worldly possessions and pledge absolute obedience to his superiors.

c.325 Mary, sister of Pachomius, organizes a number of monastic communities for women.

325 The emperor Constantine issues an edict abolishing the gladiatorial games, but they are sporadically revived.

Licinius, enabling Constantine to reunite the empire under his rule.

330 Having taken four years to build Constantinople on the site of Byzantium, Constantine makes it the new capital of his unified empire, superseding Rome.

364 The emperor Valentinian officially divides the empire. Valentinian remains emperor of the west, while his brother Valens becomes emperor of the east.

376 Pressed by the Huns to the east, the Visigoths seek the protection of the Roman Empire. They are resettled across the Danube, but grow angry at the treatment they receive and soon rise up in arms.

378 At Adrianople, mounted Visigoths rout Roman foot soldiers, kill Valens, and advance to the walls of Constantinople.

379 Theodosius, proclaimed emperor of the east by Gratian in the west, placates and makes allies of the Visigoths.

391 Theodosius reinstates Christianity as the official religion of the empire.

395 With the death of Theodosius, the Roman Empire permanently splits between east and west.

395 The Visigothic king Alaric invades Greece, but is driven back by the Vandal Stilicho leading Western Roman troops.

St. Augustine

---

315 The triumphal Arch of Constantine is erected in Rome to celebrate the emperor's victory at Milvian Bridge.

391 Theodosius issues an edict purging pagan texts, which leads to the burning of the last of the two great libraries at Alexandria, the Serapeum. Rioting Christians pillage the library's books.

399-414 Fa Xian embarks on a pilgrimage along the Silk Road to India, returning to China by ship. He describes his trip in *A Record of the Buddhist Countries*.

---

384 Jerome translates the Bible into a Latin edition called the Vulgate.

395 As the Roman Empire splits into western and eastern halves, so does the Christian church. Roman Christianity remains under the authority of the pope, while Eastern Orthodoxy develops under the patriarch of Constantinople.

397-398 Augustine, the bishop of Hippo (near Carthage), writes his *Confessions*, an autobiographical account of his early life and his conversion to Christianity.

---

groves from harmful insect pests. This is the first documented record of biological pest control.

c.325 In his *Collections*, Pappus of Alexandria records and advances the geometric knowledge of his time. His exhaustive book is the best existing source for the now-lost works of such influential ancient mathematicians as Euclid, Archimedes, and Apollonius.

c.375 Basil, bishop of Caesarea, founds the first public hospital there.

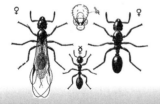

c.370 St. Ambrose introduces the singing of hymns to his church in Milan.

394 The Olympic Games held this year become the last (until the modern era) when the emperor Theodosius orders them banned.

The Body Politic

407 The Suevi, Vandals, and Alans overrun and plunder Gaul, then continue westward, settling in Spain.

407 Needed elsewhere, the remaining Roman troops are withdrawn from Britain, ending its status as a Roman province.

408 A jealous Western emperor Honorius has Stilicho killed. Born a Vandal, Stilicho embodied the leashed barbarian vigor on which Rome now ironically depends.

408 Supported by barbarian allies angry with Honorius's anti-Teutonic policies, Alaric the Bold leads a Visigothic invasion of Italy and marches unopposed to Rome. Only a ransom saves the city.

410 When political negotiations with Honorius (ensconced in Ravenna) break down, Alaric again marches on Rome and this time sacks the city.

414 After wedding the emperor's captured sister, Alaric's successor Ataulf agrees that, for land to settle in Gaul, the Visigoths will fight the Suevi, Alans, and Vandals—Rome's enemies in Spain.

429 Led by King Gaiseric, 80,000 Vandal warriors and their families cross the Mediterranean at Gibraltar and invade sparsely defended Roman North Africa.

433 Attila unites the Hun tribes under his rule and begins a series of annual

Arts & Architecture

Religion & Philosophy

413-426 Augustine writes *The City of God* to rebut the charge that Rome's decline is due to its embrace of Christianity.

428 Nestorius becomes patriarch of Constantinople, a post in the Eastern church akin to that of the pope in Rome.

431 Bishop Cyril of Alexandria chairs the Third Ecumenical Council at Ephesus, at which Nestorius is branded a heretic. A rival council condemns Cyril.

432 St. Patrick travels to Ireland as a missionary to convert the Irish.

Science & Technology

c.400 Scholars in Alexandria begin using the word *chemistry* to refer to the science of changing matter.

410-485 Life of Proclus, the most important of the later Neoplatonist philosophers. Proclus is best known for his com-

mentaries on the works of Plato, but he also comments on Book I of Euclid's *Elements* and the works of a number of classical astronomers.

415 The Neoplatonist philosopher Hypatia is dragged from her chariot,

Daily Life

c.400 Introduced to Rome by raiding barbarians, butter begins to supplant olive oil. The Hun equestrian lifestyle soon leads to a shift from togas to trousers.

444 A plague, probably bubonic, sweeps through Britain, ravaging the population

and rendering the Britons vulnerable to invasion and conquest.

c.450 Refugees fleeing the marauding Huns are forced to seek asylum on a few islands of silt and mud bordering the northern Adriatic. Within a short time,

plundering raids with his army of Huns and Germans.

435 Rome makes a costly peace with the Vandals, ceding them rich lands in North Africa that are the empire's granary.

438 The *Codex Theodosianus* collects the multiplicity of Roman statutes into a single body of law in sixteen books.

439 The Vandals seize Carthage.

449 Following the withdrawal of the Romans and a terrible plague, raids by Angles, Saxons, Picts, Irish, and Frisians culminate in the settlement of southeastern Britain by the Jutes.

451 When Attila invades Gaul, he is beaten for the first time at the battle of Chalons by a Roman army of Visigoths, Franks, and Burgundians under Aetius.

452 Attila sacks northern Italy, but he turns away from Rome when Pope Leo I marches to meet "the Scourge of God." That winter (453), Attila dies suddenly.

455 The Vandals sack Rome. Leo cannot stop them, but his negotiations with Gaiseric save the city from burning.

476 The barbarian Odoacer becomes king of Italy, dismissing the last puppet emperor Romulus Augustulus and formally ending the Western Roman Empire.

Attila the Hun

c.450 The Maya found Chichen Itza in the Yucatan (Mexico). Its ruins are among the most important in Central America. Public buildings include elaborate stone pyramids and wooden galleries supported by stone columns that are carved to resemble serpents.

c.450 The mausoleum of Galla Placidia, sister of the Western Roman emperor Honorius, is built in Ravenna. The tomb takes the form of a cross (cruciform) with a dome over the center. It is perhaps the earliest example of this type of Christian architecture.

440 Leo the Great becomes the bishop of Rome (until 461) and the first pope in the modern sense, defending Christian civilization against barbarian invaders.

451 The Fourth Ecumenical Council, meeting at Chalcedon, determines that

Christ represents two natures, one divine and one human, in a single person. Those who reject this doctrine are called monophysites. Monophysite churches include the Armenian church, the Egyptian Coptics, the Ethiopians, and the Jacobite church in Syria.

stripped naked, and scraped to death with oyster shells by a mob of Christian fanatics. The daughter of Theon of Alexandria, who edited an important edition of Euclid, Hypatia is the only woman among the first rank of Greek philosophers and mathematicians.

c.450 Antioch becomes the first city to illuminate its streets at night, using torches for lighting.

476 Proclus is made director of the famous Academy in Athens, founded by Plato circa 390 BC.

however, these exiles transform the lagoon's tiny community of fishing huts into the brick metropolis of Venice.

c.450 Legend has it that St. Patrick first teaches the Irish how to distill whiskey from grain about this time.

400-476

c.2500 BCE **–c.1500** BCE	The Indus Valley civilization of northwest India flourishes under the Harappa culture (c.2300 BCE - c.1700 BCE), which practices goddess worship.
c.1500 BCE	Nomadic Aryans migrate to the Indus Valley, bringing with them (from the Russian steppe) the horse, the chariot, and the Sanskrit language. The origins of Hinduism can be found in the fusion of the Aryans' Indo-European creed with indigenous Harappa theology.
	The Aryan priestly class of Brahmins (named after the god Brahma, the creator of the universe) spreads its new religion among the non-Aryan chieftains, who look to the Brahmins as arbiters of status in the new caste-based society. Because the Brahmins' literacy supports their position at the top of Indian society, this process of conversion is later termed Sanskritization.
c.1200 BCE **–c.1000** BCE	With its recension circa 900 BCE, the *Rigveda* formalizes the earliest literary and historical records of Vedism, from which Hinduism develops. Its 1,028 hymns reflect a polytheistic system of heavenly deities, the chief gods being Indra, Varuna, Agni, and Surya. The most important ritual described in the *Rigveda* involves a potion called *soma*, probably made from a hallucinogenic mushroom, that is offered to the gods before being ingested by the priests and sacrificers.
	The "Hymn of the Person" in the last of the ten books of the *Rigveda* divides Indian society into four classes, each symbolized by a different body part. The priest Brahman represents the head; the warrior Rajanya (later Kshatriya), the arms; the peasant Vaishya, the torso; and the servant Shudra, the legs.
c.1000 BCE **–c.500** BCE	A number of derivative Vedic works appear, the most important of which being the *Samhita* hymns devoted to specific deities; the scholarly *Vedanga* commentaries; the *Brahmanas*, which explain Vedic ritual; and the *Aranyakas*, which speculate on the mystical role of sacrifice in the cosmic order. The latter reflect the growing influence of mysticism on Hindu thought.
c.700 BCE **–c.500** BCE	The composition of the *Upanishads* marks the beginning of mystical Hinduism. These philosophic works, literally "sittings near a teacher,"

reflect a search for mystical knowledge of the afterlife. Of particular concern is the new doctrine of the transmigration of souls, according to which the human soul is reborn after death into a new human or animal form.

The oldest of the *Upanishads*, the *Brhadaranyaka*. attributes this doctrine of *samsara* [reincarnation] to the sage Uddalaka Aruni. The *Brhadaranyaka* also expounds the doctrine of *karman* [the actions of the individual], according to which the soul receives a happy or unhappy rebirth depending on the life it has recently led. Many of those dissatisfied with Vedic ritual turn to the ascetic life of the hermit and, leaving the urban enclaves, begin to wander in search of a release [*moksha*] from the eternal circle of transmigration.

c. 600 BCE Despite the undercurrent of ascetic mysticism, the grand pageant of Vedic ritual continues with the codification of social behavior, as determined by the Brahmins. The *sutras*, literally "threads," collect aphorisms that instruct readers in the performance of sacrifices and domestic rituals. Class behavior is specifically addressed in the four *dharmas*: one *dharma* [law] for each of the four Hindu classes described in the *Rigveda*'s "Hymn of the Person."

c.500 BCE Resistance to the ritualism of the Brahmins, who fail to address the issue of transmigration, peaks with the development of sects that renounce Vedism and turn instead to leaders who claim to have found a release from reincarnation. The most important of these are Siddhartha Gautama, the Buddha, and Nataputta Vardhamana, known as Mahavira, the founder of Jainism.

A large number of wealthy merchants join these groups, which challenge the Vedic social order. They are attracted by the greater role played by the participant than in orthodox Vedism because, being virtually devoid of ritual, they are much less expensive to support.

Finally, as asceticism becomes increasingly widespread, the Brahmins develop the doctrine of the four *ashrams* [dwellings] in response. This teaching divides adult male life into four chronological periods: those of the celibate religious student, the married head of a household, the forest hermit, and the wandering monk. The Brahmins' attempt to preserve the social order by restricting asceticism to late middle age is only partially successful.

c.200 BCE The composition of the *Mahabharata* corresponds to a decline in the worship of Brahma and a rise in the cult of the god Vishnu. The *Mahabharata*'s linked vignettes tell the story of heroes in the process of discovering their *dharma*. Most of the explicit religious material can be found in an interlude, the *Bhagavad Gita*, which takes the form of a dialogue between the hero Arjuna and his charioteer Krishna, an incarnation of Vishnu. Although only 700 lines long, the *Bhagavad Gita* is probably the most influential Indian religious text. As the two opposing armies of the *Mahabharata* stand poised to fight, Arjuna lays down his arms rather than battle his kin. This action causes Krishna to reprove Arjuna for refusing to do his duty according to the *dharma* of his class.

Although the text specifically attacks the Buddhist principle that release from transmigration comes only after action [*karma*] has been rejected, Krishna suggests other possible means of release, including the discipline of the task (*karma-yoga*), the discipline of meditative insight (*jñana-yoga*), and the discipline of devotion to God (*bhakti-yoga*).

The *Ramayana*, written about the same time, tells the story of the exiled Prince Rama, whose wife Sita has been kidnapped by the evil Ravana. With an army of monkeys led by his simian friend Hanuman, Rama rescues Sita and is later restored to his kingdom, where his subsequent reign is held up as a model of social harmony.

Both of these Hindu epics, the *Mahabharata* and the *Ramayana*, attempt to resolve the contemporary conflict between ascetic means of *moksha* and Vedic forms of ritual in favor of the Vedic social order. Later Vedic theology proceeds from this point.

c.200 Manu writes the first and most important of the *Dharma-sastras*, which are systematized versions of the *sutras*. Manu's eclectic work includes discussions of the Hindu creation myth as well as explanations of marriage rites and dietary laws among other juridical subjects. The *Dharma-sastras* perpetuate traditional social distinctions as they provide the four Hindu classes with their first practical religious morality.

c.320 –c.535 During the Gupta Empire, two primary sects of Hinduism gain recognition: the Vaishnavas, who worship Vishnu, and the Shaivas, devotees of Shiva. In addition, the 18 volumes of the *Puranas* appear. These encyclopedic works standardize Hindu mythology, providing elaborate genealogies of the religion's gods and heroes. While the Vedic texts remain restricted to adult males of the three higher classes, the *Puranas*, available to all, become the scripture of the common folk. The *Bhagavata-Purana*, written much later (circa 900) is easily the most popular, becoming the source text for much of India's medieval literature.

c.500 The *tantras* evolve out of a renewed cult of the mother goddess (Shaktism), which exists outside Brahmin ritual. Tantric texts teach that *moksha* may be obtained through the repetition of sacred words (*mantras*) and by meditating on symbolic designs (*mandalas*).

c.800 Shankara becomes a famous philosopher of Vedanta, the most important of the Six Schools of Hindu theology developed during the past five centuries. His work, which provides the first systematic intellectual framework for Hinduism, attempts to rid Hindu religious practice of superfluous Brahmin-directed ritual.

1486 –1533 The life of Chaitanya, the most important leader of the *bhakti* movement. Beginning with the invasion of Sind (712), which led to the Muslim domination of northern India, Islam exerted an influence upon Hinduism, most obviously found in the highly emotional *bhakti* [devotional] rituals.

1813 The British East India Company, which has previously excluded Christian missionary activity from colonial India, changes its policy in response to pressure from the evangelical movement in England. Fifteen years later, Rammohan Ray founds the Brahmo Samaj [Society of God] to reform Hinduism. Ray's successor as leader of the Brahmo Samaj will be Devendranath Tagore, whose son Rabindranath Tagore (1861-1941) becomes the greatest poet of modern India.

1836 –1886 Life of the mystic Ramakrishna, who concludes that "all religions are true," and therefore even idolatry is to be respected as long as it meets the needs of the individual believer. Ramakrishna's teachings allow educated Hindus to accept the more absurd aspects of their faith without having to believe in them literally.

c.1800 BCE   According to tradition, Abraham forms a covenant with Yahweh, the one true god and creator. In exchange for the Hebrew patriarch's devotion, Yahweh promises Abraham both plentiful offspring and the land of Canaan (modern Israel and Lebanon) in which to raise them. Abraham's family has been living in the town of Harran in northern Mesopotamia.

c.1650 BCE   During the time traditionally assigned to Abraham's grandson Jacob (also called Israel), a famine in the land of Canaan induces the seminomadic Hebrews to migrate south to Egypt, where they are ultimately enslaved.

c.1250 BCE   According to the Old Testament, the shepherd Moses, acting as the instrument of Yahweh, leads the enslaved Hebrews out of Egypt, an event celebrated each year during Passover. Following the Exodus, Yahweh renews the Covenant he made with Abraham and delivers to Moses on Mount Sinai the Ten Commandments (also known as the Decalogue), which regulate the conduct of the people toward their god. After 40 years of wandering in the desert, during which time Yahweh miraculously sustains the 12 tribes of Israel with manna from heaven, Moses leads his people back to the same land of Canaan that Yahweh once promised to Abraham.

c.1200 BCE   After the Israelites' conquest and resettlement of Canaan, highlighted by Joshua's legendary victory at Jericho, the rule of the judges begins. During this time, the ark of the Covenant resides at Shiloh.

c.1020 BCE   Saul becomes the first king of Israel after his victory over the neighboring Ammonites. His authority derives both from popular acclamation and from divine selection (through the judge Samuel). The dual nature of Saul's mandate partially resolves the dispute between those who consider the king to be Yahweh's instrument for the defeat of the pagan Philistines and those who view secular kingship as an affront to the kingship of God. Saul and Samuel come into conflict, however, when Saul is forced to accommodate himself to the theocratic will of Samuel, by whose authority (as representative of the old order) Saul was initially invested.

c.1000 BCE   The new king David makes the monarchy spiritually independent by claiming that Yahweh has made a covenant with him (and his descendants in the Davidic line) that parallels Yahweh's Covenant with the people of Israel. The dynasty of David becomes therefore, for political purposes, the means by which Yahweh will shape the destiny of the Jewish people. During his reign, David greatly extends the Jewish state by conquest and, taking Jerusalem, makes it the national capital. Transporting the ark there, he makes plans for a temple to house it, thus uniting the two covenants symbolically. But the tradition of a portable tent shrine proves too difficult to supplant, and David is forced to shelve his plans.

c.961 BCE –c.933 BCE The reign of David's son Solomon. As king of Israel, he constructs the first Temple in Jerusalem to house the ark of the Covenant. Solomon also takes many foreign wives for diplomatic purposes, building and maintaining shrines to their native cult religions on the Mount of Olives. Although Solomon neither practices idolatry himself, nor imposes his wives' beliefs upon the people, these shrines outrage zealous Jews, who consider them to be a violation of the sanctity of the holy land of Yahweh. These religious differences, as well as certain secular disputes, lead the northern tribes to secede from the kingdom of Israel circa 922 BCE—that is, shortly after Solomon's death. The northern kingdom retains the name Israel, while the southern Davidic kingdom is called Judah.

c.850 BCE Ahab, the king of Israel, marries Princess Jezebel of Tyre, who brings with her priests to staff an elaborate temple to Baal that Ahab builds for her in Samaria, the northern capital. The strenuous objections raised by Jewish purists, led by Elijah, provoke Jezebel to begin persecuting the Hebrew prophets (polytheists being generally tolerant, except in self-defense). Eventually, Elijah challenges the Baal worshipers to a test on Mount Carmel to determine whose god is the true God. When the Baal cultists fail the test, Elijah has them executed.

c.750 BCE A century of border wars between Israel and Aram (modern Syria) ends when Assyrian invaders from northeastern Mesopotamia force the Arameans to focus on a more immediate threat. In Israel, rejoicing at the cessation of hostilities is expressed by the construction of lavish temples and private mansions. Responding to the dissolution they perceive in Israelite society, a new generation of prophets emerges. First among them is Amos, who denounces the corruption and indifference of Israel's ruling class, which he predicts will result in the oppression of the Israelites by an angry Yahweh.

c.742 BCE   In the southern kingdom of Judah, where King Ahaz has sought to appease the Assyrians rather than join the Israelite-Aramean alliance against them, the prophet Isaiah warns that Assyria will be the "rod of God's wrath" that punishes Judah for its godlessness. Isaiah also prophesies that after conquering Judah, Assyria will then arrogantly exceed its divine mandate and be broken on Judah's mountains, resulting in the renewal of Israel under an ideal Davidic king. Another prophet, contemporary to Isaiah, named Micah issues similar warnings, although in much more apocalyptic language.

c.721 BCE   Assyria captures the Israelite capital of Samaria, having taken Gilead and Galilee a decade earlier (733 BCE-732 BCE) along with Aramean Damascus. The prophet Hosea interprets the conquest as a "forgetting of God."

c.710 BCE   Chastened by the fall of the northern kingdom and fearing Micah's prophecy, King Hezekiah of Judah carries out reforms designed to eliminate idolatry and placate Yahweh.

c.701 BCE   The Assyrian king Sennacherib marches to suppress a western rebellion led by Hezekiah and Babylonian insurgents. When the Assyrians easily overwhelm Judah, Hezekiah sues for peace, offering tribute, but Sennacherib holds out for the surrender of Jerusalem. Hezekiah turns for guidance to Isaiah, who prophesies that Jerusalem will not fall into heathen hands. Inspired by Isaiah, Hezekiah refuses to submit—and, for some unknown reason, Sennacherib decides to return home, content with the transformation of Judah's countryside into a vassal state of Assyria.

c.640 BCE   The reign of the reform king Josiah of Judah, who takes advantage of
–609 BCE   Assyria's degeneration to conduct extensive political and religious reforms aimed at ending pagan practices and restoring the Davidic empire.

c.605 BCE   After Nebuchadnezzar's defeat of the Egyptians at Carchemish, the prophet Jeremiah identifies the Babylonian king as the incarnation of his earlier prophecies that an invader from the north will subjugate Judah and destroy the Temple at Jerusalem. When it becomes clear that the Babylonians are unstoppable, Jeremiah preaches submission as the only means of survival (causing him to be jailed for demoralizing the populace). Meanwhile, the disconsolate Ezekiel prophesies that only the cleansing of the Temple through its total destruction will permit a reconciliation with Yahweh.

586 BCE   Nebuchadnezzar captures Jerusalem, burning the Temple and deporting the bulk of Judah's population to Babylon, beginning the Babylonian Captivity. Deprived of the sanctuary provided by the Temple, the displaced Jews emphasize non-Temple-related rituals such as observation of the Sabbath and ritual circumcision. Their exile lasts until 538 BCE, when Cyrus the Great of Persia subdues the Babylonians and permits the Jews to return to Jerusalem, where the Temple is rebuilt (completed 516 BCE).

444 BCE   The Persian king Artaxerxes I grants Ezra a charter to enforce the Torah as the law of the Persian province that now includes a greatly reduced Judah.

332 BCE   With his victory at Tyre, Alexander the Great wins control of Palestine, which becomes part of the Hellenistic kingdom of Ptolemy in Egypt after Alexander's death. Ptolemy permits the Jews considerable religious and political freedom.

c.250 BCE   The Torah (the first five books of the Old Testament, also known as the Pentateuch) is translated into Greek (the Septuagint).

198 BCE   After conquering Palestine, the Seleucid king Antiochus III continues the Ptolemaic policy of tolerance toward the Jews. His decision is made easier by the fact that around this time, Hellenized Jews gain control of the high priesthood. As high priest (175 BCE-172 BCE), Jason establishes Jerusalem as a Greek city with Greek educational institutions. Jason's ouster by an even more Hellenistic group, led by Menelaus, causes a civil war, in which Antiochus IV decisively intervenes on the side of Menelaus.

167 BCE   Antiochus IV sacks Jerusalem and pillages the Temple, lately transformed by the wealthy Oniad family of high priests into a bank. Antiochus's subsequent proclamations against Judaism lead to the revolt of Mattathias and his sons, known alternatively as the Maccabees and the Hasmoneans, whose activities are supported by rural peasants and the urban masses.

c.563 BCE The birth of Siddhartha Gautama, the semilegendary Buddha [Awakened One], in the kingdom of the Shakyas on the border between present-day India and Nepal. Being the son of King Shuddhodana, Siddhartha belongs to the ruling Hindu *kshatriya* [warrior] caste. Inspecting the infant, the sage Asita smiles and then weeps, happy in his recognition that the child will one day become a *buddha* but sad at the realization he will not live to witness the child's enlightenment. Concerned with the predictions of the Brahmins that his son will become a wandering ascetic, Shuddhodana proceeds to raise the young prince in great splendor (and isolation from the suffering of the common people) so that he might choose to lead a worldly life.

c.534 BCE According to Buddhist tradition, on a carriage ride beyond the palace walls, the sheltered prince is disturbed by the sight of an elderly man afflicted by his age. Enquiring as to the man's condition, Siddhartha is told that all men are subject to the enfeeblement of age if they live long enough. Another day, after Siddhartha sees a diseased man, his charioteer explains to him that all men are subject to illness as well. On a third excursion, the prince comes upon a corpse for the first time. Finally, on a fourth trip, Siddhartha meets a wandering *sadhu* [holy man], without any material wealth, yet possessing a noble and serene demeanor in the midst of the worldly misery all around him. These experiences cause the prince to consider the problem of human suffering for the first time, after which he renounces his life of privilege and adopts the discipline of asceticism.

c.528 BCE After practicing severe bodily deprivation while residing for nearly six years at Urvela, Siddhartha realizes that self-mortification will not lead him to the sought-after state of *nirvana* [absolute truth]. This decision causes his five companions to abandon him, wrongly convinced that Siddhartha has chosen to revert to his previous life of affluence.

Some evenings later, sitting cross-legged beneath a bodhi tree (*Ficus religiosa*) at a place now called Bodhgaya, Siddhartha determines not to rise until he has attained enlightenment. Buddhist legend describes this struggle for enlightenment metaphorically as a battle against the demons of Mara, who rules the world of passion. As a result of his victory against Mara, the Buddha gains enlightenment, including the knowledge of his past lives as a *bodhisattva* [one who aspires to be a *buddha*]. The Buddha also gains the ability to see the passing away and rebirth of being that comprises *samsara*, the Hindu doctrine of reincarnation.

Some weeks later, the Buddha travels to Isipatana, where his former companions now reside, and delivers to them his first sermon. He describes the Noble Eightfold Path, the "middle" path between self-indulgence and self-mortification. He also reveals the Four Noble Truths: human existence is suffering; suffering is caused by selfish desire; a release from suffering exists (*nirvana*); and the Noble Eightfold Path is the way to its attainment. At the end of this sermon, the five monks agree to become the Buddha's first disciples.

c.483 BCE According to tradition, the first Buddhist council meets at Rajaghra immediately after the death of the Buddha. During this council, *arhats* [monks] systematize Buddhist doctrine. The monk Upali directs composition of the *vinaya* [monastic discipline], while Ananda supervises the compilation of the *dharma* [divine law]. Although there are both memorizers and commentators at work in the *sangha* [Buddhist community] at this time, the Buddhist scriptures exist in their normative form as an oral tradition.

c.340 BCE The Buddhist religion splits into two sects that later develop into the schools of Mahayana [Greater Vehicle] and Hinayana [Lesser Vehicle], also called Theravada [Way of the Elders] because—of the two—it is more closely linked to the original teachings of the Buddha. The Theravada school of Buddhism later becomes predominant in Sri Lanka and Southeast Asia. For at least the next millennium, however, the division does not preclude Mahyanists and Hinayanists from living and worshiping side by side in the same monasteries.

c.272 BCE The reign of the celebrated Buddhist emperor Ashoka in India, who converts
−232 BCE to the faith after witnessing the carnage brought about by his conquest of the Kalinga country on the Indian east coast. Renouncing military means, Ashoka adopts a policy of "conquest by *dharma*." Soon Ashoka undertakes the construction of *stupas* [Buddhist temples] and monasteries, as well as pillars inscribed with his understanding of Buddhist doctrine. Most famous among these Rock, or Pillar, Edicts is that found on the lion capital of the pillar at Sarnath, which becomes India's national emblem.

c.246 BCE Ashoka convenes the third Buddhist council at Patna. According to some accounts, this council completes the Buddhist scriptural canon, known as

c.246 BCE
(continued)

the *Tripitaka* [Three Baskets]. Included are the *Vinaya Pitaka* [Basket of Discipline], which includes the monastic code; the *Sutra Pitaka* [Basket of Teachings], which includes the instructional sayings of the Buddha; and the *Abhidharma Pitaka* [Basket of Higher Teachings], which systematizes the philosophy implicit in the Buddha's teachings. After the completion of the *Tripitaka*, with which the Theravadins are more closely associated, the council sends missionaries throughout India (and to other countries) to spread the Buddhist faith. These include Ashoka's son and daughter, Mahinda and Sanghamitta, who bring Theravada Buddhism to Sri Lanka.

c.150 BCE

Perhaps written by Nagasena himself, the *Milinda-pañha* describes a debate between this Therevadin Buddhist scholar and Menander, the Hellenistic ruler of Bactria. An important noncanonical commentary on the *Tripitaka*, it also represents a significant achievement in Indian prose writing. The *Milinda-pañha* includes the famous analogy that, just as the parts of a chariot put together properly constitute the chariot, so do the component parts of an individual constitute the totality of that individual. There is no additional element holding the individual together.

c.60

Merchants and monks traveling the Silk Road carry Buddhism to China, where groups of expatriate Buddhists gather in the Han capital of Loyang.

220 –589

During the Period of Disunity that follows the collapse of the Han Dynasty, Buddhism spreads rapidly throughout China in response to war and the general chaos that grips the country.

372

Buddhism spreads from China to Korea, which lies well within China's political sphere of influence.

c.400

The Indian priest and scholar Kumarajiva, captured by Chinese raiders, translates scores of Buddhist texts into Chinese. Perhaps the most important of these is the *Lotus Sutra*, a popular Mahayana scripture that later becomes the central document of an important school of diaspora (non-Indian) Buddhism. Named after the mountain in southeast China where its doctrines are first propounded, this school will be known in Chinese as Tian Tai and in Japanese as Tendai.

c.520 The Indian monk Bodhidharma travels to China, where his teachings form the basis for the meditative Chan (in Japanese Zen) school of Buddhism, which also shows the influence of Daoism.

552 Buddhism spreads from China through Korea to Japan, where it is proclaimed the state religion in 594.

580 –907 During the Sui and Tang dynasties in China, Buddhism supplants Confucianism as four distinctly Chinese schools flourish: Hua Yen [Flower Adornment], Jing Tu [Pure Land], Tian Tai [White Lotus], and Chan.

c.650 Shan Dao systematizes the Pure Land school of Buddhism in China. His work later inspires Honen to found a Pure Land sect in Japan.

792 –794 Tibetans hold the Council of Samye to determine whether they should follow Indian or Chinese forms of Buddhism. After a debate between devotees of two prominent sects, the Tibetans choose a hybrid of the Mahayana and Tantric schools prevalent in northern India at the time. The Tantric school, also known as Vajrayana [Thunderbolt Vehicle], became fully established in India circa 600 as a means to sudden enlightenment through the practice of yoga and magic rituals.

1160 After the followers of Mahayana and Tantric Buddhism come into conflict with the orthodox Theravada sect in Sri Lanka, the Council of Anuradhapura bans all non-Theravada schools.

1192 –1333 Zen flourishes in Japan during the Kamakura Shogunate, in part because its discipline appeals to the ruling samurai warrior class. The two primary sects are the Rinzai school identified with the monk Eisai (12th century) and the Soto school of Dogen (established circa 1244).

c.1200 The decline of Indian Buddhism, which began about the time of the first Muslim invasion (712), reaches the point at which Buddhism virtually disappears from India.

477-1453

The Body Politic

479 Xia Daozheng founds the Qi Dynasty in southern China, but the presence of rival families precludes imperial unity.

481 Clovis becomes king of the Franks, beginning Merovingian rule in France.

486 Defeating Syagrius, Clovis takes Roman Gaul, making Soissons his capital.

493 Theodoric the Ostrogoth wrests control of Italy from Odoacer.

c.500 The Britons (perhaps under the battle leader Arthur) defeat the Saxons at Mount Badon, although this skirmish barely checks the Anglo-Saxon conquest of England [Angle-land].

507 At Vouillé, Clovis routs the Visigoths, annexing the kingdom of Toulouse.

511 Clovis dies, leaving his four sons to continue Frankish expansion as joint rulers of a single realm.

527 Succeeding his uncle Justin as the Eastern Roman emperor, Justinian makes plans to reconquer the west.

532 The Franks defeat the Burgundians at Autun and subsequently subjugate the Burgundian kingdom (by 534).

533 Justinian sends an army under Belisarius to North Africa, where it conquers the kingdom of the Vandals.

Arts & Architecture

477 Kasyapa, who becomes king of Ceylon after killing his father, builds a palace at Sigiri [the Lion's Rock].

c.500 At Cholula, the Toltecs build the largest of the Central American pyramids, using sun-dried bricks and earth.

532-537 The Eastern emperor Justinian rebuilds the Hagia Sophia (founded by Constantine) in Constantinople. Designed by Anthemius of Tralles and Isidorus of Miletus, the church is considered the finest example of Byzantine architecture, combining the central dome of

Religion & Philosophy

478 Japanese devotees of Shinto first build the shrines of Ise, which are then rebuilt every twentieth year. They are to Shinto what Mecca is to Islam.

482 Eastern emperor Zeno issues the *Henoticon*, an attempt at reconciling the

eastern and western churches, which the pope rejects.

484 Pope Felix III excommunicates Patriarch Acacius of Constantinople because he endorses the *Henoticon*, beginning a schism that lasts until 519.

Science & Technology

c.517 Aryabhata, the Indian mathematician and astronomer who first separated the two disciplines, produces his manual of astronomy.

c.520 Aryabhata and his colleague Varamihara invent the decimal system.

c.520 Dionysius Exiguus introduces the practice of marking time in relation to the birth of Christ, although it will not be accepted for some time.

524 In his *Institutiones arithmeticae*, the Roman statesman Boethius compiles

Daily Life

c.500 The practice of *sati* [suttee], in which a widow is sacrificed on the funeral pyre of her husband, undergoes a revival in India after the Hindu priesthood gives it religious sanction. The term *sati* comes from the Sanskrit meaning "good woman" or "true wife."

42

535-40 Overthrowing Ostrogothic rule in Italy south of the Po, Belisarius captures and occupies Rome and Ravenna.

552-553 Justinian sends Narses to reverse a Gothic counteroffensive in Italy. At Busta Gallorum, Narses decimates the Ostrogoths and returns Italy to the control of the Eastern Empire.

561 With the death of Clotaire, Clovis's only surviving son, the reunited kingdom passes to Clotaire's four sons, whose dissension ends Frankish imperialism.

567 The Frankish kingdom separates into the sovereign realms of Austrasia, Neustria, and Burgundy (until 751).

568 The Lombards are forced out of the Alföld [Great Plain of Hungary] by the Avars, who were themselves chased from central Asia by the Turks. King Alboin leads his people into Italy, where they found a kingdom of duchies (until 774).

580 Yang Jian proclaims himself the emperor Wen Di, establishing the Sui Dynasty and reuniting China by 589.

591 After decades of border clashes between Persia and the Eastern Romans, civil unrest in Persia forces Chosroes II to abandon his throne. When Chosroes entreats Constantinople for help, Emperor Maurice's army restores the Persian king to power, and a period of peace follows.

Clovis

---

early Christian churches in Greece with the nave and aisles of Roman basilicas.

548 Work is completed on the Church of San Vitale, begun by Theodoric but completed by Justinian after his capture of the Ostrogothic capital of Ravenna, which has become a center of learning and the arts rivaling Constantinople.

594 Gregory of Tours dies, leaving his *Historia francorum* [*History of the Franks*], an invaluable chronicle of events from the beginning of time through 591.

---

524 Awaiting death for treason, the Roman statesman Boethius writes *De consolatione philosophiae*, which remains influential throughout the Middle Ages.

529 Benedict of Nursia founds the Benedictine order of monks at Monte Cassino.

552 Koreans bring Buddhism to Japan.

589 Arian bishops accept the Roman Catholic faith at the Council of Toledo.

590 Gregory I becomes the first monk to ascend to the papacy.

---

much of what is known about mathematics into four topics—arithmetic, music, geometry, and astronomy—which he calls the *quadrivium*.

c.547 The monk Cosmas Indicopleustes writes *Christian topography* after sailing from Suez to Ceylon along the route of the spice trade.

c.550 Alexander of Tralles practices medicine and writes *De lumbricis*, one of his many books on internal medicine and therapy.

---

c.529 The pro-Christian emperor Justinian closes the Academy, founded by Plato in Athens circa 390 BC, along with other "pagan" schools.

529 Justinian issues the *Codex Vitus*, a collections of civil laws that emphasizes the emperor's authority and establishes an imperial bureaucracy.

532 Constantinople's Basilica Cistern, possibly designed by Anthemius for Justinian, is the largest of the underground tanks used for storing water.

The Body Politic

602 A bitter general, Phocas, deposes the Eastern emperor Maurice. Chosroes II of Persia declares war soon thereafter.

610 Heraclius dethrones Phocas and founds the Heraclian Dynasty (until 711). With his reign, the Eastern Roman Empire becomes the Byzantine Empire, adopting Greek as its official language.

611-616 The Persians capture Antioch, Damascus, Jerusalem, and Egypt, taking the Holy Cross back to Ctesiphon.

618 Aided by the Turks, Li Shihmin overthrows the Sui and founds the Tang Dynasty in China (until 906), known for its civil reforms. Li rules as Gao Zu.

620 Pulakesin II of the Chalukya Dynasty thwarts Harsha, ruler of northern India, in his moves southward. These two kings control nearly the entire subcontinent.

c.624 Three hundred Muslims under Muhammad defeat more than a thousand Meccans at the battle of Badr, a turning point in the Arabs' religious civil war that gains Islam many converts.

626 Avars, Slavs, and Persians besiege Constantinople unsuccessfully as the Byzantine Empire continues to withstand attacks on most of its frontiers.

627 Heraclius decisively defeats Chosroes II at Nineveh, leading to the

Arts & Architecture

c.600 Pope Gregory I endorses the *schola cantorum*, a Roman music school at which a form of liturgical music (the Gregorian chant) develops.

c.600 The Seven Pagodas are built in India south of Madras. The monuments, each carved out of a solid block of granite, are characteristic of the Dravidian architecture of the region.

c.625 The ship-burial of the Anglo-Saxon king Raedewald at Sutton Hoo, Suffolk, includes a treasure of Byzantine coins

Religion & Philosophy

601 Pope Gregory I makes the missionary monk Augustine the first archbishop of Canterbury. Having first arrived in England four years earlier, Augustine has already converted King Ethelbert of Kent and founded a Benedictine monastery at Canterbury.

604 Japanese crown prince Shotoku issues the *Constitution of Seventeen Articles* codifying Buddhist law.

c.622 Muhammad flees his native Mecca after he is persecuted for denouncing paganism and preaching the monotheis-

Science & Technology

633 Archbishop Isidore of Seville completes his encyclopedia of the sciences. Isidore also writes histories, theological treatises, and works on astronomy and meteorology, in which he collects much of the physical and natural philosophy of his time.

c.662 At a monastery in Mesopotamia, Severus Sebokht oversees the translation and exchange of scientific writings from Greek, Indian, and Arab sources. The monks introduce Greek astronomy to the Arabs and advance the adoption of the Hindu system of decimal numeration.

Daily Life

c.610 An Italian monk invents pretzels to reward children who learn their prayers.

626-49 During the reign of Tang emperor Tai Zong, professional bureaucrats come to replace the hereditary aristocracy in the royal court of China.

king's murder by Persian nobles and the demise of the Sassanid Empire in Persia.

634-44 During his reign, the Caliph Umar converts the nationalist Arabian state into an Islamic empire, conquering Jerusalem, Syria, Mesopotamia, and Egypt as part of a decade-long holy war. His troops found Fustat (Cairo) in 640.

639 The last independent Frankish king, Dagobert, dies. His successors are puppets controlled by strongmen with the title *majordomo* [mayor of the palace].

642 After a decisive victory at Nehavend, Umar proceeds to incorporate the vestiges of Persia into his caliphate.

645 Nakatomi Kamatari defeats the Soga and establishes the Fujiwara as Japan's imperial family.

680 Yazid succeeds his father Muawiya as ruler of the Arab caliphate, but his claim is disputed by al-Husain, son of the former caliph Ali. The issue is settled at Karbala, where Yazid defeats the followers of al-Husayn, later known as Shiites. The battle's date, October 10, becomes a Shiite holiday and al-Husain's tomb there a pilgrimage site.

687 The Austrasian mayor of the palace Pepin II reunites the Frankish territories after defeating the mayor of Neustria-Burgundy at Tetry.

Gregory I

---

and a number of Anglo-Saxon items that display considerable skill in metalworking and enameling.

c.680 The English herdsman Caedmon writes his *Hymn*, based on a dream. His verses are the first example of Christian

poetry composed in the Old English vernacular.

691 Abd al-Malik builds the Dome of the Rock in Jerusalem to enclose the sacred rock from which Muhammad is said to have ascended into heaven.

---

tic religion of Islam. His flight to Yathrib (later Medina) is known as the *hijra*, and it marks Year 1 of the Muslim Era.

630 After establishing a theocracy in Medina, Muhammad returns with a Muslim army to conquer Mecca.

632 The Koran compiles the words of the late prophet Muhammad.

681 Meeting at Constantinople, the Sixth Ecumenical Council rejects as heresy the belief that Christ had two natures but one will, which is known as monothelism.

---

c.670 Syrian architect Callinicus develops a flammable liquid that will be used by the Byzantines to defend Constantinople against naval sieges. Known as "Greek fire," the petroleum-based substance is thrown aboard enemy ships, enveloping them in flames.

c.690 Paulus Aegineta writes on the sciences in his *Synopsis of medicine in seven books*, which is collectively known as the *Epitome.* The sixth book of the series contains the most advanced information on surgery available during this time.

---

644 The first windmill appears in Persia for the purpose of grinding corn.

648 In his *Memoirs on Western Countries*, Xuan Zang writes of his extensive travels as a Buddhist pilgrim throughout China and India.

692 In Constantinople, the Trullan Synod denounces pagan festivals and customs including the theater, the circus, soothsayers, and jugglers.

695 Abdalmalik mints the first coinage within the Arab caliphate.

600-699

c.570 The birth of Muhammad in Mecca, a major trading and religious center for the pagan tribes of the Arabian peninsula. A pagan sanctuary called the Kaaba assures the safety of those who come to buy and sell at the many fairs. The prosperous merchants of Mecca exercise monopolistic control over the lucrative east-west trade between India and the Mediterranean. As wealth becomes centralized, however, the tribal leaders' traditional commitment to the less fortunate members of their clans declines.

c.595 On a trading journey with his uncle Abu Talib, Muhammad manages the goods of a well-to-do, 40-year-old widow named Khadija. She is so impressed with his abilities that she offers him marriage. With his acceptance, the 25-year-old Muhammad obtains capital enough to become independently wealthy.

c.610 According to Islamic tradition, Muhammad has a vision of the angel Gabriel, during which he hears a voice telling him he is the "Messenger of God." The Qadr [night of glory] marks the beginning of Muhammad's status as the Prophet. He receives further revelations (messages from Allah) at frequent intervals until his death.

c.613 Although at first perturbed by his vision, Muhammad now begins to preach publicly the faith of Islam, which literally means "surrender" (in this case to the will of Allah). Occasionally, Muhammad and his (perhaps 39) followers worship at the Kaaba. There, the Prophet repeats his revelation that Allah expects gratitude for Meccan prosperity, a gratitude that Allah wishes expressed as generosity toward the poor. Muhammad warns that on the Last Day, people will be judged according to their deeds in this life and assigned, on that basis, to spend eternity either in heaven or hell.

c.615 Active opposition to Muhammad appears in response to his implicit criticism of Mecca's wealthy merchant class. A year later, Abu Jahl organizes a commercial boycott of Muhammad's clan, but the policy fails after three years when the boycotting clans realize they are harming their own financial interests as well.

About this time, according to Islamic tradition, 80 Muslims migrate to Abyssinia (modern Ethiopia) to escape persecution. Muhammad, of course, remains in Mecca.

c.619 On the death of Abu Talib, another of Muhammad's uncles assumes leadership of the Hashim clan. This uncle, Abu Lahab, who has close ties to Mecca's wealthiest merchants, withdraws from Muhammad the support of the clan, thus leaving the Prophet vulnerable to attack as long as he continues to preach the faith of Islam in Mecca.

c.621 During the summer, 12 men from Yathrib, making their annual pilgrimage to the Kaaba, secretly reveal themselves as Muslims to Muhammad. Upon their return to Yathrib, they begin to proselytize on his behalf.

c.622 **June** Seventy-five pilgrims from Yathrib travel to Mecca, where they confess their faith in Islam and swear an oath to defend Muhammad as though he were a member of their own clan. These become known as the Pledges of al-Aqaba. Muhammad now bids his followers in Mecca to relocate to Yathrib.

September 24 Using little-traveled roads to escape assassination plots, Muhammad himself makes his way to Yathrib, which changes its name to Medina in his honor. Muhammad's journey becomes known as the *hijra* [Hegira], which literally means the severance of clan ties. The Islamic calendar begins with this year. Scholars later speculate that contact with the Hebrew population of Yathrib exposed the Arab residents to Jewish messianic beliefs that are realized with the arrival of Muhammad, whom the Arabs hope will settle a recent (and destructive) civil war (circa 618).

The Constitution of Medina, agreed to by Muhammad and the Muslims of Medina, calls for a confederation among eight local clans as well as the displaced Meccans. The document withholds from Muhammad specific authority over the local clans, but that comes later as a result of the Prophet's military victories. The Jews of Medina, who refuse to recognize Muhammad's messianic status, are not parties to the agreement.

c.623 Muhammad personally leads three *razzias* [raids] against Meccan caravans passing near Medina on their way to Syria. All three raids fail when Muslim traitors reveal Muhammad's movements to the Meccans.

c.624 **January** A small band of Muslims with sealed orders successfully raids a caravan from Yemen. In doing so, Muhammad's followers violate the pagan

c.624
(continued)

concept of sanctity, which signals to the merchants of Mecca the seriousness of the threat posed by Islam.

January Muhammad breaks with the Jews of Medina, no longer willing to make concessions to them in the hope that they might accept him as their savior. Proclaiming the specifically Arab nature of Islam, Muhammad commands Muslims who have been facing Jerusalem in prayer henceforth to face Mecca.

March 15 Leading a force of 315 Muslim raiders, Muhammad encounters near Badr a force of perhaps 800 Meccans guarding a caravan returning from Syria. At least 45 Meccans are killed (including Abu Jahl) and 70 taken prisoner, while only 14 Muslims die. Muhammad points to this victory as a confirmation of his destiny.

625

March 21 Abu Sufyan leads 3,000 Meccans against Medina in retaliation for the defeat at Badr. Though Muhammad intends to withdraw within Medina's forts, invulnerable to contemporary Arab weapons and tactics, farmers whose crops are being destroyed convince him to fight.

March 23 Attacking Muhammad's camp at Uhud, the Meccans are beaten back with heavy losses. Although the Muslims have just completed an all-night march from Medina, they pursue the fleeing Meccan infantry until a Meccan cavalry attack scrambles the field, making impossible a decisive victory for either side. Muhammad's support among the Muslims is weakened, however, when some of his followers wonder why, if Badr was a sign of Allah's support, Uhud should not be interpreted as sign of Allah's abandonment of the Muslims. Fortunately for Muhammad, the inability of the Meccan army to enforce its pledge to make the Muslims pay several times over for the deaths at Badr makes clear the Prophet's rising power.

627

April After two years of preparation for this decisive campaign, Abu Sufyan leads 10,000 men to Medina, where they besiege the oasis. When the siege fails after two weeks, Muhammad's civil and religious authority is significantly strengthened.

628

March Having seen himself in a dream making a pilgrimage to Mecca, Muhammad sets out to make that dream a reality. Accompanied by 1,600 men, the Prophet halts marches to Mecca, halting at al-Hudaybiya on the city's outskirts. There, he negotiates a treaty with the Meccans. In exchange for an end to the hostilities, the municipal leaders agree to permit a Muslim pilgrimage to Mecca the following year.

629 **March** During the pilgrimage to Mecca permitted by the Treaty of al-Hudaybiya, Muhammad and his uncle al-Abbas become sufficiently reconciled for Muhammad to take al-Abbas's sister-in-law as a wife. It has long been Muhammad's practice to consolidate political relationships through marriage, either to himself or his daughters.

November An attack by allies of Mecca on allies of the Muslims causes Muhammad to renounce the Treaty of al-Hudaybiya and prepare for war.

630 **January** Muhammad and 10,000 Muslims march on Mecca, which surrenders with little resistance once Muhammad promises a general amnesty. The Prophet thus returns to Mecca not as a military conqueror, but as a proven religious leader. Upon entering the city, he destroys the pagan idols in the Kaaba and rededicates the shrine to Islam. Many Meccans subsequently convert to the Muslim faith.

632 **June 8** Muhammad's death at Medina, for which no provisions have been made, causes a crisis within Islam and Arab politics. One of the Prophet's fathers-in-law, Abu Bakr, becomes the first caliph, literally "successor." Abu Bakr quickly puts down regional revolts and orders the compilation of the Quran [Koran], which collects Allah's words as revealed to Muhammad.

656 **June 17** The murder of the third caliph Uthman leads to the accession of Ali, the Prophet's son-in-law, who attempts to suppress the corruption he has inherited and return to the Islamic ideals of social justice.

661 With Ali's murder, the Syrian governor Muawiya becomes the fifth caliph. Muawiya has lately been directing a civil war against Ali, allegedly in retaliation for the murder of his kinsman Uthman. This conflict, which Muawiya skillfully quiets, flames again after his death (680) and results in the great Islamic schism between followers of the late caliph Ali (Shiites) and those of his own clan (Sunnis).

The Body Politic

711 After capturing Carthage (698) and converting the North African Berbers (702), invading Arabs and their new Berber allies cross to Spain at Jabal al-Tariq [Gibraltar] and conquer the Visigothic kingdom there. The Muslims in Spain later become known as Moors.

714 Amid the anarchy following the death of Pepin II, his illegitimate son Charles Martel (the Hammer) seizes Austrasia (717) and then defeats the Neustrians at Soissons (719).

717 Byzantine general Leo the Isaurian deposes the usurper Theodosius III and rules as Leo III, founding the Isaurian Dynasty (until 820). In the first year of his reign, Leo withstands a Muslim siege of Constantinople, using Greek fire to establish naval dominance.

718 By holding out against the Moors in the celebrated cave of Covadonga, Pelayo of the Asturias, the last Christian leader in Spain, begins the *reconquista*.

732 The Moors invade western France, but Charles Martel defeats them at Poitiers, ending Arab expansion into Europe.

741 Charles Martel dies, leaving the Frankish kingdom to his sons Carloman and Pepin III. When Carloman enters a monastery in 743, Pepin III becomes the sole ruler of Charles Martel's realm.

Arts & Architecture

c.700 The Old English epic *Beowulf* is composed about this time.

c.700 An unknown author, once believed to be Caedmon, carves *The Dream of the Rood*, an Old English poem about the Crucifixion, into the Ruthwell Cross.

c.700 Monks illuminate the manuscripts of the Lindisfarne Gospels at the scriptorium of the monastery on the island of Lindisfarne. In Ireland, sometime later in this century, the Irish school of calligraphy produces its finest work, the illuminated *Book of Kells*, which con-

Religion & Philosophy

726 Shamed by the iconophobic example set by monotheistic Islam, Byzantine emperor Leo III prohibits the worship of images and relics.

730 Pope Gregory II excommunicates Leo III in punishment for Leo's iconoclas-tic decrees. This leads to a final breach between the eastern and western churches, which separate formally into the Eastern Orthodox and Roman Catholic faiths.

756 Pepin III grants lands taken from the Lombards to Pope Stephen II, establishing

Science & Technology

725 In China, the astronomer Yi Xing and Liang Lingzan, an engineer, construct a water clock with an escapement that makes it tick.

751 In driving the Chinese from Samarkand, the Arabs capture skilled arti-sans who teach their new masters the ancient Chinese secret of making paper.

782 Charlemagne founds the Palatine school, at which Alcuin introduces the *quadrivium* division of mathematics developed by Boethius in 524.

Daily Life

c.730 The stirrup makes its way westward via an unknown route from China to Europe, where Charles Martel may have been the first to recognize its usefulness in cavalry combat, perhaps even utilizing the stirrup in his victory over the Arabs at Poitiers in 732.

748 The first printed newspaper appears in China at Beijing.

756 The Moors begin the systematic irrigation of Spanish river valleys.

c.770 Horseshoes appear in Europe.

750 Descendants of an uncle of Muhammad overthrow the Umayyad Dynasty, massacring nearly the entire royal clan. The Abbasid Dynasty now rules all of the caliphate (until 1258), except Spain.

751 In exchange for Frankish protection against a Lombard military threat, Pope Zacharias agrees to the deposition of the last of the Merovingian puppet kings and the crowning of Pepin III by St. Boniface as the first of the Carolingian Dynasty (until 987).

756 Escaping to Spain, Umayyad prince Abd al-Rahman defeats the weak emir Yusef outside Córdoba and founds an Umayyad emirate there (until 961).

757-96 The reign of Offa the Great, king of Mercia, during which time he annexes Kent and East Anglia and is named *Rex Anglorum* [King of England] by the pope.

763 The construction of Baghdad signals a shift in Arab interests to the east.

774 Charlemagne, the son and heir of Pepin III, interrupts his conquest of the Saxons to annex the Lombards, who were again threatening the papal state.

778 After Charlemagne mounts an abortive invasion of Moorish Spain, Basques ambush his retreating army at Roncevaux and kill his nephew Roland, an episode later recounted in the *Song of Roland.*

The Venerable Bede

tains the Gospels in Latin, along with local records.

712 The scribe Yasumoro creates the *Kojiki* [*Record of Ancient Matters*], aided by Hiyeda no Are, a court lady who has committed Japan's history to memory.

731 The Venerable Bede writes his *Ecclesiastical History of the English People*, the foremost source for the history of ancient England.

c.750 Du Fu and Li Bai, among the finest of China's poets, write concurrently.

a papal state and with it, the temporal power of the pope.

781-790 Alcuin of York resides at the court of Charlemagne, where he plays a leading role in the Carolingian scholarly renaissance, reintroducing to the Franks

the knowledge preserved in British monasteries.

787 At Nicaea, the Seventh Ecumenical Council addresses the iconoclasm controversy, restoring the veneration, though not the worship, of images.

789 Charlemagne introduces a new system of weights and measures including the royal foot as a standard unit of length.

793 With the opening of the first paper factory in Baghdad, papyrus and parchment soon disappear from the Arab world.

779 The first Chinese book on tea, the *Cha Jing*, appears. Tea has gained popularity during this century because it has been found that boiling water kills harmful bacteria that may be present.

793 The Chinese introduce a tax on tea.

793 The Japanese found the city of Heian (later renamed Kyoto), moving the imperial capital there in 794. This marks the beginning of the Heian period of Japanese history during which the Fujiwara, Minamito, and Taira families compete for the throne.

The Body Politic

800 Pope Leo III crowns Charlemagne Holy Roman Emperor in Rome on Christmas Day, reflecting the new political order in western Europe and supplanting Byzantine authority, much to the displeasure of the Byzantine empress Irene.

809 Caliph Harun al-Rashid (of *Arabian Nights* fame) dies during one of the many campaigns the Abbasids fight in order to preserve their dissipating empire.

813-833 Reign of the Abbasid caliph al-Mamun in Baghdad, who succeeds to the throne by deceitfully murdering his brother, yet presides over an unrivaled period of achievement in Arabian science and literature.

814 With Charlemagne's death, his son Louis the Pious becomes Holy Roman Emperor. Though politically weak, Louis continues the Carolingian renaissance, supporting the monastery schools set up by Alcuin at Tours, Corbie, and Fulda.

c.840 Having first crossed to the Shetland Islands circa 790, Viking raiders now move south. The Norse despoil Scotland and Ireland, while Danes maraud in England, seizing and holding land as they can.

843 The Treaty of Verdun resolves the succession dispute among the sons of the late Louis the Pious, dividing the Carolingian Empire into three parts.

Arts & Architecture

c.820 Line drawings in the Utrecht Psalter show the transition of string instruments from classical forms into the violin and guitar.

c.830 An unknown author composes the *Heliand*, an Old Saxon poem that retells the story of Jesus in the style of a Germanic epic. The story varies little from traditional Scripture, except that Jesus is cast as a king with his apostles as warriors.

c.830 Chronicles of Charlemagne's life and exploits begin to appear, the best

Religion & Philosophy

c.813-33 Syrian Christians translate the classic works of Aristotle from the original Greek into Syriac and thence into Arabic. These translations soon find their way to Toledo, which the Moors have made into a European center of learning. It is from Toledo that, in later centuries, the works of Aristotle are reintroduced to western civilization.

c.820-891 Life of Photius, patriarch of Constantinople, who makes official the schism between the eastern and western churches (867). Also, his *Bibliotheca*, a

Science & Technology

815 The science library Bayt al-Hikma is founded in Baghdad.

827 Ptolemy's *Great astronomical composition* appears in Arabic as the *Almagest*, Euclid's *Elements* having already been translated circa 800.

c.830 Muhammad ibn Musa al-Khowarizimi's *Al-jabt wa'l muqabala*, known in the West as the *Algebra*, gives methods for solving equations of the first and second degree with positive roots. The name *al-Khowarizimi* is later anglicized into the mathematical term *algorithm*.

Daily Life

c.800 The Japanese begin to cultivate a new medicine, tea, which the priest Saicho has brought back from Buddhist temples he has been visiting in China.

c.800 The French develop Brie cheese and serve it at the court of Charlemagne.

c.850 Jews who have recently settled among the Germans begin to speak Yiddish, a hybrid language derived from Hebrew and the local German dialects.

c.850 According to legend, coffee beans are discovered in East Africa by the

Charles the Bald obtains most of France, Louis II takes Germany, and Lothair retains the rest, including Italy and the title of Holy Roman Emperor.

850 Allying himself with the Bulgarians and Byzantines, the Moravian prince Rastislaus transforms a loose confederation of Slavs into the Christian kingdom of Great Moravia.

867 Byzantine emperor Basil I founds the Macedonian line (until 1054) and begins rebuilding his empire's army.

868 Egypt becomes independent under the Tulunids, as the Abbasid Caliphate declines at the expense of local emirs.

c.870 In colonizing newly discovered Iceland, the Norse reduce their capability to assault England.

871-899 Reign of Alfred the Great in England, during which he forces a stand-off with the Danes. Northumbria, East Anglia, and parts of Mercia temporarily become the Danelaw, while London and western Mercia are added to Alfred's kingdom of Wessex.

886 Holy Roman Emperor Charles III leads an army against Norse raiders in Paris, only to pay the Norse a large ransom in exchange for a peaceful withdrawal and permission to plunder Burgundy. Charles himself is deposed one year later.

Alfred the Great

---

known of which being the *Vita Karoli Magni*, a history collected by the court scholar Einhard, based on his 23 years of service to the Frankish king.

845-852 Caliph al-Mutawakkil builds the world's largest mosque at Samarra,

which can shelter 100,000 worshipers. Its spiral minaret recalls the ziggurat.

c.890 Among the earliest literature to appear in French is the *Cantilène de Ste. Eulalie*. Previous works had been in a language closer to Latin.

---

compilation of ancient writings, provides the only information available on some classical authors.

862-866 While chief of the palace school of Charles the Bald, Johannes Scotus Erigena writes *De divisione naturae*, in

which he describes the nature of the universe and God's place within it. Equating religion with philosophy and emphasizing reason, Erigena's teachings challenge established Catholic dogma and lead to friction with church authorities who consider his work heretical.

c.850 Work on the astrolabe typifies Arab advances in the field of astronomy.

886 King Alfred the Great of England begins keeping time using a system of six candles that, burning at a regular rate, last one full day.

Arabian goatherd Kaidi, who notices their invigorating effect on his goats.

863 Byzantine missionaries Cyril and Methodius leave on a journey to convert the Moravian Slavs. To further their work, they translate biblical passages into

Slavonic, using an alphabet adapted from Greek. This new alphabet, which comes to be known as Cyrillic, replaces older Serbian writing.

879 Farmers in Italy's Po Valley originate Gorgonzola cheese.

The Body Politic

906 Chased from the Russian steppe by the Patzinak Turks (892), the nomadic Magyars reach the Hungarian Alföld and soon conquer the Great Moravian kingdom.

907-60 A Mongol invasion ends Tang rule in China. The era of the Five Dynasties follows, with none achieving supremacy.

911 In exchange for an end to his plundering raids, Charles the Simple of France grants the Viking Rollo land at the mouth of the Seine that becomes Normandy [Land of the Northmen].

912 Igor inherits the principality of Russia, united by his father Oleg the Wise after 882.

912-61 Reign of Abd al-Rahman III, during which Umayyad rule reaches its height in Spain.

913 Shiite descendants of the Prophet's daughter, Fatima, found the Fatimid Dynasty in North Africa, yet they immediately begin making plans to return east in the hope of regaining a place at the center of the Islamic world.

919 Duke Henry of Saxony becomes king of the Franks and Saxons in Germany, uniting the duchies against the Magyars, whom he defeats at Riade in 933.

955 Henry's son Otto ends the Magyar threat with a decisive victory at the

Arts & Architecture

910 The Cluny monastery represents an early attempt at architecture in the Romanesque style.

c.920 The monk Ekkehard writes the *Waltharius*, an epic poem in Latin about the wars between the Visigoths and the

Huns. It describes the experiences of three young adventurers: Walter of Aquitaine, the Frankish prince Hagen, and the Burgundian princess Hiltegund.

961-976 The Spanish caliphate builds a great mosque at Córdoba, which has

Religion & Philosophy

904-963 During a period in papal history known as the "pornocracy," Theodora and her daughter Marozia of Rome's most powerful family use their influence to install as pope Marozia's lover Sergius III. Later, John XI, the bastard son of Marozia and Sergius, assumes the papacy.

910 William the Pious of Aquitaine founds a monastery at Cluny. Led initially by the Benedictine abbot Berno (910-926) and then by Odo (926-944), Cluny becomes the leading proponent of monastic reform within what has been an increasingly corrupt church.

Science & Technology

c.900 The books of the alchemist Abu Bakr al-Razi describe in detail many practical chemical procedures.

c.925 Abu Uthman translates the comments of Pappus of Alexandria on Book X of Euclid's *Elements*. This translation now

provides the only extant source for this volume of Euclid's work.

c.940 The Dunhuang star map uses for the first time a Mercator-style projection, which Mercator himself will not develop until 1568.

Daily Life

c.919 The Chinese invent gunpowder as a fuel for bombs. It later arrives in the West by way of the Mongols.

c.920 The draft harness for horses, invented in China sometime after the third century, makes its first appearance

in the West, quadrupling the load that a horse can pull effectively.

929 In Prague, Wenceslas of Bohemia, the Christian king immortalized in the famous Christmas carol, is murdered by his pagan brother, Boleslav.

Lechfeld. The German king then attempts to rebuild Charlemagne's empire, while the Magyars settle in Hungary.

960 Tai Zu becomes the first emperor in China's Song Dynasty (until 1279).

962 The Saxon Otto becomes the first non-Frank to be crowned Holy Roman Emperor by the pope.

968 Dinh Bo Linh drives the Chinese from Annam (modern-day Vietnam), which remains a sovereign state until 1407.

969 After a number of unsuccessful attempts, the Fatimids finally take Egypt, moving their capital from Mahdiya to Cairo. Their increasing neglect of their North Africa holdings, however, forces Morocco into an alliance with Umayyad Spain.

976 Basil II Bulgaroktonos [Slayer of Bulgars] ascends to the Byzantine throne and continues his empire's military revival by resisting the Bulgar king Samuel, eventually annexing the West Bulgarian Empire in 1014.

978 The vizier al-Mansur seizes power and strengthens Umayyad rule in Spain.

987 Hugh Capet becomes king of France, founding the Capetian Dynasty there (until 1328).

Wenceslas of Bohemia

become the leading center of European intellectual life.

968 Hrosvitha, a Benedictine nun from Gandersheim, writes *Carmen de gestis Oddonis*, a chronicle in verse of the Ottos and their German imperial family. She is also known for her biblical drama and plays about the lives of the saints.

976 Firdousi begins 35 years of work on the *Shahnama*, a verse history of Persia. Its renewal of ancient themes instantly makes it the Persian national epic.

987 Vladimir of Russia sends envoys to study various religions. They report back that "there is no gladness among [the Bulgars], only sorrow and a great stench." Among the Germans, they find "no beauty." In Constantinople, however, they are awestruck by the Hagia Sophia. Vladimir converts to the Eastern Orthodox faith upon their return.

999 The French scholar Gerbert becomes Pope Sylvester II, adopting a favorable attitude toward feudalism as bishops assume many of the attributes of lords.

940-998 Life of Abu al-Wafa, the foremost mathematician of his time, whose work on spherical trigonometry is based more on Indian models than Greek.

968-977 Abu Mansur al-Muwaffaq writes the *Liber fundamentorum pharmacologiae*, which classifies nearly 600 cures (some gathered during trips to India and Persia) and includes an elementary discussion of pharmacological theory.

988 The Arab sultan Sharaf al-Dawla builds a new observatory at Baghdad.

c.977 At Baghdad, Vizier Abu al-Dawla founds a hospital of 24 doctors, who use drugs from all over the known world.

982 Investigating the story of a large island far to the west, the Icelandic Viking Eric the Red discovers Greenland.

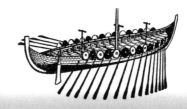

The Body Politic

1008 Mahmud of Ghazni annexes the Punjab to his Turkish Muslim realm in India.

1013 Once Ethelred the Unready flees to Normandy, Edmund Ironside leads England in its defense against invading Danes.

1016 With the defeat of Edmund, Canute of Denmark becomes king of England (until 1035) and later Norway (1028).

1040 Macbeth murders Duncan and replaces him as king of the Scots.

1042 Edward the Confessor becomes the last Anglo-Saxon king of England, but Godwin of Essex objects to the many Normans the king appoints to high office.

1046 When the papacy disintegrates into a quarrel among three rival popes, Henry III of Germany intervenes and installs Clement II, who then crowns Henry Holy Roman Emperor.

1055 The Seljuk Turks take Baghdad, completing their conquest of Iran and Iraq. By 1070, the Seljuk Sultanate will rival that of the Abbasids at their peak.

1066 With Edward's death, Godwin's son Harold becomes king. As William of Normandy prepares to cross the Channel, Harold Hardrada invades from Norway. After beating Hardrada at Stamfordbridge, Harold Godwinson rushes south to Hastings, where William kills him.

Arts & Architecture

c.1004 The Japanese noble lady Sei Shonagon writes *Pillow Sketches*, a diary of social conventions and aristocratic life during the Heian era.

1030 Benedictine monk Guido of Arezzo, called the father of modern music, travels

to Rome to teach Pope John XIV. Guido is credited with developing the staff for musical notation and with naming the first six notes of the scale.

1063 Work begins on the Church of San Marco in Venice, built in the Byzantine

Religion & Philosophy

1041 Atisha arrives in Tibet, where he revives Buddhism (suppressed for 200 years) and establishes the Dalai Lama.

1046 The council called by Henry III to install Clement II also outlaws simony, the buying and selling of church offices.

1054 The final break between the eastern and western churches, known as the Great Schism, comes when Pope Leo IX and Patriarch Michael Cerularius exchange insults and excommunications over temporal political issues and possibly certain unresolved theological ones.

Science & Technology

1005 The Fatimids establish a scientific academy and observatory at Cairo.

1030 The Arab physician Avicenna writes his five-volume *Canon of Medicine*, which will be considered for centuries among the most important medical texts.

1079 Persian mathematician and astronomer Omar Khayyam, a disciple of Avicenna, revises the Muslim astronomical tables so that the Seljuk calendar will keep better time than the Gregorian calendar. Omar also writes a collection of quatrains translated in the nineteenth

Daily Life

c.1000 In the spirit of his father Eric the Red, Leif Ericson sails west and discovers North America (probably Newfoundland), which he names Vinland.

c.1000 The Neapolitans create *pieca*, an ancestor of pizza.

c.1000 Persians, or perhaps central Asian merchants, introduce the seven-day week to China. Previously, the most common week in China has been ten days long.

1066 Halley's Comet is seen in England and associated with the Norman victory.

1071 At Manzikert, the Byzantines lose Anatolia to the Seljuks, shifting the balance of power in the Middle East.

1085 Fighting for Alfonso VI of Castile, the mercenary Rodrigo Diaz de Vivar (El Cid) recaptures Toledo from the Moors.

1090 The Assassins, a Shiite sect known for political violence, occupy the fortress of Alamut, within Seljuk territory yet independent of Seljuk rule.

1094 Extending the *reconquista*, El Cid captures Valencia from the Muslims. He will fight as a soldier of fortune for both sides, but his legend (*The Poem of the Cid*) refers only to his Christian duty.

1095 Consenting to a Byzantine request, Pope Urban II preaches the First Crusade against the Arabs and Turks at the Synod of Clermont.

1096 Anxious to liberate the Holy Land, twenty thousand weaponless Christians join the People's Crusade at Constantinople, but marching on the Seljuk Sultanate of Rum, they are slaughtered.

1097 French and German nobles leading private armies besiege and capture Nicaea. An even greater victory at Dorylaeum leaves Anatolia open to them.

1099 Using movable towers, the crusaders climb Jerusalem's walls and take the city.

Harold Godwinson

Romanesque style with marble floors and walls and decorated with mosaics.

c.1070 Probably commissioned by William the Conqueror's half-brother Odo, the *Bayeaux Tapestry,* a 220-foot-long linen needlework, celebrates William's

victory at Hastings, depicting various scenes of the battle.

c.1095 Probably the work of the Norman poet Turold, *Chanson de Roland* [*Song of Roland*] is the first of the popular poetic cycles known as the *chansons de geste*.

1075 Favoring not merely a church free of state control but a church that controls the state, Pope Gregory VII declares that the investiture of clergy is a matter reserved to the church alone, thus denying kings the right to appoint the bishops within their realms.

1076 A furious Henry IV convenes a synod at Worms to oust Gregory, whose response is excommunication. When Henry's support begins to fail, he is forced to seek the pope's forgiveness at Canossa. Later, in 1084, his power regained, Henry marches on Rome and deposes Gregory by force.

---

century by Edward Fitzgerald as *The Rubaiyat of Omar Khayyam.*

1086 Shen Gua's *Dream Pool Essays* outline the principles of erosion, uplift, and sedimentation that form the basis of earth science.

1076 As a special privilege for nobles, William the Conqueror institutes beheading as the punishment for capital crimes (until 1747), superseding the more commonplace hanging. Waltheof, earl of Northumberland, is the first Englishman beheaded.

1082 The Byzantines reward Venice's aid against the Normans with trading favors.

1086 Agents of William I compile the Domesday Book, an inventory of England, which records the owners and value of all the land so that taxes may be levied.

1000-1099

The Body Politic

1143 Zangi, the Turkish emir of Mosul, assaults the Christian crusader state of Edessa, which falls in 1144.

1145 The French king Louis VII takes the crusading vow on Christmas Day, and St. Bernard of Clairvaux soon convinces Germany's Conrad III to join Louis (1146) for the Second Crusade.

1147 English ships sailing to the Second Crusade help newly independent Portugal (1139) take Lisbon from the Moors.

1147-1149 The Second Crusade achieves little in the Holy Land after Louis and Conrad make an impolitic decision to attack Damascus, a potential ally.

1150-1172 The Shiite Almohads supplant the Almoravid Berbers in Spain. The Almoravids had come to Spain circa 1086 to help the Moors against Alfonso VI of Castile, after the disintegration of Umayyad rule there in 1031.

1154 Ending a 19-year succession fight, Henry of Anjou becomes Henry II of England, the first Plantagenet king. With his queen, Eleanor of Aquitaine, Henry controls more than half of France as well as England (the Angevin realm).

1169 Despite Christian opposition, Zangi's son Nureddin wins Egypt from the Shiite Fatimids, but political disunion with Nureddin's Sunnis lingers.

Arts & Architecture

1100-1150 Cambodians build the pyramidal temple of Angkor Vat, the best preserved example of Khmer architecture. Nearby is the ancient royal city of Angkor Thom, with palaces and temples built in the ninth century under king Jayavarman III at the height of the Khmer Dynasty.

1150-1182 Chrétien de Troyes writes the earliest Arthurian romances for members of the French royal court, where his patron is Count Philip of Flanders.

1170-1204 Walther von der Vogelweide is the best-known of the *Minnesänger*,

Religion & Philosophy

1121 A monk at Cluny since being mutilated for his secret marriage to Hèloïse, Peter Abelard is charged with heresy for his writings, including *Sic et non*, which challenges church doctrine by presenting opposing views without any attempt at reconciling them.

1122 Pope Calixtus II and German emperor Henry V agree to the Concordat of Worms, ending the investiture controversy.

1162 Henry II makes his chancellor Thomas à Becket archbishop of Canterbury. Becket surprisingly defends the church.

Science & Technology

c.1100 Chinese astronomers build a stone planisphere that correctly demonstrates the causes of solar and lunar eclipse.

c.1100 The Persian mathematician Omar Khayyam becomes the first person to solve the general cubic equation.

Daily Life

c.1100 According to tradition, the fork is introduced to Europe by the wife of the Venetian doge Domenico Silvio.

1107 The Chinese invent a multicolor printing process in order to make paper money harder to counterfeit.

1120 Hugh de Payens founds the order of the Knights Templar to guide and protect pilgrims to the Holy Land.

1140 The Norman king Roger II decrees that only physicians holding government licenses may practice medicine.

1171 When the last Fatimid caliph dies, Vizier Saladin becomes sole ruler of Egypt. Upon Nureddin's death (1174), he founds the Ayyubid Sultanate, uniting Egypt and Syria under Sunni rule.

1176 The victory of the Lombard League at Legnano forces the German emperor Frederick I Barbarossa to submit to the Peace of Constance (1183), which recognizes the League's independence.

1187 Saladin defeats the Latin king of Jerusalem at Hattin, culminating his own *jihad* [holy war] to recapture the city.

1189 Frederick Barbarossa begins the Third Crusade, but dies abruptly (1190).

1191 Richard I Coeur de Lion [the Lion-Hearted] of England and France's Philip II arrive in the Holy Land, where they capture Acre but proceed little farther. Philip returns to France, while Richard negotiates with Saladin, who agrees to permit pilgrimages to Jerusalem (1192).

1192 Minamato Yoritomo, the first of the Japanese shoguns (who control puppet emperors), founds the Kamakura Shogunate (until 1333). In the feudal wars that follow, retainer knights called *samurai* fight for competing shoguns.

1192-1194 Leopold of Austria kidnaps Richard I en route to England. Emperor Henry VI then holds Richard for ransom.

Richard the Lion-Hearted

---

who wander through Germany singing songs of love, faith, and patriotism.

1174-1184 After a destructive fire, William of Sens rebuilds Canterbury Cathedral in the Gothic style, previously unknown in England.

1174 The campanile beside the cathedral at Pisa, built on unstable ground, begins to lean soon after construction.

1196 Richard the Lion-Hearted builds the formidable Château Gaillard to defend his French lands against Philip II.

1170 Knights loyal to Henry II murder Thomas à Becket in Canterbury Cathedral.

1190 Rabbi Moses Ben Maimon [Maimonedes] issues his *Guide of the Perplexed*, a philosophical work applying Aristotelian reasoning to current Jewish thought. His

purpose is to renew the Jewish faith and combat assimilation in Islamic Spain.

1198 Death of the Moorish philosopher Averroës, whose reading of Aristotle led him to the heresy that knowledge is based on reason and not faith.

1111 Abelard of Bath writes *Questiones naturales*, an early stab at scientific method that covers some topics advanced by the Arabs including meteorology, optics, acoustics, and botany. He later translates al-Khowarizmi's *Astronomical tables* from Arabic into Latin (1126).

1175 Gerard of Cremona translates Ptolemy's *Almagest* from Arabic into the Latin used by medieval scholars.

c.1180 Burgundio of Pisa translates various treatises by Galen from the original Greek into Latin.

---

c.1150 The Chinese develop fireworks.

1170 The practice of *seppoku*, or ritual suicide, begins in Japan.

c.1176 The Old London Bridge across the Thames, made of stone, replaces an

even older timber bridge. Houses built on the new stone bridge have a tendency to burn down, but they are quickly rebuilt.

1189 Across the Yong Ding River, the Chinese build a bridge that is still heavily used by auto traffic.

1100-1199

The Body Politic

1202 A Fourth Crusade gathers at Venice, where the knights intend to board ships for Egypt. When they cannot pay the agreed-upon fare, the doge offers the crusaders passage in exchange for their help in taking the Adriatic port of Zara. From there, the crusaders are further diverted by the Venetians to Constantinople.

1204 To suit the Venetians' commercial purposes and out of antipathy for the Greeks of Constantinople, the crusaders replace the Byzantine Empire there with a Latin one. They return home without fighting a single Turk.

1211 Genghis Khan conquers the Qin Empire in northern China. Before his death in 1227, the Mongol leader will establish an empire spanning Asia from the Pacific to the Black Sea.

1212 Defeated at battle of Navas de Tolosa, the Almohads abandon Spain, while the victorious Christian kings restrict the remaining Moors to Granada.

1212 Fifty thousand teenagers join the Children's Crusade, believing their innocence will make them stronger than knights. The vast majority never return.

1214 Philip II defeats John I of England and his allies at Bouvines, enabling him to integrate into France English-held lands against which he has long plotted.

Arts & Architecture

c.1200 German literature flourishes under the influence of Wolfram von Eschenbach (*Parzival*) and his well-known contemporary Gottfried von Strassburg (*Tristan*), who author mystical and symbolic versions of epic Arthurian romances.

1230 Guillaume de Lorris writes the first part of the French poem *Roman de la Rose*, finished some 40 years later by Jean de Meun. Numbering more than 19,000 lines, this allegory subtly investigating every aspect of love is translated widely, remaining popular for centuries.

Religion & Philosophy

1208 Demonstrating his great secular power, Pope Innocent III launches the Albigensian Crusade to root out heresy in the south of France.

1208 After a rigged vote denies his friend Stephen Langton the archbishopric of Canterbury, Innocent III excommunicates John I and places England under interdiction. John relents, accepting Langton in 1213.

1261 The Eastern Orthodox church is reestablished at Constantinople.

Science & Technology

1202 The *Liber abaci* of Italian mathematician Leonardo Fibonacci marks the introduction of Arabic numerals to Europe. His extensive study of fractions includes many applications of arithmetic to practical, especially commercial, problems.

1252 Arab and Hebrew astronomers complete a new set of planetary tables, named after the Christian king Alfonso X (the Learned) of Spain. The Alfonsine Tables, as they come to be known, are considered the best available until the sixteenth century.

Daily Life

c.1200 Venetian and Genoese middlemen profitably trade European textiles for Oriental spices imported by Arabs.

1265 Having defeated Henry III at Lewes (1264), Simon de Montfort convenes the first English Parliament.

c.1275 Spectacles are invented, possibly by Roger Bacon.

c.1280 Venice begins coining gold ducats (*ducatus Venetiae*), which become an internationally accepted currency and make Venice the Continent's banker.

1215 English nobles force John I to sign the Magna Carta, which limits his monarchical power (especially regarding taxation) and mandates trial by jury.

1228-1229 German emperor Frederick II, excommunicated for malingering (1227), leads the Sixth Crusade, securing Bethlehem, Nazareth, and Jerusalem.

1244 The Mamluk general Bibars retakes Jerusalem from the Christians for the final time. Six years later, the Mamluks overthrow the Ayyubids and found their own sultanate in Egypt (until 1517).

1251 Mongols establish the realm of the Golden Horde in Russia.

1256 Lübeck and other northern German cities meet to form the Hanseatic League for the mutual protection of trade.

1258 Mongols from the Persian Ilkhanate sack Baghdad, finishing off the Abbasids, and then head for Egypt, where the Mamluks repulse them at Ain Jalut (1260).

1261 Michael VIII Palaeologus retakes Constantinople, ending the Latin Empire.

1280 Kublai Khan founds the Mongol Yuan Dynasty in China (until 1368) after conquering the Song.

1291 The Mamluks conquer Acre, the last Christian outpost in the Holy Land.

Marco Polo

1260 Italian Gothic sculptor and architect Niccola Pisano completes the marble pulpit for the Baptistery in Pisa.

c.1290 Giovanni Cimabue, mentor of Giotto, paints his masterpiece *Madonna and Child with Prophets and Angels* in

Florence's Church of Santa Maria Novella. Cimabue's innovations in composition, along with his use of light and color, make him the leading artist of his time.

1296 Work begins on the Duomo, Florence's cathedral (completed in 1436).

1274 St. Thomas Aquinas dies, leaving uncompleted his *Summa theologica*, which unites theology and philosophy within a Christian framework. Influenced by the rediscovered writings of Aristotle, Aquinas points out that reason can be used to explain that which faith accepts.

1280 The most widely read scholar of his time, Albertus Magnus dies, having written extensively on both theological and Aristotelian issues.

1294 Boniface VIII replaces a puppet at Naples and moves the papacy back to Rome.

---

c.1257 Culminating fifty years of university expansion, Robert de Sorbonne founds a celebrated college bearing his name at the University of Paris (established circa 1200 by Philip II), which has become the most influential university in Christendom.

1278 English scientist Roger Bacon is imprisoned for heresy (until 1292) for attacking the ignorance and vices of the clergy. Bacon is widely known for his advocacy of experimental science, which he regards as complementing rather than opposing religion.

1295 Adopting Simon de Montfort's plan, Edward I convenes the Model Parliament.

1295 Marco Polo returns to Venice, having spent two decades traveling the Asian continent. While in China, he sojourned at the court of Kublai Khan.

1200-1299

THE MIDDLE AGES

The Body Politic

1300 Osman I breaks away from the collapsing Seljuks. The Ottoman Empire he founds rules Turkey until 1923.

1302 Philip IV (the Fair) convenes the Estates-General for the first time so that France's feudal lords can show support for his dispute with Boniface VIII.

1314 Robert Bruce defeats Edward II of England at the battle of Bannockburn, establishing Scotland's independence.

1327 Edward II's wife, Isabelle of France (daughter of Philip the Fair), conspires with dissatisfied English nobles to depose her husband, who is replaced by their son Edward III.

1328 Isabelle's brother Charles IV dies without a male heir, ending the Capetian line. A council of nobles, ruling that the crown cannot pass through women, chooses Philip VI as king, beginning the Valois Dynasty (until 1589).

1337-1453 The Hundred Years' War begins when Philip VI and Edward III dispute each other's claim to the French throne. Erasing the French navy at Sluys (1340), England quickly controls the Channel.

1346 At Crécy, French knights charge English longbowmen 16 times, losing 1,542 noblemen. The English, who lose but 50, later take Calais (1347), which they use as a port of entry until 1559.

Arts & Architecture

1304-1374 Life of the Italian lyricist Petrarch, who writes much of his poetry to Laura, a woman he sees in church.

1306 The Gothic artist Giotto begins his greatest work, the fresco cycle on the walls of the Arena chapel in Padua.

1314 Dante Alighieri writes *The Comedy*, an allegorical journey through Hell, Purgatory, and Paradise.

1353 Giovanni Boccaccio writes the *Decameron*, a collection of stories set during the Black Death.

Religion & Philosophy

1303 During a dispute over the French king's ability to tax the clergy, Philip the Fair kidnaps Boniface VIII, who has threatened excommunication. Supporters force the pope's release, but Boniface, broken, dies a year later, after which the papacy submits to France.

1309 A former archbishop of Bordeaux, Pope Clement V moves his seat to Avignon in southern France, beginning the "Babylonian Captivity" of the papacy.

1367-1370 Urban V moves the papacy back to a dilapidated Rome but, conclud-

Science & Technology

1300 Pierre Pipelart builds the first public mechanical clock in Paris, based on the designs of the English cleric Bortholomew of London. The new mechanical clocks are driven by a weight whose descent is controlled by an escapement. Chinese clocks of this period also use escapements, but they still employ water as a power source.

1323 Pope John XXII threatens with excommunication any churchgoer practicing alchemy because alchemists "present a false metal for gold and silver."

Daily Life

c.1300 The *Nibelungenlied* combines the sagas of various German tribes into a single, unified Germanic legend.

c.1300 The Dutch fisherman William Beukelszoon discovers how to cure herring by gutting and salting the fish.

1325 Ibn Batuta of Tangier, the greatest of Muslim travelers, begins a journey that takes him to India, Ceylon, and China, returning to Fez in 1349.

c.1325 Aztecs establish Tenochtitlán on the site of modern Mexico City.

1354 The Ottoman Turks capture Gallipoli, their first foothold in Europe.

1356 Edward, the Black Prince of Wales, overwhelms the French at Poitiers.

1358 Burdened by the hardships of war, French peasants rise up against the hated nobility in the *Jacquerie*.

1368 Mongol Yuan ruler Togan Temur flees before Zhu Yuanzhang, who as Hong Wu founds the Ming Dynasty (until 1644).

1369 The Muslim convert Timur takes over the Mongol Jagatai Khanate, beginning a half-century of conquest in central Asia, Ilkhanate Persia, and Europe.

1381 Wat Tyler leads a popular revolt against the Statute of Laborers (1351), winning its repeal and other concessions.

1389 The Ottomans crush a Balkan host at Kossovo, as the impatient sultan Bayezid takes control of the region by 1396, accelerating Ottoman gains in Europe.

1395 Timur breaks up the Golden Horde khanate of Toktamish in central Russia.

1397 With the Union of Kalmar, Margaret of Denmark unites all of Scandinavia.

1399 Henry of Bolingbroke overthrows Richard II and becomes Henry IV, first of the House of Lancaster (until 1461).

Margaret of Denmark

1354 The just-completed Alhambra palace in Granada becomes the greatest example of Moorish architecture in Europe.

c.1360 The quick pace and wit of *Gawain and the Green Knight* marks a high point in Middle English romance.

1370-90 William Langland writes *Piers Plowman*, an allegory set in contemporary England.

1387-1400 Geoffrey Chaucer writes *The Canterbury Tales*, a spectrum of stories told by travelers on a pilgrimage to Canterbury.

---

ing that the church's business cannot be run there, returns to Avignon.

1377 In another attempt to move back to Rome, Gregory XI comes to the same conclusion that Urban V had, but dies before he can return to Avignon. Roman

mobs quickly force the election of Urban VI, an Italian pope committed to staying in Rome. The College of Cardinals soon revokes Urban's election and names Clement VII "anti-pope" at Avignon, beginning the Great Schism of the West (1378-1417).

---

c.1330 William of Occam's *Summa totius logicae* proposes that, of several explanations for a phenomenon, the simplest should be taken. This presumption, later identified as Occam's razor, becomes one of the founding principles of the scientific method.

c.1340 Boccaccio correctly explains the existence of fossils by deducing that the sea once covered the earth.

1346 The Hundred Years' War battle of Crécy marks the earliest recorded use of small cannon, probably of forged iron.

1346 Carried from the Volga probably by trading ships, the Black Death ravages Europe, killing 20 million people.

1351 England's Statute of Laborers fixes wages to resolve a labor shortage brought on by years of war and plague.

The Body Politic

c.1400 Pachacutic Inca rules a South American empire made up of modern-day Peru, Ecuador, and Chile.

1400 Welsh nationalist Owen Glendower joins allies of the deposed Richard II in an unsuccessful uprising against Henry IV.

1402 Picking a fight with Bayezid, the Tartar warlord Timur diverts the Ottoman army from a siege of Constantinople and defeats it at Angora. Then Timur's army, which runs on plunder, sacks the cities of the Turks one by one.

1415 On St. Crispin's Day (OCT 25), the army of Henry V defeats a French host four times its size at Agincourt, using the same strategy Edward III did at Crécy. Longbowmen devastate the French men-at-arms, who sacrifice 5,000 knights of noble birth, while the English lose 13.

1420 With the Treaty of Troyes, Henry V marries Catherine, daughter of French king Charles VI, and becomes heir apparent to the French throne—thus bypassing Charles's own son, the Dauphin.

1422 The infant Henry VI becomes king of France and England when his royal father (Henry V of England) and grandfather (Charles VI of France) die in the same year. Nationalist French territories south of the Loire, however, choose to recognize the Dauphin as king.

Arts & Architecture

1420 Filippo Brunelleschi begins work on the huge dome of the cathedral in Florence, which has posed an insurmountable problem to medieval architects. Ancient Roman engineering remains unavailable to Brunelleschi, so he invents a new double-dome system to manage the task.

c.1424 Of disputed authorship but often credited to Thomas à Kempis, *The Imitation of Christ* becomes the most widely read and influential work of its time.

1432 Flemish painter Jan van Eyck completes the altarpiece at Ghent, including

Religion & Philosophy

1400 The English Parliament passes the *De heretico comburendo*, a law that punishes relapsed heretics by burning them at the stake. The law is directed at the Lollards, followers of the Oxford theologian John Wycliffe (c.1320-1384), who opposed the church on transubstantiation, on its secular authority, and on its extensive landholdings. Wycliffites favored secular itinerant priests, who would preach the Bible (using a hitherto unavailable English translation, completed in 1388) rather than the promulgations of a corrupt church of Rome.

Science & Technology

1409 A type foundry in Korea produces the first book printed with metal type, anticipating Johann Gutenberg and Peter Schöffer by nearly five decades.

1414 In a Swiss monastery, monks discover an ancient manuscript containing the lost text of Vitruvius's Roman engineering text, *De re aedificatoria*.

1418 Portugal's Prince Henry the Navigator builds an observatory at Sagres in order to compile astronomical tables for use in navigation.

Daily Life

c.1400 As the development of heavy cannon influences new ship design, the idea of a navy—that is, ships built exclusively for warfare—begins to take hold.

1403 Upon ascending to the throne, Chinese emperor Yong Luo, third in the Ming line, commissions the colossal *Yong luo da dian*. This encyclopedia of Chinese knowledge, completed in 1408 by a 2,169-member staff, fills 917,480 pages in 22,937 separate sections.

c.1415 Lanterns light London's streets.

1428 General Le Loi expels the Chinese, who have briefly regained Annam (1407), and founds a dynasty that lasts in one form or another until the French colonize Indochina circa 1800.

1429 The peasant maid Joan of Arc, who claims to hear the voices of saints urging her on, raises the English siege at Orleans and leads an army that turns the English back at Patay. That same year, she escorts the Dauphin to Reims, where he is crowned Charles VII of France.

c.1430 The Aztec Moteuczoma [Montezuma] brokers an alliance with the Alcohuas and the vanquished Tepanecs creating an Aztec empire in central Mexico.

1431 French clerics conspire with her English captors to burn Joan of Arc at the stake in Rouen after she is declared a heretic for wearing men's clothes.

1434 Cosimo the Elder becomes the first Medici ruler of Florence.

1453 At Castillon, the French regain Aquitaine, ending the Hundred Years' War. The English have already lost Normandy (1450), but they retain Calais.

1453 Using siege engines, the Ottomans of Mehmet II (the Conqueror) reduce the walls of Constantinople, unbreached since their construction a millennium earlier, and take the city, renaming it Istanbul.

Joan of Arc

the magnificent central panel, *The Adoration of the Mystic Lamb*. Producing the first important paintings using oil paints, van Eyck also develops secular portraiture with his realistic paintings of *A Man in a Red Turban* and *Giovanni Arnolfini and His Bride*.

1440 The Florentine artist Donatello completes his bronze *David*, the first major nude sculpture since those of classical antiquity, which serve as his inspiration. Unlike other works of the time, which were designed to fit specific church niches, the *David* is freestanding.

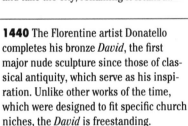

1411 Excommunicated for his Lollard sympathies, Jan Hus of Bohemia begins preaching the superiority of the Bible.

1414-1417 The Council of Constance ends the Great Schism of the West with the recognition of Martin V as pope.

c.1420 The Mongolian Turk Ulugh Beg founds an observatory at Samarkand. Its star catalog, the *Zij Ulugh Beg*, becomes famous throughout Europe.

1420 Granular gunpowder appears, leading to rapid improvements in artillery.

1436 With his *Trattato della pittura,* Italian mathematician Leone Battista Alberti becomes the first to apply geometric principles to the laws of pictorial perspective. In his *De re aedificatoria*, he develops perspective in relation to architecture.

1416 Prince Henry the Navigator of Portugal founds a school of navigation.

1431 Portuguese sailors find the Azores because, in returning from gold expeditions to Africa, they must swing far out into the Atlantic to pick up favorable winds.

1446 The hand gun, resembling a handheld cannon or bazooka, comes into practical use.

1449 Thomas Brightfield builds a water closet that flushes using water piped from a cistern.

1454-1648

The Body Politic

1454 Henry VI suffers a prolonged fit of insanity, during which Richard of York serves as regent of England (also during 1455-1456). Although enmity exists over which man has the better claim to the throne, Richard refrains from seizing power, despite the obviously inept government of the Lancastrians.

1459 As Henry's Queen Margaret plans an attack, Richard strikes first, beginning the Wars of the Roses (until 1485). Richard is routed at Ludford, but Margaret's overly harsh treatment of the defeated Yorkists earns them public sympathy.

1460 JUL 10 Landing in Kent, the exiled earl of Warwick, Richard Neville, crushes the Lancastrians at Northampton. Richard of York then declares his right to the crown and calls for Henry's deposition.

1460 DEC 30 Marching against the queen, Richard of York is killed at Wakefield. The Lancastrians give no quarter, killing their prisoners and displaying Richard's head over the gates of York.

1461 The Yorkists proclaim Richard's heir to be Edward IV, who founds the House of York (until 1485).

1462-1492 Rule of Lorenzo de' Medici in Florence. He presides over the reconciliation of the Italian trading states and the blossoming of Renaissance art.

Arts & Architecture

1454 A printed *Bible of 42 lines* appears in Mainz, at first attributed to Johann Gutenberg but now credited to Peter Schöffer (and possibly Johann Fust). Gutenberg did print the earlier 31-line *Letter of Indulgence*. These printings begin the era of movable type in Europe.

c.1460 Andrea Mantegna begins painting the Camera degli Sposi [Newlyweds' Chamber] in Mantua's Gonzaga Palace. Using complex perspective and the exact replication of architectural details, he creates the first *trompe l'oeil* interior decoration of the Renaissance.

Religion & Philosophy

c.1454 After conquering Constantinople, Ottoman emperor Mehmet II transforms the Hagia Sophia, the seat of Eastern Orthodoxy, into a mosque.

c.1454 Cosimo de' Medici welcomes to his palace in Florence many Greek schol-

Science & Technology

1464 German mathematician and astronomer Johann Müller, known as Regiomontanus, writes *De triangulis omnimodis*. The first important treatise on trigonometry by a European, Regiomontanus's work reflects both Arab and classical Greek influences.

1472 JAN Regiomontanus studies a great comet, calculating its daily parallax using a method developed by Florentine astronomer and cartographer Paolo dal Pozzo Toscanelli. Regiomontanus's observations establish the foundation for modern cometary astronomy.

Daily Life

c.1454 Borrowing from Moorish and Persian designs, Italian potters glaze their majolica in four lustrous colors: cobalt, purple, green and yellow.

c.1454 Mokha (Yemen) becomes an export center for the Arab coffee trade.

1455 The first bowling alleys appear in England, often connected to taverns. The game soon becomes popular with bettors.

1463 An English law compels men's coats to cover their buttocks, but the demands of fashion render the law unenforceable.

1463 Pope Pius II preaches, but fails to launch, a latter-day crusade to recapture Constantinople from the Ottoman Turks.

1465 The Yorkists capture Henry VI and imprison him in the Tower of London, apparently resolving the dynastic succession in favor of the House of York.

1467 Edward IV breaks with Richard Neville, earl of Warwick, whose defeat of the Lancastrians made Edward king. Partisans of Warwick lead an uprising, imprisoning Edward (1469), but the king regains his freedom and chases Warwick to France (1470), whereupon Warwick conspires with his erstwhile enemy Queen Margaret to restore Henry VI.

1469 OCT 19 Isabella, heir to Castile and Leon, marries Ferdinand of Aragon, ensuring the future unification of Spain.

1470 Warwick returns to the south of England, which rises up against Edward IV, who flees to Holland and the court of Charles the Bold. Warwick restores Henry VI, but reserves rule to himself.

1471 APR 13 Returning to England with a mercenary army, Edward IV defeats and kills Warwick at Barnet. Three weeks later at Tewksbury (MAY 3), Edward finishes off the Lancastrians. He then orders the execution of all possible Warwick and Lancaster heirs and has Henry VI murdered in the Tower (MAY 21).

Johann Gutenberg

c.1474 William Caxton publishes *The Recuyell of the Historyes of Troye*, the first book printed in the English language. Caxton continues to write, translate, and print popular and literary books until his death in 1491. He translates and publishes a printed edition of *Morte Darthur* in 1477 and one of Chaucer's *Canterbury Tales* the following year. Caxton's enterprising use of the new printing technology makes him a wealthy man, as the English upper classes flock to purchase literary works printed in their own language.

ars who have fled to Italy after the fall of Constantinople.

1462-1482 Florentine scholar Marsilio Ficino directs the Platonist Florentine Academy, advancing humanism under the patronage of Cosimo de' Medici.

1473 The printing of Lucretius's *De rerum natura* [*On the nature of things*] (written in 57 BC) promotes the popularity of ancient Greek and Roman texts. Taking advantage of the new printing technology, many classical works are translated and published at this time.

1474 In letters to Christopher Columbus, Paolo dal Pozzo Toscanelli discusses the distance from Lisbon to Asia by way of the Atlantic Ocean. Although his 3,000-mile estimate is wildly inaccurate, it nevertheless persuades Columbus to consider the journey feasible.

1464 The first money-lending shop charging interest opens in Orvieto.

1464 The French found a postal service.

1469 Makers of shoes called pattens establish a guild in England. Built with thick wooden or cork platforms, pattens keep women's feet above the muck that clogs Europe's streets. In the next century, the patten will evolve into the gilded Venetian *chopine*. The *chopine*'s platforms will be so high (up to two feet) as to require a walking attendant.

1454-1474

The Body Politic

1477 AUG 18 Hapsburg emperor Maximilian I marries the daughter of Charles the Bold, who has just inherited her father's dukedom of Burgundy and The Netherlands, confounding the attempts of Louis XI of France to annex these lands.

1478 JAN 14 The citizens of Novgorod accept Grand Duke Ivan III of Muscovy as their sovereign. Ivan thus extends his realm to include all of northern Russia from Lapland to the Urals.

1480 Ivan III stops paying tribute to Khan Ahmed of the Golden Horde, who responds with military force. Ivan holds out until the onset of winter compels the Tartar army to retire south.

1480 Ferdinand and Isabella establish the Spanish Inquisition as a means of asserting their absolute authority in matters both religious and secular.

1481 A rival khan kills Khan Ahmed as he prepares a second attack against Ivan III. Ahmed's death plunges the Golden Horde into chaos and releases Muscovy from the Tartar yoke. Ivan soon takes the imperial title of *tsar*.

1483 JUN 16 Richard of Gloucester imprisons the two young sons of his recently deceased older brother Edward IV in the Tower of London. Then, filling the city with his troops, he proclaims himself King Richard III (JUL 9). A week later, the

Arts & Architecture

1481 Leonardo da Vinci's unique treatment of his group subject in the *Adoration of the Magi* marks a turning point in Renaissance art. In the *Last Supper* (1497), considered the first painting of the High Renaissance, Leonardo develops his new perspective even further.

c.1485 For the Medicis of Florence, Sandro Botticelli paints his masterful *Birth of Venus*, inspired by contemporary poetic interpretations of ancient myth.

1495 Hieronymus Bosch paints his imaginative triptych, *The Garden of*

Religion & Philosophy

1476 Preaching on the corruption of the clergy, the shepherd Hans Böhm builds a following of more than 50,000 German villagers. But when his followers stop paying their taxes, the archbishop of Mainz has Böhm burned at the stake and his church at Nicklashausen destroyed.

1483 Having been convinced by Thomas Torquemada to create the Inquisition, Ferdinand and Isabella make him the Grand Inquisitor of Spain. In the next year, Torquemada issues instructions that permit accused heretics to be tortured until they confess.

Science & Technology

1477 In *The Ordinall of Alchimy*, Thomas Norton discusses the philosopher's stone, capable of transmuting lead into gold.

1478 The *Treviso Arithmetic*, the first printed mathematical work, teaches rules for performing common calculations.

1480 Leonardo da Vinci sketches a practical parachute. Da Vinci's contributions to scientific knowledge also include his observation of capillary action (1490), his drawings of a clock with a pendulum (1494), and his imaginative helicopter (sketched circa 1500).

Daily Life

1475 Louis de Berquem perfects the art of "brilliant" diamond cutting.

1481 Portuguese explorers found Elmina in present-day Ghana, providing a direct route to the African gold fields previously serviced by the Berbers.

1488 Searching for a new spice route, Bartholomew Diaz of Portugal becomes the first European sailor to round the Cape of Good Hope at Africa's southern tip.

1492 OCT 12 Seeking a transatlantic route to India, Christopher Columbus

nephews die mysteriously and are buried beneath the Tower.

1485 AUG 22 At the battle of Bosworth Field, the Lancastrian heir Henry Tudor (later Henry VI) defeats the forces of Richard III, who is killed, thus ending the Wars of the Roses and beginning the Tudor line (until 1603).

1488 FEB 14 Responding to the imperial decay, German princes form the Swabian League and create a national guard to protect them from foreign incursions.

1492 JAN 2 Muslim Granada surrenders to Ferdinand and Isabella, whose assurance of toleration is quickly forgotten.

1492 In keeping with the spirit of intolerance fostered by the brutal Inquisition, Ferdinand and Isabella expel the Jews from Spain.

1493 MAY 4 Pope Alexander VI draws a line of longitude 100 leagues west of the Azores. He then grants to Spain all new territories to the west of this line and to Portugal all discoveries to the east.

1499 The 19-year-old Sufi Ismail captures Tabriz and proclaims himself the first Safavid shah of Persia.

1499 SEP 22 With the Treaty of Basel, Switzerland gains its independence from the empire of the Hapsburgs.

Leonardo da Vinci

Earthly Delights, addressing contemporary concerns of human folly and morality.

1498 Fleeing the chaos of Florence after a French invasion, Michelangelo travels to Rome, where he begins to sculpt his *Pietà* for St. Peter's.

1498 German printmaker Albrecht Dürer creates the bound woodcut series *Apocalypse* with text printed on the reverse of each page. His frontispiece of the author, St. John the Evangelist, gains recognition for woodcut engraving as a true form of art.

1484 Pope Innocent VIII's bull *Summis desiderantes affectibus* calls for the persecution of witches in Germany.

1489 Jakob Sprenger and Heinrich Krömmer publish the *Hexenhammer*, an inquisitor's guide to the persecution of witches.

1490 Aldus Manutius founds the Aldine Press in Venice, dedicating himself to publishing classical Greek philosophy.

1498 The populist monk and prophet of doom Savonarola is tortured and then burned at the stake in Florence.

1489 The + and - signs for addition and subtraction appear for the first time in a treatise by Johannes Widmann.

1492 Using inaccurate Ptolemaic data (instead of Marco Polo's), Martin Behaim builds the first globe in Nuremberg.

1494 *Summa de arithmetica, geometria, proportioni, et proportionalità* by Luca Pacioli compiles the mathematical knowledge of the time, with a particular emphasis on commercial application. Pacioli elaborates on the double-entry bookkeeping used in Venice and Genoa.

---

sights the Bahamas and becomes the first European to reach the New World.

1498 MAY 20 Vasco da Gama completes the work of Diaz and finds the new spice route, dropping anchor off the Indian city of Calicut.

1475-1499

1474 Corresponding with cartographer Paolo dal Pozzo Toscanelli, Christopher Columbus becomes convinced that the riches of Asia lie across the Atlantic Ocean just a few thousand miles from Europe. Believing the world to be round, Columbus essentially reasons that, because it is a long way from Spain to Asia by land (east), it must be a short trip by sea (west).

1486 After he is refused by the king of Portugal (1484), Columbus submits to the Spanish court of Ferdinand and Isabella his plan for an expedition to find a westward route to Asia. The queen's confessor, Bishop Hernando de Talavera of Avila, forms a commission to study Columbus's proposal.

1490 Delayed in its work by Columbus's secrecy and imprecision, the Talavera commission finally advises against the expedition.

1492 **January** Despite Talavera's report (and Columbus's exorbitant demand for 10% of the commerce resulting from his discoveries), Ferdinand and Isabella agree to fund the effort.

August 3 Leaving from Palos, the 40-year-old Columbus sails west aboard his flagship, the 117-foot *Santa Maria*. Also under Columbus's command are two 50-foot caravels, the *Niña* and the *Pinta*.

August 6 Rudder trouble with the *Pinta* has Columbus suspecting sabotage.

August 12-September 6 Columbus stops at the Canary Islands, where the *Pinta*'s rudder is repaired and his three ships take on supplies.

September 25 The *Pinta*'s captain spots land, but what he actually sees is a dark squall on the horizon. Mistaken land sightings become frequent.

October 7 Flights of birds flying to the southwest convince Columbus to change his course in that direction. He also raises the reward offered by Ferdinand and Isabella for the first crew member to sight land.

October 11-12 Late at night, Columbus thinks he sees light on the horizon. A few hours later, about two in the morning, the *Pinta*'s cannon fires a shot signaling that land has been sighted. Columbus later claims the reward for himself, asserting the validity of his midnight "sighting."

October 12 Columbus arrives at Guanahani in the Bahamas, convinced that he has landed at "the end of the Orient." Despite evidence of gold among the natives (whom he calls "Indians"), Columbus leaves quickly because he believes Cipango [Japan] to be only a short distance away.

October 23 Continuing his search for the land "where gold is born," Columbus sails for Cuba, which the islanders have described to him and Columbus believes must be Japan. The admiral sends interpreter Luis de Torres ashore to interview the "grand khan," but all he finds are natives smoking a weed (tobacco), which the Spaniards consider a bizarre practice.

November 21 The *Pinta* disappears before a strong easterly wind. Columbus worries that its captain has sailed for Spain to steal from him the glory of his discovery. In search of the *Pinta*, Columbus discovers an island he names Hispaniola (modern Haiti).

December 5 Columbus hosts a meal for the islanders' chief. Although the two men cannot yet converse, Columbus later writes that the chief has told him "the whole island was mine to command."

December 24 During a Christmas Eve fête at which Columbus's crew celebrates with some 2,000 islanders, a strong gale blows the *Santa Maria* aground, smashing it against the rocky shoreline. Columbus interprets the wreck as a divine message to leave behind the crew of the *Santa Maria* in a settlement that he establishes and calls Villa de la Navidad.

1 4 9 3   **January 4** Leaving 39 sailors behind on Hispaniola with ammunition and enough food to last a year, Columbus sets sail for Spain on the *Niña*.

January 6 The *Pinta* reappears. Columbus at first rejects the captain's explanations, threatening to hang him, but the admiral soon relents.

February 14 Rough weather separates the two ships. Fearing that the *Pinta* has already sunk, Columbus writes an account of his discoveries, seals it in a barrel, and casts it overboard—lest the storm sink his ship, too, and thus prevent news of his glorious achievement from ever reaching Spain.

March 4 Columbus sights Portugal. Anchoring in the mouth of the Tagus River, he is received with great honor at the court of the Portuguese king on March 9.

1493
(continued)

March 15 The *Niña* returns to its home port of Palos, Spain, where Columbus receives an exuberant welcome. Three days later, the *Pinta* appears.

April Ferdinand and Isabella receive Columbus at Barcelona, where they rise to greet him and offer him a stool on which to sit beside them.

September 25 Columbus launches his second voyage from Cádiz. The fleet of 17 ships, carrying over a thousand men, has been largely financed by cash and property confiscated from Spain's recently expelled Jews.

November 3 Taking a more southwesterly course than he did previously, Columbus sights land off Dominica. Soon, his ships discover Guadeloupe and Puerto Rico. Arriving finally at Hispaniola, Columbus learns that the men he left behind have been murdered. Before he leaves the ruined settlement, Columbus orders a search for gold these men might have buried.

December After Columbus founds the first permanent European settlement in the New World, named Isabella after the queen, he sends a messenger back to Spain with a self-serving report. News of the massacre at La Navidad, however, shocks the court, considerably weakening his position there.

1494

March 29 Columbus returns from a two-week survey of the island to find the crew ready to mutiny against his incompetent brother Diego, whom Columbus had left in charge. The admiral deals harshly with the rebels, ordering several of them hanged.

May 5 During another tour around his islands, searching for the Asian mainland, Columbus discovers Jamaica.

June 13 Returning to Hispaniola via Cuba, Columbus becomes convinced that Cuba is indeed the mainland. He makes his crew swear an oath to this effect, threatening to have their tongues cut out should they recant.

March 24 Back in Isabella, Columbus and his brother Bartholomew lead an expedition to "pacify" the natives. Five hundred prisoners are soon shipped off to Spain as slaves in lieu of gold, which has not been plentiful.

1495

October Juan de Aguado arrives at Hispaniola, sent there by Ferdinand and Isabella to report independently on Columbus's actions as governor.

Aguado finds the natives at the point of rebellion because of a severe gold tax imposed by Columbus. The two men struggle for control of the colony.

1 4 9 6 **March 10** Columbus and Aguado sail for Spain on different ships, both built on Hispaniola. They arrive at Cadiz ón June 11.

1 4 9 8 **May 30** After regaining his status at court, Columbus embarks on his third voyage to the New World, sailing from Sanlúcar.

July Venturing farther south, Columbus nearly stumbles on the mouth of the Amazon, but instead discovers Trinidad and then the Venezuelan mainland, which he mistakenly believes to be another island.

August Columbus arrives in Hispaniola to find one of his subordinates in rebellion against his brother Bartholomew. Columbus settles the matter with an execution, but news of his poor stewardship reaches Spain, where Ferdinand and Isabella decide to replace him as governor with the courtier Francisco de Bobadilla.

1 5 0 0 **August 23** After more than a year's delay, Bobadilla arrives in Hispaniola, where he takes command. When Columbus refuses to accept Bobadilla's authority, the explorer is arrested and shipped back to Spain in chains.

November Ferdinand and Isabella order that Columbus, who has just landed at Cádiz, be set free and restored to a position of dignity, but they specifically forbid his return to Hispaniola.

1 5 0 2 **May 9** Columbus sails from Cádiz on his final voyage. On June 15, he discovers Martinique. Then, despite the royal ban, he heads for Hispaniola, where the new governor denies him admission to the harbor at Santo Domingo. Columbus sails on, fighting mutinies along the way. In one letter to Ferdinand and Isabella, he claims to be ten days from the river Ganges.

1 5 0 3 **June 23** Columbus finds himself stranded on Jamaica. He perseveres for nearly a year before help arrives from Hispaniola the following June. Landing in Spain on November 7, 1504, Columbus returns a broken man.

1476   The greedy pope Sixtus IV extends the authority of indulgences to cover souls in purgatory. Indulgences are the most flagrant of the spiritual abuses currently practiced by the increasingly corrupt Roman Catholic Church. Backed by papal authority, they allow wealthy penitents to purchase the practical component of the sacrament of penance for a fee. Negotiations are handled either by accredited papal agents (the itinerant indulgence sellers) or by the financial house of Fugger of Augsburg.

1514   The greedy and unscrupulous Medici pope Leo X offers another in his series of special indulgences, supposedly intended to raise money for the construction of St. Peter's Basilica in Rome. But Leo has made a secret arrangement with Albert, archbishop of Mainz. Greatly in debt after having spent a considerable sum purchasing his ecclesiastical office, Albert will receive half of the German proceeds from this "jubilee" indulgence that claims to make the purchaser "cleaner than Adam before the Fall."

1517   **October 31** Augustinian monk and university professor Martin Luther nails 95 theses to the great wooden door of All Saints Church in Wittenberg. These theses, which represent the evolving thought of the German theologian, attack corruption within the Catholic Church, especially regarding the sale of indulgences. Although Luther's intention at this time is to rehabilitate the Church, not break with it, his symbolic act is traditionally considered to be the beginning of the Protestant Reformation.

1518   When news of Luther's slap reaches Rome, Pope Leo X orders the head of Luther's Augustinian order to discipline the vexatious monk. When this proves futile, Leo tries to work through Luther's secular master, Elector Frederick the Wise of Saxony, but this policy also fails. What Leo has neglected to consider is that, with the current upsurge in nationalistic feeling, religious authority has become inextricably entangled with secular political considerations.

1519   Luther debates Johann Eck, a scholar well known for his argumentative nature, at Leipzig's castle of the Pleissenburg. Eck skillfully manipulates Luther into the damaging admission that his interpretation of Scripture has caused him to doubt the authority of the Council of Constance (1414-1418), which condemned the Bohemian reformer Jan Hus and burned him at the stake. The pope has been moving slowly against Luther because he has no wish to offend Frederick the Wise, one of seven electors who will soon choose the new German emperor.

1520   **June 15** Leo X issues the bull *Exsurge Domine [Cast out, Lord]* against Luther's writings, announcing that a "wild boar has entered the Lord's vineyard" and condemning Luther as a heretic. Leo demands that Luther recant within 60 days or face excommunication.

During the summer, Luther writes two controversial manifestos. *Address to the Christian Nobility of the German Nation* recalls the many German grievances against the papacy and concludes that Rome's unwillingness to change legitimizes secular intervention. *A Prelude Concerning the Babylonian Captivity of the Church*, written for an ecclesiastical audience, directly attacks papal religious authority.

1521   **January 3** After Luther openly defies the pope's command that he submit to the judgment of Rome, Leo X issues a second bull excommunicating him.

April 18 Appearing before Emperor Charles V at the Diet of Worms, Luther refuses to recant unless he can be convinced of his error either by Scripture or by reason. Unwilling to turn against his conscience, Luther reportedly concludes, "Here I stand. I can do no other." Although his simple defiance captures the imagination of Europe, an unsympathetic Charles issues the Edict of Worms, declaring Luther to be an outlaw and banning his writings. Rather than risk war between the emperor and the princes supporting him, Luther submits to a simulated kidnapping and escapes to the castle of the Wartburg, near Eisenach.

1522   Huldrych Zwingli begins the Swiss Reformation in Zurich with challenges to fasting and clerical celibacy. Zwingli acts independently of Luther, but shares the German's reliance on Scripture as the sole spiritual authority as well as Luther's belief in justification by faith (rather than by the Catholic combination of faith and works).

September Luther publishes a German translation of the New Testament, which he follows up in 1534 with a translation of the Old Testament derived from the original Hebrew.

**1524
−1525**

The Peasants' War temporarily distracts Catholic emperor Charles V from resolving the mounting problem of Lutheran heresy. Although the revolt's leaders are inspired by his writings, the socially conservative Luther disowns their rebellion against secular authority in *Against the Murdering and Thieving Hordes of Peasants*.

About this time, a number of young, radical intellectuals in Zurich split from Zwingli and found a new sect based on uncompromising adherence to scriptural authority. Their most distinctive ritual is adult baptism, on the basis of which they are called Anabaptists. Because of their extremism, the Anabaptists are generally persecuted by Catholics and Lutherans alike.

1526

Forced by the political situation into compromising his firmly Catholic beliefs, Emperor Charles V adopts a policy of religious toleration at the Diet of Speyer.

1529

April 19 At the second Diet of Speyer, the Lutheran princes of Germany read a protest against the decision made by Charles V and the Catholic princes to rescind the toleration granted in 1526. The Lutherans insist that if forced to choose between God and Caesar, they will choose obedience to God. Henceforth, their opponents call them Protestants.

October At a meeting in Marburg intended to create a unified Protestant front, Luther and Zwingli engage in the Marburg Colloquy, during which they debate the meaning of the Eucharist. Zwingli asks how Christ can be present in the bread and wine. Luther replies that if God commanded him to eat crabapples and manure, he would do it.

1530

Philip Melanchthon represents the Lutherans at the Diet of Augsburg, from which Luther is barred by the Edict of Worms. Melanchthon's *Augsburg Confession*, one of the most impressive works of the Reformation, explicates Lutheran beliefs and unites the Protestant princes, who form a defensive league at Schmalkalden in anticipation of Catholic aggression.

1532

The Turkish invasion of Hungary leads to the Religious Peace of Nuremberg, which establishes a truce between Catholics and Protestants until the convocation of a general church council or the next meeting of the Reichstag.

1534 After Pope Clement VII refuses to grant Henry VIII a divorce from his first wife, Catherine of Aragon, Henry renounces papal authority and establishes the Church of England, with the king as its spiritual head. His action begins the English Reformation.

1536 In Basel, 27-year-old John Calvin publishes the first edition of his *Institutes of the Christian Religion*, which soon becomes the most widely accepted treatise on Protestant theology.

1541 −1564 Calvin heads a sternly theocratic regime in Geneva, modeling many of his institutional reforms on the ideal society of Thomas More's *Utopia* (1516).

1545 **December 13** Pope Paul III convenes the Council of Trent to clarify ambiguities in Catholic doctrines challenged by the Protestants. Nationalist political problems force the council to adjourn in 1547. It reconvenes in 1551 and meets until Maurice of Saxony's revolt against Charles V forces another adjournment. The final convocation begins when Pius IV reopens the council in 1562.

1546 −1547 Charles V defeats the Schmalkaldic League, temporarily derailing the German Reformation, which also suffers the death of Luther in 1546.

1549 *The Book of Common Prayer* offers a Protestant liturgy in English.

1555 Despite the protests of Charles V, the Diet of Augsburg recognizes the right of Protestants to coexist peacefully with Catholics in the German Empire. Its decision becomes known as the Religious Peace of Augsburg.

1563 The Counter-Reformation begins with the formal dissolution of the Council of Trent. The purge of abuses undertaken by the reform pope Paul IV (1555-1559) makes possible this resurgence of Catholicism—which Luther had, on his deathbed, considered to be fatally wounded. Of extraordinary assistance in the Catholic rejuvenation are the Jesuits, whose disciplined and well-educated order Ignatius Loyola founded in 1539.

The Body Politic

1502 Spain begins to expel those Moors who refuse to convert to Christianity.

1515 The Ottoman Turks declare war on Egypt (MAY) and soon capture the Egyptian dominion of Syria (AUG).

1516 Ferdinand of Spain dies, leaving as his only surviving heir his mad daughter Joanna (who had once been married to the late son of Hapsburg emperor Maximilian). When Joanna is declared incompetent, the throne passes to her 17-year-old son Charles. Besides Spain itself, Charles's vast inheritance will include Burgundy, The Netherlands, and the hereditary Hapsburg lands in Austria, as well as Spain's colonies in the New World.

1517 JAN 20 Ottoman emperor Suleiman I takes Cairo, becoming sultan of Egypt and ending the Mamluk Dynasty there (since 1250).

1517 OCT 31 German theologian Martin Luther nails his 95 theses criticizing the Roman papacy to the door of the church at Wittenberg, thus beginning the Protestant Reformation in Europe.

1519 MAR 4 The conquistador Hernando Cortes lands 700 soldiers on the Mexican coast. As his men advance, the natives flee in terror—if not of the Spaniards' horses, then of their artillery fire. Some believe the invaders to be divine immortals in the image of the white Aztec god

Arts & Architecture

1501-1504 Michelangelo sculpts the *David* to represent the ideal Florentine man, at peace yet poised to defend himself against a prodigious foe.

1503 Leonardo paints the *Mona Lisa*, his portrait of a Florentine official's wife.

1505 Pope Julius II commissions Donato Bramante to design a new Church of St. Peter in Rome. Work continues under Bramante until 1514.

1508 Julius II hires Raphael to decorate the papal apartments of the Vatican.

Religion & Philosophy

1506 Johann Reuchlin publishes a Hebrew lexicon and grammar that contributes greatly to Old Testament scholarship.

1509 Johann Pfefferkorn convinces Emperor Maximilian I to impound all the Jewish books in Germany. When Reuchlin

argues for the protection of these works, the Inquisition puts him on trial.

1511 The renowned Dutch humanist and scholar Desiderius Erasmus publishes his acerbic satire *In Praise of Folly* privately in Paris.

Science & Technology

c.1502 Peter Henlein builds the first spring-driven pocket watch, known as the Egg of Nuremberg.

1504 Columbus intimidates the Jamaican natives using Regiomontanus's *Ephemerides astronomicae* to predict an eclipse.

1507 Acclaimed cartographer Martin Waldseemüller publishes a map of the world on which he identifies the New World as *America*, after Amerigo Vespucci. Although Vespucci explored the continent, he may not have (as Waldseemüller believed) discovered it.

Daily Life

1513 Spaniard Juan Ponce de Leon explores Florida after serving as the first governor of Puerto Rico.

1513 Portuguese explorer Vasco Nuñez de Balboa crosses the Isthmus of Panama and discovers the Pacific Ocean.

Quetzalcoatl. Arriving at Tabasco, Cortes learns of the immense wealth of the Aztec Empire under Montezuma II.

1520 Cortes establishes a garrison at Veracruz, burning his ships to show his men that they must either conquer or perish. He then searches out Montezuma at the Aztec capital of Mexico City. Meanwhile, Aztecs attack Veracruz and learn that the Spanish are, in fact, not gods. Hearing news of the raid, Cortes boldly storms the palace and takes Montezuma captive. When a Spanish force under Narvaez sails to relieve Cortes of his command, Cortes marches from Mexico City to meet his compatriot, whose army he defeats and then commandeers.

1520 JUL 7 At the plain of Otumba, Cortes annihilates the pursuing Aztecs, assuring his subjugation of Mexico. After assembling an army of conquered provincials, Cortes returns to Mexico City, which he besieges until its fall several months later (1521, AUG 21).

1520 OCT 23 Despite the objections of Francis I of France and Pope Leo X, Charles of Spain is crowned at Aix, becoming German emperor Charles V.

1521 MAY Charles V denounces Martin Luther in the Edict of Worms. Because of Charles's Spanish blood, many German princes side with Luther, spiriting him away to safety at the castle of the Wartburg.

Martin Luther

1508-1512 Michelangelo paints the ceiling of the Sistine Chapel.

c.1512 The foremost composer of the early sixteenth century, Josquin des Près writes *A Dirge for Five Voices* in memory of his deceased music master.

1515 Titian completes Giorgione's nude *Sleeping Venus*, beginning a secular era in European art during which visual aesthetics matter as much as subject.

1516 Ludovico Ariosto publishes his lively romance *Orlando Furioso*.

1513 Florentine statesman Niccolò Machiavelli completes *The Prince*, his classic study of the best methods for getting and keeping political power.

1516 Thomas More's *Utopia* describes the ideal society of a supposedly newly

discovered land. More uses this ruse to avoid retribution for his criticisms of corruption and vice among the powerful.

1522 Preaching strict adherence to Scripture, Huldrych Zwingli leads the Reformation in Switzerland.

1514 Nicholas Copernicus begins work on his new heliocentric theory, which enrages the church by challenging long-held dogma about the earth's place at the center of the universe. His *De revolutionibus orbium coelestium* is wisely withheld until his death in 1543.

1517 Italian physician Girolamo Fracastoro examines fossilized mussels he has found in rocks quarried for the citadel of San Felice in Verona. Fracastoro concludes that the remains must be of animals that lived in the area during the distant past.

1514 Landing at Guanzhou, the Portuguese open trade relations with the Chinese.

1517 A Spanish bishop visiting Haiti complains to King Charles of the natives' forced labor, suggesting that Africans might be better suited to the heavy work.

Accepting the advice, Charles ships 4,000 Africans to the New World, thus beginning the slave trade with the Americas.

1521 The crew of Ferdinand Magellan completes the first circumnavigation of the world. Magellan is killed en route.

1500-1524

THE RENAISSANCE

The Body Politic

1525 FEB 24 Following his invasion of Italy (1524), Francis I meets Charles V at Pavia, where Charles's army smashes the French and takes Francis prisoner.

1526 Henry VIII of England begins to contemplate divorcing Catherine of Aragon, an aunt of Charles V, because she has yet to produce a male heir.

1526 APR 19 A resurgent clan of Timurids under Babar of Ferghana (modern-day Turkestan) defeats the Delhi sultanate of Ibrahim at Panipat, founding the Mogul Dynasty in India.

1526 AUG 29 Succumbing to the Ottoman forces of Suleiman I (the Magnificent) at Mohacs, Hungary loses its independence (until 1918). Suleiman eventually cedes a portion of the country to Charles V's brother Ferdinand, who controls the Hapsburg lands in Austria.

1527 MAY 6 An imperial army of 30,000 German and Spanish mercenaries sacks Rome, devastating the Eternal City and imprisoning Pope Clement VII, who has opposed Charles V's supremacy in Italy.

1529 AUG 3 In return for the emperor's support in resisting the Reformation in Germany, Clement VII submits to Charles V, who uses his influence with the pope to deny Henry VIII's request for a divorce from his aunt Catherine of Aragon.

Arts & Architecture

1526-1528 Jacopo Carrucci da Pontormo paints the *Visitation*, a prime example of the bold Mannerist style that emphasizes form and color over content.

1532 François Rabelais publishes his burlesque classic *Gargantua* to such popular acclaim that he follows up his success with *Pantagruel* one year later.

1537 German painter and printmaker Hans Holbein becomes permanently ensconced at the English court of Henry VIII after painting Thomas Cromwell's portrait.

Religion & Philosophy

1525 Inspired by Luther, German peasants rebel against clerical privilege. Luther himself disavows them and sanctions government suppression of the uprising.

1529 After the second diet of Speyer refuses them tolerance, Germany's Lutheran princes appeal to Emperor Charles V, calling themselves "Protestants."

1535 JUL 6 Henry VIII has Thomas More beheaded for refusing to accept the king as both the temporal and spiritual leader of England.

Science & Technology

c.1530 The German Paracelsus creates a system of medicine independent of the prevailing classical and Arabian schools. Relying on the Neoplatonist notion that every disease can be treated with an antagonistic alchemical substance, he anticipates modern chemical medicine.

1535 A five-year mathematical challenge ends when Niccolò Tartaglia finally solves a cubic equation. He generalizes his method by 1541.

1538 In Toledo, two Spaniards holding a lit candle descend into water beneath an

Daily Life

1528 Venice's Aldine Press publishes Baldassare Castiglione's *Il libro d'oro*, describing the ideal Renaissance man.

1531 Portugal's John III orders surveys of the coast off Rio de Janeiro in order to expedite the colonization of Brazil.

1530 DEC A group of Protestant German princes forms the Schmalkaldic League in opposition to Charles V's order that the lands of Protestants be confiscated.

1532 The Spanish adventurer Francisco Pizarro murders the Inca king Atahualpa as a prelude to conquering all of Peru.

1533 Flouting the pope, the puppet archbishop of Canterbury Thomas Cranmer voids Henry VIII's marriage to Catherine of Aragon and sanctions his secret wedding to Anne Boleyn two months earlier.

1534 Parliament affirms the Act of Supremacy, establishing the Church of England with Henry VIII as its head.

1541 John Calvin establishes a Protestant theocracy in Geneva.

1547 JAN 16 Ivan IV Grozny [the Terrible] crowns himself tsar of Russia.

1547 Upon the death of Henry VIII, his nine-year-old son (by his third wife Jane Seymour) becomes King Edward VI of England (until 1553). Because Edward is a minor, the king's uncle Edward Seymour, duke of Somerset, rules the country as regent in his stead.

1548 AUG 15 Six-year-old Mary Queen of Scots (daughter of the late James V) arrives in France following her betrothal to the four-year-old Dauphin.

Francisco Pizarro

1544 Luis Vaz de Camoens begins his patriotic Portuguese epic *Lusiads*, the first to employ a wholly modern theme.

1545 Mannerist sculptor Benvenuto Cellini begins his 18-foot-high statue of *Perseus with the Head of Medusa*.

1546 Reconstruction of the Louvre begins in Paris, using plans by Pierre Lescot in the Italian Renaissance style.

1546 Michelangelo becomes the chief architect of St. Peter's, supervising construction until his death in 1564.

1536 The dissolution of the monasteries begins when Henry VIII makes confiscation of monastical lands state policy.

1536 John Calvin publishes his classic *Institutes of the Christian Religion*, which defends the lofty goals of Protestantism.

1539 Ignatius Loyola forms the Society of Jesus (Jesuits) in response to what he deems to be a Protestant threat.

1545 Pope Paul III convenes the Council of Trent to settle doctrinal disputes and rally Catholics against the Protestants.

---

inverted kettle. Their emergence, with the candle still burning, anticipates the invention of the diving bell.

1542 Using dissection, Andreas Vesalius completes the first systematic and comprehensive book on human anatomy.

1545 Girolamo Cardano publishes his *Ars magna*, which includes Tartaglia's solution to the general cubic equation (now mistakenly named for Cardano). This formula marks the first definitive triumph of Renaissance mathematicians over their classical predecessors.

1540-42 Francisco Vasquez de Coronado explores the southwestern United States. He records sighting a prairie bison, Zuñi pueblos, and the Grand Canyon.

1541-1542 Leaving from Mexico, Hernando de Soto explores the Mississippi.

1525-1549

The Body Politic	**1552** AUG 2 Aided by the French, Maurice of Saxony revolts against Charles V, forcing the Treaty of Passau, which promises religious freedom to German Lutherans.

1554 Mary I weds Charles V's son Philip and restores Catholicism to England. Many Protestants, including exhumed corpses, are burned at the stake.

1555 SEP 25 The Religious Peace of Augsburg grants each German prince the right to choose Lutheranism or Catholicism for himself and his subjects.

1556 A frustrated Charles V cedes the Spanish inheritance to his son Philip II. Then Charles abdicates in favor of his

brother Ferdinand, whom Pope Paul IV refuses to recognize as German emperor.

1558 NOV 17 Elizabeth I becomes queen upon Mary's death. Refusing a foreign husband, she champions "England for the English" and begins the Elizabethan Age.

1559 JUN 30 At a joust celebrating the Treaty of Cateau-Cambrésis (ending the Italian wars), a lance blow fatally wounds Henry II of France. His teenage son Francis II succeeds him, with the duke of Guise and the cardinal of Lorraine serving together as regents.

1560 Succeeding a despotic regent, Akbar begins the greatest of Mogul reigns. |
| **Arts & Architecture** | **c.1554** *La Vida de Lazarillo de Tormes*, the first picaresque novel, appears in Spain, satirizing contemporary society.

1557 AUG 10 After routing the French, Philip II of Spain vows to build a new palace and monastery dedicated to St.

Laurence. The granite Escorial, begun seven years later, becomes one of the most admired structures in Europe.

1562 The players of the Inner Temple present the first English tragedy to Queen Elizabeth. Authors Thomas Norton and |
| **Religion & Philosophy** | **1559** John Knox returns from Geneva to promote Calvinism in his Scottish homeland. A year later, the Confession of Faith abolishes papal authority there.

1563 Queen Elizabeth approves the 39 Articles that form the basis for a new,

independent Calvinist state church in England.

1563 The Catholic Counter-Reformation begins with the conclusion of the third session of the Council of Trent at which the Jesuits affirm papal centralism. |
| **Science & Technology** | **c.1550** Building on the pioneering work of Vesalius, Gabriel Fallopius describes the female reproductive system (Fallopian tubes), while Bartolemeo Eustachio, an accomplished engraver, depicts the components of the inner ear, including the Eustachian tube that bears his name.

1551 Although not admitting heliocentrism, Erasmus Reinhold nevertheless calculates his widely used astronomical *Tabulae prutenicae* using Copernican principles.

1551-1558 Konrad von Gesner's *Historium animalium* begins modern zoology. |
| **Daily Life** | **c.1550** Ambroise Paré develops many surgical innovations, including the use of ligatures to control bleeding (allowing large-scale amputations) and the treatment of gunshot wounds with bandages instead of the hot oil that has been commonly applied.

1553 Mention of the potato first appears in Pedro Cieça's *Chronicle of Peru*.

1553 The Chinese lease Macao to the Portuguese as a trading post. Then, four years later, the Chinese restrict European trade to that island. |

1560 When Francis II dies, his French-bred wife Mary returns to the throne of Scotland hoping that Catholic support in England will gain her that throne as well.

1562 MAR 1 Two hundred French Huguenots (Protestants) are massacred at Vassy by the Catholic Guises, plunging France into a series of bloody religious wars.

1567 Philip II sends the brutal duke of Alba to repress Dutch Protestants. Alba's tribunal, the Council of Blood, prompts the Dutch war of independence.

1571 OCT 7 At Lepanto, the Christian Maritime League scuttles the Ottoman fleet, halting its eastern advance.

1572 Akbar drives the Afghans out of Bengal, securing for himself the largest dominion yet of any Mogul emperor.

1572 AUG 24 As Huguenot leader Henry of Navarre prepares to marry the king's sister, Catholics manipulated by the queen mother murder 50,000 Protestants during the Massacre of St. Bartholomew.

1572-1573 Commanding the *Swan* and the *Pasha*, the English pirate Sir Francis Drake harasses Spanish shipping off Panama, winning a huge booty of silver.

1573 Oda Nobunaga defeats the last Ashikaga shogun (since 1338), beginning the creation of a new Japanese empire.

Elizabeth I

Thomas Sackville base *Gorboduc*, inspired by an English legend, on Seneca's model of tragedy.

1566 *Gammer Gurton's Needle*, considered the first English comedic drama, is performed at King's College, Cambridge.

1564 Archbishop of Canterbury Matthew Parker first uses the term "Puritan" to describe those who believe the Church of England has not turned far enough away from Roman Catholicism. The Puritans observe a strict code of religious discipline and a simple style of life.

1568 In order to force the Moors to give up Islam, Philip II demands that Moorish children be taught by Catholic priests, provoking a rebellion in Granada.

1574 Spaniards hold the first *auto-da-fé* (the Inquisitional sentencing ceremony).

1560 Giambattista della Porta, who writes on the closely allied subjects of magic and science, founds the first scientific society, the *Academia secretorum naturae*. The Inquisition forces him to disband the group, however, when it brings him to trial for practicing black magic.

1568 Gerardus Mercator first publishes the map projection that bears his name.

1569 Using a huge celestial globe, Danish astronomer Tycho Brahe defines a system for measuring astronomical movements based on right ascension and declination.

1558 Sent by Philip II to investigate Mexican plant life, Francisco Fernandes returns to Spain with the tobacco plant.

1558 Sir Thomas Gresham articulates the economic law, named after him, that "bad money drives out good."

1562 English admiral John Hawkins seizes a Portuguese slave ship and, sailing it to the New World, begins the English slave trade with Spain's colonies.

1565 St. Augustine, Florida, becomes the first European colony in North America.

1550-1574

The Body Politic

1576 NOV 3 Antwerp suffers the "Spanish Fury," during which Philip II's soldiers riot over a lack of pay (his treasury being depleted). This rampage produces the Pacification of Ghent, at which The Netherlands unites behind William of Orange to expel the Spanish troops.

1578 AUG 4 The army of Abd al-Malik slays Sebastian I at Ksar el-Kebir as the Portuguese king vainly attempts to invade Morocco. Philip II wins the ensuing succession fight by force, uniting Spain and Portugal in 1581 (until 1640).

1579 JAN 5 Philip II's governor in the Netherlands, Alexander Farnese, convinces southern Catholic nobles to join the League of Arras. Northern Protestants respond with the Union of Utrecht (JAN 29), which claims independence (as the United Provinces) in 1581. The southern Walloon provinces later become Belgium.

1586 The Protestant queen Elizabeth expels the Spanish ambassador from England for his Catholic intrigues against her.

1587 Edward Babington conspires with Mary Stuart (deposed from her Scottish throne in 1568) to murder Elizabeth. When the queen discovers the Catholic plot, she has Mary executed (FEB 8).

1587 Emperor Hideyoshi orders all Christian missionaries to leave Japan.

Arts & Architecture

1578 Raphael Holinshed's *Chronicles of England, Scotland and Ireland* along with Thomas North's version of Plutarch's *Lives of the Noble Greeks and Romans* (published 1579) later become the primary sources for many of Shakespeare's plays.

1578 El Greco, the Greek student of Titian and Tintoretto, completes his masterpiece *The Burial of Count Orgaz*.

1580 French writer Michel de Montaigne publishes an entirely new form of literature, his first collection of *Essays*.

Religion & Philosophy

1576 MAY 6 The Peace of Monsieur ends France's fourth war of religion, but its call for religious toleration everywhere (except Catholic Paris) leads to the formation of the Catholic League, which dedicates itself to the eradication of Protestantism in France.

Science & Technology

1582 Pope Gregory XIII adopts the Gregorian calendar. Placing the spring equinox at March 11, he orders the "removal" of ten days that have accumulated since the Julian calendar reform of 46 BC. Thus, the day after October 4, 1582, becomes October 15, 1582.

1584 Giordano Bruno publishes a new view of the universe based on Copernican principles. The Inquisition later burns him at the stake for heresy (1600).

1597 AUG 4 Writing to German astronomer Johannes Kepler, Galileo Galilei admits

Daily Life

1576-77 James Burbage builds London's first playhouse.

1580 SEP Sir Francis Drake returns to Plymouth after two-and-a-half years of sailing, having achieved the second circumnavigation of the globe.

1580 Russian hunters, searching for animals with which to supplement their fur trade, begin to explore Siberia.

1584 By order of its senate, Venice establishes the first public bank in Europe, the Banco di Rialto.

1588 JUL The Spanish Armada sails for The Netherlands, its mission being to carry the duke of Parma's army across the Channel in the misguided hope that this invasion will spark a Catholic rebellion in England. Unfavorable winds and a flotilla of small, mobile ships under Francis Drake, however, prevent the Spanish fleet from even reaching Parma's camp.

1589 With Henry III's assassination, the Huguenot Henry of Navarre becomes King Henry IV of a divided France, beginning the Bourbon Dynasty there.

1592 Japanese emperor Hideyoshi orders an (unsuccessful) invasion of Korea as a prelude to humbling China.

1593 JUL 25 Henry IV's conversion to Catholicism ends the religious wars in France.

1597 Infuriated by Chinese insults and condescension, Hideyoshi launches a second Japanese invasion of Korea, which disintegrates after his death (1598).

1598 APR 13 Henry IV proclaims the Edict of Nantes, granting toleration (outside of Paris) to the Huguenots, thus assuring them both rights and privileges.

1598 MAY 2 Henry IV's war to expel the Spaniards ends in mutual exhaustion with the Peace of Vervins, confirming the hastening decline of Spain, and uniting France.

Mary Stuart, Queen of Scots

1588 Already known for uniting Titian's colors with Michelangelo's designs, the Venetian Mannerist master Tintoretto receives a commission to paint the colossal *Paradise*, the largest work ever undertaken on canvas. Completed, it stands 74 feet by 30 feet.

c.1589 William Shakespeare writes his first play, *Love's Labour's Lost*. From this point on, he will average two plays a year until 1613.

1590 Edmund Spenser publishes the first three books of his epic *Faerie Queen.*

1576 French philosopher Jean Bodin publishes his *Six livres de la République*, probably the most important work on political science since Aristotle's *Politics*. Four years later, his *Démonomanie des sorciers* castigates those who do not believe in witchcraft.

1580 Robert Parsons and Edmund Campion found the first Jesuit mission in England, from which they agitate against Elizabeth in favor of Spain.

1597 Richard Hooker's *Laws of Ecclesiastical Polity* defends Anglican theology.

that he accepts Copernican theory. But fearing persecution and ridicule, he will not yet state his beliefs publicly.

c.1597 Galileo invents the first thermometer using a glass tube filled with air and water.

1584 Sir Walter Raleigh's men explore the eastern seaboard of North America and name a vast area of it Virginia after the unmarried Queen Elizabeth.

1585 Raleigh establishes England's first North American colony at Roanoke.

1586 Sir Francis Drake introduces tobacco smoking to the English court, where the novelty quickly takes hold among Elizabeth's courtiers.

1589 William Lee invents the first knitting machine (the stocking frame).

1575-1599

The Body Politic

1603 James VI of Scotland, son of Mary Queen of Scots, succeeds Elizabeth, becoming James I of England, the first Stuart king. He relaxes, then reimposes, Elizabeth's restrictions on Catholics.

1605 Catholics, Guy Fawkes among them, conspire (but fail) to blow up the king and Parliament in the Gunpowder Plot.

1605 Tsar Boris Godunov dies without an heir, beginning the chaotic and savage Smuta [Troubled Times] in Russia.

1609 SEP 22 Spain's government orders the complete expulsion of the Moors. Their brutal deracination devastates Spain's cultural and economic life.

1610 MAY 14 The assassination of Henry IV brings to the throne his nine-year-old son Louis XIII, during whose reign absolutism will be established in France.

1611 Though both Danes and Poles claim succession, Gustavus II Adolphus takes the crown of Sweden, bribing the Danes and forming an alliance with the Poles, both countries being eager to exploit Russia during its Troubled Times.

1613 With Poles and Swedes in Moscow and Novgorod, and the rest of Russia in anarchy, a popular assembly installs Michael Romanov as tsar. He evicts the Poles and later makes peace with Gustavus II, ceding him Finnish lands (1617).

Arts & Architecture

c.1600 Kabuki theater develops when a Japanese Shinto priestess organizes a troupe to stage bawdy farces.

1600 Caravaggio completes his *Calling of Saint Matthew*, using naturalistic rather than idealized human forms.

1605 Miguel de Cervantes's *Don Quixote* ridicules the chivalric tradition.

1607 Claudio Monteverdi produces his first opera *Ariana* seven years after Jacopo Peri's *Euridice* became the first dramatic performance set to music.

Religion & Philosophy

1601 JAN 24 Although many missionaries had failed before him, Matteo Ricci gains entry to the Chinese capital of Beijing at the invitation of the secluded emperor's wives. The mission Ricci establishes there provides the basis for all Roman Catholic study in China.

Science & Technology

1604 Tycho Brahe's former assistant (and heir) Johannes Kepler concludes that the orbit of Mars is elliptical.

1608 OCT 2 Hans Lippershey petitions for the exclusive rights to his new invention, the seven-power telescope.

1609 Inspired by news of Lippershey's invention, Galileo makes his own telescope. After some hasty refinements, he obtains a magnification of 32 times.

1609 Kepler publishes his *Astronomia nova*, a foundational work of modern

Daily Life

c.1600 The first European coffee houses open in Venice and Constantinople.

c.1600 Chinese tea is popularized in Europe by Dutch traders, although the beverage had been known to their Portuguese rivals as early as 1517.

1600 DEC 31 Queen Elizabeth charters the English East India Company with exclusive trading rights for all markets east of the Cape of Good Hope for a period of 15 years. She intends for the company to compete with the Dutch for the lucrative spice trade.

1618 Bohemia's Protestant estates refuse to confirm as king Austria's Catholic archduke, the Hapsburg Ferdinand. The Thirty Years' War begins when Ferdinand (elected German emperor in 1619) calls in an army of Catholic allies to take the Bohemian throne by force.

1620 DEC 11 The *Mayflower,* carrying 120 pilgrims in search of religious freedom, lands in Plymouth, Massachusetts.

1623 James I of England, who has been pursuing an alliance with Spain, sends his son Charles to Madrid to negotiate a marriage to the Spanish infanta. When the Spanish demand that the prince convert immediately and liberate all Catholics in England, Charles returns home, urging his father to make war on Spain and assuring Parliament that not even a Catholic wife could make him grant toleration to English Catholics.

1624 Becoming affianced to Henrietta Maria, the sister of French king Louis XIII, Charles grants precisely what he had promised Parliament one year earlier he would never concede: toleration to English Catholics.

1624 Cardinal Richelieu becomes first minister in France during the reign of young Louis XIII. The regency has thus far been marked by perpetual intrigue and incompetence.

Ben Jonson

1610 Peter Paul Rubens' *Raising of the Cross* reflects an Italian influence but remains distinctly Northern European.

1610 Ben Jonson's *The Alchemist*, along with *Volpone* (1606), establishes him as a playwright second only to Shakespeare.

1616 English architect Inigo Jones designs the Queen's House at Greenwich in the Venetian style of Andrea Palladio.

1623 William and Isaac Jaggard publish the first collection of Shakespeare's plays, known as the First Folio.

1611 The King James Version of the Bible is published. This English translation took 47 scholars seven years to create.

1612 Bartholomew Legate (MAR 18), leader of the fanatical Seekers, and the Baptist Edward Wightman (APR) are the last Englishmen burned at the stake for their religious beliefs.

1612 Shoemaker Jakob Boehme's *Aurora* makes him the center of a philosophical circle at Görlitz, until the Lutheran pastor denounces him as a heretic.

---

astronomy, which includes a detailed proof of heliocentrism.

1614 The Scottish mathematician John Napier publishes the world's first discussion of logarithms with complete tables for their use.

1616 MAY 26 The Holy Office bans the works of Copernicus and orders Galileo not to discuss Copernican theory.

1620 Francis Bacon's *Novum Organum* refutes Aristotelian logic in favor of an inductive scientific method.

1604 Samuel de Champlain establishes the first French colony in North America.

1609-1610 Henry Hudson explores the bay and river named after him while seeking a northwest passage to China for the Dutch East India Company.

1614 Dutch merchants build a few crude cabins at the southern end of Manhattan Island for fur trading with the Indians.

1621 Plymouth governor William Bradford invites local Indians to join the Pilgrims in the first Thanksgiving.

The Body Politic

1625 Charles I inherits a Parliament unwilling to support his military escapades in Spain and France. The king dissolves the session each time it challenges him.

1628 Charles I recalls Parliament to fund the relief of besieged Huguenots at La Rochelle (which falls to Richelieu in 1629). The House of Commons replies with the Petition of Right, limiting the king's prerogatives. Having no other source for the money, Charles submits, then dissolves Parliament again in 1629.

1637-1638 Reacting to harsh persecution, 30,000 Japanese Christians seize Shimabara and hold the fort there for three months against a shogunal army aided by Dutch naval power. With the recapture of Shimabara, Christianity effectively vanishes from Japan. The Portuguese, suspected of complicity, are expelled, leaving only the nonproselytizing Dutch, who have assured the emperor that persecuting Christians will not preclude pursuing trade.

1637-1638 When Charles I, continuing his suppression of Puritans, imposes a new Prayer Book, the Scots rise up, forcing the king to choose submission or war.

1640 APR Charles calls the Short Parliament, the first since 1629, to fund a Scottish war, but dissolves it when its members demand a redress of grievances, the war not being worth the trouble.

Arts & Architecture

c.1625 Rembrandt van Rijn produces the earliest self-portraits in his lifelong effort to reveal the inner self.

1632 Shah Jahan orders the construction of the Taj Mahal in Agra to house the remains of favorite wife Mumtaz Mahal.

1632 Rembrandt paints *The Anatomy Lesson of Dr. Tulp*, winning fame in Amsterdam as well as numerous commissions.

1633 Hoping to ward off the plague, the village of Oberammergau in Bavaria pledges to perform a passion play every

Religion & Philosophy

1628 Thomas Hobbes translation of Thucydides's *The Peloponnesian War* inspires him to study philosophy.

1629 Hapsburg emperor Ferdinand II issues the Edict of Restitution, ending the Danish phase of the Thirty Years' War at the expense of the Protestants, who are required to restore Catholic lands acquired since 1552.

1633 Archbishop of Canterbury William Laud begins persecuting non-Anglican Protestants, including the Puritans.

Science & Technology

1626 MAR Stuffing a chicken with snow to see how temperature affects bacteria formation, Francis Bacon catches a cold that develops into fatal bronchitis.

1628 William Harvey announces his discovery of the circulation of blood.

Daily Life

1626 The Dutch West Indies Company gains a trade monopoly for North America, causing a rush of colonists to Manhattan.

1626 Hunters kill the last auroch, an ancestor of the domesticated cow, in a Polish forest.

1630 Sir John Suckling invents cribbage.

1632 Boston becomes the capital of the Massachusetts Bay Colony.

1634 The English Parliament makes forgery a capital offense.

1640 NOV Invading Scots force Charles to convene the Long Parliament. Relying on the Scottish military threat to force Charles's agreement, the Puritan Parliament claims the head of Strafford, the most skillful of English absolutists.

1642-1645 The civil war between royalist Cavaliers and Puritan Roundheads ends at Naseby with the victory of Oliver Cromwell's New Model Army.

1644 With the imperial army guarding the northern frontier against the Manchus, rebel leader Li Zicheng marches into Beijing unopposed. Chong Zhen, the last of the Ming emperors (since 1368), hangs himself in the palace gardens.

1644 A disloyal general opens a gate in the Great Wall, allowing an overwhelming Manchu army to sweep into China. Ousting Li Zicheng, the Manchus install Shunzhi as the first Qing emperor (until 1911).

1648 OCT 24 The Peace of Westphalia ends the Thirty Years' War, with France and Sweden aggrandizing themselves at the expense of a now hopelessly fragmented Germany.

1648 Instigating a second civil war, Charles I makes compromise impossible. Cromwell's quickly victorious army puts the king on trial for his life, which he loses (1649, JAN 20), leaving Cromwell to rule England.

Galileo Galilei

---

tenth year. Thousands travel there each decade for the nine-hour performance.

1635 L'Academie Française is founded to purify the French language. Work begins four years later on a colossal dictionary (first published in 1694).

1636 François Mansart, designer of the classical Orléans Wing of the Château de Blois, becomes France's royal architect.

1642 Rembrandt paints *The Nightwatch* at the height of his craft, but his wife's death dampens his prospects and spirit.

1636 The General Court of Massachusetts votes £400 for the foundation of a college in New Towne (renamed Cambridge, after the English university town). When the Puritan minister John Harvard bequeaths £780 to the college in 1639, the school thereafter bears his name.

1641 René Descartes' *Meditations* attempts to logically prove God's existence.

1644 NOV 25 John Milton allows his deliberately unlicensed *Areopagitica* to appear in London. This prose work rebukes parliament for censorship.

1632 JAN Galileo publishes his *Dialogue concerning the two chief world systems*, in which one character argues convincingly for the Copernican system. The church sees through Galileo's charade, however, and threatens him with torture, forcing Galileo to renounce the work publicly.

1637 René Descartes publishes his *Discourse on method* as a preface to three scientific works, one of which introduces modern analytical geometry.

1643 As he invents the barometer, Evangelista Torricelli discovers vacuums.

1637 Japanese emperor Iemitsu forbids his subjects to leave Japan.

1642 When the English Civil War begins, Puritan-controlled Parliament orders all public theaters closed, although crude, bawdy dramas continue at country fairs.

1642 Frenchman Blaise Pascal invents the first adding machine.

1647 Following the example set by a native of Bayonne, French troops at Ypres affix steel daggers to their muskets, creating the first bayonets.

1625-1648

1618 Protestant Bohemia refuses to recognize the monarchical rights of Catholic archduke Ferdinand of Austria, which have been transferred by the recently concluded Treaty of Prague (1617) with Philip III of Spain, a fellow Hapsburg. Instead, Bohemia's estates throw out Ferdinand's deputies in the Defenestration of Prague and, raising an army, invade Austria. With the help of the mercenary corps of Ernst von Mansfeld, the Bohemians appear before Vienna itself. But the advance stalls, and in a major political blunder, the Bohemians choose Frederick, the Protestant Elector of the Palatinate, for their king. This draws into the war on Ferdinand's side the Catholic League led by Maximilian of Bavaria, the Spanish Hapsburgs, the pope, and even the Protestant Saxons, who object to Frederick's promotion. For similar reasons, the remaining German Protestant states in the north declare themselves neutral, thus depriving Bohemia of her natural allies.

1620 **November 18** The Catholic League army, fighting under Count Tilly, crushes the Bohemian rebels at the Battle of the White Mountain. Mansfeld's army, however, remains in the field, surviving on plunder.

1622 Tilly harasses Mansfeld in Alsace until the Dutch, losing ground to the Spanish under Spinola, invite Mansfeld to relieve them. He does, and then marches to East Friesland, where he allies himself with the Lower Saxon Circle (1623). Soon Tilly marches north to contain this threat. In the years that follow, England, the Dutch United Provinces, and Denmark will rally to the Protestant cause along with Catholic France, because Richelieu considers the Hapsburgs a much greater threat than Lutheranism.

1625 Supported by the subsidies of his allies and eager to assert Danish authority over the German North Sea ports, Christian IV of Denmark takes Lower Saxony under his protection.

1626 **April 25** A specifically Hapsburg army raised by Albrecht von Wallenstein, Ferdinand's proconsul in Bohemia, defeats Mansfeld's army at the Bridge of Dessau.

August 27 When English subsidies fail, Christian IV realizes he can no longer afford to continue his methodical campaign of attrition. Forced onto the offensive, he attacks Tilly at Lutter, where the Danes are totally defeated. Meanwhile, Wallenstein follows Mansfeld to Hungary, where he has taken up arms with the Transylvanian prince Gabor Bethlen. Wallenstein forces both to submit to a truce that disarms Bethlen and requires Mansfeld to leave the country. With these triumphs, opposition to the imperial army ends until 1630.

1629 Christian IV signs the Edict of Restitution, ending the Danish phase of the Thirty Years' War. The edict restores 150 ecclesiastical properties that have come into Protestant possession since the Convention of Passau (1552). Fearing that the growing imperial power of Ferdinand can only lead to a loss of religious freedom, the Protestant states of northern Germany call upon Gustavus II Adolphus of Sweden to replace their defeated Danish champion. Meanwhile, brokering a peace between Sweden and Poland, Cardinal Richelieu himself schemes to bring Sweden into the war. As an enticement, Richelieu offers to pay the young king a 200,000-ducat annuity to invade Germany.

1630 **June** Combining (as had Christian IV) religious and territorial motives, Sweden's king Gustavus lands an army at Peenemünde, renewing armed conflict with the Catholic forces of Tilly and Wallenstein.

1631 **January** In consummating his secret alliance (the Treaty of Bärwalde) with Sweden, Richelieu seriously underestimates the degree to which Gustavus's own ambitions (Swedish and Protestant) are beyond French control. The Swedish king rallies the German Protestants so successfully that the Hapsburgs and their Catholic allies, on the brink of splitting apart, are forced back together to defend themselves.

September 17 At Breitenfeld, Tilly's men rout a Saxon army allied to Gustavus, but the imperial attack breaks on the Swedish flank, and the Swedes drive Tilly from the field with heavy losses. Marching west to the Rhine, Gustavus winters in Mainz, where he raises a huge German army for an invasion of Bavaria and Austria during the next campaigning season.

1632 **November 16** Although Gustavus is slain at the battle of Lützen, the Swedes force Wallenstein's army to retire, affirming the new balance of

1632
(continued)

power in Germany. The death of Gustavus, however, marks the peak of Swedish influence and leaves the Protestants without a champion, ironically assuring the direct entrance of France into the war against the Hapsburgs.

1634

February 25 Following a failed coup d'etat in which he tries to make peace with the Swedes and Saxons, Wallenstein is assassinated at Eger by Ferdinand's Spanish allies. All possibilities for reconciliation between Catholics and Protestants die with him.

September 6 Spain agrees to lend Ferdinand the army of the Cardinal Infante, which is passing through Germany on its way from Italy to the still rebellious Netherlands. That army entrenches at Nördlingen with Ferdinand's troops, where they are attacked by half as many Swedes and Germans. Losing 17,000 men, the previously invincible army of Gustavus perishes at Nördlingen.

1635

May 30 John George of Saxony signs the Peace of Prague with Ferdinand. The treaty reinstates Lutheranism in those German principalities where it existed in 1627. A number of Protestant princes follow the Saxon example, but others with lands they have yet to recover continue the war. Much of this sparring becomes insignificant, however, when Richelieu finally declares war on Spain. On a strategic scale hitherto unknown in the war, Richelieu arranges to isolate the Spanish Netherlands and then sends his main force to face the army of the Cardinal Infante. But the cardinal overextends himself in his attempt to fight on two fronts, leading to a standoff. From this point on, the Thirty Years' War shifts in character from a religious war to a political struggle.

1636

Reinforced by an army composed mostly of Bavarians, the Cardinal Infante invades France from the northwest, capturing Corbie and threatening Paris, until a Dutch menace in the north limits the Spanish advance. For the next five years, France fights wars on four fronts (Belgium, Germany, Italy, and Spain) and, unable to focus its strength anywhere, trades frontier towns with its principal antagonist, Spain.

1637

Ferdinand III succeeds his late father, but he is forced to cede additional power to the German electors (despite the backing of Spain) in return for their confirmation of him as emperor.

1 6 4 0 First the Catalans, who have been pressed hard by the French, and then the Portuguese, who are merely seizing the opportunity, revolt against Spain's Castilian government. Portugal reestablishes its independence under a king of the House of Braganza (DEC). Meanwhile, France makes progress on the Belgian frontier, Louis XIII having himself forced the capitulation of the strategic fortress of Arras (AUG 8).

1 6 4 1 **December** Peace negotiations begin at Münster and Osnabrück in Westphalia.

1 6 4 2 **December 4** Cardinal Richelieu's death prevents him from witnessing the fulfillment of his foreign policy, which has recently been quite successful thanks to the efforts of Bernard of Saxe-Weimar in Alsace and the Swedish generals Banér and Torstensson in northwestern Germany.

1 6 4 3 **May 14** With the death of Louis XIII, the throne passes to his four-year-old son Louis XIV. The French Parlement appoints the queen mother as regent, and she chooses the Sicilian Cardinal Mazarin as both her chief minister and her lover. Mazarin adopts Richelieu's master plan for a joint French-Swedish campaign against Ferdinand III's ally Bavaria and steadfastly carries it out despite a number of setbacks.

May 19 The 21-year-old duke of Enghien, commanding the northern French army, assaults the famous Spanish infantry at Rocroi. The *tercios* courageously stand their ground, but they are eventually annihilated in a series of cavalry charges, ending the Spanish threat in the north.

1 6 4 8 **May 17** At Zusmarshausen, a combined army of Frenchmen (under Turenne) and Swedes (under Wrangel) finally breaks the Austrian-Bavarian army. Meanwhile, another Swedish force besieges Prague.

October 24 Ferdinand III authorizes his plenipotentiaries to sign the Peace of Westphalia, ending the Thirty Years' War and destroying all hope of an absolutist Hapsburg empire. Religious freedom and political decentralization prevail in Germany, while France (in Alsace) and Sweden (on the Baltic) make major territorial gains, and Switzerland and the United Provinces have their independence formally recognized.

Presto.

1649-1789

The Body Politic

1649 The Rump Parliament abolishes both the monarchy and the House of Lords, proclaiming a commonwealth under the Council of State. The poet John Milton is named secretary to the council, which is led by Oliver Cromwell.

1649 The Peace of Rueil ends the Fronde of Parlement, during which the French legislative and judicial branches of government have rebelled against the war-related financial burdens placed upon them by Cardinal Mazarin.

1652-1654 Harassment of maritime trade characterizes the first of three Anglo-Dutch wars between the world's two great naval powers.

1652 OCT 21 Louis XIV returns to Paris when the Fronde of the Princes—led by Louis de Bourbon, the prince of Condé—disintegrates. Condé flees to Spain, with whom France continues to wage war despite the Peace of Westphalia.

1653 APR 17 When the Rump Parliament fails to carry out the army's political agenda, including the abolition of tithes and legal reform, Cromwell uses the military to dissolve it.

1653 16 DEC Under the terms of the Instrument of Government, Cromwell becomes lord protector of England . The Instrument, the nation's first constitution, also grants limited religious tolera-

Arts & Architecture

1649 FEB 13 John Milton's *The Tenure of Kings and Magistrates* defends the right of commoners to depose their sovereign (in this case, Charles I).

c.1650 The minuet, reputedly adapted from a French folk dance, becomes popu-

lar among the French and English aristocracy.

1653 Izaak Walton publishes the first edition of *The Compleat Angler*. A former ironmonger, the Royalist Walton fled London early in the civil wars, moving

Religion & Philosophy

1651 Thomas Hobbes publishes his masterpiece *Leviathan*, in which he argues the necessity of a strong central government to counter the savage impulses of unrestrained man, whose life Hobbes characterizes as "solitary, poor, nasty, brutish, and short."

1656 OCT The Quaker preacher John Nayler, who believes himself to be a reincarnation of Christ, leads his followers through Bristol in a procession that imitates the entry of Jesus into Jerusalem. Nayler is arrested, tried, and convicted of blasphemy.

Science & Technology

1650 Otto von Guericke invents an air pump, which he uses to create a vacuum between two metal hemispheres. In his famous demonstration, von Guericke pumps the air from the joined sphere until the vacuum is so strong that even teams of horses cannot pry the sphere apart.

1653 Responding to pleas from gamblers, Blaise Pascal and Pierre de Fermat begin to study the mathematics of games of chance, leading to probability theory.

1654 Grand Duke of Tuscany Ferdinand II improves Galileo's glass thermometer

Daily Life

1652 The first coffeehouses open in London after they have already become popular in Vienna and Constantinople.

1653 During the first Anglo-Dutch War, Dutch settlers in New Amsterdam build a wall to protect themselves from a feared

English invasion. The pathway along this northern boundary eventually becomes known as Wall Street.

1657 A Frenchman brings the secret of chocolate to London. The Spanish had first encountered the drink at the court of

tion, but not to Catholics or Anglicans. Although the document calls for a republican form of government, Cromwell's reliance on the army to maintain control makes his rule a de facto military dictatorship.

1655 English admiral William Penn captures the island of Jamaica from the Spanish, leading to a war with Spain that causes Cromwell to form a realpolitik alliance against Spain with Catholic France under Mazarin.

1657 Refusing the crown offered to him by Parliament, Cromwell consolidates his power as lord protector, which is made a hereditary position.

1658 SEP 3 Richard Cromwell becomes lord protector upon the death of his father, beginning a power struggle between Parliament and the army.

1659 Unable to control the army, Richard Cromwell resigns his office. In search of legitimacy now that the protectorate has ended, the army reconvenes the Rump Parliament it had dissolved in 1653.

1659 NOV 5 The Treaty of the Pyrenees finally ends the war between Spain and France. Louis XIV acquires enough territory to make the Rhine his eastern frontier, and he also becomes engaged to the Spanish infanta Marie-Thérèse, eldest daughter of Philip IV.

John Milton

---

back to his native Staffordshire, where he has spent much of his time fishing.

1656 Cyrano de Bergerac's sci-fi fantasy *Histoire comique des états et empires de la lune* suggests rocket travel as one of seven ways to reach the moon.

1658 OCT 24 After gaining a reputation in the provinces, Moliére presents Pierre Corneille's *Nicomède* before Louis XIV. The play fails to move the king, but a second piece, Moliére's *Le Docteur amoureux*, wins him the patronage of the king's brother, the duke of Orleans.

1656 Patriarch Nikon of the Russian Orthodox Church convenes a synod on liturgical reform. Asserting that Russian worship has strayed too far from the Greek model, he orders the conformation of all Russian liturgical practice to the Greek. This creates a schism with "Old

Believers," who claim Turkish conquest has proven the Greeks' decline.

1656-1657 Eighteen letters in defense of Antoine Arnauld, a Jansenist on trial for attacks against the Jesuits, comprise Blaise Pascal's *Les Provinciales*.

(circa 1597), sealing the water within the glass tube so that changes in air pressure do not affect its readings.

1656 Christiaan Huygens invents a new clock that uses a pendulum to turn the gears. The regular motion of the pendu-

lum makes Huygens' mechanism a breakthrough in timekeeping.

1659 Huygens, the first to observe Mars closely, notices a dark spot. Tracking it as Mars rotates, he calculates the Martian day to be 24½ hours long.

Montezuma, but they kept its means of concoction a secret for nearly a century before the French began importing cocoa beans early in the seventeenth century.

1658 New Amsterdam forms the first colonial police force.

1649-1659

The Body Politic

1660 APR 4 The exiled prince Charles, son of the executed king Charles I, signs the Declaration of Breda, which promises both a general amnesty and liberty of conscience for all Englishmen if the monarchy is restored.

1660 MAY 8 Accepting the Declaration of Breda, Parliament restores the monarchy in the person of Charles II, who returns to England on May 25.

1660 DEC 1 Parliament passes the first of the mercantilist Navigation Acts, requiring that nearly all cargo shipped to and from England be hauled by English ships. The acts (1660-1663) are designed to damage the Dutch carrying trade.

1662 Eight-year-old Kangxi succeeds his father as Qing emperor of China (until 1722). Although the Qing are foreigners (from Manchuria), Kangxi quickly adopts Chinese customs and practices, including the teachings of Confucius. He studies under the Jesuits, however, because of the scientific and technical knowledge they offer.

1664 Charles II grants a charter to his brother James, the duke of York, for all lands between the Connecticut River and Delaware Bay. The lands between the Hudson and Delaware rivers are then transferred by James to his cronies Lord John Berkeley and Sir George Carteret, who name the tract New Jersey.

Arts & Architecture

1664 MAY Moliére's initial presentation of his comedy *Tartuffe,* about a pious crook, causes a scandal that forces him to withdraw the play for five years.

c.1665 Jan Vermeer's self-portrait, *Allegory of Painting*, pays almost scientific attention to pictorial detail and the characteristics of light.

1665 John Milton finishes his poetic epic *Paradise Lost*. On its publication, John Dryden reportedly remarks, "This man cuts us all out, the ancients too."

Religion & Philosophy

1661 John Eliot's translation of the New Testament into Algonquian becomes the first Bible to be published in North America.

1661-1665 During the ministry of Edward Hyde, first earl of Clarendon, Parliament passes four acts, known as the Clarendon Code. The Corporation Act (1661) excludes from municipal office all who have not taken the sacraments at an Anglican church. The other three acts similarly oppress Nonconformists (also called Dissenters).

Science & Technology

1661 Using a microscope, Marcello Malpighi confirms Harvey's hypothesis that small vessels (capillaries) carry blood from the arteries to the veins.

1662 Charles II charters the Royal Society for the Promotion of Natural Knowledge. Its journal, *Philosophical Transactions* (begun in 1665), will provide the principal international forum for new discoveries in the natural sciences.

1662 Robert Boyle discovers that a gas's volume varies inversely with its pressure.

Daily Life

1660 JAN 1 Samuel Pepys makes the first entry in his famous diary, which gives a thoroughly detailed portrait of upper-class life in Restoration London.

1661 Massachusetts prohibits the use of wampum as legal tender.

1662 John Graunt writes *Natural and Political Observations Made upon the Bills of Mortality,* in which he analyzes London's death records. Graunt's study, one of the earliest in statistics (known then as political arithmetic), provides the first actuarial tables.

1664 SEP 8 Governor Peter Stuyvesant surrenders Dutch control of New Amsterdam to an English fleet sent by the duke of York, after whom the colony is soon then renamed.

1665 FEB Although hostilities have been ongoing for nearly two years, England chooses to make formal the second Anglo-Dutch War, of which the Navigation Acts have been a principal cause. With this declaration, France allies herself with the Dutch.

1667 JUL 21 The Peace of Breda concludes the second Anglo-Dutch War, which essentially ended with the burning of the English fleet in the Thames in June. According to the terms of the treaty, England will retain the New Netherlands, the Dutch will keep Surinam and their African Gold Coast possession, while the French stand to regain Acadis (Nova Scotia) from the English.

1667 Louis XIV's invasion of the Spanish Netherlands, beginning the War of Devolution, frightens the United Provinces (the Dutch Netherlands) into an alliance with the English and the Swedes. This Triple Alliance forces the French king to agree to peace with the Treaty of Aix-la-Chapelle (1668). Louis XIV's claim to the Spanish Netherlands had been based on the lineage of his Spanish Bourbon wife.

Louis XIV

1666 Antonio Stradivari, a pupil of Nicolò Amati, begins to place his own labels on the violins that he makes.

1666 After the Great Fire destroys many of London's important churches and public buildings, architect Christopher Wren begins to receive plentiful commissions to rebuild them.

1669 Hans Jacob Christoph von Grimmelshausen issues the first part of *Simplicissimus*, his popular novel written in the Spanish picaresque style.

1665 JUN Baruch Spinoza, one of the Enlightenment's premier rationalist philosophers (along with Descartes and Leibniz), nears completion of his *Ethica*, but gives up the work when it becomes clear that anti-Semitism in Europe will prevent its publication.

1665 Using a compound microscope of his own design, Robert Hooke discovers that cork is composed of many tiny compartments, which Hooke calls *cells.*

1665 Plague closes Cambridge University, forcing recent graduate Isaac Newton to return home. During the two years of contemplation that follow, Newton lays the foundation for his calculus, concludes that white light is actually an intermingling of colored light, and derives the inverse-square law crucial to his theory of universal gravitation.

1664-1665 London experiences a plague that, at its worst, kills thousands each week and virtually closes the city, already feeling the pinch of a war with the Dutch. The epidemic continues off and on until the Great Fire of 1666 flattens the city.

1665 The French government carries out the first modern census in Quebec.

1666 SEP 2-5 The Great Fire savages four-fifths of London, but the rebuilding that quickly follows makes London the most modern city in the world.

1660-1669

The Body Politic

1670 MAY 20 Without renouncing the Triple Alliance, Charles II signs the secret Treaty of Dover, pledging to support Louis XIV's forthcoming invasion of the United Provinces in exchange for a subsidy (Charles being in great debt). Louis offers an additional subsidy if Charles will convert to Catholicism.

1671 JAN 18 Leading a company of nearly 2,000 English buccaneers, Captain Henry Morgan defeats a large Spanish army and sacks Panamá, one of the chief cities of the Spanish Main.

1672 MAR Louis XIV declares war on the Dutch, who block his invasion by cutting the dikes and flooding the land.

1672 On the verge of bankruptcy, Charles II declares war on the Dutch so that he can begin to collect the French subsidy.

1673 AUG 30 With the ouster of Jan de Witt, William III of Orange becomes the new Dutch *stadtholder*. He quickly builds a new anti-French coalition, including the Austrians and Spain.

1673 Parliament's passage of the Test Act, which excludes Catholics and Dissenters from national office, breaks up Charles II's pro-French group of ministers known as the Cabal.

1674 The pro-Dutch, pro-Anglican earl of Danby becomes England's chief minister

Arts & Architecture

1673 John Dryden's *Marriage A-la-Mode*, a Restoration comedy of manners, dramatizes the contemporary battle of the sexes.

1673 Dietrich Buxtehude begins his *Abendmusiken* concerts of vocal and instrumental music at St. Mary's in Lübeck.

1675-1711 Christopher Wren rebuilds St. Paul's Cathedral, drawing on Italian and French styles for inspiration.

1677 Within eight months of the first performance of his tragedy *Phèdre*, Jean Racine abandons the commercial theater.

Religion & Philosophy

1670 Blaise Pascal's *Pensées*, published posthumously, includes Pascal's wager, which relates the human condition to a game of chance: one can either bet on or against the existence of God. Pascal argues that betting on the existence of God is the only reasonable choice.

Science & Technology

1673 Gian Domenico Cassini, director of the Paris Observatory, uses parallax to find the distance to Mars and thereby gauge the size of the solar system.

1673 The French expedition to South America that helps Cassini with his parallax also finds that pendulums swing slower near the equator. Newton later claims this proves the earth's oblateness, as predicted by his theory of gravity.

1675 Using many of the same sources, Gottfried Wilhelm Leibniz achieves a pre-

Daily Life

1673 JAN 1 New York governor Francis Lovelace establishes both a postal route and mounted mail service between New York City and Boston. The Boston Post Road becomes the first important highway in the colonies. The mail service takes three weeks.

1673 Father Jacques Marquette and Louis Joliet explore the Mississippi River as far as the Arkansas, finding that it flows through hostile Spanish territory.

1674 The last description of a live dodo is published. A large, flightless bird native

and immediately negotiates the Treaty of Westminster, ending hostilities between the English and the Dutch. Danby later arranges the marriage of the duke of York's Protestant daughter Mary to William of Orange.

1678 The Treaty of Nijmegen ends the war between the French, the Dutch, and their allies, with France receiving the Franche-Comté from Spain.

1678 SEP Titus Oates reveals to the popular London magistrate Edward Godfrey the details of an alleged Popish Plot to kill Charles II and replace him with his Catholic brother James. When Godfrey dies mysteriously, near panic ensues.

1678 NOV 28 On the day the duchess of York's secretary is found guilty of treason, Oates accuses the Catholic queen Catherine of treason before the bar of the House of Lords. The Popish Plot scandal unravels, however, when Oates's many lies begin to be exposed.

1679 Parliament passes the Habeas Corpus Act restricting the detention of people accused of civil or criminal misconduct.

1679 The terms *Whig* and *Tory* are first applied to the major parliamentary parties. The middle-class Whigs, heirs of Cromwell, support the nation's republican institutions, while the conservative Tories prefer an absolutist monarchy.

Baruch Spinoza

1678 Puritan minister John Bunyan publishes *The Pilgrim's Progress*, his allegorical novel about a Christian's pilgrimage to the Celestial City. Bunyan's tale is widely considered to be the greatest and most representative of contemporary Puritan works.

1678 Charles Le Brun, creator of the Louis XIV style, paints the ceiling of the Hall of Mirrors at the Palace of Versailles, which he designed.

1679 The former samurai Matsuo Basho writes his first haiku.

1670 Spinoza's *Tractatus theologico-politicus*, published anonymously in Amsterdam, argues that the Bible should be interpreted morally and not factually, because the divine inspiration of the prophets extended only to the moral doctrines they preached.

1672 Although Charles II has not yet announced his conversion (as provided for by the Treaty of Dover), he does make the Declaration of Indulgence, extending religious toleration to Catholics. Charles later recants the edict when Parliament becomes suspicious of his popish motives.

---

liminary calculus independent of the unpublished work of Newton.

1675 Microscope pioneer Anton van Leeuwenhoek discovers the first life too small to be seen by the unaided eye. He calls these protozoa *animacules*.

1678 Christiaan Huygens counters Isaac Newton's particle theory of light with his own wave theory.

1679 MAR Leibniz introduces binary numeration, in which every number is expressed using the digits 0 and 1.

---

to Mauritius, the dodo will soon be driven into extinction by European sailors and the cats and dogs they have introduced to the island.

1677-1691 As Louis XIV's secretary of war, the marquis de Louvois molds the

French army into a force after which all European armies will soon be modeled. His reforms include promotion by merit, regular supplies and paychecks, the founding of training academies, and the establishment of the Hôtel des Invalides in Paris for elderly retired soldiers.

1670-1679

The Body Politic

1681 Charles II dissolves Parliament at the height of the Exclusion Controversy, after Whigs led by Shaftesbury insist that the king's Catholic brother be excluded from the line of inheritance. The Whigs' choice, offered during the Parliament of 1680, is Charles's illegitimate Protestant son, the duke of Monmouth.

1681 MAR 4 William Penn receives a proprietary charter from Charles II granting him what is now the state of Pennsylvania. Penn intends to establish a colonial haven there for his fellow Quakers and other religious refugees.

1683 SEP 12 With German help, Polish king Jan Sobieski defeats the Ottoman army of ambitious grand vizier Kara Mustafa. Devoted to the principle that a busy army promotes domestic peace, Mustafa had been besieging the Austrian capital of Vienna for two months. After Mustafa's defeat, the Europeans, sensing an opportunity, form the Holy League to press their advantage into Hungary.

1684 JUN 21 Charles II revokes the charter of the Massachusetts Bay Colony after Puritan authorities there go too far in discriminating against Anglicans.

1685 FEB 16 With his brother's death, James II becomes king. Monmouth attempts a revolt, but his allies are beaten easily and punished in the Bloody Assizes.

Arts & Architecture

1680 After Moliére's death (1673), his troupe merges with a company playing at the Theâtre du Marais. This combined company then joins with that of the Hôtel de Bourgogne to found what becomes France's first national theater company, the Comédie-Française.

1681 John Dryden's *Absalom and Achitophel* satirizes the intrigues of the earl of Shaftesbury, who has schemed to make Charles II's bastard son the royal heir.

1687 SEP 26 Venetian artillery blows up the Parthenon, which Turks holding out

Religion & Philosophy

1680 Cotton Mather preaches his first sermon in his father's Boston church.

1683 Louis XIV orders the *dragonnades,* during which soldiers billeted with Protestant families have permission to behave as brutally as they please.

1685 Louis XIV's revocation of the Edict of Nantes (proclaimed 1598) culminates two decades of government hostility toward the Huguenots. His decision prompts half a million, including important army officers, to leave France for neighboring Protestant states.

Science & Technology

1682 Edmund Halley observes a comet and later notices that its path matches those recorded in 1456, 1531, and 1607. Halley predicts it will return in 1758.

1684 Though Newton developed his version before Leibniz turned his energies to mathematics, it is a paper by Leibniz that first makes the calculus public.

1686 John Ray issues the first volume of his *Historia plantarum*, which classifies 18,600 plant species, laying the groundwork for Carolus Linnaeus (1737).

Daily Life

c.1680 The Benedictine monk Dom Pierre Pérignon develops a process for making champagne in the cellars of the Haut Villiers abbey. His insistence on secrecy, however, breeds rumors that the Devil plays a role in the manufacture of this sparkling wine.

1680 APR William Dockwra institutes the Penny Post in London. Dockwra's service insures and delivers parcels weighing up to one pound for a one-penny fee.

1680 Acting under the direction of Robert Boyle, who has just discovered

1688 NOV 5 At the invitation of prominent Whigs and Tories, William of Orange lands in England to claim the throne of his father-in-law James II, whose queen has recently (and unexpectedly) given birth to a male Catholic heir. James II's flight to France (DEC 11), prompted by extensive desertions from his army, completes the Glorious Revolution.

1689 Parliament offers the English crown jointly to William III and Mary II subject to certain conditions set forth in the Declaration of Rights (passed FEB 13), which defines the relationship between the monarchy and Parliament. The new law precludes a monarch from unilaterally making or suspending laws. It also pro-hibits taxation and the maintenance of a standing army without the specific consent of Parliament. Finally, it guarantees freedom of speech and a trial by jury. William accepts the throne so that he can further his life's work: containing Louis XIV in France.

1689 Following the French invasion of southwestern Germany, England joins the League of Augsburg, forming the Grand Alliance against the absolutist Sun King Louis XIV. Despite this weighty opposition, the French army, recently rebuilt by the marquis de Louvois, devastates the Palatinate. Suffering worst are the cities of Heidelberg, Worms, Mannheim, and their environs.

Isaac Newton

---

on the Acropolis have been using as a powder magazine.

1689 Henry Purcell writes his miniature opera *Dido and Aeneas* for a performance at a girl's school in Chelsea. Purcell and Jean-Baptiste Lully, who controls the court music of France, dominate this otherwise stagnant period in opera.

1689 The last great Dutch landscape painter, Meindert Hobbema, paints his Baroque masterpiece *The Avenue at Middleharnis*.

1687 Samuel Pufendorf publishes *De habitu religionis christianae ad vitam civilem*, in which he argues the civil superiority of the state over the church. Pufendorf reserves, however, the right of self-government to the church and that of liberty to the individual.

1687 Newton publishes his *Philosophiae naturalis principia mathematica*, widely considered to be the greatest scientific work of all time. In it, Newton uses his famous theory of gravitation to explain planetary motion. The *Principia* also articulates Newton's three laws of motion: that a body tends to remain at rest unless a force compels it to move; that acceleration is proportional to the force causing it; and that for every action, there must be an equal and opposite reaction. Newton has developed his calculus to express these laws mathematically.

---

phosphorus, Godfrey Haukwitz makes the first matches, striking together pieces of phosphorus to light splints of sulfur-dipped wood. The danger and expense of the phosphorus, however, limits the practical application of Haukwitz's method.

1682 APR 9 Robert La Salle reaches the mouth of the Mississippi River, claiming the land he has traversed for France.

1688 Lloyd's of London has its origins in the gatherings of merchants at Edward Lloyd's coffeehouse in Tower Street.

The Body Politic

1690 JUL 1 At the battle of the Boyne, William and Mary put down a French-aided rebellion of Irish royalists, known as Jacobites for their persistent loyalty to deposed king James II.

1690 AUG 24 Job Charnock of the British East India Company settles Calcutta.

1692 MAY 19 A combined English and Dutch fleet destroys the new French navy at the battle of Cape La Hogue.

1696 JUL 18 Tsar Peter I (the Great) captures the Black Sea port of Azov, long held by the Crimean Tartars, clients of the Ottoman Turks. The Russians had joined the Holy League a decade earlier (1686), but were able to contribute little until Peter completed the construction of Russia's first navy in 1695.

1697 The Treaty of Rijswijk ends the War of the Grand Alliance. The foundation of the peace is the restoration of the Treaty of Nijmegen (1678). There are several new provisions, however, among them France's recognition of William III's place as rightful king of England and its acquisition of the Caribbean island colony of St. Domingue (the western half of Spanish Hispaniola, later renamed Haiti). For their part, the Dutch win the right to garrison border fortresses in the Spanish Netherlands as a deterrent against future French aggression.

Arts & Architecture

1691 The plays of Pedro Calderón de la Barca are collected and published posthumously in an extremely high-quality edition. A published collection of an author's work is so rare that this book contributes to the recognition of Calderón as the greatest of Spanish dramatists.

1696 Marie de Rabutin-Chantal, the marquise de Sévigné, dies having written volumes of memorable letters to her daughter, circulated as early as 1673.

1697 Charles Perrault, a prominent member of the Académie Française,

Religion & Philosophy

1690 Following his return to England after the Glorious Revolution, John Locke publishes his two most important works, written while living in exile in Holland. Locke's *Essay Concerning Human Understanding*, a work of epistemology, is among the first to take note of current scientific research, while his *Two Treatises of Government* defends the Glorious Revolution. The *Second Treatise*, in particular, argues that when an absolutist government interferes with the rights of life, liberty, and property, the people can justly rebel.

Science & Technology

c.1690 Denis Papin, who built the first steam digester (pressure cooker) in 1679, notices that the pressure created within the cooker tends to raise the lid. Applying this observation, Papin speculates on the potential use of steam to drive a piston set within a cylinder.

c.1695 Georg Ernst Stahl develops his concept of phlogiston, which he believes to be the cause of burning and rusting. Johann Joachim Becker had proposed the existence of a "fat earth" with many of the same properties (1669), but Stahl's theory borrows more directly from the

Daily Life

c.1690 While attempting to improve the chalmeau, a single-reed woodwind used in folk music, Johann Christoph Denner develops the clarinet.

1692 The town of Salem, Massachusetts, holds its famous witch trials after stories told by a West Indian slave, Tituba, induce hysteria among a group of adolescent girls. Claiming they have been possessed by the Devil, the girls accuse three Salem women (including Tituba) of witchcraft. Nineteen are eventually convicted and hanged.

1698 JUN While in Vienna negotiating a continuation of the anti-Turkish alliance, Peter the Great learns of yet another revolt of the *streltsy* [king's bodyguards] in Moscow. He returns there immediately and puts down the rebellion harshly, executing hundreds of the musketeers, exiling the rest, and then dissolving the corps. With his power newly consolidated, Peter begins to order Western-style reforms along the lines of those he observed during his Grand Embassy to Europe (1697-1698).

1698 A new Tory coalition, placed in power by the latest parliamentary elections, votes substantial reductions in the armed forces. Disgusted at what he con-siders the ingratitude of the English, William III threatens to abdicate.

Peter the Great

1699 JAN 26 The Treaty of Karlowitz ends 16 years of fighting between the Turks and the Holy League. Its terms, which generally reflect the capitulation of the sultan, include the formal transfer of Hungary to the Austrian emperor.

1699 Having obtained Azov (and thereby access to the Black Sea), Tsar Peter now turns his attention northward, where he must confront Sweden if he is to obtain a port on the Baltic. To further this end, Peter forms an alliance with Augustus II of Poland-Saxony and Denmark's Frederick IV.

---

writes *Contes de ma mere l'oye* [*Tales of Mother Goose*] for his children.

1698 In his *Short View of the Immorality and Profaneness of the English Stage*, the English bishop Jeremy Collier attacks Dryden, Congreve, and others for under-mining popular morality with their sympathetic presentations of vice.

1699 François Fénelon, archbishop of Cambrai, writes the allegorical *Les Aventures de Télémaque*, filling it with veiled attacks on the French court.

1693 Increase Mather's *Case of Conscience Concerning Evil Spirits Personating Men* defends his (and his son's) role in the Salem witchcraft trials.

1694 German emperor Leopold I grants a charter to the University of Halle, widely considered to be the first modern university. Though Halle is created as a center for the Lutheran intelligentsia, its most notable academics, Christian Thomasius and August Hermann Francke, open up the university to a wide range of progressive, secular thought.

Aristotelian notion of a combustible property that can be lost and regained.

1698 Military engineer Thomas Savery patents the first practical steam engine, called the Miner's Friend because it can pump water from coal mines.

1694 Parliament creates the Bank of England to raise money for a new war.

1697 Peter I makes his Grand Embassy to Europe. Traveling under an assumed name, he becomes so enamored of Western culture that, returning to Moscow in 1698, he forbids the long beards popular among Russian men (but not fashionable in Europe). Peter himself clips the beards of his key imperial officials.

1699 New Orleans holds the first Mardi Gras festival in North America.

1690-1699

1700 NOV 1 On his deathbed, the Spanish Hapsburg king Charles II (Carlos the Bewitched) names Philip of Anjou as his sole heir. Philip's claim is based on his grandfather Louis XIV's marriage to the Spanish infanta (arranged by the 1659 Treaty of the Pyrenees). William III of England has twice tried to arrange a peaceful partition of the vast Spanish holdings between France and Hapsburg Austria, but the possibility of obtaining the entire Spanish prize proves too great for Louis. Knowing that it means war, he nevertheless accepts the inheritance on behalf of his grandson. The Grand Alliance hastily reforms, this time including England, The Netherlands, Austria, and most of the German Empire.

1700 NOV 20 In a decisive battle, the 18-year-old Swedish king Charles XII thrashes the Russian army at Narva. The defeat does not deter Peter the Great, however, who has engineered the Great Northern War (until 1721) in order to win a port on the Baltic Sea.

1701 MAR Louis XIV invades the Spanish Netherlands, formally beginning the War of the Spanish Succession.

1702 MAR 8 When William III dies, Mary's sister Anne becomes queen as provided for by the Act of Settlement (1701), which prohibited Catholic succession. The act further specified that, with Anne's death, the crown should first pass to

c.1700 Wang Hui, greatest of the Chinese painters known as the Four Wangs, completes his 53-foot scroll painting *Ten Thousand Miles of the Yangzi*.

1700 MAR Known for clever, biting portrayals of Restoration affectation, William

Congreve presents his greatest comedy of manners, *The Way of the World*, at Lincoln's Inn Fields. Although the work will later be regarded as the most accomplished of its time, the initial production of the play flops, and Congreve never writes another.

1700 Connecticut establishes the smallest colonial civil unit thus far, the school district, in an effort to promote elementary education.

1702 Cotton Mather publishes his two-volume *Magnalia Christi Americana*, an

ecclesiastical history of North America from the colonization of New England to the present day. Although the work is frequently inaccurate, it transforms its author, the son of noted Puritan minister Increase Mather, into the most popular of contemporary colonial writers.

1704 Because of a bitter plagiarism dispute with Robert Hooke following his presentation of the *Principia* to the Royal Society, Newton waits until Hooke's death to publish the *Opticks*, which compiles nearly 40 years of Newton's research into light and colors.

1705 Because of the high cost of using horsepower to pump water out of mines, Thomas Newcomen works for ten years to improve the Savery steam engine. Newcomen's completed machine operates at low steam pressure, using atmospheric pressure instead to drive the piston.

1702-1714 During Queen Anne's reign, facial hair is seen as comic or loathsome, so men go beardless. Those with mustaches are assumed to be foreigners.

c.1705 Daniel Twining becomes a tea and coffee merchant in London. Tea con-

sumption in England soon rises to an average of two pounds per person per year.

1706 A new regulation limits the deer season on Long Island, where a year-round open season has nearly extinguished the deer population.

Sophia, Protestant granddaughter of James I, and then to her heirs in Hanover.

1703 JUN 29 Having taken several Baltic forts while Charles XII occupied himself in Poland, Peter the Great founds a new Russian capital at the mouth of the Neva River that becomes St. Petersburg.

1704 JUL 24 Sir George Rooke captures Gibraltar and claims it for Queen Anne.

1707 MAR 4 The Act of Union joins the kingdoms of England and Scotland into a united kingdom of Great Britain.

1707 SEP After the Swedish army invades Saxony, the elector Augustus II signs the Peace of Altranstädt, surrendering the Polish crown to Stanislas Leszczynski, a protégé of Charles XII.

1709 JUN 27 Peter the Great crushes the Swedish army at Poltava after Charles XII is forced to endure a difficult winter in the Ukraine. He never recovers.

1709 SEP 11 John Churchill, the earl of Marlborough, and the Austrian prince Eugene lead the Grand Alliance in its victory over the French at Malplaquet, one of the bloodiest battles of the war. Marlborough had earlier won stunning victories at Blenheim (1704) and at Ramillies (1706), where he evicted the French from the Spanish Netherlands.

William III

---

c.1702 Antoine Watteau, the 18-year-old son of a roof tiler, leaves for Paris, where he becomes one of the most appealing painters of the Rococo.

1705 OCT Johann Sebastian Bach obtains a month's leave from his duties as a church organist in Arnstadt so that he can walk the 200 miles to Lübeck for one of Buxtehude's *Abendmusiken* concerts.

c.1709 Replacing the plucking mechanism of a harpsichord with a hammer system, Bartolomeo Cristofori invents the piano.

1706 The Deist writer Matthew Tindal publishes *The Rights of the Christian Church* anonymously. In it, Tindal attacks the trappings of high religion (both Catholic and Anglican), favoring instead a rational approach to Christian ethics which, being reasonable, make revelation superfluous. In 1710, the House of Commons orders the book burned.

1707 Edward Llwyd's comparative study of Celtic languages in *Archaeologica Brittanica* goes unnoticed until his theories are vindicated a century later.

1708 Abraham Darby finds that coke works just as well in iron-smelting furnaces as charcoal. Darby's discovery leads to the replacement of wood with coal as the primary industrial fuel source, advancing the Industrial Revolution and easing the deforestation of England.

1707 During the last eruption of Mount Fuji, the entire summit explodes into flames, causing several inches of ash to settle on the ground for miles around.

1707 The British government rescinds an ordinance that recommends branding a criminal's face as a fit punishment for petty theft. Two years later, torture is also abolished by Parliament.

1707 Mechanics in Philadelphia band together to oppose the competition presented by hired black slaves.

The Body Politic

1711 JUL 11 When Peter the Great finds his army surrounded by Turks on the Prut River, he sues for peace, agreeing to return the port of Azov. The Ottomans have declared war on Russia at the urging of Sweden's Charles XII, who escaped to Turkey after the battle of Poltava (1709).

1711 OCT The new Tory government in England begins separate peace negotiations with the French, believing that the war economy has favored Whig moneyed interests over Tory landed ones.

1713 APR 11 The Peace of Utrecht ends the War of the Spanish Succession. Philip V (Philip of Anjou) retains Spain and its colonies, but agrees not to pursue any union with the Bourbon throne in France. Additionally, Spain cedes Gibraltar to Great Britain and grants the English a monopoly on the slave trade with its American colonies. France cedes its colonies in Newfoundland, Nova Scotia, St. Kitts, and the Hudson Bay to Britain, and a collateral commercial treaty pledges an end to piracy. The remainder of the Spanish holdings in Europe, including the Spanish Netherlands and southern Italy, are delivered to Austria.

1713 Austrian emperor Charles VI, lacking a male heir, issues the Pragmatic Sanction in an attempt to maintain the future integrity of the Hapsburg possessions. He spends the remainder of his

Arts & Architecture

1711 Soon after Richard Steele folds his anti-Tory *Tatler,* he and Joseph Addison make a new start with *The Spectator*.

1713 With political tensions running high near the end of Queen Anne's reign, Alexander Pope distances himself from the Whig circle of Addison and Steele. Instead, he forms the Scriblerus Club with fellow Tories Jonathan Swift, John Gay, and John Arbuthnot.

1717 George Frederick Handel writes his occasional piece *Water Music* while com-

Religion & Philosophy

1710 Cotton Mather states the purpose of his life in *Essays to Do Good*, which instructs the reader in humanitarianism.

1710 In *Principles of Human Knowledge*, George Berkeley declares that there is no material substance to things, that they are merely ideas which have existence only in the mind of the observer.

1710 In the *Théodicée,* Leibniz states his belief that this is the best of all possible worlds because God made it that way in the image of His own perfection.

Science & Technology

1714 The British government creates a Board of Longitude, which offers a prize of £20,000 to the first person who can develop a marine clock accurate enough to determine, within 30 miles, the longitude at sea. Contemporary pendulum-based clocks are useless on the ocean because the rolling of the waves disturbs the pendulum's swing.

1714 Gabriel Daniel Fahrenheit encloses mercury in a sealed glass tube, creating the first modern thermometer. He then calibrates the tube so that its readings

Daily Life

c.1710 After Johann Friedrich Böttger and Ehrenfried Walter von Tschirnhaus discover the secret of true (Chinese) porcelain, Augustus the Strong of Saxony spirits them away to a secret factory in Meissen, where the process is improved. Porcelain from Meissen will dominate the European market until the rise of French Sèvres porcelain circa 1756.

1718 One of the brilliant women of her time, Lady Mary Wortley Montagu returns from Constantinople, where her husband has been ambassador. She brings with

reign seeking international consent to the edict, which specifically provides for succession along the female line, so that Austria might remain an undivided state. The emperor does indeed die without a male heir, but he fathers a daughter, Maria Theresa, in 1717.

1714 The treaties of Rastatt and Baden end the fighting between France and Austria that has briefly defied the Peace of Utrecht. With these treaties, Charles VI reaffirms the agreements reached at Utrecht and settles the border dispute between the two nations.

1714 AUG 1 With the death of Queen Anne, Elector George Louis of Hanover becomes King George I of England, as provided for by the Act of Settlement (1701). The House of Hanover will rule Great Britain until 1901.

1715 SEP 1 The Sun King Louis XIV dies after a 54-year reign, the longest of any European monarch. His 5-year-old great-grandson Louis XV succeeds him. Philip of Orleans serves as regent during Louis XV's minority, while the *ancien régime* develops in France.

1715 DEC James II's son James Stuart (the Old Pretender) arrives in Scotland to lead another Jacobite Rebellion, already begun by John Erskine, the earl of Mar. Both flee to France one month later.

Gottfried Wilhelm Leibniz

---

posing at the court of George I, the first of the Hanover kings.

1717 Antoine Watteau presents his masterful second version of *L'Embarquement pour l'île de Cythère* to the Académie Royale. Watteau's *fêtes galantes* mark a departure from the classicism that had dominated the court of Louis XIV.

1719 Daniel Defoe writes one of the first extended works of fiction, but his experiment proves successful when *Robinson Crusoe* sells out immediately.

1711 The third earl of Shaftesbury's *Characteristics of Men, Manners, Opinion, Times* argues the Deist position that the reality of the universe proves God's existence, making formal religion unnecessary. It also attacks Hobbes, claiming that man is inherently moral.

1715 MAR 8 Louis XIV announces that he has succeeded in removing all traces of Protestantism from France.

1715 Clement XI refuses to allow missionaries in China to "accommodate" Christian teachings to Chinese cultural traditions.

---

can be recorded quantitatively. The temperature he designates as 0° is the coldest he can achieve in his laboratory mixing salt and ice with water.

1715 *Linear Perspective* by English mathematician Brook Taylor presents the first general discussion of the principle of the vanishing point.

1717 Recognizing that malaria is most common in swampy areas, Giovanni Lancisi relates its transmission to mosquitoes and suggests that swamps be drained.

---

her a method of smallpox inoculation that she uses successfully on her children.

1718 Disguised as a workman, John Lombe makes sketches of the methods used by Italian silk throwing mills, using those sketches to open the first English mill.

1710-1719

The Body Politic

1720 Chinese Qing emperor Kangxi, fresh from military adventures in Mongolia, conquers Tibet after besieging Lhasa. A Jesuit missionary there later comments on the minimal plunder taken by the Chinese.

1720 The Treaty of Stockholm ends the war between Prussia and Sweden, granting Pomerania to Prussia and thus guaranteeing Prussia's predominance in northern Germany.

1720 New York governor William Burnet establishes trade relations with the local Indians in order to minimize any influence the French might have been cultivating with these neighboring tribes.

1720 The South Sea Bubble, a financial scheme by which England has tried to reduce its national debt, bursts. When it was formed in 1711, the South Sea Company was given certain trading monopolies, extended in 1713 to include the Spanish slave trade granted to Britain by the Peace of Utrecht. In exchange, the company agreed to assume a portion of Britain's debt. When the price of South Sea stock began to fall in September, Parliament launched an investigation, implicating Chancellor of the Exchequer John Aislabie (later imprisoned). Sir Robert Walpole, who originally opposed the scheme, regains power and offers a plan to revive public confidence in the government (DEC).

Arts & Architecture

1721 MAR 24 As the musical director at Köthen, Bach finishes the *Brandenburg Concertos*, keeping in mind the limitations of his prince, who plays the gamba.

c.1725 Japanese printmaker Okumura Masanobu introduces innovative woodblock techniques. His vivid multicolor prints later influence European impressionism.

1726 Jonathan Swift returns to England with the manuscript of *Gulliver's Travels*, which he tells Alexander Pope is designed to "vex the world rather than divert it."

Religion & Philosophy

1725 Giambattista Vico, a harbinger of cultural anthropology, publishes the first edition of his magnum opus *Scienza Nuova*, in which he attempts to join history and social science into a single science of humanity. Vico's work will later influence Goethe, Comte, and Marx.

1726 After clashing with a fatuous member of a leading French family, Voltaire is beaten, imprisoned, and then deported to England (until 1729).

1729 The first permanent Jewish congregation in the colonies is established in

Science & Technology

1721 Applying a technique first developed in Constantinople, Boston physician Zabdiel Boylston inoculates 241 people during a virulent smallpox epidemic. Boylston injects a weak strain of the smallpox in order to build up enough immunity to preclude a severe attack.

Daily Life

1722 Dutch admiral Jakob Roggeveen discovers Easter Island in the South Pacific on Easter Sunday. His crew finds the native population worshiping huge carved stone statues. After Roggeveen's single day's stay, no Europeans returned to the island until the Spanish in 1770.

1723 The colonial coffee industry begins in Martinique, where a bush stolen from the French Jardin Royal is planted.

1723 It takes Benjamin Franklin four days to travel the 100 miles from Philadelphia to New York.

1721 SEP 10 The Treaty of Nystad ends the Great Northern War, ceding to Russia the Baltic coast and reducing Sweden to a second-rank power in Northern Europe.

1722 MAR 8 At the head of an army raised in Afghanistan, which was once ruled by Persian Safavids and then by Indian Moguls, Mahmud invades the Persian capital of Isfahan. Shah Hosain acknowledges defeat in September, when he recognizes Mahmud as the de facto sovereign of Persia. Hosain's fugitive son Tahmasp II, however, escapes to Russia, where he makes a treaty with Peter the Great, ceding Russia Persia's rich northern provinces in exchange for Peter's help in driving out the Afghans.

1725 FEB 8 When Peter the Great dies, his second wife Catherine succeeds him. The previous May, Peter had crowned her empress of Russia despite the Russian tradition of male-only succession.

1725 Mahmud's death leaves the Persian throne to his cousin Ashraf, who maintains Afghan rule over Persia until 1730, when Nadir Kali, the commander of Tahmasp II's new army, deposes him.

1726 Cardinal André Hercule de Fleury becomes chief minister in France (until 1743). His policies, with those of Walpole in England, help maintain peace between Vienna and Madrid, while Europe continues its financial recovery.

Johann Sebastian Bach

1726 Alexander Pope completes the task he had set for himself in 1713 of translating Homer's *Iliad* and *Odyssey*. The £10,000 he earns from the project allows him to live comfortably and write without having to concern himself with the demands of a patron.

1728 JAN 29 At its debut, John Gay's *Beggar's Opera* proves so popular that it drives Italian opera off London's stages.

1729 Bach's *St. Matthew Passion* leads to a renewed interest in vocal works on a greater scale than the cantata.

New York City. The members build a synagogue on Mill Street in the next year.

1729 NOV John Wesley becomes head of a religious study group at Oxford University, known as the Methodists because of their methodical approach to devotion.

1724 Peter the Great founds the Academy of Sciences, attracting to Russia many leading European mathematicians, including Daniel Bernoulli and Leonhard Euler.

1728 Applying new, more scientific principles, Pierre Fauchard's *The Surgeon*

Dentist describes how to fill an infected tooth using gold, tin, or lead.

1729 Stephen Gray discovers that electricity can travel over great distances without any apparent movement of matter, meaning it must be weightless.

1724 Barbers meeting in Boston decide to set uniform prices for shaves and wigs.

1728 JUL 13 Danish navigator Vitus Bering sails from Kamchatka on an expedition commissioned by Peter the Great to determine whether Asia and North

America are joined by land. In August, he discovers the Bering Strait.

1729 James Franklin and his brother Benjamin start the *Pennsylvania Gazette*, which becomes the *Saturday Evening Post* in 1821.

1720-1729

The Body Politic

1732 JUN 9 King George II grants a royal charter to philanthropist John Edward Oglethorpe for the founding of Georgia, the last of the 13 original colonies. As Oglethorpe envisions it, Georgia will be a refuge for both debtors and the persecuted of Europe. Among its earliest settlers are German Lutherans, Portuguese Jews, and Scottish Highlanders–all religious refugees. Georgia will also serve a geopolitical function in blocking the northward expansion of Spanish Florida into the Carolinas.

1732 General Nadir Kali dethrones Shah Tahmasp II, declaring himself shah in 1736 and thus ending Safavid rule in Persia (since 1499).

1733 MAY 17 Parliament passes the first Molasses Act, which places prohibitive tariffs on molasses and rum shipped to America from the French and Spanish West Indies. Enacted to protect British sugar plantations in the Caribbean, these rarely paid duties encourage widespread smuggling as well as the bribery of customs officials.

1733 After the death of Augustus II of Poland-Saxony, Austria and Russia announce that they favor the succession of his son Augustus III to the Polish throne. Meanwhile, a group of Polish nobles chooses former king Stanislas Leszczynski (AUG 26), whose daughter has married Louis XV of France. Leszczynski,

Arts & Architecture

c.1730 Architects John Wood the Elder and his son John Wood the Younger redesign the English spa town of Bath in the Palladian style. After two royal visits in 1734, the city, presided over by the social dandy Richard (Beau) Nash, becomes the height of fashion.

c.1730 A rivalry between Marie Sallé and Marie Camargo draws public attention to the Parisian ballet. Camargo is the first to dance in a shortened skirt and heelless slippers, which permit greater leg extension and lead to the development of leaps such as the *entrechat*.

Religion & Philosophy

1733 Voltaire's *Letters Concerning the English Nation* praises England's constitutional government and shows the empiricist influence of John Locke.

1733-1734 Alexander Pope composes his philosophical *Essay on Man* in verse.

1734-35 In Northampton, Massachusetts, Jonathan Edwards leads a religious revival of such pitch that daily commerce nearly breaks down. Edwards calls the movement a "Great Awakening," a term that is soon applied to religious revivals throughout the colonies.

Science & Technology

1733 Charles DuFay discovers that while two charged amber rods repel each other, one charged rod attracts charged glass. To explain this, DuFay posits two types of electricity. Disagreeing, Benjamin Franklin suggests that electricity is but a single fluid: its presence positively charges an object, while its absence creates a negative charge.

1733 MAY 26 John Kay patents his flying shuttle, which allows one weaver to work faster than two could previously. Weavers quickly adopt Kay's invention but refuse

Daily Life

c.1730 Architect William Kent begins designing innovative naturalistic gardens to accompany his formal Palladian-style buildings. Kent's landscape designs soon come to compete with the fantasy arrangements and ornate topiaries favored in baroque Europe.

1730-1735 Reports of vampire sightings abound in Hungary.

1731 In Philadelphia, Benjamin Franklin founds America's first subscription library to make books easily available to the members of his club, the Junto.

originally placed on the Polish throne by Sweden's Charles XII (1707), has the support of France, Spain, and Sweden. During the War of the Polish Succession that follows, Russian troops besiege Leszczynski at Danzig until he renounces his claim (JUN 1734), while France uses the conflict as an excuse to aggrandize itself at German and Austrian expense. Promising not to seize the Austrian Netherlands (and thereby keeping England and The Netherlands neutral), the French army marches on the Rhine.

1736 Qian Long becomes emperor of China (until 1796). He later wages successful campaigns against Turkestan and the Gurkhas of Nepal.

1738 The Treaty of Vienna formally ends the War of the Polish Succession. Sicily and Naples are transferred from Austria to Spain's Don Carlos, while Lorraine is granted to Leszczynski, with the provision that the territory will pass to France upon his death. In return, France agrees to the Pragmatic Sanction.

1738 Captain Robert Jenkins displays to Parliament his severed ear, cut off by a Spanish colonial naval patrol. The resulting public outcry against Spain, England's new commercial rival in the Americas, forces Parliament to declare the War of Jenkins' Ear (OCT 1739), but the conflict is quickly eclipsed by the Austrian succession controversy.

Jonathan Edwards

1730 After seven years at Leipzig's Thomaskirche, Bach complains that he is not earning as much as he was led to expect because there are too few funerals.

1735 William Hogarth holds back *A Rake's Progress*, engravings of a country girl's corruption in London, until Parliament grants copyright protection to artists.

1738 At 53, Domenico Scarlatti publishes the first of his 555 sonatas for the harpsichord that greatly expand its technical and musical possibilities.

1736 FEB 5 John Wesley arrives in Georgia at the invitation of the governor.

1738 MAY 24 While listening to Luther's analysis of the *Epistle to the Romans*, John Wesley has revealed to him the Methodist doctrine of salvation by faith.

to pay him royalties. After losing all his money in unsuccessful patent infringement cases, Kay dies in poverty.

1735 John Harrison submits his first marine chronometer, known as Number One, to the British Board of Longitude.

1737 The *Systema naturae* of Carolus Linnaeus revolutionizes taxonomy. His most significant innovation is the grouping together of species exhibiting similar traits into a single genus. Related genera are then grouped into families, and related families into classes.

1732 The first regularly scheduled stagecoach line in North America opens between Burlington and Amboy in New Jersey.

1732 DEC 19 Franklin issues the first *Poor Richard's Almanack*, which continues as an annual series until 1757.

1734 New York maids unionize to protest the abuses of their mistresses' husbands.

1735 The Friendly Society for the Mutual Insurance of Houses Against Fire, the first colonial fire insurance company, begins operating in Charleston.

1730-1739

1740 In the American tradition of echoing European conflicts with half-hearted wars amongst themselves, the colonial subjects of England and Spain escalate the border fighting along the Georgia-Florida frontier. Governor James Oglethorpe of Georgia strikes a bold, but unsuccessful blow when he attacks the Spanish fortress at St. Augustine, Florida (besieged MAY-JUL). Although Oglethorpe is forced to retire, the fighting continues sporadically until the War of the Austrian Succession is finally resolved.

1740 OCT 20 Austrian emperor Charles VI dies. According to the terms of the Pragmatic Sanction (1713), his daughter Maria Theresa succeeds him.

1740 DEC 16 Frederick II (the Great) of Prussia invades Silesia. Using an outdated dynastic claim as an excuse, the invasion is a poorly disguised attempt to enlarge Prussia at the expense of a weakened Austria under Maria Theresa. Frederick's occupation of Silesia triggers the long-feared War of the Austrian Succession, which pits Prussia, France, Spain, Bavaria, and Saxony against Austria, Britain, Holland, and Hanover.

1741 APR Frederick the Great defeats an advancing Austrian army at Mollwitz, consolidating his control of Silesia, while a French-Bavarian army seizes Prague with the help of the Saxons and continues advancing as far as Linz.

1740 Samuel Richardson publishes his innovative novel *Pamela* in the form of letters written by the title character.

1742 APR 13 George Frederick Handel's *Messiah* is first performed at a subscription concert in Dublin.

1745 William Hogarth issues his much-anticipated series of engravings entitled *Marriage à la mode*, a satire on the marital customs of the upper classes.

1747 APR Samuel Johnson's friend David Garrick takes over London's Drury Lane

---

1740 On his accession to the Prussian throne, Frederick II (the Great), who has corresponded with Voltaire, begins to practice an enlightened form of monarchy. He abolishes torture, grants complete religious tolerance, and attempts to administer justice fairly.

1741 As the Great Awakening sweeps through New England, driven by evangelists preaching emotional sermons of "terror," Jonathan Edwards makes his own contribution to the religious fervor with the sermon "Sinners in the Hands of an Angry God."

---

c.1740 Benjamin Huntsman develops the crucible process for making steel.

1742 Rejecting the Fahrenheit scale, Anders Celsius devises the centigrade scale, setting water's freezing point at 0°C and its boiling point at 100°C.

1745 Ewald Georg von Kleist constructs the first Leyden jar to store captured static electricity. The device becomes identified with the University of Leyden after Peter van Musschenbroek independently builds a similar condenser there a few months later.

---

c.1741 British metallurgist Charles Wood finds platinum in South America and brings the first sample of this rare metal back to England.

1741 JUN 4 Vitus Bering and Alexei Chirikov, each commanding his own ship,

sail from Kamchatka as part of Russia's Great Northern Expedition to map the Arctic coast of Siberia. Blown off course and separated by a storm, Chirikov discovers the Aleutians, while Bering enters the Gulf of Alaska (AUG 20) and sights North America.

1742 JUN 11 With the Treaty of Breslau, Austria makes a separate peace with Prussia, ceding nearly all of Silesia. Maria Theresa then forms an alliance with Saxony against Bavaria.

1745 JUN 16 British regulars and colonial militia capture the French Canadian citadel at Louisburg in the only major action of King George's War, which is the name given to the War of the Austrian Succession in the colonies.

1746 APR 16 At Culloden, the duke of Cumberland's army defeats the forces of Charles Edward Stuart. Also known as the Young Pretender and Bonny Prince Charlie, Charles Edward is the son of the Old Pretender James Stuart. His defeat ends the Jacobite Rebellion of 1745, which had roused Scotland against King George II in the last armed attempt to restore the Stuarts.

1748 OCT 18 Anxious for peace, Great Britain pushes through the Treaty of Aix-la-Chapelle, which ends the War of the Austrian Succession. Nearly all of the captured territories are returned, except for Silesia, which is retained by Prussia (as provided for by the 1745 Peace of Dresden ending the second Silesian war). Furthermore, all parties agree to recognize Maria Theresa as the legitimate Hapsburg heir in accordance with the Pragmatic Sanction.

Frederick the Great

Theater, which he raises from insolvency with popular revivals of Shakespeare.

1748 Archaeological excavations begin at Pompeii, the ruins of which were discovered two centuries earlier by an architect digging a water tunnel.

1749 Henry Fielding's laboriously plotted *Tom Jones* provides the most complete vision yet of what a novel can be.

1749 Friedrich Klopstock's religious and highly emotional epic poem *Der Messias* causes a sensation.

1748 Montesquieu's *Spirit of the Laws* classifies governments according to their animating principles: virtue for republics, honor for monarchies, and fear for tyrannies. His work also advances the first argument for the separation of legislative, judicial, and executive powers, which will influence American constitutional thought enormously.

1749 *An Enquiry Concerning Human Understanding* articulates David Hume's quest for a scientific epistemology. In it, he distinguishes between fact and experience.

1747 In his *Reflections on the general cause of winds*, Jean Le Rond d'Alembert uses partial differential equations for the first time. Also about this time, d'Alembert becomes associated with Diderot's *Encyclopédie*. His introduction, the *Discours préliminaire* (1751), is considered to be among the defining documents of the Enlightenment.

1748 The Académie Française authorizes the *Carte géométrique de la France*, the first map ever produced by a national geographic survey.

1749 Giacobbo Rodriguez Pereire presents a sign language he has developed to the Academie Française. Falling in love at the age of 18 with a deaf-mute girl, he thereafter devoted his life to creating a system of communication for those who could neither hear nor speak.

1740-1749

THE ENLIGHTENMENT

The Body Politic

1750 With the Treaty of Madrid, Spain recognizes Portugal's claims to Brazil, leading to subsequent colonial reforms. Over the next two decades, the Portuguese marquês de Pombal grants native Indians the same legal status as European settlers and moves the Brazilian capital to Rio de Janeiro.

1752 Emperor Qian Long suppresses an anti-Chinese rebellion in Lhasa as control of Tibet passes from the Dalai Lama to imperial commissioners.

1754 MAY 28 After diplomatically asking the French to evacuate British-claimed lands in the Ohio River Valley (1753), George Washington, then a 22-year-old lieutenant colonel, returns with 160 militiamen to make the trespassers leave. The French and Indian War begins when Washington attacks a reconnaissance party near the French outpost at Fort Duquesne. Washington's troops are quickly surprised, captured, and released only when Washington signs a document admitting his fault.

1756 JAN The Convention of Westminster initiates a military alliance between Britain and Prussia. Meanwhile, France makes the diplomatic revolution complete when it accepts a rapprochement with Austria. The Anglo-French rivalry in North America contributes significantly to this European realignment.

Arts & Architecture

1750 Giovanni Tiepolo travels to Würzburg, where he paints a famous cycle of frescoes above the grand stairway of the Residenz there.

1755 Johann Winckelmann writes his influential *Reflections on the Imitation of Greek Works in Painting and Sculpture*, which provides the theoretical basis for the neoclassical movement that soon spreads through Europe.

1757 In reaction to baroque style, Jacques-Germain Soufflot designs the

Religion & Philosophy

1751-1765 Under the leadership of Denis Diderot and Jean Le Rond d'Alembert, the French *Encyclopédie* becomes an intellectual crusade on a monumental scale, a Versailles of philosophy. As Voltaire says, this 53-volume work "seems to reproach mankind's brief life span."

1755 Nine years after signing a contract with a consortium of London booksellers, Samuel Johnson completes the first *Dictionary of the English Language*. His mammoth, epochal work includes 43,500 words illustrated by 118,000 quotations. The verb "to take," for example, is shown

Science & Technology

1752 Investigating digestion, René de Réaumur makes a hawk swallow small capsules made from metal mesh and filled with meat. When the hawk regurgitates the capsules, Réaumur finds that the meat has been partially dissolved by a yellowish liquid (gastric juices), convincing him that digestion proceeds chemically and not mechanically.

1752 During a thunderstorm, Benjamin Franklin performs his famous kite experiment. Attached to Franklin's kite is a pointed wire and a conductive silk thread.

Daily Life

c.1750 The first Conestoga wagon hauls up to six tons. It later evolves into the prairie schooner, which proves indispensable to America's westward expansion.

c.1750 The hooped whalebone petticoat becomes so fashionable in London that architects design new, outwardly curving stairway balustrades to compensate for the skirt's enormous width.

1752 Franklin develops the first lightning rod, which he installs atop his own house on Philadelphia's Market Street.

1756 JUN 20 Bengali soldiers capture and imprison 146 Europeans, only 23 of whom survive a single night in what comes to be known as the Black Hole of Calcutta. Sacking the city, the Bengalis capture Fort William, base of the British East India Company.

1756 AUG Learning that the Russians, Austrians, and French are plotting against him, Frederick the Great of Prussia launches a preemptive invasion of their ally Saxony, thus beginning the Seven Years' War.

1757 After the collapse of the Whig government, William Pitt (the Elder) assumes the political leadership of Great Britain and aggressively pursues the colonial war in North America.

1759 The Chinese limit international trade to the port of Guanzhou [Canton], where foreign merchants are required to conduct business through the *cohong*, a guild of Chinese merchants who enjoy monopolies on tea and silk.

1759 SEP 13 British major general James Wolfe ends the French and Indian War in North America when he defeats the French army of the marquis de Montcalm on the Plains of Abraham outside Quebec. Both men are killed during the battle. The capital of New France surrenders five days later.

Voltaire

Panthéon in Paris, perhaps France's most significant neoclassical structure.

1759 Voltaire's philosophical novel *Candide* satirizes blind optimists who believe that this is the best of all possible worlds.

to have 113 transitive senses in addition to 21 intransitive ones.

1758 Claude-Adrien Helvétius's *On the Mind* becomes instantly scandalous for its vigorous attacks on all forms of religious morality. Its public burning precipitates a crisis among Voltaire's circle of Philosophes.

1759 Christoph Nicolai, Gotthold Lessing, and Moses Mendelssohn found the great journal of the German Enlightenment, *Allgemeine deutsche Bibliothek*.

When Franklin puts his hand near a metal key tied to the end of the thread, the key sparks, thus proving that lightning is a form of electricity.

1753 Euler announces his solution to a classic problem in topology, the Seven Bridges of Königsberg. He shows that it is impossible to cross all the bridges once without crossing one of them twice.

1758 DEC 25 The sighting of Halley's Comet confirms the late astronomer's prediction that the comet would return.

1752 Handel's trumpeter John Shore invents the tuning fork.

1755 Frustrated at having to invert his needle while sewing, Charles Weisenthal invents a double-pointed needle with an eye in the center, which provides the basis for the later development of the sewing machine.

1759 Josiah Wedgwood starts a ceramics factory and begins creating the fine earthenware that will later earn him the post of official potter to the Crown.

1762 JAN 5 After the combined Russian and Austrian armies nearly destroy Prussia at the battle of Kunersdorf (1759, AUG 12), Frederick the Great is saved when, with the death of the Russian tsarina Elizabeth, her unstable nephew Peter III comes to power. An admirer of Frederick, Peter miraculously makes peace with Prussia and places 18,000 Russian troops at Frederick's disposal.

1762 JUL 9 Royal guard regiments led by her lover Grigory Orlov depose Peter III in favor of Peter's wife Catherine, who rules until 1796. Catherine II (the Great) reclaims the troops lent to Frederick, but declines to renew Russia's military alliance with Austria.

1762 Wary of British encroachments made possible by the French and Indian War, the Ottawa chief Pontiac organizes an alliance among the Great Lakes tribes. The surprise attacks they launch against British outposts become known as Pontiac's Rebellion. Pontiac's initial success convinces other tribes to join the confederacy, but the most important forts (Detroit, Niagara, Pitt) hold out until British reinforcements arrive. Pontiac is finally forced to sign a peace treaty in July, 1766.

1763 FEB 10 Britain, France, and Spain (a late entry on the French side) consent to the Treaty of Paris, which ends the Seven Years' War. According to its provisions, France cedes all of Canada as well

1761 At the height of his career, adored ballet soloist Gaetano Vestris remarks, "There are but three great men in Europe: the king of Prussia, Voltaire and I."

1762 The first volume of *The Antiquities of Athens* by architects James Stuart and

Nicholas Revett spurs European neoclassicism and contains the first suggestion that Roman architecture derives from Greek and not vice versa.

1762 On his first Austrian tour, six-year-old prodigy Wolfgang Amadeus Mozart

1762 In addition to writing for the *Encyclopédie*, Jean-Jacques Rousseau publishes his philosophical novel *Émile* on education and *The Social Contract*, which begins with the oft-quoted sentence, "Man was born free, but he is everywhere in chains." Rousseau goes on

to present his theory of the general will as the analogue of individual will (but representing society as a whole).

1762 When she hears that Denis Diderot is being harassed by the French authorities, Catherine the Great, set on making

1762 John Harrison's Number Four chronometer loses only five seconds during a trip to Jamaica, exceeding the standards set for the Board of Longitude prize.

1764 James Hargreaves devises the spinning jenny, the first machine to spin

multiple threads. The output is suitable only for weft, but the jenny remains a crucial advance over the spinning wheel.

1764 The University of Glasgow hires James Watt to fix a malfunctioning Newcomen steam engine. Puzzled by its

1760 Joseph Merlin of Belgium popularizes roller-skating.

1762 John Montagu, the fourth earl of Sandwich, has sliced meat and bread brought to him during a 24-hour binge at the gaming table, so that he can continue

to play as he eats. The dish is thereafter called the *sandwich*.

1767 Daniel Boone makes his first trip to the Cumberland Gap. Eight years later, he blazes the Wilderness Road through this legendary Appalachian pass.

as its territories east of the Mississippi to England, while Spain yields Florida in exchange for the return of Cuba and Manila, which have been seized by the British. The treaty, which humbles France, makes Britain the preeminent world power.

1763 FEB 15 The peace treaty between Prussia and Austria signed at Hubertusburg calls for Frederick to evacuate Saxony while retaining Silesia.

1764 Parliament passes the Revenue Act to pay off Britain's £130 million war debt. The new law, also known as the Sugar Act, establishes tariffs on a wide range of goods, including sugar, coffee, and

molasses. The new tariff on molasses is actually lower than the unenforced tariffs of the Molasses Act (1733), but American radicals such as Samuel Adams denounce the duties as improper taxation without representation.

1765 To replace the objectionable Sugar Act, Parliament passes the Stamp Act, which levies a tax on all paper goods and documents used in the colonies. The colonists react with the Stamp Act riots.

1769 Gurkha prince Prithvi Narayan Shah conquers the Nepal Valley, making his new capital at Kathmandu. His realm forms the basis for the modern state of Nepal.

Catherine the Great

---

enjoys such a triumph at the imperial court in Vienna that he begins a grand tour of Europe the following year.

1765 Horace Walpole's *The Castle of Otranto* begins the vogue for Gothic romances in England.

1765 François Boucher, whose festive paintings typify French Rococo taste, becomes first painter to King Louis XV.

c.1766 Jean-Honoré Fragonard paints *The Swing*, a masterful *fête galante* in the style of Boucher.

---

her country more cosmopolitan, invites Diderot to work on his *Encyclopédie* in Russia under her protection.

1764 Cesare Beccaria's *Crimes and Punishment* argues innovatively that criminal punishment should only be harsh

enough to maintain public order, pointing out that the certainty of punishment is much more important than its severity.

1765 Sir William Blackstone issues the first volume of his preeminent *Commentaries on the Laws of England*.

---

waste of steam, Watt adds a number of improvements, including a condenser (1765, MAY), that make the engine at least three times more efficient.

1769 Richard Arkwright patents a water frame for spinning warps. Because the

machine is too large and costly for use in cottages, its development leads to a shift from home to factory production.

1769 Engineer Nicolas-Joseph Cugnot builds a steam-powered tractor for hauling artillery, the first automobile.

1768 The Admiralty appoints James Cook to command the Royal Society's expedition to the Pacific. Cook's orders are to convey the scientists to Tahiti, so that they can view the transit of Venus across the sun. Cook's ship, the HMS *Endeavour*, is a refitted coal hauler.

1760-1769

The Body Politic

1770 MAR 5 Five colonists are killed when British soldiers fire on a mob of rioting Bostonians. Samuel Adams calls it a "massacre."

1772 Prussia and Austria demand that Russia, already fighting the Turks in the Crimea, partition its satellite Poland. Having little choice but to accede, Russia grants Galicia to Austria and Pomerania to Prussia.

1772 With the aid of his Finnish guard, Gustavus III unseats Sweden's parliament and founds an absolutist but enlightened monarchy there. His social reforms end serfdom and expand Sweden's industrial base, making him a national hero.

1773 DEC 16 Sons of Liberty dressed as Mohawks dump 340 chests of British tea into Boston Harbor to protest the tea monopoly recently granted the British East India Company. An aghast Parliament responds with the Intolerable Acts, closing the port of Boston and ending colonial self-rule in Massachusetts.

1774 MAY 10 Upon the death of the unpopular ruler Louis XV, his grandson Louis XVI becomes king of France. His queen, Marie Antoinette, is the daughter of the Austrian empress Maria Theresa.

1774 With the Treaty of Kuchuk Kainarji, Turkey cedes the north shore of the Black Sea to Russia.

Arts & Architecture

c.1770 Thomas Gainsborough paints *The Blue Boy* in homage to Anthony Van Dyck.

1771 Benjamin West's greatest success in painting historic subjects comes with his *Death of General Wolfe*, for which he innovatively chooses a modern scene.

1774 Johann Wolfgang von Goethe captivates Europe with his first novel, *The Sorrows of Young Werther*, a tragic story of hopeless love.

1775 *The Barber of Seville* by Pierre-Augustin Caron de Beaumarchais fea-

Religion & Philosophy

1770 In jail during a period of religious intolerance in England, Ann Lee has a vision that only through celibacy can Christ's kingdom be achieved. Four years later, another vision instructs this Shaking Quaker to emigrate to America. There, thousands of her followers found Shaker communities in upstate New York and western Massachusetts.

1771 Editors complete work on the first edition of the *Encyclopaedia Brittanica*, which is widely considered to be an advancement over Diderot's work. For

Science & Technology

1772 Pooling cash, Antoine Lavoisier and his colleagues buy a diamond, which they heat until it burns, proving that diamonds and coal are chemically identical.

1774 Joseph Priestley discovers oxygen when he heats a red precipitate of mer-cury. Priestley calls his discovery "dephlogisticated air."

1775 John Wilkinson builds a machine of unprecedented accuracy to bore cannon barrels. Watt uses it instead to perfect the cylinders in his steam engine.

Daily Life

c.1770 Irritated by her lover Louis XV's low regard for women chefs, the comtesse du Barry has one secretly prepare a meal so tasty that Louis hires her. As a reward, the comtesse demands "nothing less than the *cordon bleu*," thus originating the term for high culinary achievement.

1775 APR 18 Paul Revere rides from Boston to alert the countryside that British troops are marching on Concord, where intelligence reports have led them to believe munitions are being stored. The next morning, British redcoats and American Minute Men exchange a volley across Lexington Green.

1775 JUN 17 At Bunker Hill, a pyrrhic victory for the British, General Israel Putnam instructs militiamen hiding behind earthworks not to fire until they can see "the white of their eyes."

1776 JUL 4 The Continental Congress formally adopts Thomas Jefferson's final draft of the Declaration of Independence.

1776 DEC 25-26 Crossing the ice-clogged Delaware River in the middle of the night, George Washington and his Continental Army surprise the Hessian mercenaries guarding Trenton.

1777 OCT 7 With a courageous Benedict Arnold leading the way, the Continental Army routs General John Burgoyne's professional infantry corps at Saratoga. This unexpected American victory finally convinces France to enter the war on the American side.

1777 DEC 19 After the demoralizing loss of Philadelphia, Washington's Continental troops arrive at Valley Forge, where they make their winter camp.

Thomas Jefferson

---

tures the valet Figaro, who is highly critical of his master. This class-conscious comedy becomes controversial when Louis XVI objects to the play's production.

1778 John Singleton Copley's first major work, *Watson and the Shark*, employs one

of the great themes of the romantic age: man's struggle against nature.

1778-1779 Johann Gottfried von Herder, leader of the *Sturm und Drang* literary movement, prepares his collection of German popular verse, the *Volkslieder*.

---

political reasons, the *Encyclopédie* favored long, polemical entries, while the *Brittanica* achieves much greater breadth.

1773 JUL 21 In order to avoid a schism within the Catholic Church, Clement XIV dissolves the Society of Jesus (Jesuits).

1776 Adam Smith's *The Wealth of Nations* expands a study of capitalist market forces into a complete laissez-faire philosophy. The welfare of all, Smith insists, is best achieved by allowing individual citizens to pursue their own self-interest.

1777 In a paper given at the French academy, Antoine Lavoisier asserts that Priestley's "dephlogisticated air" is in fact a separate gas (oxygen). Lavoisier goes on to explain combustion, not in terms of phlogiston, but as the combination of a burning substance with oxygen.

1779 Combining the best aspects of the spinning jenny and the water frame, Samuel Crompton develops the spinning mule. Unable to afford a patent, he confides his invention to a number of factory owners, who employ it to great advantage, but pay Crompton only £60.

1777 JUN 14 The Continental Congress authorizes a flag composed of 13 white stars (set against a blue field) and 13 alternating red and white stripes.

1779 FEB 14 During a dispute over the stealing of a cutter, Polynesian natives

kill Captain James Cook on the beach at Kealakekua in Hawaii.

1779 JUL 27 The *Journal de Paris* carries a description of a bicycle prototype, the velocipede, which the rider propels by running on the ground.

1770-1779

The Body Politic

1781 MAR 1 Maryland becomes the last state to ratify the Articles of Confederation, an unsuccessful forerunner of the Constitution that lacked sufficient federal power.

1781 OCT 19 At Yorktown, Lord Cornwallis surrenders to Washington and the comte de Rochambeau the last actively campaigning British army in America, thus ending the Revolutionary War.

1783 Grigory Potemkin—Catherine the Great's lover, political partner, and the war hero of her victory over Turkey (1774)—arranges the Russian annexation of the Crimea, posing yet another threat to the Ottomans.

1783 FEB 6 Britain defeats the Spanish navy and its French ally, ending the four-year siege of Gibraltar that has produced a number of significant advances in artillery technology.

1787 The emperor of Austria, the king of Poland, and numerous others make a luxurious journey across Russia with Catherine the Great to inspect her new provinces in the Crimea. Because they travel part of the way by water, the procession becomes known as "Cleopatra's fleet," reflecting its opulence.

1787 FEB The French finance minister Charles-Alexandre de Calonne arranges an assembly of prominent nobles and

Arts & Architecture

1782 JAN 13 Friedrich von Schiller's first play *The Robbers*, decrying the suffocating formality he finds in Germany, debuts at the National Theater in Mannheim.

1783 Having been influenced by the growing neoclassicism in Rome, Antonio

Canova accepts an important commission to design the tomb of Pope Clement XIV.

1785 The presentation of Jacques-Louis David's *Oath of the Horatii* at the Paris Salon inaugurates the neoclassical movement in French painting.

Religion & Philosophy

1781 Immanuel Kant publishes *The Critique of Pure Reason*, the first of three commanding "critiques" that become the cornerstones of Kantian philosophy. Kant's work attempts to reconcile the rationalism of Descartes with the empiricism of Locke and Hume. Kant,

who is notoriously unreadable, describes this first *Critique* as "dry, obscure, contrary to all ordinary ideas, and on top of that prolix."

1783 In *Jerusalem*, Moses Mendelssohn explores his commitment to both Judaism

Science & Technology

1781 MAR 13 William Herschel observes what he at first believes to be a comet, but later decides is the planet Uranus.

1781 James Watt invents a sun-and-planet gear to turn the reciprocating motion of his steam engine into rotary motion.

1782 The Montgolfier brothers light a fire beneath a large paper bag. As the air inside heats up, the balloon rises.

1784 Henry Cavendish discovers water to be a compound of hydrogen and oxygen. Therefore, it cannot be an element.

Daily Life

1783 NOV 21 Jean-François Pilâtre de Rozier and the marquis d'Arlandes make the first manned balloon flight in a craft designed by Joseph and Étienne Montgolfier. They sail over Paris for 23 minutes, burning straw and wool to keep the air inside the balloon hot.

clerics to consider solutions to the government's financial crisis. This body rejects all proposals to tax the privileged classes, and instead calls for the convocation of the Estates-General. The three estates represented by the Estates General—the nobility, the clergy, and the people—have not met since 1614.

1787 MAY 25 The Constitutional Convention meets in Philadelphia, charged with substituting a more federalized system for the obviously inadequate Articles of Confederation. The completed document, characterized by Montesquieu's separation of powers (1748), is submitted to the states for ratification on September 17.

1789 JUN 20 The populist Third Estate, meeting independently on the Versailles tennis courts, swears not to disperse until it has produced a new constitution for France. Louis XVI sends for troops.

1789 JUL 14 Alarmed by rumors that the soldiers en route to Versailles plan to put down the Third Estate, a Parisian mob storms the Bastille to capture the armaments stored there.

1789 AUG 26 The National Constituent Assembly, formed after the Tennis Court Oath, adopts the Declaration of the Rights of Man, which proclaims the rights of "liberty, property, security and the resistance to oppression."

Immanuel Kant

1785 Accompanied by Benjamin Franklin, sculptor Jean-Antoine Houdon travels to Virginia to execute a commission for a statue of George Washington.

1785 Angelica Kauffman uses herself as the model for *Cornelia, Mother of the*

Gracchi. Her self-portraits also present the artist as "Painting" personified.

1787 Using a method he calls "illuminated printing," British mystic William Blake publishes his verse in the illustrated volume *Songs of Innocence.*

---

and rationalism. Interpreting Judaism as a religion of reason, he places it above Christianity in this respect.

1783 Mennonites in Lancaster County, Pennsylvania, are accused of treason for feeding destitute British soldiers.

1789 Jeremy Bentham, the founder of utilitarianism, publishes his best-known work, *An Introduction to the Principles of Morals and Legislation*. Bentham's signature argument is that society's goal should be the greatest happiness for the greatest number.

1785 Antoine Lavoisier formulates his law of conservation that matter can neither be created nor destroyed.

1785 Charles de Coulomb shows that the force between two charged bodies obeys the same inverse-square law as gravity.

1787 Experimenting with balloons, Jacques Charles discovers that for all gases, volume and temperature vary directly.

1788 Joseph-Louis Lagrange's *Mécanique analytique* establishes mechanics as a branch of mathematical analysis.

1784 Placing musket balls and a bursting charge inside a common artillery shell, Lieutenant Henry Shrapnel invents the Shrapnel shell. Detonating in flight, the explosive charge shatters the shell, raining the balls and shell fragments down onto the target. This new techno-

logy kills so effectively that Shrapnel is promoted to Lieutenant-General.

1787 Claude Bertholent demonstrates the highly effective bleaching properties of chlorine, an element discovered 13 years earlier by Karl Wilhelm Scheele.

1780-1789

1763 The conclusion of the Seven Years' War, called the French and Indian War in America, finds the colonists reveling in the ascendancy of the British Empire. Never has their allegiance been felt so deeply, but the £130 million war debt run up by Prime Minister William Pitt has yet to be addressed.

1764 **May 24** Boston radical Samuel Adams lectures a town meeting at Faneuil Hall on the subject of the Sugar Act, which has been passed by Parliament at the suggestion of Prime Minister George Grenville. The Sugar Act calls for tariffs on a wide range of goods. Adams insists that Parliament has no right to use trade regulation as a means of raising revenue. Speaking after him, James Otis coins the phrase "no taxation without representation."

1765 Willing to compromise, Grenville proposes the Stamp Act, which levies a tax on all documents in the colonies, from newspapers to college diplomas. Stamp Act riots in nearly every port city on the east coast greet news of the new law's passage and force its repeal one year later.

1767 Parliament continues its campaign to raise colonial revenue with the Townshend Acts, which impose import duties on a few selected items including tea. The British believe that the money spent defending America during the French and Indian War should be returned to the treasury through American taxes, regardless of colonial resistance.

1770 **March 5** A violent mob corners a redcoat standing guard outside Boston's Custom House. Members of a rescue party, acting specifically against orders, fire into the crowd, killing five. Sam Adams calls it a "massacre."

1773 **December 16** Radicals dressed as Mohawk Indians board tea ships in Boston Harbor and dump their cargo overboard. This act of defiance comes in response to Parliament's recent grant of a monopoly on tea to the debt-ridden East India Company. Patriots have warned the British that, as long as the monopoly remains in effect, no tea ships will be permitted to land. Other colonies soon hold "tea parties" following the Boston example. In response, Parliament passes the Coercive Acts (also known as the Intolerable Acts). These new laws close the port of Boston until restitution is made for the ruined tea and end, for all practical purposes, colonial self-rule in Massachusetts.

1774   **September 5-October 26** The first Continental Congress meets at Carpenter's Hall in Philadelphia to demand the repeal of the Coercive Acts and the removal of British troops from Boston. The delegates agree to continue the widespread boycott of British goods until the colonists' demands are met.

1775   **April 18** Joseph Warren, one of the few high-ranking patriot leaders still in Boston, sends Paul Revere on his midnight ride to Lexington to warn Samuel Adams and John Hancock that the British are coming.

        April 19 On its way to investigate intelligence reports of a patriot arms depot near Concord, a British advance guard under Major John Pitcairn encounters a company of 70 Minute Men off to the side of the road on Lexington Green. Their skirmish begins the military phase of the American Revolution.

        May 10 Ethan Allen and his band of ruffians, the Green Mountain Boys, capture Fort Ticonderoga and its small British garrison without a fight. At the southern tip of Lake Champlain, Ticonderoga occupies a key strategic position along the traditional invasion route from Canada.

        June 15 The second Continental Congress unanimously appoints Virginia planter George Washington as commander-in-chief of the Continental Army.

        June 17 The British respond to the bold occupation of the Charlestown peninsula with a frontal assault against American fortifications on Breed's Hill, which the American commanders have mistakenly identified as Bunker Hill. The British strategy, intended to unnerve the raw militiamen, proves overly optimistic. After two failures, a third charge up the hill succeeds only when the Americans retreat, having run out of ammunition. Although the British win, the wounded and dead amount to half their 2,200-man force.

1776   **January 9** Thomas Paine publishes the pamphlet *Common Sense*, which becomes the most widely read piece of writing in the colonies after the Bible.

        March 17 Once Washington installs cannon captured at Ticonderoga atop Dorchester Heights, the British evacuate Boston. Washington makes an agreement with the British commander Sir William Howe not to fire on the departing redcoats in exchange for Howe's pledge not to burn the city.

1776
(continued)

June 28 Believing Tory (loyalist) support to be more active in the south, the British send a naval expedition to Charleston, South Carolina. But William Moultrie leads a spirited defense of the harbor, which scuttles British plans for a southern campaign. One of Moultrie's cannonballs even rips off the breeches of British admiral Sir Peter Parker.

July 4 The Continental Congress formally adopts the Declaration of Independence, whose primary author is Thomas Jefferson of Virginia.

August 22 William Howe lands 15,000 men at Gravesend Bay off Brooklyn, beginning the battle of Long Island. Washington falls back to Manhattan during the night of August 28-29 and continues his retreat northward.

September 20 Fully one-quarter of British-held New York City burns to the ground. Howe suspects patriot sabotage. When Connecticut schoolmaster Nathan Hale is brought before the general on charges of espionage, Howe sends Hale to the gallows as an example of what happens to spies.

December 25-26 Having been chased south through New Jersey and across the Delaware River by pursuing British troops, Washington decides to risk a counterpunch against Hessians wintering in Trenton. Recrossing the Delaware during a blinding nighttime snowstorm, the Continentals launch a dawn attack that catches most of the German mercenaries still sleeping off the alcohol they consumed during Christmas celebrations the night before.

1777

July 6 As part of Britain's strategy to cut off New England from the rest of the colonies along the Champlain-Hudson axis, a 10,000-man army under "Gentleman Johnny" Burgoyne captures Ticonderoga, forcing its broken garrison south. The British plan calls for Burgoyne to rendezvous at Albany with armies led by Barry St. Leger (traveling east along the Mohawk River) and Howe (coming up the Hudson from New York City). But St. Leger is stopped at Fort Stanwix, while Howe, believing that Burgoyne can handle matters on his own, instead ships his troops south, where he hopes to crush the rebellion by capturing the rebel capital of Philadelphia.

September 11 The British attack the American position on the north bank of Brandywine Creek, where Washington has chosen to make his stand in defense of Philadelphia. Lord Cornwallis turns the American right flank, but Howe's chronic hesitation allows Washington to make a hasty but orderly retreat. Congress abandons Philadelphia on September 19.

September 19 Burgoyne's army advances on American troops under Horatio Gates, which have gathered atop Bemis Heights, near Saratoga. Benedict Arnold's division meets the British at Freeman's Farm, where his unrelenting attacks nearly win the day before British reinforcements under the German mercenary general Baron von Riedesel arrive. The zealous Arnold is later confined to his quarters after he accuses Gates of losing the engagement through excessive caution.

October 7 Determined to prove the superiority of the British forces, Burgoyne again advances on the Americans. Hearing the musket fire, Arnold disobeys Gates's order confining him to quarters and leads the Continental troops to victory. Burgoyne's surrender ten days later shocks the world and finally convinces France, which has already been supplying the colonists with covert aid, to enter the war openly on the side of the Americans.

December 17 Washington's army arrives at Valley Forge, where it constructs huts for its winter quarters.

1780 **March 29** Reviving their southern strategy, the British besiege Charleston. General Benjamin Lincoln surrenders the coveted port on May 12.

September 21 A disgruntled Benedict Arnold meets secretly with Major John André, sent to him by British general Henry Clinton to arrange the surrender of Arnold's West Point command. André is captured making his return to New York, but confusion among the Americans gives Arnold time to escape.

1783 **May** Having been repulsed in the Carolinas, Cornwallis arrives in Virginia, where he briefly skirmishes American troops under the marquis de Lafayette before settling down into the deep-water port of Yorktown.

August 21 Washington and the comte de Rochambeau begin moving their troops secretly from New York to Virginia. Meanwhile, the French fleet under Admiral de Grasse sails for the Chesapeake Bay.

September 5 Off the coast, the French navy defeats the British fleet, thereby winning control of the Chesapeake and trapping Cornwallis in Yorktown.

October 19 A besieged and bombarded Cornwallis surrenders to Washington the last of the actively campaigning British armies in the colonies.

1787 **May 25-September 17** Instead of merely amending the Articles of Confederation, the Constitutional Convention meeting in Philadelphia drafts an entirely new document.

1789 **March 4** The Congress holds its first session under the new Constitution.

1791 The first ten amendments to the Constitution, collectively known as the Bill of Rights, protect individual freedoms not specifically addressed in the Constitution. The **First Amendment** provides for the separation of church and state, freedom of religion, freedom of speech, and freedom of assembly. The **Second Amendment** establishes the right to bear arms. The **Third Amendment** restricts the quartering of soldiers in private homes. The **Fourth Amendment** prohibits unreasonable search and seizure. The **Fifth Amendment** assures the rights to due process and protection against self-incrimination. The **Sixth Amendment** guarantees the right to a speedy and public trial by an impartial jury. The **Seventh Amendment** extends the right to a trial by jury to suits at common law. The **Eighth Amendment** prohibits cruel and unusual punishment. The **Ninth Amendment** states that rights not enumerated in the Constitution are retained by the people. The **Tenth Amendment** states that all powers not granted to the federal government by the Constitution are reserved to the states and to the people.

1798 The **Eleventh Amendment** removes from federal jurisdiction those cases in which a citizen of one state (or a foreign country) sues a different state.

1804 The **Twelfth Amendment** revises the procedure by which electors vote for the president and vice president.

1865 The **Thirteenth Amendment** abolishes slavery.

1868 The **Fourteenth Amendment** grants citizenship to all people (including former slaves) born in the United States and mandates for all citizens equal protection under the law. The amendment also prohibits Confederates who once swore (and then broke) constitutional oaths from again holding federal office. Finally, it repudiates the Confederate war debt.

1 8 7 0   The **Fifteenth Amendment** forbids the denial or abridgement of the right to vote on the basis of race, color, or previous condition of servitude.

1 9 1 3   The **Sixteenth Amendment** empowers Congress to impose taxes on income.

The **Seventeenth Amendment** provides for the direct election of senators by the people of each state, rather than by their state legislatures.

1 9 1 9   The **Eighteenth Amendment** prohibits the manufacture, transportation, and sale of intoxicating liquors for beverage purposes.

1 9 2 0   The **Nineteenth Amendment** extends the vote to women.

1 9 3 3   The **Twentieth Amendment** moves the date of the presidential inauguration from March 4 to January 20 and shifts the beginning of the congressional term from the first Monday in December to January 3.

The **Twenty-First Amendment** repeals Prohibition (established by the Eighteenth Amendment in 1919).

1 9 5 1   The **Twenty-Second Amendment** limits the president to two terms in office.

1 9 6 1   The **Twenty-Third Amendment** grants representation in presidential elections to residents of the District of Columbia.

1 9 6 4   The **Twenty-Fourth Amendment** forbids poll taxes in federal elections.

1 9 6 7   The **Twenty-Fifth Amendment** provides for an orderly transfer of power in the case of presidential disability.

1 9 7 1   The **Twenty-Sixth Amendment** extends the vote to all citizens 18 years of and older.

1789-1797	**George Washington**	Atlas of America, Old Fox, Father of His Country
1797-1801	**John Adams**	Duke of Braintree, Old Sink or Swim, His Rotundity
1801-1809	**Thomas Jefferson**	Red Fox, Pen of the Revolution
1809-1817	**James Madison**	Sage of Montpelier, Father of the Constitution
1817-1825	**James Monroe**	Last of the Cocked Hats
1825-1829	**John Quincy Adams**	Old Man Eloquent, Second
1829-1837	**Andrew Jackson**	Old Hickory, King Andrew the First
1837-1841	**Martin Van Buren**	Little Magician, Petticoat Pet
1841	**William Henry Harrison**	Old Granny, Old Tippecanoe
1841-1845	**John Tyler**	His Accidency
1845-1849	**James Knox Polk**	Napoleon of the Stump
1849-1850	**Zachary Taylor**	Old Rough and Ready
1850-1853	**Millard Fillmore**	American Louis Philippe, Wool-Carder President
1853-1857	**Franklin Pierce**	Handsome Frank, Purse
1857-1861	**James Buchanan**	Old Buck, Ten-Cent Jimmy
1861-1865	**Abraham Lincoln**	Honest Abe, Great Emancipator
1865-1869	**Andrew Johnson**	Sir Veto, Tennessee Tailor
1869-1877	**Ulysses Simpson Grant**	Butcher from Galena, Uncle Sam
1877-1881	**Rutherford Birchard Hayes**	Granny Hayes, His Fraudulency
1881	**James Abram Garfield**	Canal Boy, Preacher President
1881-1885	**Chester Alan Arthur**	Elegant Arthur, Our Chet

1885-1889	**Grover Cleveland**	Buffalo Hangman
1889-1893	**Benjamin Harrison**	Little Ben, Grandfather's Hat
1893-1897	**Grover Cleveland**	Uncle Jumbo
1897-1901	**William McKinley**	Idol of Ohio, Wobbly Willie
1901-1909	**Theodore Roosevelt**	Great White Chief, Teddy
1909-1913	**William Howard Taft**	
1913-1921	**Woodrow Wilson**	Professor
1921-1923	**Warren Gamaliel Harding**	
1923-1929	**Calvin Coolidge**	Silent Cal
1929-1933	**Herbert Clark Hoover**	Chief
1933-1945	**Franklin Delano Roosevelt**	F.D.R., Boss
1945-1953	**Harry S. Truman**	Give 'Em Hell Harry, Haberdasher Harry
1953-1961	**Dwight David Eisenhower**	Ike
1961-1963	**John Fitzgerald Kennedy**	J.F.K.
1963-1969	**Lyndon Baines Johnson**	L.B.J., Landslide Lyndon
1969-1974	**Richard Milhous Nixon**	Tricky Dick
1974-1977	**Gerald Rudolph Ford**	Jerry, Junie
1977-1981	**James Earl Carter**	Jimmy
1981-1989	**Ronald Wilson Reagan**	Great Communicator, Gipper, Dutch
1989-1993	**George Herbert Walker Bush**	Poppy
1993-	**William Jefferson Clinton**	Bubba, Slick Willie

1 8 0 3 In *Marbury v. Madison*, Chief Justice John Marshall, writing for a unanimous Court, rules that a section of the Judiciary Act of 1789 is unconstitutional. He thus establishes the process of judicial review, which reserves to the Court the final say as to whether an act of Congress is constitutional.

1 8 1 9 In *Dartmouth College v. Woodward*, argued by Dartmouth graduate Daniel Webster, the Court establishes protections against state interference in business contracts.

In *McCulloch v. Maryland*, the Court rules that a prohibitive tax placed by Maryland on the Second Bank of the U.S. is unconstitutional. Marshall's logic is that the power to tax means the power to destroy. Therefore, in taxing the bank, Maryland infringes on Congress's mandate to make all laws "necessary and proper" to execute its Article I powers. In upholding the legality of the bank, which was not specifically authorized in the Constitution, the Court legitimizes Alexander Hamilton's doctrine of "broad construction."

1 8 5 7 In *Dred Scott v. Sandford*, Chief Justice Roger B. Taney's opinion denies the slave Dred Scott the right to sue for his freedom, because blacks are not citizens and therefore have no standing with the court.

1 8 9 5 Describing the income tax as a "communistic threat" to property, the Court declares it unconstitutional in *Pollock v. Farmers' Loan and Trust Co.*

1 8 9 6 In *Plessy v. Ferguson*, the Court upholds racial segregation as long as equivalent facilities are provided for both whites and blacks. This "separate but equal" doctrine sanctions the Jim Crow laws of the South.

1 9 1 1 Employing the "rule of reason" in *Standard Oil Co. of New Jersey v. U.S.*, the Court decides to dissolve John D. Rockefeller's oil trust, not because of its size, but because it unreasonably restrains trade.

1 9 1 9 In *Schenck v. U.S.* involving the Espionage Act of 1917, Justice Oliver Wendell Holmes, Jr., introduces the "clear and present danger" test as a means of determining when free speech might legally be restricted.

1935 With its decision in *Schecter Poultry Corp. v. U.S.*, the Court strikes down the National Industrial Recovery Act, one of the cornerstones of Roosevelt's New Deal, because it unconstitutionally delegates legislative power to the executive branch.

1938 In *Erie Railroad v. Tompkins*, the majority opinion of Louis Brandeis rules that, in cases involving citizens of two or more states, the Court must uphold the applicable state law rather than a "federal common law."

1954 The unanimous decision of the Warren Court in *Brown v. Board of Education* overturns the "separate but equal" doctrine enunciated in *Plessy v. Ferguson* (1896) in relation to public schools.

1961 In *Mapp v. Ohio*, the Court rules that illegally obtained evidence must be excluded from state as well as federal trials.

1962 With *Baker v. Carr*, the Court orders that election districts in Tennessee be redrawn, overturning *Colegrove v. Green* (1946), which had ruled that disproportional representation was a "political question."

1963 *Gideon v. Wainwright* establishes the right of an indigent defendant accused of a felony to legal counsel provided by the state.

1964 In *New York Times v. Sullivan*, the Court rules that public officials can win libel suits against the press only when they can prove either prior knowledge that a report is false or a reckless disregard for the truth.

1966 In *Miranda v. Arizona*, the Court rules that suspects must be informed of their constitutional rights prior to questioning by police.

1973 Building on the right to privacy established in *Griswold v. Connecticut* (1965), the Court's 7-2 decision in *Roe v. Wade* articulates a constitutional right to an abortion during the first trimester of pregnancy.

1774 **May 10** Louis XV dies of smallpox. Although popular at the outset of his rule, the king has more recently become the object of public disdain. Late in his reign, Louis XV accepts the view of his minister Joseph-Marie Terray that France must rationalize its baroque tax system, which exempts most of the privileged classes. But his attempts at reform are resisted by the privileged Parlement of Paris. In fact, the monarchy has become so unpopular that even the bourgeoisie refuse to accept reform under the king's auspices. Louis XV's grandson succeeds him as Louis XVI.

1781 Although Louis XVI's genial charm initially regains some favor for the monarchy, his star falls precipitously during the Affair of the Diamond Necklace, through which his wife Marie Antoinette is indirectly disgraced. The case involves the Prince de Rohan, a cardinal, who bribes a woman he believes to be the queen with a diamond necklace. Napoleon later cites this episode as the real beginning of the French Revolution.

1783 The successful conclusion of the American war dramatically increases France's prestige, but its cost doubles the French national debt. To service this debt, finance minister Jacques Necker borrows heavily. Necker cannot levy new taxes because of the king's precarious political situation. The monarchy now faces opposition from both the privileged classes, who oppose change, and the bourgeoisie, which demands radical financial reform. Having alienated both constituencies, Louis's government now moves from crisis to crisis without any real hope of restoring its influence.

1787 **February** Concluding that new loans will no longer meet the state's needs, Necker's successor Charles-Alexandre de Calonne convenes at Versailles the Assembly of Notables in the hope that its privileged members will finally accept financial responsibility for the nation. Unfortunately, the assembly decides to place the blame on monarchical mismanagement and has Louis replace Calonne with one of its own members, the atheistic cardinal Loménie de Brienne.

May After reversing himself and adopting Calonne's conclusions, Loménie dismisses the Assembly of Notables when it also refuses to listen to him. In August, Loménie continues his desperate measures with the exile of the reactionary Paris Parlement to Troyes. However, the breakdown of the governmental machinery, particularly in relation to the collection of taxes, forces the Parlement's recall in September.

1788 **May 8** When the Paris Parlement invalidates a stamp tax ordered by Louis XVI to save the state treasury from bankruptcy, the king again exiles the assembly. But once more unable to sustain his actions, Louis recalls the Parlement within the month.

August 8 Finally forced to recognize his own impotence, Louis XVI agrees to call the Estates-General, which has not been convened since 1614. At that time, it met as three bodies with the First Estate representing the clergy; the Second Estate, the nobility; and the Third Estate, the people. The opening session of the new Estates-General is set for May 1, 1789.

September 25 Confirming its status as a bastion of reaction, the Parlement declares that the Estates-General will again meet as three separate bodies, thereby diminishing the influence of the Third Estate.

December 27 At the urging of Necker, lately returned to power, King Louis overrules Parlement, decreeing that the estates will meet separately, but that the Third Estate will have as many deputies as the other two estates combined.

1789 **April-May** Riots throughout rural France reflect a general decline in law and order. Peasant attacks on grain convoys become common as the price of bread soars following the unusually poor harvest of 1788.

May 5 During the opening session of the Estates-General at Versailles, the Third Estate, anxious to set a precedent that all votes should be taken in common, insists that the council's powers be verified in common.

June 17 The Third Estate declares itself the National Assembly, prompting Louis to bar these deputies from their chamber. In the days that follow, reform-minded nobles and clergy join the National Assembly's deliberations.

June 20 Barred from their chamber, the members of the National Assembly gather on the tennis courts at Versailles, where they swear an oath not to dissolve until they have produced a new constitution for France. Within the week, Louis orders 20,000 soldiers to Versailles.

June 27 Once a majority of the clerical deputies defects to the National Assembly, King Louis relents in his opposition and invites the remainder of the clergy and the nobility to join that body, which proclaims itself the National Constituent Assembly on July 9.

1789
(continued)

July 14 Alarmed by rumors that the king has ordered his troops to crush the Third Estate, and emboldened by the dispossessed peasants who have lately flocked to the city, a Parisian mob storms the Bastille, symbolic fortress of the absolutist *ancien régime*, and captures its armory.

July 20-August 6 Although somewhat groundless, the Great Fear grips France. Responding to perceived threats from brigands and conspiring aristocrats, frightened peasants transform their panic into aggression, which leads them to storm the castles of their lords and burn the records of their feudal obligations. Unwilling either to condone the peasants or to abandon them for an alliance with the aristocracy, the Constituent Assembly hesitates.

August 4 Allying themselves with liberal nobility, Third Estate delegates to the Constituent Assembly vote for an abolition of feudalism more semantic than real. Its legal structure is done away with, but without land reform, feudalism carries on as a system of economic organization.

August 27 The Constituent Assembly adopts the Declaration of the Rights of Man and of the Citizen, which calls for social distinctions based on talent and virtue (rather than birth) and argues for taxation to be distributed fairly according to each citizen's ability to pay.

November 2 The Constituent Assembly tries to ease the continuing financial crisis by placing clerical property "at the disposal of the nation." On December 19, 400 million livres' worth of confiscated church property goes on sale.

1790

July 12 The passage of the Civil Constitution of the Clergy reorganizes the Catholic church in France as a national institution whose bishops and parish priests will be elected in the same manner as secular officials.

1791

April 13 Pope Pius VI condemns the Civil Constitution of the Clergy, causing a schism between papists in France and those Catholics who support the revolution. This split mirrors a similar division within civil society between royalists and the bourgeoisie, who still hope for a constitutional monarchy although neither the feudal lords nor the peasantry will agree.

June 20 About midnight, dressed as a valet, Louis XVI leaves the Tuileries with his family, hoping to escape the country. The next night, he is arrested at Varennes and returned to Paris. Louis' flight appears to prove the incompatibility of aristocratic and bourgeois interests, ending any hope of establishing a constitutional monarchy in France.

August 27 Responding to the pleas of royalist emigrés, the Hapsburg emperor Leopold II (brother of Marie Antoinette) and Prussia's Frederick William II issue the joint Declaration of Pilnitz, in which they threaten to restore the French monarchy by force.

October 1 With the Constitution of 1791 now in effect, the newly chartered Legislative Assembly supplants the National Constituent Assembly. Both the bourgeois Girondins (who come to control the assembly) and the aristocracy begin to agitate for war with Austria. The nobility hopes that a defeat might spark a counter-revolution.

1792 **April 20** The Legislative Assembly declares war on Austria. As the Girondins expect, the crisis renews revolutionary fervor among the populace.

August 10 When the Girondins prove unable to manage the war, working-class radicals establish the revolutionary Paris Commune. Suspending the Constitution of 1791, they institute universal suffrage, which replaces a system by which the vote was restricted to those paying a certain level of tax.

September 20 The newly elected National Convention meets for the first time on the same day that inspired French troops turn back a combined Austrian-Prussian army at Valmy.

September 21 The Convention votes unanimously to abolish the monarchy, but a split later develops within the bourgeois delegation between the Montagnards and the conservative Girondins. Being but a small, radical minority, the Montagnards choose to ally themselves with the powerful popular movement of the *sansculottes* [lower-class artisans].

December 11 The Convention puts Louis XVI on trial for treason. On January 14, 1793, he is found guilty by a unanimous vote, but the vote on the imposition of the death sentence, taken in a relentlessly long roll call, is much closer: 387 votes in favor to 334 against.

1793 **January 21** The execution of Louis XVI radicalizes the Convention, which now turns to the Montagnards and Maximilien Robespierre for leadership.

1790-1899

The Body Politic

1791 JUN 20-21 As power shifts from the aristocracy, Louis XVI attempts to flee France, but he is arrested at Varennes and returned to Paris. Throughout Europe, worried monarchists begin to persecute Jacobins in their own countries who support the French Revolution.

1792 APR 20 To meet a Hapsburg threat, France declares war on Austria, and then on its ally Prussia. Austro-Prussian troops soon cross the border.

1792 AUG 10 Convinced that the king has betrayed France to the queen's Austrian relatives, revolutionaries storm the royal living quarters in the Tuileries and imprison Louis XVI.

1792 SEP 20 In response to the demands of the bourgeois Girondins, the new National Convention meets to abolish the monarchy. On the same day, French troops turn back the invading Austro-Prussian army with a determined stand at Valmy.

1793 JAN 21 Louis XVI is executed by order of the National Convention. The vote on his guilt was unanimous, but the death sentence passed only by a narrow margin (387-334).

1793 JAN 23 After the Poles proclaim a new constitution, Russia and Prussia sign a treaty calling for the Second Partition of Poland. Tadeusz Kosciuszko organizes a nationalist revolt in 1794, but its suppres-

Arts & Architecture

1791 MAY 16 James Boswell's *Life of Samuel Johnson*, the first full-scale biography, is published in London.

1791 SEP 30 Mozart's final opera *Die Zauberflöte* debuts two months before his death. His *Requiem* remains unfinished.

1791 The marquis de Sade (from whose name *sadism* derives) publishes his scandalous erotic classic *Justine*.

c.1792 Gilbert Stuart's portraits of George Washington help establish an American school of portraiture.

Religion & Philosophy

1790 Although he endorsed the American Revolution, Edmund Burke condemns the French as unacceptably extreme in *Reflections on the Revolution in France.*

1791-1792 Outraged by Burke's conservatism, Thomas Paine publishes *The*

Rights of Man in two parts, defending democracy and republican principles.

1792 Johann Gottlieb Fichte, a disciple of Kant, issues his *Essay toward a Critique of All Revelation,* which concerns the possibility of religious belief.

Science & Technology

1791 Luigi Galvani announces the results of experiments in which he applied electricity to the severed legs of frogs. Alessandro Volta rejects Galvani's theories of "animal electricity," but his data leads directly to Volta's development of the battery in 1799.

1792 William Murdock distills coal gas, using it to light his office and his home.

1793 APR Eli Whitney invents the cotton gin, a machine for cleaning seeds from cotton that revolutionizes the American textile industry.

Daily Life

1793 Jean-Pierre Blanchard makes the first aeronautic parachute jump (from a balloon). He survives, but breaks a leg.

1795 Through his influence, Scottish physician Sir Gilbert Blane makes the use of lime juice mandatory throughout the

British navy. From this scurvy inhibitor comes the slang term *limey*.

1795 Responding to a prize offered by the French Directory, Nicolas Appert begins developing a storage process for food by which the food is first cooked and

sion leads to the Third Partition (1795), which dismembers the country entirely. Poland disappears from the maps of Europe until 1918.

1794 JUL 27 The National Convention overthrows Robespierre, who as leader of the Committee of Public Safety carried out the Reign of Terror.

1794 Farmers in western Pennsylvania revolt against a tax on whiskey imposed by the Congress. Wielding the new federal power recently provided by the Constitution, President Washington raises an army larger than the one he commanded during the Revolution and puts down the Whiskey Rebellion.

1795 OCT 5 Napoleon Bonaparte disperses a royalist force marching against the National Convention, saving the First Republic. Having proved his loyalty to the Directory, Napoleon receives command of the French army in Italy (MAR 1796).

1797 OCT 17 The Peace of Campo Formio, forced by the success of Napoleon's Italian and Austrian campaigns, ends the War of the First Coalition (Austria, Prussia, The Netherlands, and Britain). Only the sea war with Britain continues.

1799 NOV 9 The Coup of 18 Brumaire, masterminded by the director Emmanuel-Joseph Sieyès, topples the Directory and installs Napoleon as First Consul.

Marie Antoinette

1793 *The Death of Marat* makes neoclassical painter Jacques-Louis David the most admired artist of the French Revolution.

1798 Alois Senefelder invents the process of lithography by which a press transfers an image, drawn on limestone, onto paper. Lithographs become a popular medium for journal illustration during the nineteenth century.

1798 William Wordsworth and Samuel Taylor Coleridge publish *Lyrical Ballads*, beginning the English romantic movement.

1792 Mary Wollstonecraft writes *A Vindication of the Rights of Woman*, protesting the common assumption that women exist only to be men's playthings.

1794 The first part of Thomas Paine's *The Age of Reason* appears while Paine lingers in a French prison for his opposition to the execution of Louis XVI.

1798 Thomas Malthus's *Essay on Population* points out that population growth would outrun growth in the food supply were it not for war and famine.

1795 France's new revolutionary government formally adopts the metric system.

1796 MAY Performing the first vaccination, Edward Jenner deliberately infects a boy with cowpox in order to preclude a smallpox infection.

1798 Henry Cavendish's experiment measures the specific gravity of the earth.

1798 Pierre Simon Laplace completes the first volumes of his *Mécanique celeste*, a work of celestial mechanics second only to Newton's *Principia* (1687).

then stored in a vacuum. Appert uses glass jars, but his method will later be applied to tin cans.

1799 An officer in Napoleon's army named Boussard discovers the Rosetta Stone four miles north of Rosetta, Egypt.

1790-1799

The Body Politic

1801 FEB The Treaty of Lunéville ends Austria's role in the War of the Second Coalition. Napoleon's victory at Marengo (1800, JUN 14) and Moreau's at Hohenlinden (DEC 3) have convinced the Austrians to obey Campio Formio (1797).

1802 MAR 27 France, Britain, Spain, and Holland sign the Treaty of Amiens. The peace, which ignores many sensitive issues, lasts 14 months.

1803 President Jefferson buys most of the land between the Mississippi and the Rockies from France for $15 million. The Louisiana Purchase more than doubles the size of the United States at the cost of approximately four cents per acre.

1804 DEC 2 Pope Pius VII travels to Rome to crown Napoleon emperor of France, but at the last minute Napoleon takes the crown and places it on his head himself.

1804 DEC Napoleon induces Spain to join his renewed war against Britain, hoping to contest British control of the seas, which has so far thwarted French plans to cross the Channel to England.

1805 JUL 24 Napoleon orders his Grand Armée east from Boulogne (where it has been preparing to invade England) to face the armies of the Third Coalition (Austria, Russia, and Sweden). Defeating the Austrians at Ulm, the French emperor enters Vienna on November 13.

Arts & Architecture

1800 Friedrich von Hardenberg (Novalis) writes *Hymen an die Nacht*, expressing the yearnings common to the romantic poets.

1802-1807 Jacques-Louis David paints a series of dramatic works celebrating the achievements of Napoleon.

1804 First performed in Austria, Ludwig van Beethoven's third symphony (*Eroica*) is unprecedented in its length and the size of the orchestra needed to play it.

1805 Architect Benjamin Latrobe submits two plans for the Catholic Cathedral

Religion & Philosophy

1800 Robert Owen becomes part owner and manager of the New Lanark cotton mills, which he makes into a model of enlightened capitalism and social reform.

1801 JUL 16 Napoleon and Pope Pius VII agree to the Concordat of 1801, which

establishes a modus vivendi between the church and the secular government.

1804 MAR 31 Reaffirming the gains of the French Revolution, the legal reforms of the Code Napoléon assure equal rights to all French citizens.

Science & Technology

1801 The publication of Karl Friedrich Gauss's *Disquisitiones arithmeticae* wins the 24-year-old mathematician immediate and worldwide fame.

1801 DEC 24 On Christmas Eve, a road locomotive developed by English engineer

Richard Trevithick carries the first passengers ever conveyed by steam power.

1802 The publication of Gottfried Reinhold Treviranus's *Biologie* confirms the debut of a new scientific discipline specifically given to living organisms.

Daily Life

1801 Eli Whitney demonstrates to federal officials musket manufacturing methods that introduce a major industrial innovation: interchangeable parts.

1802 Great Britain's Health and Morals of Apprentices Act is the first labor law to

protect workers (in this case, apprentices). The act requires adequate clothing, sleeping quarters, and religious instruction for these children.

1804 MAY 14 Meriwether Lewis and William Clark leave St. Louis and travel

1805 OCT 21 The British navy under Admiral Horatio Nelson destroys the French-Spanish fleet off Cape Trafalgar. Nelson's victory assures British naval supremacy for another century.

1805 DEC 2 Napoleon wins his greatest victory at Austerlitz, defeating the combined armies of Austria and Russia.

1805 DEC 25 In the Peace of Pressburg, Austria cedes Italy, as well as western Germany, which Napoleon unites in the Confederation of the Rhine (JUL 1806).

1806 OCT 14 Joining the anti-French coalition too late, Prussia's armies are overwhelmed at Jena and Auerstedt.

1807 JUN 14 Meeting at Tilsit, Napoleon and Tsar Alexander I divide continental Europe into French and Russian spheres.

1808 Congress outlaws the importation of slaves, ending the triangular trade that had brought manufactured goods to Africa, slaves to the West Indies, and rum and molasses to America.

1809 JUL 6 After once more declaring war on France, and even inflicting Napoleon's first defeat at Aspern (MAY), Austria falls at the battle of Wagram. Napoleon's victory, achieved not through cleverness but by sheer power, convinces the rest of Europe that the emperor may indeed be invincible.

Napoleon Bonaparte

in Baltimore, one in the Gothic style as well as the neoclassical design that is finally accepted.

1806 Jean Chalgrin designs Paris's Arc de Triomphe in the neoclassical style (completed 1836).

1808 Johann Wolfgang von Goethe finishes Part I of his classic *Faust*.

1808 German romantic Caspar David Friedrich paints his first works in oil. His landscapes become well known for their symbolism and powerful atmospherics.

1807 In his *Phenomenology of the Spirit*, Georg Wilhelm Friedrich Hegel begins to articulate his concept of a *Zeitgeist* [spirit] moving through history. In this volume, Hegel discusses the stages of the mind leading up to its attainment of absolute knowledge.

1804 FEB 21 Applying his steam technology to iron rails, Richard Trevithick develops a steam locomotive that hauls 20 tons of iron up a hill in Wales.

1804 Johann Friedrich Blumenbach's *Handbook of Comparative Anatomy* founds the science of physical anthropology. His cranial research leads to the division of humans by skin color into white, yellow, brown, black, and red races.

1807 Robert Fulton's steamboat, the *Clermont*, begins to ply the Hudson River.

north to the headwaters of the Missouri. From there, President Jefferson has ordered them to cross the Rockies and continue west. Lewis and Clark reach the Pacific on November 15, 1805, becoming the first explorers to do so by a land route north of the Mexican border.

1806 Responding to popular demands for new roads that might promote western expansion, Congress authorizes the construction of the federally financed Cumberland Road from Cumberland (Maryland) to Wheeling (western Virginia) on the Ohio River.

1800-1809

The Body Politic

1810 SEP 16 Warning that Mexico may soon be delivered to the godless French, Miguel Hidalgo y Castilla issues the Cry of Dolores to end Spanish rule.

1812 JUN 18 Angered by years of naval harassment, the U.S. declares war on Britain, which has been enforcing a strict blockade against France. Trade with both parties had been highly profitable to neutral American shipping.

1812 SEP 7 With a 450,000-man army, Napoleon attacks his erstwhile ally Russia at Borodino. After the battle, which settles nothing, the French emperor continues on to the abandoned city of Moscow. Having no one to fight, he orders a retreat late in October, just as the Russian winter is setting in. The grueling march back reduces the effective strength of his army to 50,000 men.

1814 APR 6 Once a provisional government under Charles Talleyrand begins peace talks with the allies converging on Paris, Napoleon realizes that defiance would be useless and abdicates. The Treaty of Fontainebleau grants him the island of Elba and a two-million-franc annuity.

1814 SEP The Congress of Vienna meets to reorganize Europe in the aftermath of Napoleon. The policies of the Austrian prince Metternich produce a relative peace that lasts until World War I.

Arts & Architecture

1810-1814 Francisco Goya makes a series of etchings, *Los Desastres de la Guerra*, that are now considered among the most powerful depictions of war ever drawn.

1812-1813 Brothers Jakob and Wilhelm Grimm issue their famous *Fairy Tales*.

1814 JAN 26 Edmund Kean's London debut as Shylock instantly makes him a star.

1816 The British Museum obtains the Elgin Marbles from the earl of Elgin, who cannibalized these statues from the Parthenon in Athens four years earlier.

Religion & Philosophy

1810 Johann Gottlieb Fichte becomes rector of the new University of Berlin, the first modern research university, which Fichte himself had designed (1807).

1811 Textile workers around Nottingham, who call themselves Luddites, undertake masked, nighttime raids to destroy the machinery that is replacing them.

1817 David Ricardo's *Principles of Political Economy and Taxation* details his laissez-faire economic doctrines, including his Iron Law of Wages.

Science & Technology

1811 In a journal article, physics professor Amedeo Avogadro states the rule that has since come to bear his name: for all gases, given the same conditions of temperature and pressure, equal volumes will always contain the same number of molecules.

1812 Diverting himself from physics and astronomy, Pierre Simon Laplace advances the probability theory of Blaise Pascal with his *Théorie analytique*.

1812 Frederic Albert Winsor founds the Chartered Gas-Light and Coke Company

Daily Life

1811 DEC 16 A massive earthquake—estimated at 8 on the Richter scale and centered at New Madrid, Missouri—devastates the Midwest, opening great fissures in the earth and causing the Mississippi River to reverse its course for several hours.

c.1815 Unknown Scottish philosopher Sir David Brewster becomes famous for his new invention, the kaleidoscope.

1815 Mount Tambora on the Indonesian island of Sumbawa erupts with such violence that clouds of volcanic dust thrown

1814 DEC 24 The Treaty of Ghent ending the stalemated War of 1812 returns all captured territory and restores the status quo between Britain and America.

1815 JAN 8 Unaware that the Treaty of Ghent has been signed, General Andrew Jackson decimates the British at the bloody battle of New Orleans.

1815 MAR 20 Abandoning his exile on Elba, Napoleon returns to Paris, where he interrupts the Bourbon Restoration.

1815 JUN 18 With his newly mustered army, Napoleon meets the duke of Wellington at Waterloo in Belgium. The French are close to victory when a

Prussian force under Gebhard Blücher, defeated two days earlier at Ligny, arrives in relief. Napoleon's second abdication ends the Hundred Days, after which he is again exiled, this time to the remote southern Atlantic island of St. Helena.

1817 JAN-FEB Argentine liberator José de San Martín leads his army on an incredible trek across the Andes, surprising the Spanish at Chacabuco (FEB 12) and freeing the Chilean capital of Santiago.

1819 AUG 7 At Boyacá, Simon Bolívar defeats the army of New Granada (Colombia). His entry into Bogotá three days later completes the revolution against Spanish rule.

Simon Bolívar

1817-1826 Thomas Jefferson and Benjamin Latrobe build the University of Virginia.

1818 Japanese print designer Katsushika Hokusai enters his most creative period. His imaginative landscapes offer a visual encyclopedia of Japanese life.

1818 Madrid's Prado art museum opens.

1819 With *Ivanhoe*, Sir Walter Scott invents the genre of historical fiction.

1819 Beethoven becomes almost totally deaf, yet lives and composes until 1827.

1818 Arthur Schopenhauer completes *The World as Will and Idea*, in which he develops Kantian philosophy on the body and the will. The distinctions he makes, especially his use of art as an example of bodily expression uncontrolled by will, later stimulate Sigmund Freud.

---

to illuminate London's streets. He lights Westminster Bridge in 1813 and, by 1816, about 25 miles of London thoroughfare.

1815 Scottish engineer John McAdam originates the practice of paving roads with crushed rock (hence *macadam*).

1815 Humphrey Davy invents the miner's arc lamp to prevent mine explosions.

1819 Physician René Théophile Laënnec writes a treatise advocating use of the stethoscope and outlining what is now known as physical diagnosis.

---

up into the atmosphere lower temperatures around the world for a year.

1815 A Dutch mechanic named Winkel invents the metronome. Johann Maelzel tries to buy the rights, but when Winkel refuses, Maelzel pirates the invention.

1819 Robert Owen convinces Parliament to prohibit the hiring of children younger than nine and to limit the workday of older children to 12 hours out of every 24.

1819 The paddleboat *Savannah* becomes the first steamship to cross the Atlantic.

1810-1819

The Body Politic

1820 MAR 3 Ending the first important battle over slavery, Congress passes the Missouri Compromise, which admits Maine as a free state and Missouri as a slave state. Rapid population growth in the North has become an important issue for the South, which finds itself losing voting power in the House of Representatives. As a result, pro-slavery southerners insist that the Senate remain evenly divided between free and slave states. In exchange, the South accepts the prohibition of slavery in the Louisiana Purchase north of latitude 36°30'.

1821 The American Colonization Society (founded 1816) establishes Liberia on the western coast of Africa as a colony for freed American slaves. The first settlement is founded in late 1822 by the Methodist minister Jehudi Ashmun.

1823 DEC 2 In his annual address to Congress, President James Monroe proclaims the Monroe Doctrine, announcing that, "The American continents ... are henceforth not to be considered as subjects for future colonization by any European power." Secretary of State John Quincy Adams, who formulated the speech, has been concerned that Spain might try to regain colonies in Central and South America that have recently thrown off the European yoke. The Monroe Doctrine becomes a cornerstone for American foreign policy in the Western Hemisphere.

Arts & Architecture

1820 John Constable exhibits *The Hay Wain* at the Royal Academy. His use of pure color will influence Eugéne Delacroix and later the impressionists.

1820 *The Sketch Book of Geoffrey Crayon*, including the stories "Rip Van Winkle" and "The Legend of Sleepy Hollow," make Washington Irving the first American writer to win acclaim in Europe.

1821 English actor Junius Brutus Booth settles in Virginia, where he has recently played *Richard III*. Several generations of

Religion & Philosophy

1821 Jean-François Champollion uses the Rosetta Stone to begin deciphering Egyptian hieroglyphics.

1821 James Mill, leader of the influential Philosophical Radicals, publishes *Elements of Political Economy*.

1824 Sequoyah invents a Cherokee alphabet, believing that writing can keep the Cherokee independent of the whites.

1824 Leopold von Ranke's *History of the Latin and Teutonic Nations from 1494 to 1514* founds modern historiography.

Science & Technology

1820 JUL 20 Hans Christian Oersted accidentally notices an electric current deflecting a magnetized needle. He calls his discovery electromagnetism.

1821 SEP Building on Oersted's work, Michael Faraday discovers a method for using charged wires to cause the continuous revolution of a magnet, thus inventing the first electric motor.

1821 The Roman Catholic Church finally removes the works of Nicholas Copernicus from the Index Librorum Prohibitorum.

Daily Life

c.1820 Missionaries ban surfing in Hawaii on the grounds that it is immodest and a waste of time.

1823 Charles Macintosh dissolves india rubber in naphtha and invents the waterproof fabric that bears his name.

1827 English druggist John Walker makes the first practical friction matches.

1828 Noah Webster publishes his dictionary, containing 12,000 words and nearly 40,000 definitions that have not appeared in a dictionary before.

1825 Work is completed on the Erie Canal, joining the Hudson River to Lake Erie and thus making barge traffic between Buffalo and New York City possible. A triumph of civil engineering, the canal had been proposed by Gouverneur Morris as early as 1800, but it took the political machinations of a former New York City mayor, DeWitt Clinton, to see the route approved. Clinton's success in building the canal helped win him several terms as governor of the state.

1825 DEC 26 Following the death of Tsar Alexander I, the Decembrists in St. Petersburg attempt to block the accession of Nicholas I. They are easily suppressed, but their martyrdom (five are executed and the rest imprisoned or banished) inspires Russian revolutionary groups for many years to come.

1828 The innovative grassroots organizing of the new Democratic party helps war hero Andrew Jackson win the presidency. Jackson's supporters stage local picnics, parades, barbecues, and tree plantings on his behalf and that of the local party slate.

1829 SEP 14 The Treaty of Edirne ends the two-year Russo-Turkish War to the territorial advantage of the Russians, presaging the Ottoman Empire's role as "the sick man of Europe," as well as the process of balkanization.

James Monroe

Booths become actors, including sons Edwin and John Wilkes.

1822 Realist Jean-Baptiste Corot begins painting with a new naturalism that comes to define the landscapes of the Barbizon school.

1826 James Fenimore Cooper's *The Last of the Mohicans* provokes great interest in the American wilderness and Indian life.

1827-1838 James Audubon publishes 435 of his original color drawings in editions of *The Birds of America*.

1827 Joseph Smith claims that the angel Moroni has appeared before him and directed him to buried golden plates. The writing on these plates, which Smith translates as the *Book of Mormon* (published 1830), describes American Indians as descendants of the ancient Hebrews.

1823 Inspired by Oersted's discovery , André Marie Ampère develops his theory of magnetism as an electric phenomenon.

1826 Nicolas Lobachevsky delivers his first lecture on non-Euclidean geometry, basing his work on the proposition that some of the postulates in Euclid's *Elements* may not be true.

1827 Georg Ohm publishes a pamphlet in Berlin elaborating the law named after him: that electric current is proportional to the difference in potential.

1828 JUL 4 Formal construction begins on the first railroad in the United States, the Baltimore & Ohio.

1828 In the second edition of his *Guide to the Rhine from Mainz to Cologne*, German printer Karl Baedeker evolves the format on which his famous travel series will be based.

1829 British colonial authorities in India make the Hindu rite of suttee (widow-burning) a criminal offense, thereby ending the practice.

1820-1829

The Body Politic

1830 JAN 19-27 Prompted by a fight over the Tariff of Abominations (1828), Daniel Webster of Massachusetts and Robert Y. Hayne of South Carolina debate states' rights before the Senate. Hayne's speeches herald the nullification controversy (1832-1833), while Webster's eloquence makes Hayne's seem treasonous.

1830 The Treaty of New Echota grants all Cherokee land east of the Mississippi to the government. Although very few Cherokee signed the treaty, and the Supreme Court soon voids it, President Jackson refuses to enforce the court's decision.

1831 Abolitionist William Garrison begins publishing *The Liberator* in Boston.

1832 Nationalist leader Giuseppe Mazzini founds Young Italy, a secret society dedicated to the movement for Italian unity known as the Risorgiment.

1833 MAR 23 The Zollverein [Customs Union] binds together 25 million Germans into an economic commonwealth, a critical step in the path to political unity.

1835 More than 10,000 Afrikaners begin the Great Trek from the Cape Colony to the Highveld and Natal. This migration makes them the first white settlers north of the Limpopo River. The Afrikaners leave for two reasons: to protest British colonial policies and to find new pasture land.

Arts & Architecture

1830 French realist Marie-Henri Beyle, known as Stendhal, writes *The Red and the Black*, with a new type of hero who remains alienated from his environment.

1830 During the opening night performance of Victor Hugo's *Hernani* at the

Comédie-Française, riots break out between neoclassicists and romantics.

1830-1848 Honoré de Balzac publishes over 50 novels comprising *La Comédie humaine*, portraying a panorama of French society beginning with Napoleonic times.

Religion & Philosophy

1830 Auguste Comte begins publishing his *Course of Positive Philosophy* (completed 1842). The positivists, led by Comte, reject society's historical dependence on theology and metaphysics and instead look to science for social reorganization on a more rational basis.

1831 Prussian general Carl von Clausewitz dies, leaving behind his unpublished *On War,* which treats war as "nothing but a continuation of political intercourse."

1831 William Miller begins preaching that the world will end "about 1843." His

Science & Technology

1831 AUG 29 Michael Faraday obtains the first evidence that electricity in one circuit can induce current in another.

1831 DEC 27 The HMS *Beagle* embarks on a five-year mission to survey the coastline of South America and the Galápagos

Islands, with 22-year-old Charles Darwin aboard as the ship's naturalist.

1834 Charles Babbage publishes his research into the "calculating machine," but this first computer, supported by government grants, is never completed.

Daily Life

1831 Cyrus McCormick builds a mechanical reaper in his father's workshop. With improvements, McCormick's machine will revolutionize farm labor.

1835 Samuel Colt perfects his famous six-shot revolver.

1835 The polka makes its social debut in Prague after Josef Neruda, observing a Bohemian peasant girl, writes down the tune and steps.

1837 Friedrich Froebel opens the first kindergarten in Blankenburg, Germany.

1836 FEB 23 The Mexican general Antonio López de Santa Anna lays siege to the Alamo, which holds out for 11 days under the leadership of Colonels James Bowie and William Travis and frontiersman Davy Crockett. On March 6, however, Santa Anna's troops overwhelm the Texans, killing nearly everyone inside the fortified mission (about 15 women and children survive). In the meantime, Texas declares its independence (MAR 2).

1838-1839 The Trail of Tears, a forced march from Georgia that relocates the Cherokee to Oklahoma, kills some 4,000 of the Indians along the way. Despite obviously inadequate food and supplies, General Winfield Scott refuses to slow the march in order to accommodate the sick and elderly.

1839 OCT 10 In the third year of a 64-year reign, 20-year-old Queen Victoria meets Prince Albert of Saxe-Coburg-Gotha at Windsor during his first court visit. Victoria proposes five days later.

1839 Moving to halt the illegal British importation of opium into China, the Chinese government seizes key warehouses in Guanzhou [Canton], precipitating the first of two Opium Wars. The British win easily, forcing China in the Treaty of Nanjing (1842, AUG 29) to pay reparations and cede five ports to Britain (including the island of Hong Kong.)

Victoria

1831 Intending to create a Russian nationalist drama based on native subject matter, Alexander Pushkin writes the play *Boris Godunov*.

1832 Pianist Frédéric Chopin's first concert makes him a celebrity in Paris.

1833-1834 Designed by Robert Mills, the Washington Monument becomes the tallest of the nineteenth-century obelisks that epitomize the romantics' lofty ideals.

1838-1840 Moscow's Kremlin Palace mixes Russian and Renaissance styles.

views later influence the formation of the Adventist Church.

1835 Alexis de Tocqueville publishes the first part of his *Democracy in America*, based on his travels with Gustave de Beaumont during 1831-1832. Tocqueville

dissects American society so acutely that his work becomes an instant classic in the field of political science.

1837 Horace Mann gives up a successful legal career to begin reforming public education in Massachusetts.

1837 SEP 2 Samuel F. B. Morse displays his first working telegraph. Current induction had convinced Morse in 1832 that intelligence could be transmitted electrically. Morse's invention provides the first means of nearly instantaneous nonvisual communication.

1838 Matthias Schleiden demonstrates that all plant tissue must be composed of individual cells, thus preparing the way for Theodor Schwann's epoch-making elaboration of cell theory in *Microscopic Investigations* (1839), which synthesizes 200 years of histology.

1837 John Deere constructs a plow with a steel moldboard that can cultivate previously untillable prairie soil.

1839 FEB 6 Louis Daguerre publishes his first daguerreotype, an early photograph produced using silver-plated copper.

1830-1839

The Body Politic

c.1845 Tens of thousands starve as potato crops fail in Ireland and Germany—but hundreds of thousands more leave in the first massive wave of emigration to the United States.

1846 Following the annexation of Texas (1845), President Polk sends troops into disputed territory along the border. When the Americans and Mexicans skirmish, Polk declares that the spilling of American blood demands retaliation. Abraham Lincoln, running for Congress, counsels caution, but war is soon declared.

1848 JAN 24 While building a sawmill for John Sutter at the junction of the American and Sacramento rivers in California, James W. Marshall discovers gold, but it takes nearly seven months before news of his strike first appears in the New York *Herald* (AUG 19). The arrival by ship of prospectors on February 28, 1849 (hence the nickname *forty-niners*), launches the Gold Rush.

1848 FEB 2 The Treaty of Guadalupe Hidalgo ends the Mexican War, establishing the Rio Grande and Gila River border and transferring to the U.S. Mexican holdings north of that line, including California. In return, fiscally unstable Mexico receives $15 million.

1848 FEB 22 Louis-Philippe of France, who has never understood the proper role

Arts & Architecture

1841 The first detective story, Edgar Allan Poe's *Murders in the Rue Morgue*, appears in *Graham's Magazine*.

1842 The Christy Minstrels begin performing minstrel shows, popularizing slave songs of the southern plantations.

1843-1850 Henri Labrouste's Bibliothèque Ste.-Geneviève in Paris is the first French building to use cast iron on a large scale.

1847 Charlotte Brontë publishes *Jane Eyre*, shocking contemporary readers with

Religion & Philosophy

1840 Søren Kierkegaard becomes engaged, but breaks off the relationship when he decides marriage is incompatible with his philosophical mission from God. Kierkegaard's works, including *Either-Or* (1843), criticize German idealism and look to Christianity, and Protestant theology in particular, for an explanation of the human condition.

1840 Ralph Waldo Emerson helps found *The Dial*, first edited by Margaret Fuller, which becomes the journal of American transcendentalism.

Science & Technology

1840 John William Draper takes the first successful photograph of the moon.

1842 Christian Doppler demonstrates the Doppler effect: that the frequency of sound waves varies as the source moves in relation to the observer.

1843 James Joule first states his theory on the mechanical equivalence of heat.

1844 MAY 24 Samuel Morse uses a government-funded telegraph prototype to send a message from Washington to Baltimore: "What hath God wrought!"

Daily Life

1844 George Williams founds the Young Men's Christian Association in London.

1844 DEC American dentist Horace Wells makes the first practical use of anesthesia when he inhales nitrous oxide before having a tooth extracted.

of a constitutional monarch, provokes riots in Paris by once again banning the meetings of opposition parties. The next day, panicky troops kill 20 protesters, whose dead bodies are paraded through the streets. On the third day of the rioting, Louis-Philippe abandons the Tuileries, while opposition deputies and socialist journalists proclaim the Third Republic from the balcony of the Hôtel de Ville. Louis Napoleon Bonaparte becomes president of the Second Republic in December.

1848 MAR Roused by the Paris uprising, revolutionary socialist sentiment sweeps Europe. In Vienna, rioters force Metternich to give up his cabinet post (MAR 13), while in Germany, nationalist demonstrations force the convocation of the Frankfurt National Assembly (MAY 18), charged with drawing up a constitution for a united fatherland. In Italy, Mazzini declares a Roman Republic (FEB 1849) and defends it with the help of Giuseppe Garibaldi. When these revolutions all fail, many question the truth of Hegel's dictum that ideas shape reality.

1848 JUL 19-20 The Seneca Falls Convention meets in upstate New York to discuss women's rights. Its Declaration of Sentiments, drafted by Lucretia Mott and Elizabeth Cady Stanton, enumerates the manifold ways in which women are oppressed, including the denial of property rights and suffrage.

Fyodor Dostoyevsky

its frank analysis of women's feelings. In the same year, sister Emily writes *Wuthering Heights*, also controversial because of its hero's helplessness.

1848 English naturalistic artists form the Pre-Raphaelite Brotherhood.

1849 APR 23 The Russian secret police arrest Fyodor Dostoyevsky, then a 27-year-old short-story writer, for allegedly revolutionary activities. Approaching the scaffold, he learns that his death sentence has been commuted to four years' exile in Siberia.

1841 Ludwig Feuerbach writes *The Essence of Christianity*, criticizing Hegel's idealism and providing an important link between Hegel and Marx.

1846-7 Following Brigham Young to Utah, the Mormons build Salt Lake City.

1848 Karl Marx and Friedrich Engels circulate the *Communist Manifesto* as the platform for the Communist League. It emphasizes Marx's view of history as a class struggle. "The proletarians have nothing to lose but their chains," Marx and Engels write.

1846 SEP 23 Searching in a region indicated by Jean Leverrier, Johann Galle discovers Neptune, confirming the find when he observes the following evening that the planet has moved. Leverrier had calculated Neptune's location from its perturbing effect on the orbit of Uranus.

1848 William Thomson, Lord Kelvin, proposes an absolute scale of temperature.

1849 Using a toothed wheel to separate a beam of sunlight into flashes, Armand Fizeau makes the first approximate calculation of the speed of light.

1845 New York City fireman Alexander Cartwright modernizes the rules of baseball, fixing the number of bases at four and placing them 90 feet apart. Cartwright also outlaws the practice of putting out base runners by "plugging" them (hitting them with a thrown ball).

1846 JAN 21 Charles Dickens becomes the first editor of the just-founded *Daily News* in London.

1849 John Gorrie's experiments in lowering the temperatures of fever patients result in the first air conditioner.

1840-1849

The Body Politic

1851 Hong Xiuquan founds the Heavenly Kingdom, thus beginning the Taiping Rebellion that takes at least 30 million Chinese lives. Hong introduces land reform, emancipates women, and commands a highly disciplined army of men and women whose difficult campaigns foreshadow Mao's Long March (1934).

1851 DEC 2 Louis Napoleon carries out a bloodless coup d'état in France, during which reactionary forces wipe out the gains of the 1848 revolution.

1852 DEC 2 After a plebiscite shows 97% support for his plan, Louis Napoleon proclaims the Second Empire and crowns himself Napoleon III.

1853 APR Russia sends an ultimatum to the Turks demanding recognition of Tsar Nicholas I's right to represent Ottoman Christians. The ultimatum cloaks Nicholas's real aim: control of Constantinople. After the sultan (in consultation with his European allies) refuses, Nicholas occupies the Danubian Principalities, beginning the Crimean War. Turkey declares war on October 14, leading Britain and France into the conflict.

1854 JAN 4 Pushing the idea of a transcontinental railroad, Stephen Douglas proposes statehood for Nebraska. When southerners object (because Nebraska would be a free state under the 1820 Missouri Compromise), Douglas suggests

Arts & Architecture

1850 As does much of Charles Dickens' work, *David Copperfield* exposes the injustice of modern industrial society.

1850 Realist master Gustave Courbet exhibits *The Stone Breakers* and *A Burial at Ornans* at the Salon, where their unrelenting depiction of the bleakness of everyday life shocks and confounds art critics attending the show.

1851 Herman Melville publishes *Moby Dick* to the ridicule of most critics, causing it to fail commercially.

Religion & Philosophy

1850 MAR Karl Marx, his wife Jenny, and their four children endure eviction and the seizure of their belongings. For the next six years, they barely subsist.

1854 The transcendentalist philosopher and essayist Henry David Thoreau writes *Walden*. Subtitled *Life in the Woods*, Thoreau's work declares his faith in the "unquestionable ability of man to elevate his life by conscious endeavor."

1854 Pope Pius IX proclaims the Immaculate Conception to be an article of faith.

Science & Technology

1850 Rudolf Clausius gives the first concise statement of the second law of thermodynamics (concerning entropy).

1852 Henri Giffard flies the first steam-powered dirigible balloon at a top speed of 6.7 miles per hour.

1854 Louis Pasteur studies wine, devising pasteurization to prevent spoilage.

1855 OCT 17 Henry Bessemer patents a method for removing impurities from molten iron. His process dramatically reduces the cost of producing steel.

Daily Life

1850 P.T. Barnum hires Jenny Lind (the Swedish Nightingale) to tour America.

1851 Isaac Singer patents his sewing machine, but a court later determines that he infringed on Elias Howe's 1846 patent. Howe's royalties eventually total more than $2,000,000 before his patent expires in 1867.

1853 Levi Strauss sails to San Francisco with heavy canvas that he sells to miners for tents. With some of his stock, Strauss makes the first jeans.

that the territory become two states. Repealing the Missouri Compromise, the Kansas-Nebraska Act permits each state to determine its own slave status.

1854 MAR 31 Commodore Matthew Perry negotiates the first commercial treaty between the U.S. and Japan at Kanagawa.

1856 MAR Russia, now under the reform-minded rule of Alexander II, agrees to the Peace of Paris, which places the Danubian territories under European control and guarantees the future integrity of the Ottoman Empire.

1857 MAR 6 The Supreme Court hands down its decision in the case of *Dred Scott v. Sandford*. Chief Justice Roger B. Taney rules that blacks cannot sue for their freedom because they are not citizens. Five other justices agree, at least as far as Dred Scott is concerned, pushing the country closer to civil war.

1859 APR 25 With the blow of a pickax, Ferdinand de Lesseps begins construction of his diplomatic triumph, the Suez Canal. Its opening (1869, NOV 17) means that cargo ships from the East will no longer have to sail around Africa.

1859 OCT 16 Fanatic abolitionist John Brown raids the federal armory at Harpers Ferry, hoping to trigger a slave revolt in Virginia.

Napoleon III

1851 Workers erect Sir Joseph Paxton's Crystal Palace, the first prefabricated building, in just nine months for London's Great Exhibition.

1854 After the U.S. opens Japan to international trade, previously unknown Japanese prints begin to influence Western ideas of color and composition.

1857 When Gustave Flaubert's highly realistic *Madame Bovary* first appears in serial form in the *Revue de Paris*, the government brings charges of immorality.

1858 FEB 11 St. Bernadette sees a vision of the Virgin Mary in Lourdes.

1859 John Stuart Mill's *On Liberty* argues that limits on individual liberty are justifiable only when they are needed to protect the liberty of others.

1856 The first remains of Neanderthal humans are found in the Feldhofen cave in Germany's Neander valley.

1858 AUG 16 After a number of false starts, the first messages are passed along a transatlantic telegraph cable.

1859 NOV 24 All 1,250 copies of the first edition of Charles Darwin's *On the Origin of Species by Means of Natural Selection* sell out on the day of publication. In the book, Darwin presents both his theory of evolution and evidence supporting its existence.

1853 The new prefect Georges Haussman begins replacing crowded streets in Paris with broad boulevards.

1853 Either George Crum or Indian Kate Moon makes the first potato chip at a hotel in Saratoga Springs, New York.

1854 Elisha Otis demonstrates his new elevator at the New York World's Fair.

1859 AUG 27 Edwin Drake strikes oil in Titusville, Pennsylvania. This oil well, the first ever, begins the oil boom soon dominated by John D. Rockefeller.

The Body Politic

1860 MAY-SEP Giuseppe Garibaldi and his ragtag nationalists conquer Sicily and Naples, while further north Piedmontese prime minister Camillo de Cavour defeats the papal forces at Castelfidardo. The following March, an all-Italian parliament meeting in Turin proclaims Victor Emmanuel II of Piedmont-Sardinia to be king of a united Italy (except the Venetian and papal states).

1860 DEC 20 South Carolina becomes the first state to secede from the Union in protest of Abraham Lincoln's election.

1861 FEB 4 A congress of seven southern states meets in Montgomery, Alabama, to form the Confederate States of America.

1861 APR 12 The Civil War begins at 4:30 AM when Confederate shore batteries open fire on Fort Sumter, the federal garrison in Charleston Harbor.

1861 Alexander II abolishes serfdom in Russia, freeing 40 million peasants but retaining the system of the *mir,* which provides for collective ownership of the land.

1862 MAY 20 The signing of the Homestead Act by President Lincoln provides 160 acres of public land to each head of a household who settles that land for five years and pays a small fee.

1862 SEP Otto von Bismarck becomes the prime minister of Prussia, his goal

Arts & Architecture

1861 Charles Garnier's design for the Paris Opéra makes it the grandest public building of the Second Empire.

1861 English designer William Morris founds Morris, Marshall, Faulkner & Company to make handcrafted furniture,

metalware, ceramics, glass, textiles, and wallpaper.

1862-1869 Leo Tolstoy writes his epic *War and Peace*. A panoramic novel of the Napoleonic wars in Russia, it has unprecedented scope.

Religion & Philosophy

1862 In *Utilitarianism*, John Stuart Mill modifies Bentham's theory by criticizing the idea that goodness only has meaning in the context of self-interest. He tries to show that a sense of obligation is not incompatible with utilitarian cost-benefit analysis.

1862 Ivan Turgenev's *Fathers and Sons* popularizes the term *nihilist,* which the character Bazarov uses to describe his inability to believe in anything.

1863 Nikolai Chernishevski's novel *What is to be Done?* influences an entire

Science & Technology

1860 SEP The first International Chemical Conference opens in Karlsruhe to resolve conflicting theories of atomic weight. The idea for arranging all the known elements into a systematic table originates with diagrams printed by Lothar Meyer for his lectures.

1860 Working separately, James Clerk Maxwell and Ludwig Boltzmann develop a formula for determining the velocity of molecules in a gas. Because each individual molecule moves at a different speed, the Maxwell-Boltzmann method calculates a statistical average.

Daily Life

1860 APR 3 The Pony Express makes the first of its semiweekly runs between St. Joseph, Missouri, and San Francisco. Each of its riders covers approximately 200 miles a day for ten consecutive days. The riders change to fresh mounts every ten miles or so.

1862 Richard Gatling develops the first machine gun, which the Union uses for the first time during the siege of St. Petersburg, Virginia (1864-1865).

1863 Tailor Ebenezer Butterick begins commercial production of the first dress-

being the unification of Germany under Prussian control.

1862 SEP 22 Lincoln issues the Emancipation Proclamation, which frees all the slaves in Confederate-held territory.

1863 JUL 1-3 Believing the only way for the South to win the war is to take the fighting to the North, Robert E. Lee and his Army of Northern Virginia march on Washington. Union troops under General George Meade intercept Lee at Gettysburg, leading to three days of bloody fighting that kill more than 50,000 men. The turning point of the battle and the war comes on the third day when Pickett's Charge fails to break through the Union lines.

1863 JUL 13-16 Antidraft riots in New York City challenge the nation's first conscription act (enacted MAR 3).

1863 NOV 19 Lincoln delivers the two-minute Gettysburg Address at the dedication of a national cemetery there. He prepares the speech on an envelope during the train ride to the battlefield.

1864 At the request of the German Confederation, Austria and Prussia go to war with Denmark over Schleswig-Holstein, but Bismarck manipulates the situation so that he ends up controlling the territory. Prussian intransigence eventually leads to war with both the Confederation and Austria (1866).

Abraham Lincoln

1862 Ivan Turgenev's *Fathers and Sons* makes him the first Russian writer to become famous throughout Europe.

1863 Napoleon III orders an exhibition of avant-garde paintings that have been rejected by the conservative judges of the

Salon. At this show, which becomes known as the Salon des Refusés, Édouard Manet exhibits his *Déjeuner sur l'herbe*, depicting two clothed men with a nude woman. The painting provokes charges of indecency, but the resulting publicity confirms the work's success.

---

generation of young Russian radicals, particularly Lenin.

1864 Cardinal Newman, one-time leader of the Oxford Movement to reform the Anglican Church, writes *Apologia pro Vita Sua* defending his conversion to catholicism.

1864 SEP 28 British and French trade-union leaders found the International Working Men's Association, later known as the First International. Though Karl Marx plays no part in organizing this group, he immediately becomes its intellectual leader.

1862 Louis Pasteur's experiments disprove earlier theories about the spontaneous generation of life.

1864 James Clerk Maxwell devises four simple equations to describe all electrical and magnetic behavior.

---

making patterns, which can be used to reproduce garments exactly. By 1871, he sells 6 million patterns a year.

1864 William (Candy) Cummings of the Brooklyn Stars throws the first curve ball against the Brooklyn Atlantics.

Skeptics claim the pitch is an optical illusion.

1864 An international conference adopts the first Geneva Convention (revised 1904, JUL 6) regarding the treatment of wounded soldiers in the field.

1860-1864

1 8 5 4   **May** Passage of the Kansas-Nebraska Act leaves to the voters of each territory the question of whether it will be admitted to the Union as a free state or a slave state. The new law, proposed by Democratic senator Stephen Douglas of Illinois, effectively repeals the Missouri Compromise of 1820, which restricted slavery in those territories of the Louisiana Purchase north of latitude 36°30'.

July 6 A coalition of Free-Soilers and Whigs, along with northern Democrats who will no longer tolerate southern control of their party, found the Republican party to address the growing fear among abolitionists that slavery will be extended to the new territories.

1 8 5 6   **May 24-25** In Kansas, the fanatic John Brown leads a band of abolitionists on a nighttime raid that kills five of their proslavery neighbors in the Pottawatamie Massacre. Brown acts in reprisal for a recent attack by Border Ruffians on the free-state town of Lawrence. Fighting between abolitionists and Border Ruffians, who want to keep slavery legal, plagues the territory now known as Bleeding Kansas.

1 8 5 7   **March 6** In the case of *Dred Scott v. Sandford*, the southern-dominated Supreme Court rules in an opinion by Chief Justice Roger B. Taney that Congress has no right to prohibit slavery in the new territories. Denying Scott's bid for freedom on the grounds that, as property, he cannot have standing with the court, the decision turns public opinion in the north against the Democrats who control the federal government.

1 8 5 9   **October 16** John Brown and 21 raiders seize the federal armory at Harpers Ferry, Virginia. Brown intends to use the weapons captured there to lead a messianic slave revolt in the south. But the townspeople bottle him up until a company of Marines, commanded by Colonel Robert E. Lee and Lieutenant J.E.B. Stuart, arrives on October 18. Brown is captured, put on trial for murder, and hanged December 2.

1 8 6 0   **May 3** The Democratic party convention in Charleston adjourns when supporters of Douglas and those of the Buchanan administration split over Jefferson Davis's demand that Congress pass laws to guarantee slavery in the new territories.

November 6 Republican candidate Abraham Lincoln wins the presidential election, defeating Stephen Douglas, John C. Breckinridge, and John Bell. Lincoln fails to win a majority of the popular vote, but he takes the electoral college easily when Douglas and Breckinridge split the Democratic vote. Even in the fourteen slave states, 124,000 more ballots are cast for the compromise candidates Douglas and Bell than for the extremist Breckinridge.

December 20 South Carolina becomes the first state to secede formally from the Union.

1861 **February 4** Meeting in Montgomery, delegates from the seven states that have already seceded (Alabama, Georgia, Florida, Louisiana, Mississippi, South Carolina, and Texas) form the Confederate States of America. Jefferson Davis becomes its first and only president.

April 12 At dawn, Confederates guns open fire on Union-held Fort Sumter in Charleston Harbor, beginning the Civil War.

April 19 Lincoln announces a blockade of southern ports designed to prevent the exportation of cotton (the basis of the Confederate economy) as well as the importation of foreign guns, clothing, and medical supplies, all of which the agrarian South cannot manufacture itself. Although the interdiction exists at first primarily on paper, it becomes highly effective by 1863.

May Forced by the attack on Fort Sumter to choose sides, four more states (Arkansas, North Carolina, Tennessee, and Virginia) reluctantly join the Confederacy.

July 21 Believing the war will be a quick one, an army of 30,000 hastily assembled Union soldiers marches out to face a Confederate force of similar size at Bull Run, just across the Potomac River from Washington. When the Confederate right under Thomas (Stonewall) Jackson breaks the federal attack and sends the raw Union recruits scurrying back to Washington, the congressmen picnicking on the hills above the battlefield realize that victory will not come as easily as they had thought.

July 25 Congress passes the Crittenden Resolution, proclaiming the goal of the war to be preservation of the Union, not the abolition of slavery.

1 8 6 2   **March 9** In the first naval battle between ironclads, the Union *Monitor* and the Confederate *Virginia* (also known as the *Merrimack*) fight to a draw off Hampton Roads, Virginia.

April 6-7 Two months after Union general Ulysses S. Grant captures Forts Henry and Donelson in western Tennessee, a Confederate army under Albert Sidney Johnston and P.G.T. Beauregard surprises Grant with a counterattack at Shiloh on Tennessee's southern border. Although Grant's 63,000-man army suffers 13,000 casualties, it wins a narrow victory. Grant feels such remorse for his woeful lack of preparation, that he considers resigning from the army. But his colleague General William Tecumseh Sherman soon talks him out of it.

June 26-July 2 Leading 100,000 Union soldiers up the James River, George B. McClellan attacks Richmond. McClellan's men get close enough to hear the bells ringing in the steeple of the Confederate capital, before Lee forces them back with heavy losses. The Confederate general's shrewd tactics during the Seven Days' Battles save Richmond from capture and reawaken the Rebels' martial spirit.

August 29-30 After a larger Union force under John Pope chases down Stonewall Jackson's army at Manassas, Lee launches a surprise attack on Pope's rear, transforming the second battle of Bull Run into a rout. Jackson's army had been raiding in the Shenandoah Valley, where Lee sent the general to relieve the pressure Pope's army had been placing on Richmond.

September 5 Lee boldly invades Maryland, leading 55,000 hungry and poorly armed troops across the Potomac in the first major Rebel foray across the Mason-Dixon Line.

September 17 At Antietam, one of the bloodiest battles of the war, McClellan fights Lee to a standstill, convincing him to withdraw.

September 22 Lincoln uses the "victory" at Antietam as a pretext for issuing the Emancipation Proclamation. Effective January 1, 1863, his executive order frees slaves held within the Confederacy (but not those in Union slave states) and changes the war goal to the abolition of slavery.

1 8 6 3   **May 1-4** The Confederates' decisive success at Chancellorsville inspires Lee to try another invasion of the North, despite the loss of Stonewall Jackson, who is accidentally shot by his own troops.

July 1-3 The failure of George Pickett's desperate charge on the third day of the fighting at Gettysburg ensures a Union victory and marks the "high tide" of both the northern invasion and the Confederacy as a whole. Lincoln delivers the Gettysburg Address at a battlefield cemetery on November 19.

July 4 Grant accepts the surrender of Vicksburg, the last Confederate stronghold on the Mississippi River, after a six-week siege. Combined with David Farragut's naval victory at New Orleans on April 25, 1862, which sealed off the southern Mississippi, the Union now splits the Confederacy in two, severing supply-rich Texas and Arkansas from the Deep South.

July 13-16 Lincoln's call for renewed conscription causes draft riots in New York City, where poor immigrants resent having to fight a war, the success of which will flood the job market with newly freed slaves. They also scorn a law permitting wealthy draftees to pay others to serve in their place.

1864 **May 5-6** Using a thick forest to give his outnumbered troops a tactical advantage, Lee inflicts unusually heavy casualties on Grant's Union army at the Battle of the Wilderness. But unlike the previous Union commanders Lee has faced, Grant refuses to withdraw. By the end of May, Grant has lost 50,000 men, but despite the carnage, Lincoln will not relieve the general. "I cannot spare this man," Lincoln says. "He fights."

June 18 After failing to take the city by storm, Grant begins a nine-month siege of Petersburg, Virginia, the "back door to Richmond." Lee's evacuation of Petersburg on April 2, 1865, precipitates his surrender on April 9 at Appomattox.

December 22 Ending his famous march from Atlanta to the sea, Sherman captures Savannah, which he offers to Lincoln as a "Christmas present." Following the concept of total war, Sherman has systematically destroyed Georgia's railways, factories, and plantations across a 60-mile front. Union strategists now believe that conquering territory and defeating Confederate armies will not be enough to end the war; only an end to the South's ability to wage war will bring peace. Meanwhile, cavalry general Philip Sheridan attacks the Confederacy's agricultural base in the Shenandoah Valley, cutting off Richmond's food supply.

1865 **April 9** Lee's surrender at Appomattox Court House ends the Civil War.

The Body Politic

1865 APR 9 Robert E. Lee's surrender to Ulysses S. Grant at Appomattox Court House, Virginia, ends the Civil War.

1865 APR 14 John Wilkes Booth shoots Lincoln in the back of the head as the president watches a performance of *Our American Cousin* at Ford's Theater.

1865 DEC 24 Confederate veterans in Pulaski, Tennessee, form the Ku Klux Klan to resist Reconstruction in the South and restore white supremacy through violent means.

1866 JUN-AUG Its victory in the Seven Weeks' War, engineered by Chief of the General Staff Helmuth von Moltke, leads to Prussia's emergence as the preeminent power in central Europe. In addition to Moltke's brilliant tactics, Prussian soldiers have been aided by breech-loading rifles that fire six shots for each fired by Austrian muzzle-loaders.

1867 FEB-MAY The Ausgleich [Compromise] demanded by Hungary after Austria's defeat in the Seven Weeks' War, leads to a dual monarchy in Austria-Hungary.

1867 MAR 2 Congress passes the first Reconstruction Act over President Johnson's veto, declaring martial law in the South. The same day, Congress also passes the Tenure of Office Act, again despite a presidential veto. The new law

Arts & Architecture

1865 Reclusive mathematician Charles Dodgson publishes *Alice in Wonderland* under the pen name Lewis Carroll.

1867 Édouard Manet and Gustave Courbet hold one-man shows at the Paris World's Fair in defiance of the Salon.

1867 A San Francisco newspaper sends Mark Twain on a steamboat trip to the Mediterranean. His dispatches are later collected into *Innocents Abroad* (1869).

1868 Architect Eugène Viollet-le-Duc's *Comprehensive Dictionary of French*

Religion & Philosophy

1865 William Booth founds an evangelical ministry in London's East End that evolves into the Salvation Army.

1866 Pierre Larousse publishes the first part of his *Grand Dictionnaire*, issued fortnightly until its completion (1876).

Science & Technology

1865 JUN Louis Pasteur's research into a French silkworm epidemic leads to his germ theory of disease.

1865 Alexander Parker treats pyroxylin (nitrocellulose) with camphor, creating the first artificial plastic.

1865 Applying Pasteur's ideas, Joseph Lister uses carbolic acid (a sewage deodorant) as an antiseptic to prevent infection in compound fractures.

1866 Austrian abbot Gregor Mendel publishes in an obscure journal an account of

Daily Life

1865 Topologist August Möbius displays the Möbius strip, a shape with just one side and one edge.

1867 John Chambers, assisted by the eighth marquess of Queensberry, draws up boxing's Queensberry rules.

1867 Alfred Nobel patents dynamite, which he creates by mixing powerful yet highly volatile nitroglycerin with a stabilizer called *kieselguhr* (diatomaceous earth). His invention soon revolutionizes the mining industry as well as railroad construction.

restricts the president's powers to appoint and dismiss federal officials.

1867 MAR 30 Secretary of State William H. Seward buys Alaska from Russia for $7.2 million. Those who consider the deal foolish dub it Seward's Folly.

1867 MAY-JUL Benito Juárez's victory at Querétaro over French forces in the service of Mexican emperor Maximilian ends the French attempt (begun in 1861) to restore the monarchy in Mexico.

1868 JAN The European intervention that follows Perry's opening of Japan (1854) weakens the prestige of the shogun Keiti to the point at which he is forced to abdi-

cate. The Meiji emperor Mutsuhito, who replaces Keiti, begins a social and political revolution that will transform feudal Japan into a modern nation-state.

1868 FEB 24 Radical Republicans in the House who oppose Johnson's Reconstruction policies vote to impeach him for violating the Tenure of Office Act. The Senate votes twice, both times 35-19, which is one vote short of the two-thirds required for conviction.

1869 MAY 10 At Promontory Point, Utah, the driving of the Golden Spike connects the Central Pacific and Union Pacific lines to form America's first transcontinental railroad.

Karl Marx

Architecture from the Eleventh to Sixteenth Century revives medieval style.

1868 American art student Mary Cassatt travels to Paris, where she becomes involved with the impressionists. Like that of Edgar Degas, her work shows the

influence of Japanese prints popularized at the Paris World's Fair.

1868-1869 Robert Browning writes *The Ring and the Book*, a series of poems that use dramatic monologues to develop the psychological analysis of a crime.

1867 Karl Marx publishes his *Das Kapital* in Berlin. Though primarily an economic analysis of the current market system, *Das Kapital* derives its extraordinary influence from Marx's discussion of historical materialism. Marx claims that this analysis, owing much to the

Hegelian dialectic, proves scientifically that communist revolution is inevitable and likely to happen soon.

1869 In *Culture and Anarchy*, literary critic Matthew Arnold indicts the crass commercialism of Victorian society.

---

his breeding experiments with peas. Ignored until 1900, Mendel's work originates the formal study of heredity.

1868 Workers digging a railroad bed uncover five prehistoric skeletons in the Cro-Magnon caves of southern France.

1868 Norman Lockyer names an unknown element found in the spectra of the sun *helium* (not found on earth until 1895).

1869 Dmitri Mendeleyev's periodic table arranges the elements according to their periodically recurring properties.

1868 Karl Siemens introduces the open-hearth method for making steel, in which spent hot gases are used to create the blast used by Bessemer to purify iron.

1869 MAR 15 Harry Wright and George Ellard organize the Cincinnati Red

Stockings, the first professional baseball team.

1869 Thomas Edison invents the stock ticker, which he sells to Wall Street for $40,000. Edison uses this new wealth to establish a laboratory in Newark.

1865-1869

The Body Politic

1870 JUL 9 France declares war on Prussia after Bismarck publishes the text of a conversation between the French ambassador and Prussian king William I at Bad Ems (the Ems Dispatch). The proximate cause of the Franco-Prussian War is Hohenzollern prince Leopold's claim (since withdrawn) to the Spanish throne. But the war's true origins are to be found in Napoleon III's fear of Prussian hegemony in Europe and Bismarck's obsession with German unity.

1870 SEP 1 The Prussian army forces the French to capitulate at Sedan, taking Napoleon III prisoner. Three days later, Parisians disgusted with the empire's humiliation found the Third Republic.

Ignoring this change in government, Bismarck besieges Paris, while Léon Gambetta escapes by balloon to organize a "war of the people" in the countryside.

1871 JAN 18 Manipulating powerful nationalist sentiments aroused by the Franco-Prussian War, Bismarck hastily proclaims William I emperor of a newly unified Germany in the Hall of Mirrors at Versailles. Bismarck's triumph is made possible by recently concluded treaties that formally establish the second German Reich.

1871 JAN 28 Paris surrenders. Four months later, the Peace of Frankfurt (MAY 10) compels France to cede Alsace-

Arts & Architecture

1870 Charles Dickens dies, leaving his unfinished *Mystery of Edwin Drood* without a solution.

1871 West Point reject James Abbott McNeill Whistler, one of the first artists to be affected by the rage for Orientalism

(*Japonisme*), paints *Arrangement in Grey and Black*. The painting later becomes known by its subject matter as *Whistler's Mother*.

1871 William Gilbert and Arthur Sullivan begin their collaboration with *Thespis*.

Religion & Philosophy

1870 JUL 18 The first Vatican Council confirms papal infallibity, but limits it to *ex cathedra* pronouncements.

1871 JUL Chancellor Otto von Bismarck abolishes the Catholic bureau of the Prussian Ministry of Culture, beginning

his *Kulturkampf* against the Catholic establishment in Germany.

1872 Karl Marx has Mikhail Bakunin and his anarchist followers expelled from the First International, splitting the revolutionary movement in Europe.

Science & Technology

1870 Named surgeon-general of the army during the Franco-Prussian War, Friedrich von Esmarch becomes an expert in triage and develops the Esmarch bandage.

1871 JAN 7 Dmitri Mendeleyev announces that the holes in his periodic table

actually represent as-yet-undiscovered elements. Three of these are later found within Mendeleyev's lifetime.

1871 The first major tunnel through a mountain, the transalpine Mont Cenis tunnel, opens to rail traffic.

Daily Life

1871 OCT 8-9 A fire, reportedly started when Mrs. O'Leary's cow kicks over a lantern, destroys most of Chicago.

1871 OCT 23 Henry Stanley of the New York *Herald* finally locates missionary David Livingstone at Lake Tanganyika.

1871 Phineas Taylor Barnum launches his collection of circus and freak acts, entitled the "Greatest Show on Earth," before a Brooklyn audience. Barnum's spectacle merges with James Bailey's circus in 1881 and finally sells out to Ringling Brothers in 1907.

Lorraine, pay reparations, and accept an occupying army.

1871 MAR Rebellious Parisians blockade the streets of the city and establish an independent revolutionary socialist government, known as the Paris Commune. French president Adolphe Thiers orders troops to lay siege to the city.

1871 MAY 21-28 During the Bloody Week, French troops commanded by Marshal Patrice de MacMahon enter Paris and regain control, massacring 20,000 Communards in the process. The failure of the socialist Paris Commune confirms Karl Marx's opinion that only Communists can lead a proper revolution.

1873 SEP 18 The failure of the nation's leading brokerage firm, Jay Cooke & Company, which has been financing the Northern Pacific railroad, triggers the financial Panic of 1873, caused by land speculation and an overabundance of paper money.

1874 Using the pretext of a scientific survey expedition, the army sends George Armstrong Custer's Seventh Cavalry into the Black Hills to search for gold. Custer's expedition clearly violates an 1868 treaty with the Sioux guaranteeing them the sacred *Paha Sapa* for eternity. When Custer's discovery of gold brings a rush of prospectors to the region, the enraged Sioux go to war.

Otto von Bismarck

1871 Italian composer Giuseppi Verdi's *Aida*, commissioned to celebrate the opening of the Suez Canal, debuts at the new Opera House in Cairo.

1871-1893 Founding French naturalist Émile Zola writes *Les Rougon-Macquart*, a group of 20 novels that tell the saga of a Second Empire family.

1874 Art critic Louisa Leroy coins the term *impressionism* after viewing Claude Monet's *Impression: Sunrise* at the first impressionist exhibition in Paris.

1872 Friedrich Nietzsche publishes his first book, *The Birth of Tragedy*. A continuing theme in Nietzsche's work will be his emphasis on the Dionysian side of human nature (characterized by unconscious, orgiastic behavior) at the expense of calm, rational Apollonian virtues.

1871 To illustrate how the second law of thermodynamics might be violated, James Clark Maxwell hypothesizes a "demon," who would separate fast (hot) gas molecules from slow (cold) ones within a closed system, thereby creating useful heat using only intelligence.

1873 JUN 15 Amateur archaeologist Heinrich Schliemann announces his discovery (near Hissarlik, Turkey) of the ruins of the legendary city of Troy, described by Homer in the *Iliad*. Schliemann's reckless excavations, however, nearly destroy the site.

1872 Aaron Montgomery Ward issues the first mail-order catalog. His one-page list expands to 240 pages by 1884. Sears Roebuck begins its own catalog in 1888.

1873 Belgian missionary Joseph de Veuster, known as Father Damien, volunteers to take spiritual charge of the leper colony on Molokai. He contracts leprosy himself in 1889.

1874 Robert Green creates the first ice-cream soda in Philadelphia. He develops the ice-cream cone thirty years later.

1870-1874

The Body Politic

1876 JUN 25 Chasing after renegade Indians, Colonel George Custer discovers an enormous encampment of Sioux and Cheyenne along the banks of the Little Big Horn River. Believing himself able to handle any number of Indians, Custer splits his regiment so that none of the hostiles can escape, and then he attacks.

1876 NOV 7 Democrat Samuel Tilden wins a plurality of 250,000 votes in the presidential election, but the Republicans refuse to concede, contesting returns from four states. After weeks of infighting, Tilden allows to stand the decision of a 15-member commission, which awards the election (probably stolen from Tilden) to Rutherford B. Hayes.

1876 Russian populists found the Land and Freedom party. Its most radical members advocate political assassination as a means of achieving political liberty.

1877 APR 12 An overreaching Britain attempts to annex the Transvaal, but its tenuous position there is shortly revealed by the Zulu War and the successful Afrikaner uprising (1880-1881).

1877 APR 24 Once again declaring war on Turkey, Russia invades Romania.

1878 MAR 3 The Treaty of San Stefano, ending the last of the Russo-Turkish wars, again confirms Russian expansion at Ottoman expense. In addition to ced-

Arts & Architecture

1875 The *Hermes* sculpted by Praxiteles is rediscovered at Olympia.

1875 Peter Ilich Tchaikovsky's *Swan Lake* debuts in Moscow, but the company has difficulty adapting to its unconventional score, and the ballet fails.

1875 George Bizet's *Carmen* opens at the Opéra Comique in Paris. It runs 37 shows, though Bizet dies after the 31st.

1876 The Bayreuth Festspielhaus opens with the debut of Richard Wagner's opera cycle *The Ring of the Nibelung*.

Religion & Philosophy

1875 Helena Blavatsky founds the Theosophical Society, a universalist religious group with an emphasis on mystical experience and the occult.

1875 Language scholar Max Müller begins his 51-volume series *The Sacred Books of the East*, which stimulates worldwide interest in Orientalism.

1876 Felix Adler, a rabbi's son, founds the Society for Ethical Culture in New York City. Adler's purpose is to promote morality independent of a supreme being.

Science & Technology

1876 Brazil's emperor tries Alexander Graham Bell's new telephone at the Centennial Exposition and makes newspaper headlines exclaiming, "It talks!"

1877 Thomas Alva Edison patents a phonograph that plays foil-wrapped cylinders.

1877 Nikolaus Otto builds the first four-cycle internal combustion engine.

1878 Thomas Edison causes gas company stocks to tumble when he announces that he will attempt to solve the filament problem of the electric light bulb.

Daily Life

1876 FEB 2 Eight teams form baseball's National League.

1877 Brothers William and Andrew Smith pioneer factory-sealed packaging to prevent unscrupulous druggists from substituting cheaper cough drops.

1879 Frank W. Woolworth opens The Great Five Cent Store in Utica, New York, which fails because of its poor location. In the same year, however, he opens another store in Lancaster, Pennsylvania, launching a chain-store empire that grows to 596 stores by 1912.

ing parts of Turkey directly to Russia, the treaty establishes independent states in the Turks' Balkan dependencies of Romania, Bulgaria, Serbia, and Montenegro. Finally, Austria receives Bosnia and Herzegovina, and Britain takes Cyprus.

1878 JUN 13-JUL 13 The Congress of Berlin, meeting to resolve the Eastern Question, revises the Treaty of San Stefano so that the Ottoman Empire remains an integral, although considerably weakened, European power. A humiliated and bitter Russia loses nearly all of her territorial gains.

1879 JAN War breaks out in the Transvaal between the British and Zulu tribesmen, who reject the Empire's colonial policies. The Zulus win an early victory, massacring British troops at Isandhlwana, but Britain's superior military defeats the Zulus in the following year.

1879 OCT 7 Austria and Germany conclude the first treaty confirming their Dual Alliance. The agreement, valid for the next five years, will be renewed repeatedly until 1918.

1879 During the nihilist trials, Russia's Land and Freedom party splits into two factions. The radical splinter group, which takes the name Will of the People, dedicates itself to the assassination of Tsar Alexander II.

George Armstrong Custer

1876 Pierre-Auguste Renoir's *Le Moulin de le Galette* exhibits compositional elements that reflect simultaneous developments in photography.

1877 Exhibiting with the impressionists for the last time, Paul Cézanne, a forerunner of cubism, breaks away from the group to emphasize structure and form in his paintings.

1877 Classicists in London found the Society for the Protection of Ancient Buildings from Injudicious Restoration.

1878 Historian Heinrich von Treitschke, a staunch imperialist and enemy of socialism, leads an antisemitic crusade against Jewish influence in Germany.

1879 Recurrent psychosomatic illnesses force Nietzsche to surrender his chair in classics at the University of Basel. He spends the next ten years at spas, writing and trying to regain his health.

1879 Mary Baker Eddy, the founder of Christian Science, begins to organize her first church in Boston.

1879 On the walls of a cave at Altamira on the northern coast of Spain, the marquis de Sautuola finds sophisticated prehistoric paintings.

1879 Walther Flemming uses red dye to stain the threadlike chromosomes of cellular nuclei. Studying the resulting "snapshots," Flemming discovers the process of cell division, which he terms *mitosis* after the Greek word for *thread.*

1879 OCT 21 Edison succeeds with a carbon filament of scorched cotton thread.

1879 Ohio saloon manager James Rilty invents the first cash register, which he calls an "incorruptible cashier," to reduce employee theft.

1879 OCT 8 Frank and Jesse James rob the Glendale, Missouri, train.

1875-1879

The Body Politic

1881 MAR 13 The radical nihilist group Will of the People assassinates Tsar Alexander II. His successor, Alexander III (until 1894), quickly institutes a much more oppressive and autocratic government, which he supports through terror imposed by means of the Okhrana, a newly created secret police.

1881 JUL 2 Frustrated office seeker Charles Guiteau shoots President James Garfield in a Washington railroad station. Garfield remains incapacitated for two months, raising constitutional questions about his ability to govern. Garfield finally dies on September 19, although he might have recovered had visiting medical specialists not constantly reinfected his bullet wound with their unscrubbed examinations.

1882 JAN 2 John D. Rockefeller and several of his wealthy associates form the Standard Oil trust. Rockefeller has been searching for years for a way to corner the oil market legally, because interstate commerce laws prohibit him from combining the operations of several oil companies in different states. Finally, his clever lawyer Samuel Dodd conceives of the trust as a means of circumventing those laws. The idea works so well that trusts are soon formed in other key industries, prompting Congressional involvement that results in the Sherman Antitrust Act (1890).

Arts & Architecture

1880 Vincent van Gogh leaves missionary work to become a painter. He has also worked as a schoolmaster and art dealer.

1881 FEB 12 Fyodor Dostoyevsky's funeral occasions a memorable outpouring of public grief in the Russian capital.

1881 Japanese women perform on the stage for the first time since the development of Kabuki (circa 1600).

1881 Richard D'Oyly Carte builds the Savoy Theater to showcase the popular comic operas of Gilbert and Sullivan.

Religion & Philosophy

1881 After Alexander II's assassination, mobs in more than 200 Russian cities attack and destroy the property of Jews, whom the Orthodox Church has accused of revolutionary activity (although only one of the nihilist assassins is a Jew). The pogroms continue for two years.

Science & Technology

1881 Louis Pasteur cultures anthrax bacteria at a high temperature, creating a weakened strain. It is the first vaccine to be artificially produced.

1881 Imprisoned for his part in the assassination of Tsar Alexander II, nihilist bomb maker Nikolai Kibalchich designs a rocket plane, but his writings languish in prison archives until 1917.

1882 Thomas Edison builds the first direct current power plant (in New York City) to power his electric light bulb.

Daily Life

1880 German-born Anton Feuchtwanger makes the first frankfurter in St. Louis. He serves it with no bun, but provides white gloves to keep his customers' fingers clean. Feuchtwanger begins using buns when his patrons neglect to return the gloves.

1881 JUL 14 Sheriff Pat Garrett kills Billy the Kid (William Bonney) in a darkened bedroom in Fort Sumner, New Mexico Territory.

1881 OCT 26 At the O.K. Corral, the Earp brothers, along with Doc Holliday, shoot it

1882 British forces occupy Egypt with the immediate aim of resolving a diplomatic dispute there. However, the British occupation persists, beginning a heated colonial rivalry with France that lasts until 1898.

1883 To counter the growing influence of the Social Democrats in Germany, Chancellor Otto von Bismarck develops a social security system, with which he hopes to appease the working classes.

1883 NOV 18 The U.S. and Canada adopt a standardized system of time zones to eliminate the confusion that has plagued travelers, whose railroad schedules generally list inconsistent local times.

1884 Concerned that colonial competition in Africa might lead to political instability in Europe, Bismarck convenes the Congo Conference in Berlin to mediate imperialist claims to the Congo Basin. All the Great Powers (Britain, France, Germany, Austria-Hungary, Italy, and Russia) agree to participate, as well as other smaller nations. The conference finally declares the neutrality of the Congo Free State (1885, FEB 5), placing the territory under the sovereignty of Belgium's Leopold II, but guaranteeing freedom of trade to all states.

1884 AUG 5 The cornerstone for the Statue of Liberty, a French gift, is laid on Bedloe's Island in New York Harbor.

John D. Rockefeller

1883 Workers complete the arduous task of building the Brooklyn Bridge. This masterwork of John Augustus Roebling, who dies accidentally at the outset of construction, becomes the world's longest suspension bridge and the first to use steel wire for cables.

1884 A publishing company owned by Mark Twain issues *The Adventures of Huckleberry Finn* and also the profitable *A Connecticut Yankee in King Arthur's Court* (1889). But Twain's *The American Claimant* fails, forcing the closing of the business and Twain into debt.

1883-1884 Sidney and Beatrice Webb, along with George Bernard Shaw, found the Fabian Society, which advocates evolutionary (rather than revolutionary) socialism. Its name refers to the Roman general Fabius, who defeated more powerful foes by avoiding pitched battles.

1884 In *The Man Versus the State*, social Darwinist Herbert Spencer suggests that Darwin's theory of evolution ("the survival of the fittest" in Spencer's assessment) implies that people who are burdens to society deserve no help because they are inherently weak.

1882 Josef Breuer uses hypnosis to treat Anna O. (Bertha Pappenheim), who has been suffering from hysterical paralysis since the death of her father.

1884 Carl Koller discovers that cocaine can be used as a topical anesthetic for eye

operations. Soon dentists begin using the drug during extractions.

1884 Hilaire Bernigaud de Chardonnet sprays dissolved cellulose nitrate (as a spider spins a web), producing the first artificial fiber, later named rayon.

---

out with the Clantons and the McLowrys for control of the town of Tombstone in the Arizona Territory.

1883 JUL 4 Buffalo Bill Cody's Wild West Show performs for the first time in North Platte, Nebraska.

1883 AUG 27 The eruption of Krakatoa (east of Java), heard as far away as Australia, darkens the sky for two days and creates tsunamis that kill 36,000.

1883 OCT 4 The Orient-Express makes its first run from Paris to Istanbul.

1880-1884

The Body Politic

1885 NOV 14 When Bulgaria and neighboring Eastern Rumelia discuss unification, Serbia declares war. Bismarck intervenes diplomatically (through Austria-Hungary) in order to prevent the fighting from evolving into a larger conflict between Russia and Austria, each of whom has a stake in the Balkans.

1886 MAY 4 As police arrive in Chicago's Haymarket Square to break up a labor rally, a bomb explodes among them, killing seven officers. Eight leading anarchists who spoke at the rally are arrested. Although the prosecutors present no evidence proving that any of these men threw the bomb, all eight are found guilty, seven receiving death sentences.

1886 SEP 4 Geronimo finally surrenders to General Nelson (Bearcat) Miles in Arizona, after which all his Chiricahua Apaches are shipped to Florida as prisoners of war.

1886 NOV 1 A new Anglo-German treaty defines spheres of influence for each party in East Africa. Meanwhile, Portugal claims the territory between Angola and Mozambique.

1886 DEC 8 Labor groups meeting in Columbus, Ohio, form the American Federation of Labor. Samuel Gompers of the Cigarmakers Union becomes the first president of the AFL, which initially represents 150,000 workers.

Arts & Architecture

1886 Vincent van Gogh moves to Paris to live with his brother Theo, an art dealer. Two years later, he moves to Arles, where he takes his own life (1890).

1886 Georges Seurat exhibits his *Sunday on the Island of La Grande Jatte*

at the last impressionist show. Seurat's pointillist style proceeds from recent scientific investigations of light and color.

1887 Sir Arthur Conan Doyle writes the first of his many Sherlock Holmes stories, *A Study in Scarlet.*

Religion & Philosophy

1887 L.L. Zamenhof constructs the artificial language Esperanto from roots commonly found in European languages, thus making it easy to learn. He intends Esperanto to be an international second language. All the words in Esperanto are spelled just as they are pronounced.

Science & Technology

1885 Gottlieb Daimler and Karl Benz independently build the first practical automobiles.

1885 Louis Pasteur uses his rabies vaccine on a human for the first time, treating 9-year-old Joseph Meister. The boy

survives, later becoming gatekeeper of the Pasteur Institute, but he kills himself in 1940 when the Nazi army in Paris orders him to open Pasteur's crypt.

1888 Former (and embittered) Edison assistant Nikola Tesla develops a system

Daily Life

1885 At Long Island's Argyle Hotel, Frank Thompson organizes the waiters into a baseball team for the amusement of the guests. The club evolves into the Cuban Giants, the first salaried black team. The players speak a gibberish in the field, hoping to pass as foreigners.

1886 Atlanta druggist James Pemberton sells an interest in his medicinal drink business, recently renamed Coca-Cola (and now cocaine-free), to Asa Candler.

1886 Clark Stanley sells snake oil from the Moki Pueblo as a cure for rheumatism.

1887 In order to maintain alliances on both his Russian and Austrian fronts after the dissolution of the Dreikaiserbund [League of the Three Emperors], German chancellor Otto von Bismarck carries out the most complex negotiations of his career. First, he renews the Triple Alliance (Germany, Austria-Hungary, Italy) for another three years (FEB 20). Then he signs the Reinsurance Treaty with Russia (JUN 18), agreeing to remain neutral in any Russian war (except one involving Austria) and to support Russia's expansionist policies in the Near East. Finally, he joins the Mediterranean Agreements among Italy, Britain, and Austria-Hungary, which maintain the status quo in the Near East.

1888 JAN 28 Germany and Italy sign a military agreement, binding Italy to assist Germany in the event of another Franco-German war.

1888 JUN 15 William II becomes German emperor (until 1918) following the death of his father. Because of the great disparity in their ages and outlooks, Bismarck loses his imperial support and thus his diplomatic influence. Kaiser Wilhelm finally dismisses Bismarck in 1890.

1888 The incorporation of the Imperial British East Africa Company leads to an intense rivalry between Britain and Germany for control of the territories adjacent to the source of the Nile.

Friedrich Nietzsche

1887 Stéphane Mallarmé publishes his *Poesies*, which spark the French Symbolist movement in poetry.

1887 Polish pianist Ignace Padrewski makes his triumphant public debut in Vienna.

1889 MAR 13 The Eiffel Tower, engineered by Alexandre Eiffel, reaches its full height of 984 feet, making it by far the tallest structure in the world.

1889 French novelist André Gide begins his *Journal*, which he keeps until 1949.

1889 JAN Friedrich Nietzsche becomes insane, after which his sister Elizabeth cares for him until his death in 1900.

1889 European socialist parties and trade unions found the Second International, which initially calls for the

achievement of social democracy through parliamentary means.

1889 Henri Bergson, the originator of process philosophy, publishes his seminal work on the nature of time, *An Essay on the Immediate Data of Consciousness*.

---

of alternating current that competes successfully with Edison's direct current generators.

1888 George Eastman invents the push-button Kodak camera. A year later, he makes the first celluloid film.

1887 The new player piano becomes a hit in saloons throughout the West, where piano players can be scarce.

1888 St. Louis Browns' owner Chris von der Ahe begins serving hot dogs and beer at his ballpark.

1888 AUG 7-NOV 10 A murderer calling himself Jack the Ripper slits the throats of seven prostitutes in London's East End, baffling the police.

1889 The 16 stories of New York's World Building make it the world's tallest.

1885-1889

The Body Politic

1890 JUN 18 Germany pushes Russia and France together when it allows the Reinsurance Treaty to lapse despite Russian efforts to renew the alliance.

1890 JUL 2 Congress passes the Sherman Antitrust Act prohibiting monopolistic trusts, such as the Standard Oil trust (1882), that concentrate economic power for the purpose of restraining trade.

1890 DEC 15 Indian police kill the unarmed Sitting Bull outside his cabin near the Grand River in South Dakota. Although the Hunkpapa Sioux chief has been living peacefully, the Indian agent for his reservation fears that Sitting Bull might join the Ghost Dance religion currently gripping the Plains tribes. As preached by Wovoka, the Ghost Dance is believed to make braves invulnerable to the white man's bullets and bring Indian ancestors back from the dead.

1892 JAN 1 Ellis Island in New York Harbor opens as a processing center for immigrants, mostly from eastern Europe.

1892 JUN 26 Workers walk out on Carnegie Steel, beginning the Homestead Strike. When the company hires Pinkertons to protect its plant in Homestead, Pennsylvania, strikers kill three guards and wound many more (JUL 6). Six days later, the governor sends in state troopers to protect Carnegie's strikebreakers.

Arts & Architecture

c.1890 Australian collector of bush songs Andrew Barton (Banjo) Paterson composes *Waltzing Matilda*.

1890 Photographer Jacob August Riis publishes *How the Other Half Lives*, a study of slum life in New York City.

1891 French painter Paul Gauguin leaves for Tahiti, where he paints his best-known works.

1891 Henri de Toulouse-Lautrec begins producing posters of the Paris dance halls and nightclubs that he frequents.

Religion & Philosophy

1890 In his masterful *Principles of Psychology*, William James enunciates the innovative idea that subjective feelings might be caused by the bodily changes that follow perception. "We feel sorry because we cry," James writes, "angry because we strike."

1890 James George Frazer's *The Golden Bough* traces the development of thought from the magical to the religious and finally to the scientific.

1891 Leo XIII issues the papal encyclical *Rerum novarum* [*Of new things*]. Its care-

Science & Technology

1890 William Stewart Halsted introduces the practice of wearing sterilized rubber gloves during surgery.

1891 George Johnstone Stoney calls recently discovered electrically charged particles *electrons*.

1892 Rudolf Diesel modifies the internal combustion engine, placing the fuel-air mixture under high pressure so that compression alone is sufficient to ignite it.

1893 George Westinghouse, to whom Nikola Tesla has sold his patents, wins a

Daily Life

1890 James B. Duke and four former competitors form the American Tobacco Company, which will control 93% of the cigarette market by 1900.

1890 AUG 6 William Kemmer becomes the first man to die in the electric chair.

1890 NOV 29 In the first Army-Navy football game, Navy wins, 24-0.

1891 To reduce the deluge of applications, the Patent Office begins to require inventors of perpetual-motion machines to supply working models.

1892 During this presidential election year, disgruntled voters organize the People's Party, known as the Populists. The party's platform advocates lower tariffs, an eight-hour workday, and currency reform.

1894 OCT 15 The infamous Dreyfus Affair begins with the arrest of Captain Alfred Dreyfus, a Jewish official in the French ministry of war, on charges of treason. Dreyfus's conviction and life sentence arouse intense public controversy when his case is linked to forgery, perjury, and antisemitism. Although Dreyfus is eventually rehabilitated (1906), his case reveals deep divisions within French society.

1894 Professor Ernst Hasse launches the antisemitic Pan-German movement to heighten nationalist consciousness and promote German territorial expansion. Pan-German ideology will later have a substantial influence on Adolf Hitler.

1894-1895 The Tonglak uprising in Korea sparks the first Sino-Japanese War as both Chinese and Japanese troops move to intervene. Using its naval power, Japan soon disables the Chinese fleet, taking key ports in Shantung and occupying Manchuria. The Treaty of Shimonoseki (1895, APR 17) creates an independent Korea, but also compels China to make territorial concessions, pay reparations, and open ports to Japanese trade.

Sigmund Freud

1891 Carnegie Hall opens in New York.

1892 A large exhibition in Berlin of oppressive paintings by the Norwegian artist Edvard Munch causes a public sensation. His work, including *The Scream* (1893), inspires German expressionism.

1893 Louis Tiffany begins making Favrile glass, spraying panes with an iron salt solution to give them a metallic sheen.

1893 Thomas Edison develops the kinetoscope, but its peep show-like reels can be viewed by only one person at a time.

---

ful yet genuine concern for the working classes earns him distinction as "the working man's pope."

1891 The International Correspondence School, the first of its kind, opens in Scranton, Pennsylvania.

---

landmark victory over Edison when he obtains the right to build the Niagara Falls power plant using alternating current.

1894 Eugène Dubois announces his discovery of *Pithecanthropus erectus* (commonly known as Java man).

1894 Breaking with Breuer over his own emphasis of sexuality, Sigmund Freud gives up hypnosis and instead encourages his patients to say whatever comes into their minds. Freud calls this process by which his patients slowly come to unburden themselves *psychoanalysis.*

1892 JAN 15 James Naismith's rules for basketball are printed in the newspaper of the Springfield (Mass.) Y.M.C.A.

1893 Henry D. Perky develops the first ready-to-eat breakfast cereal, Shredded Wheat, at a Denver vegetarian restaurant.

1893 George Ferris builds the first Ferris wheel for the Columbian Exposition being held in Chicago.

1894 Milton Hershey makes the first American candy bar, a chocolate product that he names after himself.

1890-1894

The Body Politic

1895 FEB 24 Partially as a result of the financial Panic of 1893, which depressed the sugar industry there, Cuba begins its revolt against Spanish rule.

1896 JAN 3 Anglo-German relations deteriorate when Kaiser Wilhelm II sends a telegram to Transvaal president Paul Kruger congratulating him on the defeat of Jameson's Raid, a British attempt to overthrow the Afrikaner (Boer) state. The Boers interpret the Kruger Telegram as a promise of German aid against Britain.

1896 JUL 8 William Jennings Bryan's eloquent "Cross of Gold" speech at the Democratic convention in Chicago wins him the party's presidential nomination.

Opposing the gold standard, Bryan's "easy money" policy favors silver coinage.

1896 Buying the New York *Journal* with a loan from his mother, William Randolph Hearst begins a circulation battle with Joseph Pulitzer's *World*. Their "yellow" journalism incites public pressure for military intervention in Cuba.

1898 JAN 13 Author Émile Zola publishes a letter on the front page of the *Aurore* under the headline "J'Accuse," in which he charges that the French army has covered up the truth about Alfred Dreyfus. Zola's startling attack provokes an antisemitic backlash, which leads to his arrest and conviction on charges of libel.

Arts & Architecture

1895 FEB 14 Oscar Wilde's *The Importance of Being Earnest* opens at the St. James Theater, where it charms London audiences. The same year, however, Wilde brings an unsuccessful libel action against the marquess of Queensberry, who has accused Wilde of homo-

sexuality. In the sensational trial that follows, Wilde is found guilty and sentenced to two years' imprisonment at hard labor.

1897 The Lumiére brothers open the world's first movie theater in Paris featuring their cinematograph.

Religion & Philosophy

1896 FEB Theodor Herzl, transformed into a Zionist by the Dreyfus affair, publishes a pamphlet entitled *The Jewish State*. He argues that the Jewish question is not a religious question but a political one, which should be settled by a world council of nations.

1896 Former baseball player Billy Sunday begins to hold religious revivals. His emotional sermons appeal to people displaced from the country to the city.

1899 *The School and Society*, one of John Dewey's classic works in pedagogy,

Science & Technology

1895 William Roentgen accidentally discovers radiation of extremely short wavelength, which he calls *X rays*.

1896 Testing a uranium compound for phosphorescence, Henri Becquerel accidentally discovers radioactivity.

Daily Life

1895 William and John Kellogg develop the first flaked breakfast cereal for their patients at the Battle Creek sanitarium, who are bored with oatmeal.

1895 King C. Gillette invents the first successful safety razor.

1896 APR James B. Connolly—winner of the hop, step, and jump—becomes the first Olympic champion to be crowned since 394. Americans win nine of the 12 events held at the first Olympiad of the modern era in Athens, organized by the French baron Pierre de Coubertin.

1898 FEB 15 The American battleship *Maine* mysteriously explodes as it lies at anchor in Havana's harbor. The ship has been sent to protect U.S. citizens in Cuba, where anti-Spanish riots have recently gained momentum. Newspaper headlines in America urging the public to "Remember the *Maine!*" pressure President McKinley to declare war on Spain.

1898 APR 24 As Congress prepares to draft a war resolution, having rejected Spanish peace overtures, Spain makes its own declaration of war.

1898 MAY 1 Admiral George Dewey smashes the Spanish fleet at Manila in the Philippines, taking just seven casualties.

1898 DEC 10 The Treaty of Paris ends the Spanish-American War. Spain agrees to renounce its claim to Cuba as well as to cede its colonies of Guam and Puerto Rico to the United States, which pays Spain $20 million for title to the Philippines and thus becomes a bona fide international imperialist power.

1899 OCT The Anglo-Boer war begins when voting-rights negotiations between Transvaal president Paul Kruger and British colonial officials break down. When Kaiser Wilhelm, inclined to help the vastly outnumbered Boers, learns that his navy is inadequate to the task, Germany begins a massive shipbuilding effort (1900).

Rosa Luxemburg

1897 Gustav Mahler becomes conductor of the Vienna Imperial Opera, where he sets new standards for operatic productions.

1898 German socialist artist Käthe Kollwitz publishes a series of prints sympathetically portraying the poor.

1898 Cellist Pablo Casals debuts in Paris.

1899-1904 Hector Guimard designs the Metro subway stations of Paris in the art nouveau style.

c.1899 Jazz develops in New Orleans.

---

applies his pragmatic philosophy to the educational process.

1899 Eduard Bernstein's *Evolutionary Socialism*, one of the first works of Marxist revisionism, uses statistical evidence to show that many of the economic

predictions in *Das Kapital* (1867) have not come to pass.

1899 In *Reform or Revolution*, Rosa Luxemburg refutes Bernstein, calling the German parliament a bourgeois fraud and insisting on the need for revolution.

1897 Count Ferdinand von Zeppelin begins designing a dirigible airship for the German army that will carry up to five men at a speed of 18 miles per hour.

1898 JUL Searching for an unknown element they have detected in pitchblende,

Pierre and Marie Curie isolate a trace of black powder (polonium) 400 times more radioactive than uranium. In December, they isolate an even more radioactive element (radium).

1899 Felix Hoffman perfects aspirin.

1896 Adolph S. Ochs buys the ailing *New York Times*. His new motto for the paper is "All the News That's Fit to Print."

1897 William Randolph Hearst has Rudolph Dirks create the "Katzenjammer Kids," the first newspaper comic strip.

1899 The New York Zoological Society opens a zoo in the Bronx, the largest in the world at that time.

1899 John Dorrance of the Campbell Preserve Company comes up with a process for condensing soup.

1895-1899

c.3500 BC   The **wheel,** most likely by a Mesopotamian who uses two potter's wheels and an axle to make a hauling sledge.

c.2600 BC   **False teeth,** by the Egyptian Neferites who crafts ivory, gold, and silver into crowns and bridges.

c.1300 BC   The **water clock** [clepsydra], in Egypt, a significant improvement over the sundial because it can measure time on cloudy days and at night.

c.250 BC   The **screw**, by Archimedes who invents a device to raise water from the holds of ships. The screw thread is soon applied to wine presses.

49 BC   **Abdominal surgery**, by the Indian physician Susruta who removes portions of a patient's damaged intestine, then sutures the ends using the freshly cut heads of black ants, which secrete formic acid, an antiseptic.

812   **Paper money**, by a Chinese bank for the purpose of paying taxes.

1719   **Three-color printing**, by Jakob Christoph Le Blon who patents a four-plate process to reproduce masterpieces of art.

1760   **Roller skates**, by Joseph Merlin who popularizes his invention by wearing a pair to a fancy-dress ball in London. Unfortunately for Merlin, while simultaneously playing a violin, he crashes into a giant mirror, injuring himself severely.

1793   The **cotton gin**, by Eli Whitney. The ability of the cotton gin to clean short-staple, green-seed cotton mechanically makes possible the commercial success of a plantation economy in the South.

1799   The **electric battery**, by Alessandro Volta who uses his invention to disprove Luigi Galvani's theory that only animal tissue can produce electric current. Galvani developed his theory while experimenting with severed frogs' legs during the 1780s.

1801 **Interchangeable parts**, by Eli Whitney who demonstrates his new manu-facturing method to President-elect Thomas Jefferson. Whitney's method for assembling muskets from standardized parts is the first step in mass-produc-tion manufacturing.

1803 The **steam railway locomotive**, by Richard Trevithick who later abandons the project because cast-iron rails prove too brittle for his hefty engines.

1823 **Waterproof fabric**, by Charles Macintosh who has been investigating uses for the waste products of gas works. Observing that coal-tar naphtha dis-solves india rubber, Macintosh paints the solution on wool cloth, sealing it.

1824 An **alphabet for the blind,** by 16-year old Louis Braille, a student at the institute for blind children established by Valentin Haüy in Paris. Haüy has invented an embossed type, which blind people can read, but Braille's system of raised dots allows the visually handicapped to write as well.

1831 The **mechanical reaper**, by Cyrus McCormick. Until this time, a farmer's harvest was limited by the amount of human labor available.

1837 The **postage stamp**, by British educator Rowland Hill, for mail which has previously been paid for by the recipient, not the sender.

1839 **Vulcanization**, by Charles Goodyear who has spent ten years (some in debtor's prison) searching for a way to make rubber commercially useful. He finds the answer when he accidentally drops some india rubber mixed with sulfur onto a hot stove.

1856 **Condensed and powdered milk**, by Gail Borden who thought that milk might be more easily stored by drying it.

1867 **Barbed wire**, by Lucien B. Smith, but his invention proves impractical until Joseph F. Glidden improves the design during 1873-1874. Glidden's wire becomes instrumental in controlling the movement of cattle on the Great Plains where farmers and ranchers use it to fence in the open range.

1876 The **telephone**, by Alexander Graham Bell who makes the first telephone call on March 7. "Mr. Watson," Bell says to his associate in the next room, "Come here. I want to see you."

1960

1877 The **phonograph**, by Thomas Alva Edison who improves on experimental models, which have been in development since 1857.

1878 The **microphone**, by David Hughes whose invention marks an important advance in telephony.

1879 The **incandescent light bulb**, by Thomas Edison. Although Humphrey Davy demonstrated as early as 1802 that platinum strips could be heated to produce light, work on the first practical light bulb did not become possible until the development of powerful vacuum pumps, capable of producing a sufficient vacuum inside the bulb. Working independently in England, Joseph Wilson Swan also develops a working bulb, but Edison's concurrent advances in the electrical systems necessary to power the bulb earns him the credit.

1892 The **vacuum flask** (or thermos), by the British chemist Sir James Dewar who invents the double-walled insulator so that he can store volatile liquefied gases, which would otherwise evaporate at room temperature.

1895 The first **safety razor**, by King C. Gillette, who was once advised by an employer to invent something that people could use and then throw away. As a result, the customers would always have to come back for more.

1902 **Radio**, by Reginald Fessenden, who invents a process of amplitude modification by which voices and music can be transmitted using a carrier wave emitted at a constant frequency.

1903 The **airplane**, by bicycle mechanics Wilbur and Orville Wright whose *Flyer I* makes the first powered, sustained flight at Kitty Hawk, North Carolina.

1908 The **vacuum cleaner**, by James Spangler, who subsequently sells the rights to his electrically driven suction sweeper to leather merchant W.H. Hoover.

c. 1912 The **brassiere**, by Paris couturiere Helene Cadolle, because newly shortened corsets no longer provide adequate support for the breasts.

1912 The "separable fastener," by Gideon Sundback. In 1923, B.F. Goodrich uses Sundback's invention on rubber boots, calling it the **zipper**.

1925 **Television**, by John L. Baird who transmits the first moving image with gradations of light and shade that permit the recognition of a human face.

1937 **Instant coffee**, by the Swiss food manufacturer Nestlé which markets the dried powder under the brand name Nescafé.

1947 The **Polaroid camera**, by Edwin Land. The Polaroid can develop a picture in 60 seconds.

1958 The **microchip**, by Texas Instruments engineer Jack Kilby whose invention is the first great advance in the miniaturization race.

1964 The **synthesizer**, by engineer Robert Moog, in collaboration with Wendy Carlos who popularizes the new machine with *Switched-on Bach* (1968).

1972 The **video game**, by Norman Bushnell who develops Pong.

1982 The **compact disc**, by the Sony Corporation and N.V. Phillips, working jointly to establish standards for recording, playback, and size.

The Body Politic

1900 FEB Taking the offensive against the Boers, the British under Herbert Kitchener occupy Bloemfontein. When Johannesburg (MAY) and Pretoria (JUN) fall, the war enters its guerrilla phase. Britain retaliates with a scorched-earth policy and concentration camps that provoke international outrage.

1900 JUN 12 Driven by Germany's desire to control world politics, navy secretary Alfred von Tirpitz pushes through the second Navy Law, which will double the size of the German navy within 20 years.

1900 JUN The Boxer Rebellion reaches its most violent phase, as the Boxers, a secret society whose Chinese name means "The Righteous and Harmonious Fists," move beyond isolated attacks on rural Christian missionaries to riots in Beijing. On June 18, the Empress Dowager calls for all foreigners to be killed.

1900 JUN 25 Using the Boxer Rebellion as an excuse, Russia mobilizes its army in preparation for an invasion of China. Japan, which also has plans for the annexation of Manchuria, mobilizes its troops one day later.

1900 AUG 4 A combined army of Russian, Japanese, British, American, and French troops reaches Beijing, rescuing Chinese Christians and foreigners besieged there since June 20.

Arts & Architecture

1900 L. Frank Baum's *The Wonderful Wizard of Oz* and Beatrix Potter's *Tale of Peter Rabbit* launch the careers of two beloved children's writers.

1902 George Méliès science-fiction film *Voyage dans la Lune* delights audiences with its quirky humor and use of stop-action, the first special effect.

1902 The Abbey Theater in Dublin evolves from a dramatic company established by William Butler Yeats and Lady Gregory. The Irish National Theatre

Religion & Philosophy

1900 During his exile from Russia, Vladimir Lenin begins editing the expatriate newspaper *Iskra* [*The Spark*] in order to promote his revolutionary Marxism.

1900 JAN 25 The House votes 268-50 to unseat Utah congressman-elect Brigham H. Roberts on the grounds that the polygamous Mormon has three wives.

1902 *The Varieties of Religious Experience* culminates William James's investigation into the psychology of religion. His conclusion—that religion

Science & Technology

1900 Max Planck announces the quantum theory of energy: that radiation is transmitted in small units (quanta).

1901 DEC 11 Developing Heinrich Hertz's work on radio, Guglielmo Marconi sends the first signal across the Atlantic.

1902 Karl Landsteiner isolates human blood types, making transfusions safe.

1903 Ernest Rutherford and Frederick Soddy describe radioactivity as a type of modern alchemy by which one element breaks down into another.

Daily Life

1900 APR 30 Instead of jumping to safety, engineer John Luther (Casey) Jones keeps his hand on the brake as his locomotive nears the Vaughan (Mississippi) station, where another train blocks the track. Jones dies in the crash, but saves the lives of his passengers.

6¢ AIR MAIL WILBUR AND ORVILLE WRIGHT
FIRST FREE CONTROLLED AND SUSTAINED POWERED FLIGHT BY MAN
UNITED STATES POSTAGE

1901 SEP 6 The anarchist Leon Czolgosz shoots President McKinley at the Pan-American Exposition in Buffalo. McKinley dies on September 14.

1901 SEP 7 The Boxer Protocol, forced on China by the occupying armies, implements the Open Door policy of American secretary of state John Hay.

1903 JUL 17 The exiled Social Democratic Workers' Party of Russia open its second congress in Brussels. Lenin's Bolsheviks advocate immediate revolution led by a professional vanguard, while the Mensheviks, following Marxist theory more closely, insist that capitalism in Russia must reach a more advanced stage.

1903 NOV 6 The Hay-Bunau-Varilla Treaty grants the United States canal-building rights and guarantees the independence of the new Panamanian republic, which has just seceded from Colombia (with U.S. help).

1904 FEB 8 When Russia reneges on its promise to withdraw its troops from Port Arthur in Manchuria, Japan launches a surprise attack on the Russian warships there, beginning the Russo-Japanese War.

1904 APR 8 Fearing the growth of German militarism, Great Britain and France agree to the Entente Cordiale, which resolves diplomatic tensions caused by colonial competition in Africa and Asia.

Harry Houdini

Society, which plays there, spearheads a literary renaissance featuring the works of playwrights J.M. Synge and Sean O'Casey.

1903 Working for Thomas Edison's film company, Edwin S. Porter directs the most popular film of the decade, *The Great*

Train Robbery, a western adventure notable for its quick cuts from character to character.

1904 Charles McKim models his design for the Pennsylvania Railway Station on the Roman baths of Caracalla.

---

serves a need in times of crisis—offers a means of understanding religion that neither contradicts modern science nor debases religion, as Marx had.

1904 Max Weber publishes his masterful sociological study *The Protestant Ethic*

and the Spirit of Capitalism, in which he links certain capitalist motivations to Puritan anxiety over eternal salvation and damnation. More generally, Weber argues that the truth of capitalism cannot be found merely in economic or technological analyses.

1903 Ivan Pavlov invents the term *conditioned reflex* to describe the subject of his recent research. Pavlov rings a bell each time he gives food to a dog. After 20 to 40 repetitions, the dog begins to salivate when it hears the bell, even if no food is present.

1903 DEC 17 At Kitty Hawk, N.C., bicycle mechanics Orville and Wilbur Wright make the first sustained flight in a heavier-than-air machine. Orville travels 120 feet in the 12 seconds he manages to keep the 745-pound glider (powered by a 12-horsepower engine) aloft.

---

c.1901 Conjurer Harry Houdini begins to earn an international reputation for his daring escapes from shackles.

1902 NOV 18 Brooklyn toy maker Morris Michtom takes a Clifford Berryman cartoon showing President Roosevelt refusing

to shoot a bear cub and displays it beside a stuffed brown bear that Michtom calls "Teddy's Bear."

1904 OCT 27 The New York City subway begins operating from City Hall to West 145th Street.

1900-1904

The Body Politic

1905 JAN 22 In the Russian capital of St. Petersburg, factory workers led by the priest Georgy Gapon march on the Winter Palace to present a petition to Tsar Nicholas II. Imperial troops fire on the demonstrators, killing or wounding several hundred in a massacre that comes to be known as "Bloody Sunday."

1905 MAY 27-28 In the Straits of Tsushima, a task force of Japanese ships wipes out the much larger Russian Baltic fleet. The Japanese victory astounds the world, forcing the Western powers to acknowledge that Asian nations might overturn Western colonial hegemony. In Russia, the tsar's military humiliation adds to the popular unrest.

1905 JUN 27 An officer of the Russian battleship *Potemkin* shoots and kills one of the crew members protesting rations of spoiled meat. The murder triggers a mutiny during which enraged sailors kill the captain and all but five officers. When the *Potemkin* makes port at Odessa, the crew joins in local revolutionary activity before finally surrendering the ship (JUL 8). The incident becomes a powerful symbol for Russia's Marxist revolutionaries.

1905 JUL 7 Radical trade unionists led by Big Bill Haywood found the Industrial Workers of the World, known popularly as the Wobblies, to counter the more conservative influence of Samuel Gompers' American Federation of Labor.

Arts & Architecture

1905 Isadora Duncan makes a controversial trip to Russia, where she introduces modern dance to Sergei Diaghilev. Duncan's style, developed with Ruth St. Denis, establishes modern dance as an uninhibited reaction against the balletic tradition.

1905 Photographer Alfred Stieglitz opens the 291 gallery in New York to promote modern art. Among the artists who have their inaugural shows at the 291 gallery are Auguste Rodin, Henri Rousseau, and Constantin Brancusi, as well as Stieglitz's wife, Georgia O'Keeffe.

Religion & Philosophy

1905 George Santayana, who studied under William James at Harvard, publishes *The Life of Reason*, his "biography of the human intellect." Santayana's work introduces his theory that reason is not purely intellectual, but is allied to the instincts as well.

1905 Sigmund Freud's *Three Essays on the Theory of Sexuality* shocks the medical community with its frank discussion of sexual development during childhood and its suggestion that children's erotic urges often reflect fantasies involving their parents.

Science & Technology

1905 Swiss patent examiner Albert Einstein writes five articles for the *Annalen der Physik*. In them, he presents his Special Theory of Relativity (extending Planck's quantum theory) and also develops the mathematics of energy-mass equivalence ($e = mc^2$).

1906 DEC 24 Using a method he has devised to modulate the amplitude of radio waves (so that they mimic sound waves), Reginald Fessenden broadcasts the first music ever to come out of a radio, playing "O Holy Night" on Christmas Eve and reading from the Bible.

Daily Life

1906 APR 18 A massive earthquake strikes San Francisco, causing fires that raze the city and leave hundreds of thousands homeless.

1907 SEP 12 The *Lusitania,* the world's largest steamship, completes its maiden voyage, setting a new transatlantic speed record between Ireland and New York of 5 days, 54 minutes.

1907 Health officials finally find Mary Mallon, nicknamed Typhoid Mary, in Manhattan. She was diagnosed with

1905 SEP 5 The Treaty of Portsmouth, mediated by Theodore Roosevelt, settles the Russo-Japanese War. Japan receives the Liaodong peninsula and part of Sakhalin Island, while Russia retains northern Manchuria. For his efforts, Roosevelt wins the Nobel Peace Prize.

1906 Great Britain launches the HMS *Dreadnought* with ten 12-inch guns and a top speed of 21 knots, a major event in the arms race leading up to World War I.

1906 APR Forced to accept some form of popular representation, Nicholas II allows elections for a Duma. Once seated, this limited legislature demands land reform, amnesty for political prisoners,

and equal rights for Jews, all of which are unacceptable to the tsar, who dissolves the Duma in July and reasserts absolute imperial rule.

1906 JUN 30 Urged on by Theodore Roosevelt, Congress passes the Pure Food and Drug Act and the Meat Inspection Act, which require accurate labeling and set basic sanitary practices. Supporting the president's efforts are muckraking works such as *The Jungle* (by Upton Sinclair) about the meat-packing industry.

1908 JUL 3 Starting with an army revolt in Resna, the Young Turks lead a national uprising that forces the Ottoman sultan to restore constitutional government.

Albert Einstein

1905 A new exhibition of paintings by Henri Matisse and others scandalizes visitors to Paris's Salon d'Automme. The paintings' brute two-dimensionality and vivid, unrealistic colors lead critics to dub these artists "Les Fauves" [The Wild Beasts].

1907 Pablo Picasso paints *Les Demoiselles d'Avignon* in the cubist style he develops with Georges Braque.

1909 Frank Lloyd Wright designs the Robie House, his masterpiece of the Prairie school.

1907 William James's *Pragmatism* collects a series of celebrated, standing-room-only lectures given at Columbia University on the philosophy of Charles Peirce.

1907 Conservative pope Pius X sparks controversy with his condemnation of the

modernist movement, which reinterprets Catholic doctrine in light of new philosophical and psychological theories.

1908 NOV The Gideons begin placing Bibles in rooms at the Superior Hotel in Iron Mountain, Montana.

1907 Hans Geiger constructs the first Geiger counter to measure radioactivity.

1909 Paul Ehrlich discovers the first bacteriological cure for disease (known as "Dr. Ehrlich's magic bullet," because it kills the disease and not the patient),

when he and his student Shachiro Hata find that arsenic compound 606 kills the syphilis spirochete.

1909 Leo Baekeland produces the first synthetic plastic (Bakelite) that finds widespread commercial application.

---

typhoid during a 1904 epidemic on Long Island, but had escaped quarantine.

1909 APR 6 Arctic explorer Robert E. Peary, his assistant Matthew Henson, and four Eskimos become the first people to reach the North Pole.

1905-1909

1910 MAY 31 The South Africa Act unifies and grants self-government to British colonies in the region. The new constitution, largely the work of Jan Smuts, concentrates power in an all-white parliament, thus denying representation to black Africans.

1910 AUG 22 Japan formally annexes Korea following the subjugation of Korean resistance fighters and the forced abdication of their king. The conquest of Korea establishes Japan as the preeminent military power in Asia.

1911 OCT 10 Mutinous troops in Wuchang seize control of the city, triggering revolts in other cities against imperial authority. These eventually depose the regent to the boy emperor Pu Yi in favor of newly elected president Sun Yat-sen.

1912 APR 14-15 The *Titanic,* considered unsinkable, strikes an iceberg during its maiden voyage to New York and sinks off Newfoundland. In response, federal inspectors issue new regulations (MAY 1) that require every ship to carry enough lifeboats to hold all its passengers.

1912 JUN 18 At the Republican convention, conservatives and progressives split between President Taft and former president Roosevelt. When Taft wins the nomination, Roosevelt forms the Bull Moose (Progressive) party, drawing Republican

Arts & Architecture

1911 Vasily Kandinsky, Franz Marc, and Paul Klee form the expressionist group Der Blaue Reiter in Munich.

1912 MAY 29 At the premiere of *Le Sacre du printemps* [*The Rite of Spring*], Igor Stravinsky's thunderously dissonant score so alarms its Parisian audience that the screams of the patrons drown out the playing of the orchestra. The dancers of Sergei Diaghilev's Ballets Russes continue to perform, however, as choreographer Vaslav Nijinsky gesticulates madly from the wings.

Religion & Philosophy

1910 Bertrand Russell and Alfred North Whitehead publish *Principia Mathematica*, in which they attempt to derive mathematics from purely logical principles.

1911 Anthropologist Franz Boas's *The Mind of Primitive Man* will be used to refute many of the racial superiority theories of the 1920s and 1930s.

1912 Carl Jung and Sigmund Freud split over the publication of Jung's *Psychology of the Unconscious*, which disputes Freud's theories on the sexual origins of

Science & Technology

1910 Thomas H. Morgan begins researching the genetic structure of fruit flies. His work leads him to discover the role of the X and Y chromosomes.

1911 On high-altitude balloon flights, Victor Hess discovers cosmic radiation.

1912 Pursuing new research on dietary-deficiency diseases, Casimir Funk prepares an amine compound (he calls it *vitamine*) that can prevent beri-beri.

1913 René Lorin takes out the first patent for jet propulsion.

Daily Life

1910 JUL 4 Jack Johnson, the first black heavyweight champion, beats former champ Jim Jeffries in 15 rounds in Reno, Nevada. Called the "Great White Hope," Jeffries has been coaxed out of retirement by white boxing fans unable to abide a black champion.

support and helping to elect Democrat Woodrow Wilson in a landslide.

1914 JUN 28 In Sarajevo, a Serb nationalist assassinates Austrian archduke Francis Ferdinand, setting in motion a domino effect that produces World War I.

1914 JUL 28 After presenting a humiliating ultimatum, Austria-Hungary rejects Serbia's conciliatory response and declares war, prompting Russia to mobilize in defense of fellow Slavs. When Germany calls for Russian demobilization go unheeded, Germany declares war on Russia (AUG 1) and France (AUG 3). Germany's invasion of Belgium (AUG 3) compels Britain, with no interest in Serbia, to enter

the war because of a mutual defense pact. The U.S. declares itself neutral (AUG 5).

1914 OCT 19-NOV 22 The "race to the sea" begins near Ypres, where the Allies have been trying to turn the Germans' flank. Anticipating a renewed Allied offensive, the Germans counterattack successfully on October 20. After November 11, heavy rains and the resulting mud force both sides to entrench along a stabilized front that hardly moves until late in 1918.

1914 JUN The victorious revolutionary forces of Pancho Villa and Venustiano Carranza enter Mexico City after defeating the dictatorship of General Victoriano Huerta.

Sun Yat-sen

1913 FEB 17 The postimpressionist Armory show opens in New York City, introducing the works of the European avant garde to America.

1913 NOV After receiving several rejections, Marcel Proust pays for the publica-

tion of *Du côté du chez Swann* [*Swann's Way*], the first volume in his *À la recherche du temps perdu*.

1914 While directing his second comedy for Mack Sennett, Charlie Chaplin develops his tramp character.

---

neurosis. For his part, Freud objects to Jung's movement toward mysticism.

1913 Edmund Husserl's *General Introduction to Pure Phenomenology* outlines a systematic method for investigating one's own consciousness (because, as

Descartes pointed out, consciousness is the only thing that surely exists).

1913 Sigmund Freud's *Totem and Taboo* explains how cultural norms defining what is acceptable and what is not influence human psychology.

1913 Niels Bohr develops the modern conception of the atom, according to which electrons orbit as planets do about a nuclear sun. Bohr's work owes much to Rutherford, particularly his alpha-particle bombardments of metal foil, which proved the existence of a nucleus.

1913 William Knudsen designs the first factory assembly line for the Ford Motor Company, which begins producing 1,000 low-priced Model T's a day.

1914 Andrew Ellicott Douglass introduces tree-ring dating (dendrochronology).

1911 MAR 25 A fire at a New York sweatshop, the Triangle Shirtwaist Co., kills 146 workers trapped inside the building by blocked fire exits. The tragedy leads to building code reform and increased organizing by the International Ladies Garment Workers' Union (founded 1900).

1912 Jim Thorpe wins the pentathlon and decathlon at the Stockholm Olympics, but loses his medals a year later because he played semipro baseball in 1909 and 1910.

1914 AUG 15 The 50-mile-long Panama Canal (begun 1904) opens to traffic.

1910-1914

The Body Politic

1915 MAY 7 A German submarine sinks the British liner *Lusitania* without warning, drowning 1,198 passengers. U.S. public opinion turns fiercely against Germany.

1916 FEB 21 Launching a massive attack on the fortress-city Verdun, the Germans make progress, but French reinforcements hold and, by August, turn the tide. The battle continues until the end of the year, by which time the name Verdun has come to fill the public imagination with the horrors of modern warfare. French casualties alone number 300,000.

1917 JAN 16 British intelligence intercepts the Zimmermann Telegram, in which the German foreign minister invites Mexico to enter the war as a German ally. On April 2, Wilson asks Congress for a declaration of war to make the world "safe for democracy" (passed APR 6).

1917 MAR 8 The February Revolution (its date being FEB 23 on the old Russian calendar) breaks out in Petrograd. Tsar Nicholas II abdicates March 15, after which Alexander Kerensky leads an ineffectual provisional government.

1917 APR 16 Vladimir Lenin arrives at the Finland Station in Petrograd. The Germans have allowed the exiled Lenin to return from Switzerland in a sealed train car, knowing that his Bolsheviks favor Russia's abandonment of the war.

Arts & Architecture

1915 FEB 8 D.W. Griffith's spectacular and scandalously racist film *The Birth of a Nation* opens in Los Angeles.

1916 Artists who frequent Zurich's Cabaret Voltaire begin a new anti-bourgeois, anti-aesthetic movement in reaction to the slaughter of World War I. They name it Dada by randomly opening a dictionary to the French word for *hobby-horse*.

1917 Franz Kafka believes his newly contracted tuberculosis to be a psychosomatic symptom of his own inner turmoil.

Religion & Philosophy

1918 Oswald Spengler publishes the first volume of *The Decline of the West*, a study in the philosophy of history that argues for a cyclical view of civilization. Spengler insists that every culture passes through an irreversible cycle of growth and decay.

1919 The New School for Social Research begins informally as a center for the embryonic social sciences.

1919 Karl Barth publishes *Epistle to the Romans*, which emphasizes the "otherness" of God, causing a sensation in the

Science & Technology

1915 Albert Einstein's General Theory of Relativity suggests that, as a result of the presence of matter, space is curved. This idea, though confusing, does account for irregularities in the orbit of Mercury that cannot be explained by Newtonian physics.

1916 AUG 15 Britain uses the first tanks (converted tractors) in their disastrous Somme offensive.

1917 By vibrating crystals electrically, French physicist Paul Langevin produces ultrasonic waves of a very short wave-

Daily Life

1915 "What this country really needs," Vice President Thomas Marshall declares during a tedious Senate debate, "is a good five-cent cigar."

1916 OCT 16 Margaret Sanger opens the first birth control clinic, in Brooklyn.

1918 SEP An international influenza epidemic reaches New York, Boston, and Philadelphia. Confounding health care workers, it quickly spreads through 46 states, killing nearly half a million Americans, in addition to the 20 million fatalities worldwide.

1917 OCT 14 The French execute Mata Hari after convicting the exotic dancer of passing military secrets to the Germans.

1917 NOV 6 Lenin leads the October Revolution (OCT 26 on the old calendar), which ousts Kerensky and establishes a new revolutionary Bolshevik government.

1919 JAN 15 Seizing control of Berlin, the reactionary Freikorps arrest and murder Communist extremists Rosa Luxemburg and Karl Liebknecht during the abortive Spartacist Revolt in Germany.

1919 FEB 6 The new National Assembly convenes in Weimar to write a new German constitution (adopted in July).

1919 MAR Lenin founds the Third International (Comintern) to promote worldwide revolution. His action alarms bourgeois interests, contributing to public distrust of the new Russian government.

1919 APR 13 When 10,000 unarmed Indians gather in Amritsar to protest colonial rule, British troops fire into the crowd, killing or wounding 1,500 and rousing Mohandas Gandhi to begin his *satyagraha* campaign for independence.

1919 JUN 28 The Treaty of Versailles, signed in the Hall of Mirrors, compels Germany to pay unrealistic and unfair reparations. It soon becomes a symbol of betrayal and humiliation to every German.

Kaiser Wilhelm II

1917 Marcel Duchamp signs and exhibits a urinal that he has found in the street. He calls this conceptual sculpture (entitled *Fountain*) a *ready-made.*

1919 Walter Gropius founds the Bauhaus school of architecture following William

Morris's principle of combining quality workmanship with function-driven design.

1919 John Reed, the only American to be buried in the Kremlin, writes *Ten Days That Shook the World* about the Bolshevik Revolution, to which he was a witness.

---

theological community. Barth criticizes liberal Protestantism for its growing affinity to psychology and rationalism, because neither can prove the existence of God. "Belief cannot argue with unbelief," the Swiss theologian declares, "it can only preach to it."

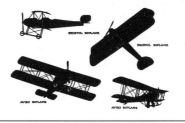

---

length. He immediately applies this discovery to submarine detection, but the war ends before sonar can be perfected.

1918 Harlow Shapley calculates the diameter of the Milky Way to be 300,000 light years (actually 100,000).

1919 Francis William Aston, an assistant to J.J. Thomson, invents the mass spectrograph, which Thomson uses to isolate two types of neon atoms with different atomic weights (neon 20 and neon 22). Their work proves the existence of stable isotopes.

1919 OCT 1-9 The Cincinnati Reds defeat the heavily favored Chicago White Sox, five games to three, in the World Series, but the victory is soon tainted by revelations that eight "Black Sox," including Shoeless Joe Jackson, conspired with gamblers to throw the games.

1919 OCT 28 Congress passes the Volstead Act over President Wilson's veto, providing an enforcement mechanism for the newly ratified Eighteenth Amendment (Prohibition). The new law defines as intoxicating (and thus bans) all beverages containing more than 0.5% alcohol.

1915-1919

1 9 1 4   **June 28** The Pan-Serbian nationalist Gavrilo Princip assassinates Archduke Francis Ferdinand, heir presumptive to the Austro-Hungarian throne, during a military inspection in the Bosnian capital of Sarajevo. Serbians have lately been demanding the annexation of territory in southern Austria-Hungary primarily populated by fellow Slavs.

July 6 Before leaving on his annual cruise to the North Cape, Kaiser Wilhelm II assures Austria-Hungary of Germany's support should Serbian aggression lead to war.

July 23 Seizing the opportunity to humiliate Serbia, Austria-Hungary delivers an ultimatum that it knows Serbia cannot accept. According to the Austrians' political calculus, the threat of German intervention will keep Serbia's powerful ally Russia on the sidelines.

July 24 Russia announces that it will not permit Austria-Hungary to crush the Serbs.

July 25 An acquiescent Serbia accepts all but two of the Austrian demands, offering to submit these particular infringements on Serbian sovereignty to international arbitration.

July 28 Having returned home the day before, Kaiser Wilhelm learns of Serbia's response to the Austrian ultimatum and immediately informs Austria-Hungary that he no longer sees any justification for war. He is too late, however. Urged on by German ministers while the Kaiser was away, Austria declares war on Serbia. Russia orders a partial mobilization.

July 30 When Austria-Hungary responds with a partial mobilization of its own on the Russian frontier, Russia orders a general mobilization.

July 31 Germany demands that Russia halt its mobilization within 24 hours and gives Russia's ally France just 18 hours to declare its neutrality.

August 1 When Russia and France ignore its demands, Germany orders a general mobilization and declares war on Russia. France mobilizes.

August 3 After declaring war on France, Germany puts in motion a 20-year-old plan, prepared by then chief of staff Alfred von Schlieffen, that begins with an invasion of neutral Belgium. Attacking from the north, the Germans hope to bypass France's fortifications along their common border.

August 4 Although Great Britain has no interest in Serbia, and no obligation to defend either Russia or France, it does have a treaty obligation to defend Belgium. Therefore, Britain declares war on Germany.

August 5 The United States declares its neutrality.

August 14 Following his woeful Plan XVII, French general J.J.C. Joffre counterattacks in Lorraine. Joffre's plan, however, seriously misjudges the Germans' strength and strategic goals.

September 5 In the Treaty of London, the Allied Powers (Britain, France, and Russia) agree not to seek a separate peace with the Central Powers.

September 6-9 In the first battle of the Marne, a French counteroffensive halts the southeastward advance of Germany's Fourth and Fifth Armies.

September 11 Unable to reduce the fortresses of Lorraine, the German general staff orders the retreat of its armies in France. The Allies give chase as far as the Lower Aisne, where the Germans make a successful stand. Both sides begin to dig systems of trenches (salients).

October 20 The German navy begins its submarine campaign against merchant shipping when a U-boat [*Unterseeboot*] sinks the steamship *Glitra* after evacuating its crew.

November 1 Russia declares war on Turkey after the Turkish fleet, led by the German warship *Goeben*, crosses the Black Sea and bombards Odessa on October 29-30. Fearing that Russia might use the war as an excuse to seize the Dardanelles, Turkey had signed a secret treaty with Germany on August 2. But Britain's entry into the war on August 4 so alarmed the Turks that they reconsidered the move, even to the point of proposing an alliance with Russia, which Russia refused.

November 22 As winter approaches and the rains begin, the first battle of Ypres settles down into trench warfare as French reinforcements finally arrive to support the British Expeditionary Force in Belgium.

1915   **February 4** After torpedoing two ocean liners without warning, the Germans declare that, from February 18, they will consider British waters to be a war zone within which all ships, neutral or not, may be subject to attack.

1 9 1 5 **February-March** Repeated French assaults on German trenches in
(continued) Champagne gain 500 yards at the cost of 50,000 lives.

April A French offensive against the German's Saint-Mihiel salient southwest of Verdun takes 64,000 lives and gains nothing.

April 22 During an attack against the Allies' Ypres salient, the Germans
use chlorine gas for the first time on the Western Front, where General
Erich Falkenhayn's strategy has Germany maintaining a defensive posture.

April 25 In response to a Russian call for help against the Turks, the
British begin landing troops on the Gallipoli peninsula on the western
shore of the Dardanelles. Mustafa Kemal (later Kemal Atatürk) leads a vigorous defense against Australian and New Zealand troops, who finally win a
bridgehead on the Aegean side of the peninsula.

April 26 Italy signs a secret treaty with the Allies, who convince the
Italians to abandon their obligations under the Triple Alliance (with
Germany and Austria-Hungary) in exchange for promises of territorial
expansion at the Austrians' expense. Italy declares war on May 23.

May 7 German U-boats sink the *Lusitania* on its way from New York to
Liverpool with 2,000 passengers and 173 tons of ammunition aboard. The
1,198 civilian deaths, including those of 128 Americans, outrages the U.S.

September At a conference of socialists in Zimmerwald, Switzerland,
internationalists decry the imperialist war and criticize those socialists
who have succumbed to "bourgeois patriotism." Most call for peace, but
Lenin and the Bolsheviks argue for transforming the war into a revolution.

September 18 Prevailing over the naval high command, Germany's civilian leadership orders a suspension of U-boat attacks against civilian targets
in the English Channel and the Atlantic. The diplomatic corps has been concerned that continued attacks will provoke America to enter the war.

September 25 Launching an offensive along the Western Front, the Allies
lose 242,000 men and the Germans 141,000, while the front fails to move.

1 9 1 6 **January 8-9** The British navy completes the evacuation of the Gallipoli
peninsula. The failed invasion has cost the Allies 213,980 lives.

February 21 Continuing Falkenhayn's strategy of victory through attrition, the Germans attack the French stronghold of Verdun. The outlying forts Douaumont and Vaux fall on February 25 and June 7, respectively.

April 25 German cruisers bombard Yarmouth and Lowestoft in an attempt to lure a manageable part of the British Grand Fleet away from its base at Scapa Flow. Admiral Reinhard Scheer's plan calls for this decoy mission to lead the pursuing British battle groups north to Norway, where the entire German High Seas Fleet can engage and destroy them.

May 30 Intercepting a German signal, the British learn of the trap and send the entire fleet from Scapa Flow to intercept the Germans at Skagerrak.

May 31 The British and German fleets fight the battle of Jutland, one of the largest naval engagements in history. The 12-hour encounter produces extensive damage and loss of life on both sides, of which the British get the worst. But the Grand Fleet's losses are not nearly enough to threaten Britain's overall naval superiority or its domination of the North Sea.

July 1 The first battle of the Somme begins when 11 British divisions attack across a 15-mile front. Convinced that a week's advance bombardment will permit his soldiers to move ahead quickly, British commander Sir Douglas Haig is shocked to find his 60,000 men, inching slowly forward under the weight of 66-pound packs, slaughtered by German machine-gun fire.

September 15 The first tanks are used by the British in their Somme offensive, but in numbers far too small to influence the fighting, which continues for two months before early rains suspend operations. In the 18-week battle, the British and French suffer 614,000 casualties and the Germans 440,000.

October 24 Counterattacking the Germans, who have been weakened by the Somme offensive, the French forces at Verdun under Philippe Pétain recapture Fort Douaumont. Fort Vaux is retaken eight days later.

1 9 1 7   **January 9** Chief of the German general staff Paul von Hindenburg and his quartermaster general Erich Ludendorff succeed in reinstituting unrestricted submarine warfare (effective February 1), which they hope will scuttle German chancellor Theobald von Bethmann Hollweg's plans for negotiating peace with the Allies.

1917
(continued)

January 16 The British Admiralty intercepts and deciphers a coded telegram from German foreign minister Arthur Zimmermann to his ambassador in Mexico. In the telegram, Zimmermann instructs the German ambassador to propose that Mexico become Germany's ally should American enter the war, in which case Mexico might recover Texas, New Mexico, and Arizona.

January 22 Soon after his reelection, President Woodrow Wilson resumes his efforts at mediation with a speech advocating "peace without victory."

February 3 Although the U.S. breaks off diplomatic relations with Germany over the resumption of unrestricted submarine warfare, American public opinion remains unwilling to support entry into the war.

February 23 The Germans consolidate their position by withdrawing from bulges along the Western Front into newly constructed fortifications behind the smoother and shorter Siegfried Line.

March 1 The text of the Zimmermann Telegram, which the British government passed to Wilson on February 24, appears in U.S. newspapers, leading to an immediate public demand for war with Germany.

April 6 In response to renewed U-boat attacks on American merchant ships, President Wilson declares war on Germany.

May 15 After German machine guns transform R.G. Nivelle's spring offensive into a fiasco, Pétain replaces him as chief of the French general staff. Pétain's first task is to put down a mutiny among 16 army corps, after which he adopts a defensive strategy until U.S. troops can arrive.

July 6 Leading a handful of Arabs against 1,200 Turks, T.E. Lawrence (Lawrence of Arabia) captures Aqaba. A thoroughly unprofessional yet highly effective soldier, Lawrence has already provoked the rebellion of Hashemite emir Husayn ibn Ali, which now threatens both Turkish control of Palestine and the vital Hejaz Railway.

July 31 While Pétain waits for the Americans, Haig launches an ill-considered offensive in Flanders. To soften up the Germans, Haig has ordered two weeks of bombardment, but the 4,500,000 shells, while announcing the British intentions, do little to harm German machine gunners safe within their concrete pillboxes. The third battle of Ypres bogs down when rains (that had long been forecast) turn the field into a swamp.

1918   **January 8** President Wilson announces his war aims in the Fourteen Points. The last point calls for "a general association of nations" to preserve the integrity and freedom of each state.

March 3 Russia signs the Treaty of Brest-Litovsk with Germany, conceding vast amounts of territory in exchange for peace, during which the Bolsheviks hope to consolidate the gains of their recent revolution.

March 21 Convinced that they must strike before the bulk of the American army arrives, the Germans launch their first major offensive since 1914.

April 21 The German flying ace Baron von Richthofen, who has shot down 80 planes during dogfights, dies on the ground, trapped in his red Fokker during an Allied attack near Amiens. Hermann Goering replaces him as squadron commander.

July 15 With a second offensive, the Germans attempt to build on the success of the first. But a counterattack, orchestrated by new Allied commander Ferdinand Foch and launched July 18, forces a hasty German retreat. By this time, U.S. troops are arriving at the rate of 300,000 per month.

August 8 Having reversed the Germans' progress, the British push ahead with a counteroffensive along the Somme, striking with 450 tanks and overwhelming the Germans' forward positions. Ludendorff, who later calls this "the black day of the German Army," begins to advocate a negotiated peace.

September 12 John J. Pershing leads an independent U.S.army against the Saint-Mihiel salient, capturing this position held by the Germans since 1914.

October 3-4 During the night, the German government sends a note to Wilson requesting an armistice and peace negotiations on the basis of Wilson's Fourteen Points.

October 29 A mutiny begins at Kiel among the sailors of the High Seas Fleet. The uprising soon escalates into a democratic revolution in Germany, culminating with the November 9 abdication of Kaiser Wilhelm II and the establishment of a provisional government under Frederick Ebert.

1919   **January 19** The Paris Peace Conference opens, leading to the signing of the Treaty of Versailles on June 28 in the Hall of Mirrors.

1917 **March 8** Factory workers mark International Women's Day (February 23 by the old Russian calendar) with protests in Petrograd over food shortages. The demonstrations soon become riots, sparking the February Revolution.

March 11-12 Nicholas II, who has been a notably ineffectual and despotic tsar, sends troops to restore order, but the soldiers refuse to fire on the crowds of people and mutiny instead. Although the tsar dissolves the moderate Duma, he quickly finds that his authority has collapsed. The Duma's leaders set up a Temporary Committee to maintain order and make democratic reforms, while the workers join with mutinous soldiers to form the revolutionary Petrograd Soviet. Socialist-controlled Soviets based on the Petrograd model soon appear throughout Russia but refrain from seizing power, believing the country to be in the throes of a bourgeois revolution.

March 13 Discussions begin between the Duma and the Petrograd Soviet.

March 14 The Petrograd Soviet issues its "Order Number One" exercising control over the army.

March 15 The Duma announces the formation of a Provisional Government, which the Petrograd Soviet has decided not to join. Prince Georgy Lvov becomes prime minister, with Constitutional Democratic party leader Pavel Milyukov as foreign minister and Alexander Guchkov of the conservative Octobrist party as war minister. The moderate socialist Alexander Kerensky of the Labor Group becomes the minister of justice and unofficial liaison to the Petrograd Soviet. In the evening, at Pskov, Nicholas II abdicates in favor of his brother Michael, who refuses the throne on March 16.

March 21 Lvov's Provisional Government arrests and detains Nicholas II.

March 25 Lev Kamenev and Joseph Stalin become the first high-ranking Bolshevik leaders to return from tsarist exile in Siberia. They endorse the Petrograd Soviet's preliminary acceptance of the Provisional Government and set about organizing their small (fewer than 30,000 members) but influential party. Meanwhile, both Vladimir Lenin in Switzerland and Leon Trotsky in New York denounce the Provisional Government.

April 10 When he is refused permission to return to Russia through Allied territory, Lenin arranges passage through Germany, which is anxious to have Russia withdraw from World War I. The Germans have the Bolshevik leader ride inside a sealed train car until he reaches the Swedish border.

April 16 Lenin arrives at the Finland Station in Petrograd, where he issues the April Theses calling for the overthrow of the Provisional Government. "All power to the Soviets!" he declares, despite the fact that the Bolsheviks are a minority there and the Menshevik majority wants no such power. Soon Trotsky, along with other left-wing Mensheviks, joins Lenin's call for a second revolution. During the next six months, Bolshevik party membership will swell to 200,000 people as food shortages continue, Russia remains at war, and the Provisional Government founders.

May 3 The publication of foreign minister Milyukov's May 1 note to the Allies promising to continue the Russian war effort triggers two days of demonstrations known as the April Days (because of the old style calendar).

May 7-12 The Bolsheviks hold a party conference. Although many members thought Lenin mad, or perhaps confused by the complexity of the situation, when he called for power to the Soviets, the party now endorses that view.

May 18 After the forced resignations of Milyukov and Guchkov, the cabinet is reorganized to include two socialist ministers whose participation has been approved by the executive committee of the Petrograd Soviet.

June 16-July 6 At the first All-Russian Congress of Soviets, delegates from the local councils meet to define a common program.

June 27 The Provisional Government sets August 30 as the date for elections to the Constituent Assembly, which will draft Russia's new democratic constitution. Major policy decisions are postponed until after the assembly's first scheduled meeting September 12.

June 29 War minister Kerensky orders a Russian offensive in Galicia.

July 16 As a German counteroffensive turns Kerensky's Galician strategy into a rout, a huge mob in Petrograd acts spontaneously on Lenin's call for a second revolution, beginning the violent July Days.

July 17 Sailors from the Kronstadt naval base join armed demonstrators as troops loyal to the Provisional Government fire on the mob. Meanwhile, the Provisional Government raids Bolshevik party headquarters and closes its newspaper *Pravda*. Lenin goes into hiding with Gregory Zinoviev.

July 18 Government troops finally restore order, ending the July Days.

July 20 Prince Lvov resigns as prime minister. Kamenev and Trotsky are among the Bolshevik leaders arrested.

July 21 Kerensky becomes the leader of a moderately socialist Provisional Government. At his direction, the Bolshevik party is outlawed.

July 23 The Petrograd Soviet announces its support for the reorganized Provisional Government.

July 31 Kerensky makes Lavr Kornilov commander-in-chief of the army. The conservatives look to General Kornilov as the one man who can permanently restore order.

August 22 Lenin escapes to Finland. Meanwhile, the government postpones elections for the Constituent Assembly.

August 25 Kerensky opens the State Conference in Moscow, at which the deep divisions between the right and the moderate left become apparent.

September Peasants impatient with the progress of reform begin to seize the estates of their landlords, while workers take control of the factories. Food shortages worsen, and the army's desertion rate increases rapidly as peasant soldiers return home to join in the land seizures. While the government struggles with legalities, the Bolsheviks enjoy great success with their "Peace, Land, and Bread" program, which responds directly to the demands of the populace.

September 7 Kornilov orders troops to Petrograd. The general claims they are needed to protect the government, but Kerensky believes the move to be the start of a right-wing coup. Reluctantly, he turns to the left for support, even to the extent of relaxing his ban on Bolshevik activity.

September 12 Kornilov's troops desert him, and the coup collapses, polarizing the right and moderate left in the coalition cabinet.

September 13 The Petrograd Soviet passes the first resolution sponsored by its new Bolshevik majority.

September 16 Kerensky calls for a Democratic Conference to consider Russia's future. Hiding in Finland, Lenin orders an armed insurrection. But the Bolshevik Central Committee, believing that power will come to the party democratically, decides to participate.

September 21 Released from jail four days earlier, Trotsky becomes chairman of the Petrograd Soviet, consolidating Bolshevik control.

September 27-October 5 On the sixth day of its deliberations, the Democratic Conference votes to constitute a Pre-Parliament to continue its work until elections for the Constituent Assembly can be held.

October 4 Under Bolshevik direction, the Petrograd Soviet passes a resolution against the Democratic Conference, declaring that the upcoming second Congress of Soviets will settle the question of power. That same day, however, the Bolshevik Central Committee decides to participate in the Pre-Parliament.

October 20 Led by Trotsky, the Bolshevik delegation walks out of the Pre-Parliament during its opening session (although the vote in favor of the walkout was a close one). Later that evening, Lenin secretly returns to Petrograd to campaign personally for armed insurrection, his letters to this effect having been generally ignored by the Central Committee.

October 22 Meeting in plenary session, the Petrograd Soviet resolves to arm the workers.

October 23 At Lenin's urging, the Bolshevik Central Committee votes 10-2 to "place the armed uprising on the agenda."

October 29 The Bolshevik Central Committee confirms its resolution of October 23 and calls for the workers to prepare for an armed seizure of power. Kamenev threatens to resign. Zinoviev also rejects the move.

November 1 Kerensky reaffirms the readiness of the government to smash the Bolsheviks should they rise against it.

November 4 The Petrograd garrison agrees to obey only those orders countersigned by the Military Revolutionary Committee set up by the Bolsheviks.

November 6 The October (by the old style calendar) Revolution begins when Kerensky sends officer cadets to close the Bolshevik newspapers, causing the MRC to sends its troops to reopen them.

November 7 Proclaiming the overthrow of the Provisional Government, Lenin attacks the Winter Palace, which falls to Bolshevik forces around midnight.

The Body Politic

1920 JAN 16 The League of Nations, created by a covenant in the Treaty of Versailles, holds its first meeting, but the refusal of the U.S. Senate to ratify the treaty considerably weakens the League's diplomatic influence.

1922 APR 7 Warren Harding's corrupt interior secretary Albert Fall secretly grants the Mammoth Oil Company exclusive rights to the Teapot Dome oil reserves in Wyoming, for which he receives a $200,000 bribe. Harding escapes personal implication in the unfolding scandal, but it adversely affects his health. A strenuous cross-country trip finally breaks him, and Harding dies exhausted in a San Francisco hotel (1923, AUG 2).

1922 OCT 31 Emphasizing the need for order, Benito Mussolini becomes the first fascist leader in Europe when his Black Shirts march on Rome to break up a general strike. Mussolini, who prefers the title *Il Duce*, soon embarks on a popular program of industrialization and massive public works.

1922 NOV 1 Turkish military leader and civil reformer Mustafa Kemal (later Kemal Atatürk) abolishes the Ottoman sultanate (since 1300). A year later, he becomes president of the new Turkish republic (proclaimed 1923, OCT 29).

1923 JAN Claiming that Germany has defaulted on its reparations payments,

Arts & Architecture

c.1920 Developed as a means of teaching socialist values, the Soviet avant-garde theater thrives until 1932, when Joseph Stalin comes to power. The constructivist artists who build the bold, industrial sets delight in technology and the possibilities of the future.

1922 Sylvia Beach, owner of the Paris bookstore Shakespeare & Co., publishes James Joyce's *Ulysses.* The U.S. Post Office has already burned sections of the work that appeared in a 1918 journal, and London authorities will soon seize the second British edition.

Religion & Philosophy

1921 *Psychological Types* presents Carl Jung's theory of two personality types: the extrovert (outward-looking) and the introvert (inward-looking).

1921 Ludwig Wittgenstein publishes his 75-page *Tractatus Logico-Philosophicus,*

largely written as he fought in the Austrian army during World War I. The book addresses the issue of how people can make themselves understood through language. Wittgenstein's answer is that they can use words and sentences as signs to create "pictures" of reality.

Science & Technology

1920 Psychiatrist Hermann Rorschach begins showing his patients accidental inkblots, asking, "What might this be?"

1921 JUL 27 Frederick Banting and Charles Best isolate the antidiabetes hormone insulin.

Daily Life

1920 JUN 8-12 The predilection for cigar-smoking among party bosses at the Republican presidential convention, especially during back-room negotiations that end with the compromise selection of Warren G. Harding, brings the phrase "smoke-filled room" into the vernacular.

1921 MAY 19 President Harding signs the Immigration Restriction Act, establishing a quota system and immigration ceiling for the first time in U.S. history.

1922 AUG 28 Radio station WEAF in New York City airs the first commercial.

France occupies the industrial Ruhr. Objecting vehemently, the Weimar government begins printing money to finance the payments, which causes such hyperinflation that bread prices rise as people wait in line to purchase some. The same dollar that bought four marks before the war buys one million in August and 130 billion by November.

1923 NOV 8-9 With the blessing of World War I commander Erich Ludendorff, Adolf Hitler attempts a coup d'etat in Munich (the Beer Hall Putsch), for which he receives a lenient prison term of five years. During the eight months he actually serves, Hitler composes the first part of *Mein Kampf* [*My Struggle*].

1924 JAN 21 Lenin's death ends his plans for economic reform and leads to a power struggle among the revolutionary leadership, particularly between Leon Trotsky and Joseph Stalin.

1924 AUG 16 Having appointed him to find a solution to the German economic crisis, the Allied Reparations Committee now accepts the recommendation of Charles G. Dawes that American loans be made to Germany. By passing American dollars through Germany to France and Britain, the Dawes Plan stabilizes the European economy. When the 1929 crash halts U.S. loan payments, however. Dawes's stopgap measure fails, and the international banking system collapses.

Benito Mussolini

1922 T.S. Eliot, the leading modernist in poetry, publishes *The Waste Land*, reducing the 800-line manuscript to 433 lines at the suggestion of Ezra Pound.

1924 André Breton's *Manifeste du surréalisme* defines this growing movement that seeks to bridge the divide between reason and madness by probing the subconscious as defined by Freud.

1924 George Gershwin composes *Rhapsody in Blue*, one of the first works to fuse jazz with symphonic techniques.

1922 John Dewey, a pragmatist in the manner of Peirce and James, completes *Human Nature and Conduct*, in which he analyzes the nature and function of habit.

1923 Gyorgy Lukács's *History and Class Consciousness* revives the philosophical side of Marxism, lately overshadowed by the economic determinism of *Das Kapital*.

1924 I.A. Richards' *Principles of Literary Criticism* helps establish the Cambridge Critics, whose methodological approach depends upon a close reading of the text.

1922 NOV 7 In the Valley of the Tombs of the Kings near Luxor, British egyptologist Howard Carter reaches the sealed entrance to the grave of the boy pharaoh Tutankhamen. Carter had discovered the first signs of this sensational find three days earlier.

1924 Aiming the new 100-inch Mount Wilson telescope at the Andromeda galaxy, Edwin Hubble resolves the outer edges well enough to spot cepheid variable stars. Using these, he calculates the galaxy to be nearly one million light years away.

1923 APR 18 Yankee Stadium opens in New York. Sportswriters call it "The House That Ruth Built," because tickets bought by the Babe's fans paid for it. The Red Sox had sold Ruth to the Yankees in 1920 for $125,000, a price that was both unheard of and a bargain.

1923 SEP 15 Ku Klux Klan violence forces Oklahoma governor J.C. Walton to declare martial law.

1924 Notre Dame goes undefeated in nine games under innovative coach Knute Rockne, who stresses the forward pass.

1920-1924

The Body Politic

1925 APR Ultraconservative army officer Paul von Hindenburg wins election as the second president of the Weimar Republic, but Germany's economic distress continues, leading to political instability.

1927 MAR As part of a Northern Expedition to conquer the Beijing government, China's Nationalist party seizes control of Shanghai and Nanjing, where Kuomintang troops loot the homes and businesses of foreigners. Some conservative Nationalists, alarmed at what they consider to be Communist excess, encourage Chiang Kai-shek, head of the Kuomintang, to expel the Communists. On April 12, Chiang's troops begin to arrest and execute their Communist allies.

1927 AUG 23 Nicola Sacco and Bartolomeo Vanzetti are executed for murders committed during a shoe factory robbery. Socialists had protested the case, arguing that the men were convicted on the basis of prejudice and their anarchist beliefs, not on the merits of the evidence presented against them.

1927 OCT Mao Zedong leads several hundred peasants into the mountains of Hunan, where he trains them in rural guerrilla warfare, beginning his 22 years in "the wilderness."

1928 JAN Stalin has Trotsky exiled to Alma-Ata in central Asia and, a year later, banished from the Soviet Union. Trotsky

Arts & Architecture

c.1925 Originating among southern blacks, the wild, jazz-age Charleston becomes America's most popular dance.

1926 MAY 5 Sinclair Lewis declines a Pulitzer, because awards make writers "safe, polite, obedient, and sterile."

1926 The founding of the Book of the Month Club introduces rural America to a new variety of literary styles.

1927 Duke Ellington's band begins a five-year engagement at the popular Cotton Club in Harlem.

Religion & Philosophy

1925 JUL 10-21 Representing the state of Tennessee, William Jennings Bryan prosecutes schoolteacher John Scopes for violating a state law that prohibits the teaching of Charles Darwin's theory of evolution. Clarence Darrow defends Scopes and, during the trial, puts Bryan on the stand to defend the law. Scopes is convicted and fined $100, but the conviction is reversed on appeal.

1926 MAY 18 The sudden disappearance of revivalist Aimee Semple MacPherson makes headlines all across the nation.

Science & Technology

1925 Wolfgang Pauli's exclusion principle explains how electrons are distributed within each shell.

1925 OCT Working in his attic, John L. Baird transmits the first television image of a recognizable human face.

1926 Erwin Schrödinger revises the concept of the atom. Assuming Louis de Broglie's theory of the wave nature of particles to be correct, Schrödinger rejects the solar-system analogy and instead visualizes each electron as a wave that curves around the nucleus.

Daily Life

1925 Clarence Birdseye perfects a means of quick-freezing food that preserves its original taste.

1926 Henry Ford continues his string of labor innovations, introducing the 40-hour work week to limit overproduction.

then travels the world until Mexico grants him political asylum in 1936. Having thus eliminated his chief rival, Stalin moves to abandon the New Economic Policy, which marked Lenin's retreat from some of his earlier Bolshevik theories about state-run capitalism. Instead, Stalin collectivizes the farms, following a tragic policy that leads to the execution of millions of peasants.

1928 OCT 10 When the second campaign of the Northern Expedition succeeds in capturing Beijing, the Kuomintang proclaims a new government at Nanjing.

1928 AUG 27 The most ambitious of the many postwar peacemaking efforts, the Kellogg-Briand Pact outlaws war as an instrument of national policy. Although Secretary of State Frank Kellogg wins the Nobel Peace Prize in 1929 for his work, the failure to provide an enforcement mechanism renders the treaty useless.

1929 OCT 29 On Black Tuesday, the U.S. stock market crashes. Hysterical stockholders, many of whom have bought stock on margin (that is, using credit), trade more than 16 million shares in a desperate effort to salvage a small piece of their paper fortunes. Some investors commit suicide rather than face bankruptcy. By December, stock market losses total more than $25 billion in value, unleashing a worldwide depression.

Babe Ruth

1927 OCT 6 Vitaphone releases *The Jazz Singer*, starring Al Jolson, the first commercially successful "talkie."

1928 Walt Disney's short *Steamboat Willie*, introducing Mickey Mouse, takes advantage of the new sound technology.

1929 Ludwig Mies van der Rohe designs the German Pavilion at the Barcelona International Exhibition in his famous International Style. The huge onyx, chrome, marble, and glass structure has no functional constraints. It could easily be a giant spatial sculpture.

When she reappears just as suddenly in Mexico, an investigation reveals that Sister Aimee ran off with a church official.

1927 The difficulty of Martin Heidegger's *Being and Time* is matched only by its immediate influence. Heidegger later adopts to Nazism and distances himself from his Jewish mentor Husserl.

1928 APR 19 With its completion, the *Oxford English Dictionary* (conceived in 1857) becomes the definitive historical dictionary of the English language.

1926 MAR 16 Robert Goddard launches the first liquid-fueled rocket.

1927 Werner Heisenberg publishes his Uncertainty Principle: the more certain one is of a particle's position, the less certain he can be of its momentum.

1927 Working back from Hubble's claim of an expanding universe, Georges Lemaître postulates the "cosmic egg" (big bang).

1928 Alexander Fleming discovers penicillin when bread mold accidentally kills bacteria he has been culturing.

1927 MAY 21 Charles Lindbergh lands at Orly, outside Paris, completing the first nonstop solo transatlantic flight aboard his monoplane *Spirit of St. Louis*.

1927 SEP 27 "Sultan of Swat" Babe Ruth hits his 60th home run of the season.

1928 MAY 11 Schenectady's WGY begins the first regular TV broadcasts. The 90-minute shows air three times a week.

1929 FEB 14 Chicago mobsters, probably sent by Al Capone, gun down Bugs Moran's gang in the St. Valentine's Day Massacre.

1925-1929

The Body Politic

1930 JAN 23 Wilhelm Frick's appointment as interior minister of Thuringia makes him the first Nazi to hold office. In the upcoming July elections, the Nazis will win six million votes. Even those who know Hitler to be a thug consider him a good defense against Bolshevism.

1930 MAR As unemployment reaches four million, Congress appropriates funds for relief programs, but Hoover refuses to approve unemployment benefits, claiming they diminish individual responsibility.

1931 SEP 18 The invasion of Manchuria, beginning with an attack on Shenyang, defines the Japanese imperialist policy that dominates Asia before World War II.

1932 NOV 8 Promising a "new deal," Franklin Roosevelt beats Hoover by a landslide and carries a Democratic majority into Congress with him. The coalition he puts together of working class, urban, minority, and southern voters will elect two generations of Democratic presidents before Ronald Reagan proves its debasement in 1980.

1933 JAN 30 At President Hindenburg's invitation, Adolf Hitler becomes chancellor of Germany. The Beer Hall Putsch has shown Hitler the benefits of achieving power legitimately, rather than by force.

1933 FEB 27 When fire destroys the Reichstag, Hitler blames the Communists

Arts & Architecture

1931 MAY 1 The steel-framed, 1,250-foot Empire State Building becomes the world's tallest structure (until 1954).

1931-1932 Inspired by a visit from Piet Mondrian, Alexander Calder begins to experiment with abstract sculpture.

Marcel Duchamp later dubs the hanging, motor-driven, geometric forms that Calder develops *mobiles*.

c.1932 As mandated by Stalin, the heroes of Socialist Realism succeed against the odds, unencumbered by flaws or tragedy.

Religion & Philosophy

1930 Wallace Fard, who emigrated to the U.S. from Mecca, founds the Temple of Islam in Detroit, preaching that blacks must prepare for an inevitable race war and giving new Arabic names to his followers to replace their "slave" names. When Fard disappears without a trace in

1934, Elijah Muhammad (originally Elijah Poole) succeeds him as leader of the Nation of Islam, also known as the Black Muslims.

1932 Karl Jaspers' *Philosophy*, which presents a systematic exegesis of existen-

Science & Technology

1930 FEB 18 Clyde Tombaugh discovers Pluto in the spot where Percival Lowell reckoned it might be.

1930 Ernest O. Lawrence invents the cyclotron, an atom smasher essential for research into nuclear structure.

1931 Studying radio static, Bell Telephone engineer Karl Lansky discovers radio emissions from outer space, thus beginning the science of radio astronomy.

1932 When James Chadwick cannot detect a new particle in a Wilson cloud

Daily Life

1931 MAR 25 Nine young black men are arrested and charged with raping a white woman in Scottsboro, Alabama. Ignoring the lack of evidence, a racist jury finds the "Scottsboro Boys" guilty, but the Supreme Court eventually overturns their conviction (1935, APR 1).

1931 OCT 24 The Port of New York Authority completes the George Washington Bridge under budget and eight months ahead of schedule.

1932 MAR 1 The kidnapping of 20-month-old Charles Lindbergh, Jr., trans-

and assumes emergency powers that allow Hermann Goering to purge the police. Meanwhile, the private Nazi militia (Sturmabteilung) begin a campaign of political terror. Not surprisingly, elections held March 5 give the Nazis the Reichstag majority they need to pass the Enabling Act, creating a de facto dictatorship.

1933 MAR 4 In his inaugural address, Roosevelt promises decisive action, and in his first hundred days, the president delivers. He signs sweeping New Deal legislation that creates the National Recovery Administration, the Tennessee Valley Authority, the Civilian Conservation Corps, and the Federal Emergency Relief Administration.

1934 AUG 19 A plebiscite held after the death of Hindenburg approves Hitler's assumption of the presidency. Though he is now both chancellor and president, Hitler prefers to be called the *Führer*.

1934 OCT 15 Having recovered from the Japanese invasion of Manchuria, Chiang Kai-shek's Kuomintang army resumes its successful assaults on rural Communist bases in central China. Breaking through the Kuomintang lines, Mao Zedong leads his pregnant wife and 100,000 soldiers on the famous Long March westward. Mao's army crosses 6,000 miles and 18 mountain ranges before reaching a safe haven in remote Shan Xi province. Only 8,000 Communists survive the march.

Franklin Delano Roosevelt

1932 Olympic swimmer Johnny Weissmuller begins his second career as Tarzan opposite Maureen O'Sullivan's Jane.

1933 Diego Rivera completes his mural *Man at the Crossroads* for Rockefeller Center. Its depiction of a figure closely resembling Lenin, however, leads to public calls for the work's destruction.

1933 Forty-year-old Mae West, recently jailed on obscenity charges, makes her film debut in *She Done Him Wrong*, adapted from her Broadway play *Diamond Lil*.

---

tialism, shares many concerns found in Heidegger's work, but the friendship between the two men ends with Heidegger's entry into the Nazi party.

1934 Arnold Toynbee publishes the first volume of his *Study of History* in reaction to pessimistic works such as Spengler's *Decline of the West* (1918). Toynbee declares that civilizations grow through the response of creative minorities to challenges. Thus, a society's decline occurs not inevitably, but only when its leaders fail to act creatively.

---

chamber, he concludes that it must have a neutral charge and calls it a neutron.

1932 Edwin Land, a Harvard student on leave, develops Polaroid, a sheet of plastic embedded with crystals that polarize light.

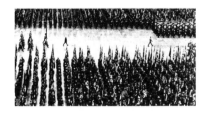

---

fixes the country. A $50,000 ransom is paid as America holds its breath, but the baby is found dead on May 12.

1933 MAR 12 Franklin Roosevelt begins his "fireside chats," the first of which concerns the reopening of the nation's banks, closed by the president during the previous week to prevent runs.

1934 JUL 22 FBI agents shoot Public Enemy Number One John Dillinger as the gangster leaves the Biograph Theater in Chicago.

1930–1934

The Body Politic

1935 APR 8 The Emergency Relief Appropriation Act funds the Works Progress Administration, which will provide jobs for more than two million unemployed workers building roads, bridges, parks, and other public works.

1935 SEP 15 The Nazi Nuremberg Laws strip Jews of their German citizenship.

1935 OCT Mussolini's invasion of Ethiopia reverses the positive image of Fascist Italy in Europe and the U.S.

1936 JUL 17 The Spanish Civil War begins when fascist general Francisco Franco mutinies against the recently elected left-wing republican government.

1937 FEB 5 President Roosevelt proposes the reorganization of the Supreme Court, prompting conservatives to accuse him of trying to stack the court with liberals.

1937 APR 26 German planes horrify the world by obliterating the Basque village of Guernica. Franco denies Nazi involvement, but Goering admits in 1946 that Guernica was a test of German air power.

1937 DEC 13 Five months after the start of the Sino-Japanese War (begun JUL 7), invading Japanese forces massacre 200,000 civilians in the "rape of Nanking."

1938 MAR 11 In the Anschluss, German troops roll into Austria, where they are

Arts & Architecture

1936 Benny Goodman forms a jazz trio, the first to be racially integrated, with Teddy Wilson and Lionel Hampton.

1937 Nazis organize the Entartete Kunst [Degenerate Art] exhibit in Munich to defame the works of Bolsheviks and Jews.

The show includes works by Kandinsky, Picasso, and psychotic mental patients.

1937 Pablo Picasso's *Guernica* expresses his rage at the carnage of the Spanish Civil War. He choose as his subject the brutal bombing of a defenseless town.

Religion & Philosophy

1936 A.J. Ayer's *Language, Truth and Logic* provides a bridge between British linguistic analysis and the logical positivism of the Vienna Circle.

1938 In *The Culture of Cities*, Lewis Mumford uses his study of urban life to

explore the relationship between culture and technological change.

1938 Benedetto Croce calls *History as the Story of Liberty* the definitive form of his "philosophy of spirit" developed through his writings in *La Critica* (found-

Science & Technology

1935 Antonio Egas Moniz performs the first prefrontal lobotomy in an attempt to cut off severely disturbed mental patients from past associations.

1937 Alan Turing shows that mathematical problems can be solved mechanically

as long as they can be broken down into tasks that a machine can perform.

1939 When the AM radio moguls ignore his new static-free technology, Edwin Armstrong spends $300,000 of his own money to build the first FM radio station.

Daily Life

1935 MAY 24 The Reds beat the Phillies, 2-1, in the major leagues' first night game at Cincinnati's Crosley Field.

1935 SEP 8 Louisiana governor and populist ideologue Huey Long is assassinated inside the state capitol in Baton Rouge.

1936 The U.S. finishes second to Germany at the Berlin Olympics, but Jesse Owens wins four gold medals, rebutting Hitler's theories of racial superiority.

1937 MAY 6 In the first coast-to-coast radio broadcast, Herbert Morrison reports

greeted by cheering crowds. Two days later, Hitler announces the reunification of Austria with the German Reich.

1938 SEP 30 Britain, France, Germany, and Italy agree at Munich that Germany will annex the Czech Sudetenland, ostensibly because three million ethnic Germans live there. The real reason is that Prime Minister Neville Chamberlain believes appeasement will avert war.

1938 NOV 9-10 Nazi propaganda minister Joseph Goebbels organizes a "spontaneous" demonstration to protest the murder of a Paris embassy official by a Polish Jew. During Kristallnacht, 7,500 Jewish businesses are destroyed.

1939 AUG 23 The Germans and Soviets shock the world when foreign ministers Joachim von Ribbentrop and V.M. Molotov sign a nonaggression pact. Secret protocols outline how Eastern Europe, including Poland, will be divided once war breaks out.

1939 SEP 1 In a blitzkrieg of tanks, the German army invades Poland, sending 54 divisions into the country without a declaration of war. France and Britain, which have both signed mutual defense pacts with Poland, offer to negotiate with Germany once its troops are withdrawn. When Hitler fails to respond, the Allies issue an ultimatum. When that is ignored, they declare war (SEP 3).

Adolf Hitler

1938 JUN Superman appears in a comic book by Jerry Siegel and Joe Shuster.

1938 OCT 30 Orson Welles's *War of the Worlds* radio play about Martians invading New Jersey (delivered as a news program) causes thousands to panic.

1939 "Frankly, my dear, I don't give a damn," says Rhett Butler in *Gone With the Wind*. It is the first use of profanity in a major motion picture.

1939 Bandleader Harry James discovers Frank Sinatra working in a roadside cafe.

---

ed 1903). Croce's work is put to the test by Italian Fascism, which he resists.

1938 When Mussolini begins to adopt the Nazi's racial policies, Pope Pius XI takes a much less compromising position toward the Fascist government in Italy.

1939 Paul Müller develops the insecticide DDT, for which he wins the Nobel Prize in medicine (1948).

1939 AUG 2 Urged on by fellow emigré scientists, Albert Einstein writes to President Roosevelt, warning him to be vigi-

lant lest the newly recognized fission process lead to the development of a German atomic bomb.

1939 SEP 14 The first working helicopter, Igor Sikorsky's VS-300, makes its maiden flight.

---

the dramatic explosion of the *Hindenburg* at Lakehurst, New Jersey.

1937 JUL 2 Amelia Earhart and Frederick Noonan, flying a twin-engined Lockheed Electra, disappear over the Pacific Ocean during their globe-circling flight.

1938 Hungarian journalist Laszlo Biro develops the first practical ballpoint pen, which he patents in 1943 after fleeing to Argentina to escape the Nazis.

1938 Stockings made from the "miracle fabric" nylon go on sale in the U.S.

1935-1939

The Body Politic

1940 MAY 10 Winston Churchill replaces the discredited Neville Chamberlain as prime minister of England.

1940 AUG 20 An agent sent by Joseph Stalin uses a pickax to murder exiled Communist leader Leon Trotsky in his heavily guarded house near Mexico City.

1940 SEP 27 In a move to deter U.S. involvement in the war, the Axis powers sign the Tripartite Pact, which provides for a united front against any nation declaring war on one of them.

1940 NOV 26 The Germans begin enclosing the Jewish ghetto in Warsaw, describing the move as a "health measure."

1941 MAR 11 President Roosevelt signs the Lend-Lease Act, which authorizes the transfer of matériel (payment deferred) to nations considered vital to U.S. interests. Eventually, $50 billion in equipment will be shipped to the Allies.

1941 MAY 7 A German weather ship taken off Iceland yields secret documents relating to the German Enigma code. A U-boat captured May 9 provides both a machine and code books. The Germans never discover their loss, and soon the Allies solve the riddle of the Enigma.

1941 DEC 7 Early on a Sunday morning, Japanese bombers attack the headquarters of the Pacific Fleet at Pearl Harbor.

Arts & Architecture

c.1940 Dizzy Gillespie, Charlie Parker, and Thelonius Monk develop the improvisatory "bebop" style of modern jazz.

1940 Ernest Hemingway bases *For Whom the Bell Tolls* on his experiences as a correspondent during the Spanish Civil War.

THERESIENSTADT

Religion & Philosophy

1941 Psychoanalyst Erich Fromm's *Escape from Freedom* outlines the historical development of human freedom. In this work, Fromm argues that fascism appeals to people because its totalitarian qualities resolve many of the anxieties and insecurities of modern life.

1942 Albert Camus' *The Myth of Sisyphus* presents a sympathetic analysis of nihilism and the concept of the "absurd."

1943 In *Being and Nothingness*, Jean-Paul Sartre, the leading voice of existentialism (along with Heidegger), posits an

Science & Technology

1941 DEC 6 Following Einstein's advice, President Roosevelt authorizes atomic research under the inconspicuous title of the Manhattan Engineer District.

1942 DEC 2 For the first time, the cadmium control rods are pulled out of the

atomic pile built secretly under the University of Chicago football stadium. At 3:45 PM, Enrico Fermi confirms the presence of self-sustaining nuclear fission.

1943 Jacques-Yves Cousteau develops the aqualung, which recycles exhaled air

Daily Life

1940 SEP 16 Congress passes the Selective Service Act, establishing the first peacetime draft in U.S. history.

1941 JUL 17 Two Cleveland Indians pitchers combine to stop Joe DiMaggio's 56-game hitting streak (begun MAY 15).

1941 DEC 7 Under attack at Pearl Harbor, Chaplain Howell M. Forgy tells antiaircraft gunners on the *New Orleans* to "praise the Lord and pass the ammunition."

1941 DEC 27 The Office of Price Administration begins rationing essential com-

1942 JAN 20 At the suburban Wannsee Conference, Adolf Eichmann works out the practical details of the "final solution" to the Jewish problem.

1942 FEB 20 The president authorizes the internment of Japanese-Americans (nisei), whose property is bought up by land speculators at wickedly low prices.

1943 APR 13 Germany announces the discovery of mass graves in the Katyn forest. The 4,100 Polish officers whose bodies are uncovered there were murdered by the Soviets in 1940.

1943 APR 19-MAY 16 The Warsaw Ghetto Uprising of some 50,000 Jews (down from 500,000) convinces the Germans to close the ghetto and ship the remaining Jews to extermination camps.

1943 JUN 20-21 The migration of 300,000 southerners to war plants near Detroit produces tensions that explode into race riots, killing 35 people.

1944 JUN 6 The D-Day invasion (Operation Overlord) begins just after midnight when the largest invasion fleet in history crosses the English Channel.

1944 OCT 14 Nazi authorities force Field Marshal Erwin Rommel to commit suicide for his part in the July 20 assassination attempt against Hitler.

Winston Churchill

1941 Eugene O'Neill completes his autobiographical masterpiece *Long Day's Journey into Night* about a day in the life of a disintegrating family.

1941 RKO releases *Citizen Kane*—starring its writer, director, and producer Orson Welles— despite attempts by William Randolph Hearst to have the film, based loosely on Hearst's life, banned.

1943 Rodgers and Hammerstein's *Oklahoma!* is the first musical to integrate production numbers into the plot.

---

opposition between being, or *thingness,* and consciousness, or *nothingness.*

1943 Reinhold Niebuhr's theological treatise *The Nature and Destiny of Man*, which challenges liberal faith in the inevitability of progress, becomes extremely influential in postwar American politics. Its attitude that the world is a place often hostile to American liberal values provides the theoretical justification for many of the realpolitik policies adopted by the State Department during the Cold War.

---

through chemicals that absorb the carbon dioxide and make it breathable again.

1944 Oswald Avery and colleagues at the Rockefeller Institute announce that they have found the basic genetic material of the cell: deoxyribonucleic acid (DNA).

1944 Working with IBM, Harvard professor Howard Aiken completes the Mark I, the first modern digital computer.

1944 John von Neumann publishes *The Theory of Games,* which applies his minimax theorem (1928) to two-player games.

---

modities. Starting with rubber, the OPA next rations sugar and gasoline.

1942 JUN 22 V-mail service begins between New York and London. V-mail letters are microfilmed, sent overseas, and then reprinted before being delivered.

c.1943 Zoot suits become fashionable, arising out of the black jazz culture.

1944 JUN 22 President Roosevelt signs the Serviceman's Readjustment Act (GI Bill of Rights), which legislates education and housing benefits for veterans.

1940-1944

1939 **March 26** Germany and Poland break off talks on Hitler's demands for the annexation of Danzig and a new road through the Polish Corridor.

March 31 British prime minister Neville Chamberlain promises to defend Poland from attack. A preliminary defense agreement is signed April 6.

April 28 Hitler renounces the German-Polish Nonaggression Pact of 1934 and the Anglo-German Naval Agreement of 1935.

May 3 Stalin relieves Soviet foreign minister Maksim Litvinov, a Jew, and replaces him with V.M. Molotov, who immediately opens negotiations with the Germans, while at the same time pursuing talks with Britain and France.

May 22 Weary from military adventures in Spain and Ethiopia, Mussolini agrees to the Pact of Steel with Germany in the mistaken belief that Germany will not begin a war for at least three years.

August 23 Molotov and Nazi foreign minister Joachim von Ribbentrop sign the German-Soviet Nonaggression Pact, even though Hitler's repression of German Communism has made the pact seem inconceivable. A secret protocol divides Poland and the Baltic republics into German and Soviet spheres of influence.

September 1 Germany invades Poland employing a new, highly mobile strategy called *blitzkrieg* [lightning war]. Using the Luftwaffe [air force] and Panzer tank divisions, the Germans strike quickly and with overwhelming force.

September 3 When Hitler refuses to withdraw his troops from Poland, Great Britain and France declare war on Germany.

September 17 The German conquest of Poland is nearly complete as Soviet troops invade from the east, ostensibly to "liberate" the Slavs there.

October The French develop the first in a series of plans to counter a German offensive through Belgium similar to that which opened World War I. The French correctly consider the heavily fortified Maginot Line (along the Franco-German border) to be impregnable, but they nevertheless misjudge the Germans' route through Belgium, discounting the possibility of an attack through the heavily wooded hills of the Ardennes.

November 30 The Soviet Union attacks Finland after its demands for territorial concession are refused.

1940   **April 9** The Germans invade Denmark and Norway. Before the surrender of Finland on March 12, Winston Churchill had been advocating Allied operations in neutral Norway as a means of both supplying Finland and cutting off Germany's importation of Swedish ore.

May 10 The Germans launch their long-awaited invasion of The Netherlands (capitulates May 15) and Belgium (capitulates May 28). In Britain, Winston Churchill succeeds Chamberlain as prime minister.

May 26-June 4 Unable to arrest the Germans' march through the Low Countries, the British evacuate Allied troops from Dunkirk in northern France. Luftwaffe bombing prevents use of the harbor, but small craft manned by amateur seamen ferry 338,000 British, French, and Belgian soldiers from the beaches to the Royal Navy waiting in the English Channel.

June 10 Italy formally declares war on Britain and France.

June 14 The Germans enter Paris. Two days later, after the resignation of French premier Paul Reynaud, World War I hero Philippe Pétain forms a new government and sues for peace. An armistice signed at Rethondes on June 22 divides France between the German-occupied north and a southern zone nominally controlled by Pétain's government (installed at Vichy on July 1).

August 2 In advance of the planned invasion of England, Luftwaffe chief Hermann Goering orders massive air raids to crush British fighter power (the battle of Britain). Beginning August 8, the raids, involving 1,500 aircraft daily, primarily target Royal Air Force installations. In mid-September, however, the Blitz begins as the Luftwaffe shifts the focus of its raids to London and the civilian population (until April, 1941).

September 27 Germany, Italy, and Japan sign the Tripartite (Axis) Pact.

1941   **March 11** The Lend-Lease Act authorizes the transfer of war matériel to U.S. allies overseas. The program, originally developed to aid Britain, is quickly extended to China in April and the U.S.S.R. in September.

March 24-April 11 Sent to North Africa to relieve the struggling Italians, Erwin Rommel leads the newly formed Afrika Korps in an unexpected offensive that succeeds in recapturing Cyrenaica from the British. Tobruk alone holds out, despite Rommel's siege.

1941
(continued)

June 22 The Germans attack the Soviet Union in Operation Barbarossa. Originally scheduled for 1943, the invasion of Russia was moved up by Hitler to intimidate Britain and discourage U.S. intervention in Europe.

July 12 The U.S.S.R. and Great Britain formally become allies, although the Soviets notably refuse to commit to the restoration of prewar Poland.

August 14 Roosevelt and Churchill announce the formulation of the Atlantic Charter, which describes principles upon which peace should be based.

November 26 Secretary of State Cordell Hull sends a diplomatic note to the Japanese, demanding that they remove their troops from China and Southeast Asia. After this, the Japanese see little point in continuing negotiations.

December 6 With the Germans just 20 miles from the Kremlin, Soviet general Georgy Zhukov leads the first important Soviet counteroffensive.

December 7 The Japanese launch a surprise attack on the U.S. Pacific Fleet based at Pearl Harbor, Hawaii. All eight battleships in port are hit as 2,330 servicemen die. The fleet's three aircraft carriers, out on patrol, escape. On the same day (December 8, local time), Japanese bombers attack U.S. air bases in the Philippines, destroying more than half of the army's planes in the Far East.

December 10 The Japanese begin to land infantry on the principal island of Luzon in the Philippines. Commanding general Douglas MacArthur organizes a retreat to the Bataan Peninsula and Corregidor Island across Manila Bay.

1942

March 11 Vowing "I shall return," MacArthur leaves the Philippines for Australia. Jonathan Wainwright takes command of the U.S. forces in Bataan.

April 9 Bataan surrenders to the Japanese, who force 70,000 prisoners to walk 63 miles to a POW camp. During the course of the infamous Bataan Death March, thousands of these soldiers are executed, while others die of starvation and disease. Corregidor falls during the night of May 5-6.

April 18 Jimmy Doolittle leads a daring air raid on Tokyo that dramatically improves American morale, which has been low since Pearl Harbor. Doolittle's squadron of 16 B-25 bombers takes off from the carrier *Hornet*, then flies past Tokyo and lands behind friendly Chinese lines.

May 4-8 During the battle of the Coral Sea, the first in which the fighting is conducted entirely by carrier-based aircraft, the U.S. fleet turns back a Japanese invasion force headed for Port Moresby, New Guinea.

May 26 Despite being outnumbered nearly two to one, Rommel attacks the British Eighth Army just west of Tobruk. Much to his dismay, Rommel learns that the U.S. has reinforced the British with new Grant tanks that take out one-third of Rommel's force in a single day. On May 29, the Germans take up a defensive position in the Cauldron, from which they repel numerous British assaults with consistently heavy losses.

June 3-6 The battle of Midway begins when U.S. bombers strike a Japanese fleet headed for strategic Midway Island in the North Pacific. During the ensuing battle, a turning point in the Pacific war, the Japanese lose all four of their heavy carriers as well as most of their front-line pilots.

June 11 Rommel moves against the depleted British Eighth Army, which three days later begins a hasty retreat back toward Egypt.

July 1-17 During the first battle of el-Alamein, the British halt Rommel's advance, thereby saving Egypt.

August 7 In the first major U.S. offensive of the Pacific war, the First Marine Division invades Guadalcanal, one of the southern Solomon Islands, where the Japanese have been constructing an air base.

September The German Fourth Panzer Army unites with the Sixth Army under General Friedrich Paulus for a joint attack on Stalingrad. As the Germans push closer, however, the front becomes ever more compact, and the resistance of the Red Army stiffens.

October 23-November 4 The British Eighth Army, now under General Bernard (Monty) Montgomery, begins the second battle of el-Alamein after reinforcements raise its tank strength to 1,230 (against 210 tanks of similar quality for the Germans and Italians). Although Hitler orders the recently ill Rommel back to the front, even the Desert Fox cannot hold back the British armor.

November 8 Dwight D. Eisenhower commands Operation Torch, the first joint Allied offensive in the European theater. Torch lands more than 100,000 U.S. and British soldiers on the coast of northwest Africa in three operations near Casablanca, Oran, and Algiers.

1942
(continued)

November 13-15 An attempt by Japan to reinforce its garrison leads to the naval battle of Guadalcanal, during which Admiral William F. (Bull) Halsey disrupts the landing operation. The marines finally take control of Guadalcanal on February 8 after six months of tenacious and bloody fighting that will be repeated often during the U.S. island-hopping campaign.

November 19 Marshal Zhukov leads a decisive Soviet counterattack at Stalingrad. The encircled Paulus holds out long enough for German troops in the Caucasus to pull back, but finally surrenders on January 31.

1943

January 14-24 Meeting in Casablanca, Roosevelt and Churchill agree that the next Allied step should be an invasion of Sicily, rather than the opening of a second front in France as Stalin has long demanded. Roosevelt's spontaneous call for Germany's unconditional surrender, however, dismays those Germans working for Hitler's overthrow in the hope that his downfall might result in a negotiated peace.

February 20 Faced with Allied armies on two fronts, Rommel strikes first in the west, overwhelming the U.S. in the Kasserine Pass. But George Patton rallies the First Army and leads a counteroffensive that, linking up with Montgomery's Eighth Army, forces the surrender of Tunis on May 7. By May 12, the Allies have captured 252,000 soldiers of the vaunted Afrika Korps.

April 5 The Germans announce the discovery of more than 4,000 Polish officers buried in mass graves in the Katyn Forest, west of Smolensk. Although the Soviets deny it, they are believed to be the bodies of men missing from Soviet prison camps in eastern Poland since the spring of 1940.

April 19-May 16 During the Warsaw Ghetto Uprising, Polish Jews, who have recently learned from escapees of the gas chambers awaiting them, violently resist deportations to the Treblinka concentration camp.

July 10 Montgomery's Eighth Army and Patton's Seventh begin the conquest of Sicily with beach landings on the southern coast of the island.

July 24-25 After Mussolini reveals a German plan to evacuate southern Italy, the Fascist Grand Council votes a resolution against him, leading to Il Duce's resignation. The next day, King Victor Emmanuel III orders Mussolini's arrest and instructs Pietro Badoglio to form a new government.

August 17 The Sicilian campaign ends with the Allies' entry into Messina.

September 3 Crossing the Strait of Messina, Montgomery's Eighth Army begins the invasion of Italy. Meanwhile, the combined U.S.-British Fifth Army under Mark Clark lands at Salerno, south of Naples, on September 9. Although Montgomery encounters little resistance, his northward progress is slowed by the lack of decent roads. At Salerno, Field Marshal Albert Kesselring launches a six-day counterattack that threatens to push 165,000 Allied troops back into the Mediterranean.

September 8 The announcement of an armistice agreement between Badoglio and Eisenhower results in a German coup against the Badoglio government, during which Rome is occupied, Italian soldiers are disarmed, and Mussolini is freed to lead a new puppet government formed behind the German lines.

November 28-December 1 The Big Three meet for the first time in Tehran. Stalin renews his promise to intervene against Japan in exchange for renewed assurances from Roosevelt and Churchill that they will indeed open the long-awaited second front in France during 1944.

1944 **January 22** Blocked by the Gustav Line at Monte Cassino, the Allies land 50,000 troops behind the German lines at Anzio, just 33 miles south of Rome. Delays in crossing the Alban Hills, however, allow Kesselring time enough to mobilize his reserves for a counterattack on February 3.

May 11 The Allied attack that begins the battle of Monte Cassino succeeds in breaching the Gustav Line at a number of points, forcing the Germans to withdraw troops from Anzio and leading to a breakout there on May 26 after months spent trapped on the beaches. The Allies occupy Rome on June 4.

June 6 On D-Day, Operation Overlord lands 156,000 soldiers on the beaches of Normandy. The largest naval invasion in history, Overlord employs 5,000 invasion craft, 1,200 warships, and 10,000 planes.

June 13 The first V-1 missiles, Hitler's latest secret weapon designed by Wernher von Braun, strike London from bases in the Pas-de-Calais.

July 20 Colonel Claus von Stauffenberg plants a bomb inside a briefcase at Hitler's headquarters in East Prussia. The bomb explodes, but Hitler survives and subsequently orders the execution of 5,000 people, of whom only 200 or so are actually implicated in the assassination plot. Rommel, implicated as a conspirator, is allowed to commit suicide on October 14.

1944
(continued)

July 25 Allied troops, supported by George Patton's Third Army, break through the German lines at Avranches, cutting off German troops in Brittany and transforming the fighting into a mechanized dash to the Rhine.

July 31 When the Red Army reaches the suburbs of Warsaw, the Polish Underground rises up. The Germans rally, however, throwing back the Soviets and putting down the revolt. Meanwhile, the latest Soviet advance, covering 450 miles in just five weeks, stalls for six months on the Vistula.

August 19 The French Resistance rises against the Germans in Paris, which is liberated by a French division under Jacques Leclerc six days later.

August 21-October 7 At the Dumbarton Oaks conference, American, Soviet, British, and Chinese representatives discuss the creation of a new international organization to replace the League of Nations. The most important issues remain unresolved, however, until the San Francisco conference (April 25-June 26, 1945), which establishes the United Nations.

October 20 The U.S. lands four divisions on Leyte in the Philippines, and MacArthur has his picture taken wading ashore, thus fulfilling his famous promise to return. The battle of Leyte Gulf, which follows three days later, ends October 25 in a major defeat for the Japanese.

December 16 A surprise Panzer counteroffensive through the Ardennes achieves limited success, creating a bulge in the German front. The Battle of the Bulge ends when Patton's Third Army compels the Germans to withdraw.

1945

February 4-11 The Big Three meet for the last time at Yalta in the Crimea. At Stalin's insistence, the western Allies agree that the provisional government of postwar Poland should be formed around the Lublin committee, which Stalin controls, rather than the exiled Polish government in London.

February 13-14 Intensifying their raids as German air defenses diminish, American and British planes firebomb Dresden, of inconsequential value as a military target, killing perhaps 135,000 civilians.

February 19 Marines land on the heavily fortified island of Iwo Jima, where a Japanese fighter base threatens bombing missions aimed at Tokyo from U.S. bases in the Marianas. Although the American flag is planted on Mount Suribachi on February 22, the fighting continues until March 16.

March 9-10 Switching to nighttime raids and napalm, U.S. bombers hit Tokyo, destroying 25% of the city, killing 80,000 people, and leaving 1,000,000 homeless.

April 1 The largest amphibious operation of the Pacific war lands 60,000 American troops on Okinawa in the final prelude to an invasion of Japan. The 75,000 Japanese troops there respond fiercely with 355 kamikaze attacks. The battleship *Yamato*, the most powerful warship in the world, is sent to Okinawa with only enough fuel for the outward journey.

April 11 The western Allies reach the Elbe, but halt there because of Eisenhower's unwillingness to sacrifice the lives necessary to capture Berlin.

April 12 President Roosevelt dies at his retreat in Warm Springs, Georgia.

April 25 Having encircled Berlin, the Soviets join hands with Americans on the Elbe. Hitler prepares to make his final stand against the Red Army.

April 28 Italian partisans kill Mussolini as he tries to escape the country dressed as a German soldier.

April 30 Hitler and his mistress Eva Braun (whom he married two days earlier) commit suicide in Hitler's bunker beneath the Chancellery.

May 7 The Germans surrender to Eisenhower at his Reims headquarters. In the days before the official end to the war on May 8, 65% of the German Army of the East (1,800,000 men) move into the U.S. and British zones.

July 2 The battle for Okinawa ends with 12,000 Americans and 100,000 Japanese dead, 34 ships sunk, and 368 damaged.

July 17-August 2 At a conference in the Berlin suburb of Potsdam, Truman reveals to Stalin that the U.S. has successfully tested an atomic bomb at Alamogordo, New Mexico, on July 16.

August 6 Flying from Tinian Island in the Marianas, a specially modified B-29 named the *Enola Gay* drops an atomic bomb on the city of Hiroshima. A second bomb is dropped on Nagasaki three days later.

August 10 Japan announces that it will agree to the surrender terms outlined at Potsdam. MacArthur accepts the formal Japanese surrender on September 2 aboard the U.S.S. *Missouri* in Tokyo Bay.

The Body Politic

1945 FEB 4-11 Meeting at Yalta to discuss postwar Europe, Stalin, Roosevelt, and Churchill agree to divide Germany into zones and to support free elections in the defeated and liberated countries.

1945 APR 13 The world first learns of the Holocaust when British troops liberate Bergen-Belsen concentration camp.

1945 AUG 6 The *Enola Gay* drops the first atomic bomb used against people on the city of Hiroshima, killing 80,000. Another atomic bomb kills 40,000 people at Nagasaki on August 9.

1945 OCT 18 The International Military Tribunal holds its first session in Nurem-berg to hear the cases of Nazis accused of "crimes against humanity."

1946 MAR 5 In a speech at Fulton, Missouri, Churchill borrows a phrase from Joseph Goebbels, declaring that an "iron curtain" has descended across Europe.

1947 MAR 12 Truman announces U.S. aid to Greece and Turkey, which are both threatened by Communist rebels and Soviet expansionism. His strongly anticommunist stance becomes the Truman Doctrine.

1947 JUN 5 Secretary of State George Marshall unveils his plan for a European recovery to be financed by the U.S. The Marshall Plan provides $12 billion in aid

Arts & Architecture

c.1945 Buckminster Fuller begins work on the first geodesic dome.

1945 Eschewing the glamor and spectacle of Hollywood, Roberto Rossellini inaugurates the gritty neorealist movement in film with his *Open City*.

1947 Jackson Pollock develops his radical "drip painting" method, causing *Time* magazine to nickname him "Jack the Dripper." About the same time, Jasper Johns begins using his splatter technique. In the work of both artists, process supersedes subject.

Religion & Philosophy

1945 In *The Open Society and Its Enemies*, Karl Popper attacks historicism—the idea found in Plato, Hegel, and Marx that general laws set history's course.

1946 JUL 7 Pius XII presides over the canonization of Mother Frances Xavier Cabrini, the first American to be canonized, who ministered to poor Italian immigrants (of whom she was one).

1947 Shepherd boys accidentally discover the Dead Sea Scrolls in a cave on the northwest shore of the Dead Sea. The

Science & Technology

1947 OCT 14 Test pilot Chuck Yeager, flying an X-1 rocket plane, breaks the sound barrier for the first time.

1947 The Haloid Company (later Xerox) buys the rights to Chester Carlson's xerographic process (patented 1940).

Daily Life

c.1945 U.S. soldiers scrawl *Kilroy was here* on streets, signs, and bathroom walls all over the world. *Kilroy* refers to a personification of the average GI.

1946 A designer names his new, abbreviated two-piece bathing suit the bikini after the "ultimate impact" of the atomic bomb test at the Bikini Atoll.

1947 APR 10 Jackie Robinson becomes the first black to play major league baseball when he starts for the Brooklyn Dodgers on Opening Day.

during the next four years so that Europe can rebuild its industrial base.

1947 JUL George Kennan's anonymous article (signed "X") appears in *Foreign Affairs.* In it, he outlines the program of Communist containment that will guide U.S. foreign policy for the next 40 years.

1947 AUG 15 India wins independence after 200 years of colonial rule. The country is immediately divided into Hindu and Muslim states, the latter named Pakistan.

1947 NOV 29 The UN General Assembly votes to partition Palestine into Jewish and Arab states after the expiration of the British mandate there (1948, MAY 15).

1948 APR 1 When the Soviets blockade West Berlin, the U.S. and Britain respond with a massive two-million-ton airlift. The Soviets abandon the blockade on May 12, 1949, but deliveries continue until September so that goods can be stockpiled.

1948 AUG 15 Syngman Rhee becomes president of the new Republic of Korea, south of the 38th Parallel. To the north, Russia creates the Democratic People's Republic under Kim Il Sung (SEP 3).

1949 OCT 1 After the People's Liberation Army drives Chiang Kai-shek and his Nationalists from mainland China, Mao Zedong announces the formation of the People's Republic of China in Beijing.

Joseph Stalin

1947 The House Un-American Activities Committee holds hearings in Hollywood to ferret out alleged Communists in the movie business. Actors, writers, and directors accused by the committee of left-wing sympathies are immediately blacklisted by the studios.

1947 Tennessee Williams' steamy psychological drama *A Streetcar Named Desire* wins him the Pulitzer Prize.

1949 Miles Davis's *The Birth of Cool* album exhibits a new jazz style that will soon captivate West Coast beatniks.

---

leather-and-papyrus manuscripts prove to be of unprecedented archaeological value to biblical scholars, who begin to reconstruct the relationship between Judaism and early Christianity during the centuries just before and just after the birth of Jesus.

1948 MAR 8 The U.S. Supreme Court rules that religious education in public schools violates the First Amendment.

1949 Simone de Beauvoir's *The Second Sex* anticipates many themes and goals of the feminist movement of the 1960s.

1948 Three researchers at Bell Labs invent the transistor, which replaces the cumbersome vacuum tube and opens up the field of solid-state electronics.

1949 In "The Origin of Chemical Elements," George Gamow and Ralph

Alpher postulate a thermonuclear reaction, or "big bang," to explain the distribution of chemical elements in the universe.

1949 The National Bureau of Standards builds an atomic clock accurate to within one second in three million years.

1947 Otto Frank publishes a diary kept by his daughter Anne during the two years the family hid from the Gestapo in Amsterdam. Frank found the diary among papers collected by friends after the Gestapo raided the secret room in which the Jewish Franks were hiding. Although

Otto Frank survived Auschwitz, Anne was sent to Bergen-Belsen, where she died.

1947 Thor Heyerdahl sails the balsa-wood *Kon-Tiki* from Peru to Polynesia to prove his theory that Polynesia could have been settled by South Americans.

1945-1949

The Body Politic

1950 FEB Republican senator Joseph McCarthy claims during a speech in Wheeling, West Virginia, that there are some 205 Communist agents in the State Department. Although McCarthy never produces any proof, his charges make emotional sense to Americans who cannot otherwise explain the "fall" of China to Mao Zedong's Communists (1949).

1950 JUN 25 North Korean troops cross the 38th Parallel, invading South Korea. When the UN Security Council calls for an immediate end to the fighting, the Soviets walk out. Two days later, the Security Council (with the Soviets absent), ratifies Truman's decision to enter the war alongside South Korea.

1950 SEP 15 Landing at Inchon, General Douglas MacArthur leads UN troops in a successful counterattack against the Communists. Crossing the 38th Parallel into North Korea on October 9, MacArthur reaches the Chinese border at the Yalu River on November 20. But his drive north foolishly brings China into the war.

1950 OCT 21 Chinese forces invade eastern Tibet, overwhelming poorly equipped Tibetan troops. The Dalai Lama appeals for help to the UN, which refuses him.

1951 APR 11 Angered by MacArthur's insistence on invading China, and considering it a challenge to his presidential authority, Truman dismisses the general.

Arts & Architecture

1950 Abstract expressionist Willem de Kooning paints *Woman I*. His violent brushstrokes shock those more comfortable with delicate portrayals of women.

1951 "What are you rebelling against, Johnny?" a girl asks biker Marlon Brando

in *The Wild One*, directed by Laslo Benedek. "Whattya got?" replies Brando.

1951 J.D. Salinger's first novel *The Catcher in the Rye* captivates readers with its portrayal of Holden Caulfield's disgust with the "phony" adult world.

Religion & Philosophy

c.1950 Billy Graham becomes the chief spokesman for Christian fundamentalism, conducting internationally televised revival meetings.

1950 Arthur Koestler edits *The God That Failed*, a collection of essays by former

Communists telling of their disillusionment with the party.

1950 The title of David Riesman's *The Lonely Crowd* enters the vernacular. It is meant to signify the alienation Riesman finds in everyday modern life.

Science & Technology

1951 JUN 14 J. Presper Eckert, Jr., and John W. Mauchley demonstrate UNIVAC I, the first electronic digital computer built for commercial purposes. Eckert and Mauchley, whose business is later taken over by Remington Rand, designed UNIVAC for the Census Bureau.

1951 DEC 20 At the Idaho Falls testing station, the Atomic Energy Commission produces the first electricity obtained from a nuclear reactor.

1952 NOV 1 The U.S. secretly tests a hydrogen bomb, the first thermonuclear

Daily Life

1950 The Diners' Club introduces the first credit card.

1950 JAN 21 The jury at his second trial convicts former State Department employee Alger Hiss of perjury. Self-confessed Communist courier Whittaker

Chambers has accused Hiss of passing him secret microfilm inside a hollowed-out pumpkin.

1951 OCT 3 Bobby Thomson of the New York Giants hits a three-run homer in the bottom of the ninth inning off Ralph

1951 JUL 8 Negotiations to end the Korean War begin at Kaesong. The talks will last more than two years until an armistice is finally signed (1953, JUL 27) restoring the 38th Parallel border.

1952 APR 8 President Truman seizes the nation's steel mills to prevent striking workers from halting production. When the Supreme Court declares the seizure unconstitutional (JUN 2), Truman returns the mills. The strike continues until July, when a settlement is reached.

1953 JUN 17 Protests started by construction workers in East Berlin escalate into anti-Communist riots. Those who believed that Stalin's death (MAR 5) would

permit an easing of tensions are proved wrong when Soviet tanks crush the demonstrations.

1953 JUN 19 Julius and Ethel Rosenberg are executed following their 1951 conviction for the part they played in passing atomic secrets to the Soviet Union.

1954 APR 23 The Army-McCarthy hearings open to consider Senator Joseph McCarthy's charge that Army secretary Robert Stevens obstructed his investigation of Communists in the military. The hearings (until JUN 17) will be McCarthy's undoing. Meeting in a special session, the Senate votes to censure the junior senator from Wisconsin on December 2.

Elvis Presley

1953 Samuel Beckett's *Waiting for Godot* opens in Paris. This theater-of-the-absurd play tells the existentialist story of two men who, unable to accept that they have no purpose in life, presume the existence of a third character for whom they are waiting.

1954 JUL 6 Nineteen-year-old truck driver Elvis Presley makes his first record, "That's All Right, Mama," for Sam Phillips' Sun label in Memphis. Before Elvis, Phillips made his money recording black Delta blues acts such as B.B. King and Bobby (Blue) Bland.

1953 Psychologist B.F. Skinner's *Science and Human Behavior* presents his view that human behavior consists largely of physiological responses to the environment. His *Walden Two* (1948) depicted life in a utopian community founded on the principles of social engineering.

(fusion) device, at the Eniwetok Atoll in the Marshall Islands.

1953 James Watson and Francis Crick suggest that the structure of DNA resembles a "double helix." Their discovery opens up the field of molecular biology.

1954 FEB 23 Dr. Jonas Salk inoculates schoolchildren with a new polio vaccine.

1954 Although he played a pivotal role in developing the atomic bomb, J. Robert Oppenheimer is declared a security risk for opposing the H-bomb on moral grounds.

Branca to beat the Brooklyn Dodgers, 5-4, and win the National League pennant. Sportswriters call Thomson's blast "the shot heard 'round the world."

1952 Harvey Kurtzman edits the first issue of *Mad* magazine, his new 32-page

comic book that satirizes other comics (as well as itself).

1953 MAY 29 Edmund Hillary and his Nepalese guide Tenzing Norgay are the first to reach the summit of Everest, the highest mountain in the world.

1950-1954

The Body Politic

1955 MAY 14 The USSR and its satellites sign the Warsaw Pact, a mutual defense treaty to counter NATO (established 1949, APR 4). The treaty calls for a unified (Soviet) command structure, with Soviet troops to be stationed within the territory of each signatory nation.

1956 FEB 24-25 At the 20th Party Congress in Moscow, Nikita Khrushchev admits all of Stalin's mistakes in a speech detailing past abuses that leads to a temporary relaxation of political repression at home and hostility abroad.

1956 JUL 26 When the U.S. and Britain deny him funds to build the Aswan Dam (because he already accepts Soviet aid),

Egyptian president Gamal Abdel Nasser nationalizes the Suez Canal, intending to use canal tolls to finance the dam. Fearful for their oil supply, England and France prepare secret plans, with Israel, to regain control of the canal.

1956 OCT 23 A student demonstration against the Soviet-dominated government in Hungary turns violent once troops fire on the demonstrators. When the Hungarian army sides with the students, handing out weapons to the populace, former prime minister Imre Nagy attempts to negotiate a total withdrawal of Soviet troops. But three days after he announces Hungary's withdrawal from the Warsaw Pact (NOV 1), the Soviets send in tanks,

Arts & Architecture

1955 After flopping a year earlier, Bill Haley's "Rock Around the Clock" tops the *Billboard* charts. The difference has been the song's appearance on the soundtrack to Richard Brooks' *The Blackboard Jungle,* a film about juvenile delinquents that has provoked rioting in movie theaters.

1955 Marian Anderson, the first black to sing at New York's Metropolitan Opera, performs Verdi's *Un ballo in maschera.*

1955 Muppeteer Jim Henson develops his Kermit the Frog character for a five-minute television show, *Sam and Friends.*

Religion & Philosophy

1955 Herbert Marcuse's *Eros and Civilization* employs Freudian concepts to analyze the nature and structure of modern political society.

1955 MAY 23 The Presbyterian Church approves the ordination of women ministers.

Science & Technology

1957 Daniel Bovet wins the Nobel Prize in medicine for developing the first effective antihistamine (1937). Pharmaceutical companies unsuccessfully marketed Bovet's drug in 1949 and again in 1950 as a cure for the common cold, which it is not.

1957 OCT 4 Russia's launch of Sputnik 1, the first manmade satellite to orbit the earth, begins the space race.

1958 Arthur Shawlow and Charles Townes of Bell Laboratories apply for the first patent on a laser. Theodore H.

Daily Life

1955 Annual sales of comic books reach one billion. Meanwhile, New York State forbids the sale of crime and horror comics to minors.

1956 APR 19 The actress Grace Kelly marries Prince Rainier III of Monaco.

1957 JAN 22 The game show *Truth or Consequences* becomes the first national television program to be seen on videotape rather than live.

1957 With the end of the baseball season, the New York Giants move to San

which enter Budapest and crush the coalition government, executing Nagy and the other leaders in 1958.

1956 OCT 29 The Israeli army crosses into Egypt, advancing toward the Suez Canal. Britain and France soon join the attack. When the UN (with U.S. backing) forces a cease-fire (NOV 7), Nasser emerges as a nationalist Arab hero.

1957 MAR 25 France, Belgium, West Germany, The Netherlands, Luxembourg, and Italy create the European Economic Community (Common Market). The founding Treaty of Rome is designed to remove trade barriers and provide for coordinated economic and agricultural policies.

1958 SEP 28 A nationwide referendum in France approves a new constitution for the Fifth Republic. Charles De Gaulle becomes its first president.

1959 JAN 1 With his regime collapsing under the onslaught of Fidel Castro's guerrillas, Cuban dictator Fulgencio Batista flees to the Dominican Republic.

1959 JUL 23 Vice President Richard Nixon arrives in Moscow to attend an American exhibition there. The next day, before the opening ceremonies, he and Khrushchev argue the relative merits of capitalism and communism while standing in front of a model kitchen. The exchange becomes the Kitchen Debate.

Nikita Khrushchev

1955 Russian exile Vladimir Nabokov sets his love story *Lolita* in the motel culture of his adopted United States.

1955 SEP 30 James Dean dies in an automobile accident, crystallizing his image as a rebellious, idealistic youth.

1956 Ingmar Bergman gains international fame for his cinematic adaptation of a medieval morality play, *The Seventh Seal.*

1957 Jack Kerouac's *On the Road* about a cross-country car trip becomes the definitive work of the Beat Generation.

1955 *Tristes Tropiques* by Claude Lévi-Strauss influences literary criticism with its application of structuralist methods to the genre of literary memoir. The French anthropologist first developed these techniques in *The Elementary Structures of Kinship* (1949).

1959 Shortly after his coronation, John XXIII, in a bold and controversial move, announces plans for the first Vatican Council since 1870 in order to "bring the Church up to date." He thus becomes the first pope since the Reformation to admit that Catholicism needs reform.

Maiman will successfully operate a laser for the first time in 1960.

1959 JUL 17 Mary Leakey, working with her husband Louis in the Olduvai Gorge in northern Tanzania, discovers a human-like skull that she identifies as

Homo zinjanthropus, the earliest of its type yet found.

1959 The first transatlantic television broadcast from London to Montreal shows Queen Elizabeth II leaving for Canada to open the St. Lawrence Seaway.

Francisco, while the Brooklyn Dodgers leave Ebbets Field for Los Angeles.

1958 JAN 13 The *Daily Worker,* the organ of the Communist party in America, suspends publication. Its last headline reads, "We'll Be Back."

1959 JUL 6 New York governor Nelson Rockefeller proposes a system of bomb shelters to protect citizens from fallout in the event of a nuclear attack.

1959 DEC 19 The last Civil War veteran, Walter Williams, dies at the age of 117.

1955-1959

1954 **May 17** The Supreme Court decides unanimously in *Brown v. Board of Education* that racial segregation in public schools is unconstitutional. Reversing *Plessy v. Ferguson* (1896), Chief Justice Earl Warren rules that "in the field of public education the doctrine of 'separate but equal' has no place." Thurgood Marshall argued the case for the NAACP.

1955 **August 28** Fourteen-year-old Chicagoan Emmett Till, visiting relatives in Money, Mississippi, says "Bye, baby" to a white woman in the general store. Till is black. Three days later, two men take Till in the middle of the night and kill him. At their trial, a defense lawyer tells the all-white jury he is sure "every last Anglo-Saxon one of you has the courage to free these men." The men are acquitted.

December 1 In Montgomery, Alabama, Rosa Parks refuses to give up her seat on a city bus to a white man. After Parks' arrest, Dr. Martin Luther King, Jr., leads a boycott of the bus system that lasts from December 5 until the buses are desegregated on December 21, 1956.

1957 **January 10-11** King and black ministers meeting in Atlanta found the Southern Christian Leadership Conference to coordinate civil rights activity.

September 3 Governor Orval Faubus calls out the Arkansas National Guard to prevent nine black students from attending all-white Central High in Little Rock. When a federal court compels Faubus to admit the students, the governor announces his compliance. But he refuses to protect the Little Rock Nine, removing the National Guard and forcing President Eisenhower to send in the 101st Airborne Division to enforce the court order.

1960 **February 1** In Greensboro, four black freshmen from North Carolina Agricultural and Technical College seat themselves at the downtown Woolworth's lunch counter, which is for whites only. Although the students are refused service, they remain in their seats until closing time. Similar "sit-ins" quickly spread to 77 other cities and command national attention.

April 17 The Student Nonviolent Coordinating Committee is founded during a conference called by the SCLC to take advantage of increasing student involvement. SNCC's immediate purpose is to organize the sit-in movement.

1 9 6 1   **May 4** Thirteen Freedom Riders, six whites and seven blacks, board a Greyhound bus in Washington, D.C., bound for the Deep South. Their purpose is to test the Supreme Court's recent ruling in *Boynton v. Virginia* that segregation in interstate travel is unconstitutional.

May 14 In Anniston, Alabama, a mob attacks a bus carrying Freedom Riders, breaking its windows and slashing its tires. The bus speeds out of town, but when flat tires force it to stop, the bus is surrounded and set afire.

May 20 Alabama governor John Patterson promises to protect Freedom Riders traveling from Birmingham to Montgomery. But when the bus carrying them arrives in Montgomery, its police escort disappears, and the passengers are beaten in the worst riot yet.

1 9 6 2   **September 3** Deciding a suit originally filed in May, 1961, Justice Hugo Black upholds a federal circuit court decision ordering the University of Mississippi to admit James Meredith, a black air force veteran.

September 20 Keeping his promise that "no school in our state will be integrated while I am your governor," Ross Barnett flies to the Ole Miss campus in Oxford to turn James Meredith away personally.

September 29 At midnight, after three secret telephone conversations with Barnett during the day, President Kennedy federalizes the Mississippi National Guard and orders army troops to Memphis.

September 30 Students returning to Oxford from a football game find 300 federal marshals on campus protecting Meredith. Kennedy goes on national television to ask the people of Mississippi to obey the law. As the president speaks, the marshals are attacked with gunfire and firebombs made from Coca-Cola bottles. When it appears that they might be overwhelmed, Deputy Attorney General Katzenbach sends for the army troops waiting in Memphis. The next morning, Meredith is finally registered.

1 9 6 3   **April 3** King begins Project C (for "confrontation") in Birmingham with a march and a boycott of downtown stores. On April 10, an Alabama circuit court forbids further marches. On April 15, however, King personally leads a march and is arrested for defying the court order. In his cell, he writes "Letter from a Birmingham Jail" on scraps of toilet paper.

1963
(continued)

May 2 Six thousand children march in Birmingham, inaugurating the Children's Crusade. The next day, an enraged Commissioner of Public Safety Eugene (Bull) Connor orders police dogs and fire hoses turned on the young marchers. Pictures of Connor's brutality make news all over the world.

June 11 Emulating Ross Barnett, Governor George Wallace of Alabama fulfills a campaign promise to "stand in the schoolhouse door" to prevent integration at the University of Alabama. In response, Kennedy federalizes the Alabama National Guard and forces Wallace to step aside. That same night, Kennedy delivers on national television his strongest civil rights speech yet. Then, just after midnight, Medgar Evers, Mississippi field secretary for the NAACP, is shot and killed by a sniper as he returns home.

June 19 President Kennedy introduces a civil rights bill to Congress. Among its provisions, the bill would outlaw segregation in public accommodations and allow the attorney general to sue for school integration.

August 28 More than 250,000 people gather for a March on Washington in support of the pending civil rights bill. At three o'clock, King delivers his famous "I Have a Dream" speech on the steps of the Lincoln Memorial.

September 15 A bomb explodes at Birmingham's Sixteenth Street Baptist Church during a Sunday morning Bible class. Four girls from the class are killed by an avalanche of falling bricks.

1964

June 21 Summer volunteer Andrew Goodman and CORE workers Michael Schwerner and James Chaney are arrested for speeding near Philadelphia, Mississippi. Shortly after being released from jail, they disappear. A white New Yorker like Schwerner, Goodman is part of the Freedom Summer project, which has enlisted white northern students to help register voters for a new integrated state party, the Mississippi Freedom Democratic Party.

July 2 President Johnson signs into law the Civil Rights Act of 1964. Skillfully shepherded through the Senate by Johnson, the bill is an even stronger version of the legislation Kennedy had proposed the year before.

August 4 A $30,000 reward unearths what a month-long FBI search could not: the bodies of the missing civil rights workers. Autopsies show that Goodman and Schwerner were killed with single bullets, while Chaney, a black Mississippian, first had his skull crushed before being shot three times.

August 22 In Atlantic City, MFDP delegate Fannie Lou Hamer delivers nationally televised testimony before the Credentials Committee at the Democratic convention, challenging the right of the all-white Mississippi regulars to the state party's seats.

December 21 When Mississippi governor Paul Johnson refuses to seek state murder indictments in the Goodman, Schwerner, and Chaney killings, the Justice Department files civil rights charges against 21 men, including Neshoba County deputy sheriff Cecil Price, who is eventually convicted.

1 9 6 5   **January 18** Joining a SNCC voter registration effort already in place, King and the SCLC arrive in Selma, Alabama, looking for a success to speed President Johnson's development of new voting rights legislation.

February 4 SNCC invites Malcolm X to speak in Selma, where he tells a capacity crowd that "If the white people realize what the alternative is, perhaps they will be more willing to hear Dr. King."

February 18 Registration worker Jimmy Lee Jackson is shot at point-blank range by an Alabama state trooper during a march in Marion. His outraged SNCC colleagues discuss delivering the body to Governor Wallace, but King and the SCLC instead organize a 54-mile march from Selma to Montgomery.

February 21 Malcolm X is shot and killed by members of the Nation of Islam while delivering a speech at the Audubon Ballroom in New York City.

March 7 Despite a refusal by Wallace to allow the march, 600 protesters begin the walk, only to be met by state troopers in riot gear at the Edmund Pettus Bridge in East Selma. When the marchers fail to disperse, the police attack with tear gas. That night, all three networks interrupt their prime-time programs to show film of what looks like war on the streets of Selma.

March 9 King flies to Selma and begins a second march, despite a federal court order specifically prohibiting it. State troopers again block the way, and rather than test them, King turns the column around.

March 21-25 With the court order lifted, King leads 4,000 marchers across the Edmund Pettus Bridge. Four days later, 25,000 marchers arrive in Montgomery. King's return to the scene of the bus boycott is triumphant, but the Selma march marks the last act of a unified, inclusive movement.

1957 **October 4** The Soviet Union launches the first manmade satellite into an orbit of 228 kilometers by 947 kilometers. Sputnik 1 (meaning *fellow traveler* in Russian) is a 38-pound metal sphere with four whip aerials outside and a radio with batteries inside.

November 3 The launch of Sputnik 2 further damages U.S. prestige when it carries a dog named Laika into space. Instruments confirm that Laika survives the launch and weightlessness. As the Soviets are unable to return her to earth, however, she dies when her oxygen runs out one week later.

December 6 The failure of the Vanguard rocket, which topples off the launchpad in a humiliating fireball, allows former Nazi rocket scientist Wernher von Braun to restart his Project Orbiter, which had been shelved. The press calls the Vanguard fiasco "Flopnik" and "Kaputnik."

1958 **January 31** America launches its first satellite atop Von Braun's Juno 1 rocket. Explorer I carries a Geiger-Mueller counter provided by James Van Allen, which detects the Van Allen radiation belts.

October 11 In the first mission launched under the auspices of the newly formed National Aeronautics and Space Administration, a Thor-Able rocket carrying the lunar probe Pioneer 1 fails to reach escape velocity.

1959 **January 2** The Soviet Union begins its lunar program with the launch of Lunik I, a 165-pound sphere. Intended to hit the moon, Lunik I misses by 3,300 miles but nevertheless becomes the first space probe to escape the earth's gravity. Lunik 2 (launched September 12) becomes the first manmade object to reach the moon. Lunik 3 (launched October 4) takes nine photos of the moon's hidden far side, which are transmitted back to earth by TV.

1960 **April 1** The United States launches the first weather satellite, TIROS 1.

1961 **January 31** The chimpanzee Ham survives an early Project Mercury test flight. His suborbital mission reaches an altitude of 150 miles.

April 12 Vostok 1 carries Soviet cosmonaut Yuri Gagarin into orbit, making him the first human in space. His single-orbit flight lasts 108 minutes.

May 5 Mercury astronaut Alan Shepard becomes the first American in space when a Redstone rocket launches his *Freedom 7* capsule on a suborbital flight that lasts 15 minutes 22 seconds, reaching an altitude of 110 miles.

May 25 President Kennedy announces his plan to land a man on the moon by the end of the decade.

1962 **February 20** John Glenn aboard *Friendship 7* becomes the first Mercury astronaut to orbit the earth.

July 10 AT&T launches Telstar, the first commercially developed communications satellite, which revolutionizes television broadcasting.

1964 **July 31** After a number of early failures, Ranger 7 returns more than 4,000 pictures of the moon's surface in the 15 minutes before it crashes into the Sea of Clouds. The final three Ranger missions provide Apollo scientists with the information they need to design a lunar landing module.

1965 **March 18** Voskhod 2 cosmonaut Alexei Leonov makes the first space walk.

March 23 Virgil (Gus) Grissom and John Young complete the Gemini 3 mission, the first manned flight of the two-astronaut Gemini spacecraft, which has replaced the single-astronaut Project Mercury capsule.

June 3-7 During the Gemini 4 mission, Edward White becomes the first American astronaut to walk in space.

June 28 The first INTELSAT satellite, nicknamed *Early Bird*, goes into service. It can relay 240 telephone calls or one television channel.

July 14 Mariner 4 flies within 600 miles of Mars. The 21 television pictures it returns show no sign of Martian canals or Martian life.

1966 **January 31** After a string of five failures, the Soviet Union lands Luna 9 in the Ocean of Storms, making it the first lunar probe to land safely on the moon. A television camera transmits the first-ever pictures from the moon's surface.

1 9 6 6
(continued)

March 30 Advancing the work of the Ranger probes, Surveyor 1 makes a soft landing less than ten miles from its targeted site on the Ocean of Storms.

1 9 6 7

January 27 The UN Outer Space Treaty prohibits placing weapons of mass destruction into orbit and forbids the national appropriation of celestial bodies.

January 27 Three Apollo 1 astronauts die in a launchpad fire during a routine countdown test. The inquiry that follows reveals a huge number of safety problems that delay the Apollo program for 18 months.

1 9 6 8

December 24 Apollo 8 places the first astronauts into lunar orbit.

1 9 6 9

July 20 Apollo 11 astronauts Neil Armstrong and Edwin (Buzz) Aldrin land the lunar module *Eagle* at the Sea of Tranquility. Michael Collins remains aboard the command module *Columbia*.

1 9 7 0

April 13 Fifty-six hours into the Apollo 13 mission, an oxygen tank in the service module ruptures. During the next four days, the astronauts use the lunar excursion module as a lifeboat, while mission controllers improvise a way to use the LEM's engine to bring Apollo 13 safely back to earth.

1 9 7 3

May 14 The unmanned launch of space station Skylab 1 runs into trouble when a thin meteoroid shield deploys too early, tearing away one of the station's two main solar panels. The launch of the manned Skylab 2 mission, originally scheduled for May 15, is delayed ten days while mission specialists plan a salvage mission. The first Skylab crew boards the crippled station on May 26 and carries out makeshift repairs.

1 9 7 5

July 17 The docking of Soyuz 19 with an Apollo capsule consummates the Apollo-Soyuz Test Project, the first international manned space mission. It also marks the final use of a Saturn rocket and Apollo capsule.

1 9 7 6

July 20 Viking 1 makes the first successful soft landing on Mars.

1979   **March 5** Voyager 1 makes its closest approach to Jupiter. The probe uses nuclear power instead of solar panels because, at this distance, light from the sun is very weak.

July 11 A victim of unexpectedly high atmospheric drag, Skylab reenters the earth's atmosphere, where it breaks apart. Most of the fragments land in the Indian Ocean, but some fall on Australia. NASA had considered using the space shuttle to boost the abandoned station into a higher orbit, but delays in shuttle development make that impossible.

September 1 Pioneer 11 returns the first close-up images of Saturn, while providing data about its moons and rings that will help mission planners calculate the proper trajectories for the Voyager probes to follow.

1981   **April 12-14** John Young commands the first flight of the space shuttle. Robert Crippen accompanies him as copilot aboard the *Columbia*.

1983   **June 13** Crossing the orbit of Neptune, Pioneer 10 becomes the first spacecraft to leave the solar system.

1986   **January 28** The space shuttle *Challenger* explodes 73 seconds after launch, killing the seven-member crew.

February 20 Having turned to manned space stations after losing the moon race, the Soviet Union launches its third generation station, the Mir, which is the first to be continuously manned. Improving on the Soyuz and Salyut stations, the Mir consists of a central core to which specialized modules containing scientific experiments can be attached.

1989   **May 4** The space shuttle *Atlantis* deploys the probe Magellan, which begins a 15-month flight to Venus.

August Voyager 2 reaches Neptune after flying by Uranus in January, 1986.

1990   **August 10** Magellan enters orbit around Venus, where it proceeds to map 84% of the planet, showing details as small as 120 meters across.

The Body Politic

1960 MAY 1 The Soviets shoot down an U-2 reconnaissance plane flown by Francis Gary Powers, who ejects safely. Caught and convicted of espionage (AUG 19), Powers is held until the U.S. trades a Soviet spy for him two years later.

1960 SEP 26 John F. Kennedy and Richard Nixon meet in Chicago for the first of four nationally televised presidential debates.

1961 JAN 3 The U.S. severs diplomatic relations with Cuba after Fidel Castro nationalizes American property worth hundreds of millions of dollars. Later in the year, Congress imposes a total embargo on trade with Cuba.

1961 APR 17 A small force of CIA-trained Cuban exiles lands at the Bay of Pigs. The plan calls for a popular revolt against Castro, which never materializes. Instead, Castro's army crushes the small band, while Kennedy refuses to permit U.S. military intervention. Although Eisenhower originated the plan, Kennedy accepts full responsibility for its failure.

1961 AUG 12-13 During the night, Communist authorities construct a barbed-wire barricade, sealing off East Berlin and closing the last remaining escape route to the West. The barricade is later replaced by a concrete wall, officially referred to as the "anti-fascist security barrier" by the East German government.

Arts & Architecture

1960 Arriving in Greenwich Village, where he hopes to find his idol Woody Guthrie, Bob Dylan performs for the first time at Gerde's Folk City.

1960 FEB 7 The U.S. release of Jean-Luc Godard's unscripted film *Breathless* popularizes the French New Wave originated by Alan Resnais (*Hiroshima mon amour*) and François Truffaut (*400 Blows*).

1961 The American publication of Henry Miller's sexually frank novels *The Tropic of Cancer* and *The Tropic of Capricorn*

Religion & Philosophy

1962 JUN 11-15 Students for a Democratic Society holds its first national convention in Port Huron, Michigan.

1962 OCT 11 The 21st Ecumenical Council, popularly known as Vatican II, opens in Rome. The reforms adopted during its sessions focuses on the pastoral needs of the church and alter fundamentally nearly every aspect of life within Roman Catholicism. The changes set forth include greater lay participation in the celebration of the mass and the introduction of vernacular liturgies.

Science & Technology

1960 JAN 23 Jacques Piccard and Don Walsh descend a record seven miles in the bathyscaphe *Trieste* to the bottom of the Marianas Trench in the South Pacific.

1960 Three different observatories report the first quasar, a compact galaxy that releases light and radio waves in enormous quantities.

1961 APR 12 Soviet cosmonaut Yuri Gagarin, traveling in the five-ton space capsule Vostok 1, becomes the first human being to orbit the planet.

Daily Life

1960 MAY 19 The payola scandal peaks with DJ Alan Freed's arrest for bribery.

1960 OCT 17 Police arrest on perjury charges 14 quiz show contestants, including Charles Van Doren, who have denied receiving the answers in advance.

1961 MAY 9 FCC chairman Newton Minow calls television a "vast wasteland."

1961 MAY 1 An armed Cuban forces the pilot of a National Airlines flight from Miami to Key West to divert to Havana in the first successful skyjacking.

1962 OCT 22 Kennedy announces a naval blockade in response to aerial photos that show Soviet missile installations being constructed in Cuba. For a week, as Soviet ships approach the blockade, the world waits for news of nuclear war. Khrushchev finally backs down on October 27.

1963 JUL British diplomat Kim Philby escapes to the U.S.S.R. just as counterintelligence agents uncover his double life as a Soviet spy. Guy Burgess and Donald MacLean also prove to be Soviet moles.

1963 AUG 30 After the Cuban Missile Crisis reveals poor communication links, the Soviets and Americans establish the "hot line" between Moscow and Washington.

1963 NOV 22 Lee Harvey Oswald shoots and kills President Kennedy as he rides through the streets of Dallas. Two days later, Oswald is himself gunned down by nightclub owner and part-time mafioso Jack Ruby.

1964 MAR 16 President Johnson submits to Congress his $962.5-million War on Poverty program.

1964 OCT 14 The Soviet Central Committee ousts Nikita Khrushchev, who has never recovered from the Cuban Missile Crisis. Aleksei Kosygin replaces Khrushchev as premier, and Leonid Brezhnev takes over Khrushchev's position as Communist party chief.

John Fitzgerald Kennedy

---

signals a change in what is considered acceptable literature.

1962 Andy Warhol's paintings of Campbell's Soup cans, as well as his Brillo-pad sculptures, popularize the Pop Art movement in America.

1964 FEB 7 The Beatles fly to New York for their first U.S. tour, set to include two spots on CBS's Sunday-night variety show hosted by Ed Sullivan. "I love Beethoven," says Ringo at the airport press conference, "especially his poems." Beatlemania grips the nation.

1964 Herbert Marcuse's *One-Dimensional Man* becomes a philosophical bestseller. In it, Marcuse argues, from a Marxist-Hegelian viewpoint, that Western society inherently represses people because its use of technology to satisfy their material needs spiritually enslaves them.

1962 Rachel Carson publishes *Silent Spring*, in which she argues that widespread use of chemicals, especially DDT, threatens the environment.

1963 Dr. Michael De Bakey successfully implants a mechanical heart. Although

the patient dies, the device does improve his heart's pumping action.

1964 JAN 11 Surgeon General Luther Terry issues a government report that leads to a new warning on cigarette packages linking smoking to cancer.

1962 FEB 14 First Lady Jacqueline Kennedy leads 47 million television viewers on an intimate tour of the White House.

1962 AUG 5 A sleeping pill overdose, which the coroner rules a suicide, kills Marilyn Monroe in her Los Angeles home.

1963 Harvard University fires psychology professor Timothy Leary for using undergraduates in his LSD experiments.

1964 OCT 14 Martin Luther King, Jr., wins the Nobel Peace Prize, donating the $54,600 award to civil rights causes.

1960-1964

The Body Politic

1965 JAN 4 In his State of the Union address, President Johnson outlines the Great Society program, which includes aid for education, health care, and the arts.

1965 AUG 11-16 Rioting devastates the largely black Watts section of Los Angeles. The rampage begins when white police stop a black suspected of driving drunk.

1967 JUN 5 The Six Day War begins when Israeli planes stage a preemptive raid on 25 air bases, virtually destroying every Arab air force. Meanwhile, Israeli tanks smash through Egyptian troops in the Sinai, seize the West Bank from Jordan, and capture the Golan Heights from Syria, threatening Damascus.

1967 JUL 12-17 Race riots in Newark rage for almost a week, leaving 26 dead and over 1,300 injured. On July 23, one of the worst riots in U.S. history erupts in Detroit, leaving 43 dead and causing $200 million in property damage.

1968 MAR 31 After Eugene McCarthy nearly wins the New Hampshire primary, President Johnson announces in a televised speech that he will not commit more troops to Vietnam, that he will open negotiations for an end to the war, and that he will not seek another term as president.

1968 APR 4 James Earl Ray kills Martin Luther King, Jr., as King stands on the balcony of the Lorraine Motel in Memphis.

Arts & Architecture

1966 SEP 8 *Star Trek* premieres on NBC.

1966 Truman Capote's *In Cold Blood,* about a gruesome murder in Kansas, applies innovative journalistic techniques to novel writing, blurring the distinction between fact and fiction.

1967 Joseph Papp's New York Shakespeare Festival produces the first commercially successful rock musical , *Hair.*

1967 The Beatles' *Sgt. Pepper's Lonely Hearts Club Band* sets music critics arguing about whether or not rock and roll is art.

Religion & Philosophy

1965 OCT 4 On a trip to New York, Pope Paul VI delivers a plea for peace at the UN. He also celebrates mass at Yankee Stadium and visits the World's Fair.

1966 JUN The Roman Catholic Church ceases publication of the Index Librorum Prohibitorum [Index of Forbidden Books], which has censored Galileo among others.

1968 The encyclical *Humanae Vitae* reaffirms the Catholic Church's opposition to birth control, despite the reforms of Vatican II (ended 1965, DEC 8).

Science & Technology

1967 DEC Dr. Christiaan Barnard and a South African surgical team perform the first heart transplant. The patient, Philip Blaiberg, lives several months.

1968 FEB Anthony Hewish of Cambridge University announces the discovery of pulsating neutron stars. Astronomers at the University of Arizona make the first optical identification of a pulsar in the Crab Nebula (1960, JAN 20).

1969 Joseph Weber announces that he has observed the gravitational waves pre-

Daily Life

1965 SEP 8 Cesar Chavez leads the United Farm Workers in a strike against California grape growers.

1965 NOV 9 The failure of an automatic relay near Niagara Falls leads to a blackout across the entire Northeast.

1966 MAR 22 General Motors president James Roche apologizes to a Senate subcommittee for spying on Ralph Nader, author of *Unsafe at Any Speed* (1965).

1967 JAN 14 Self-proclaimed "freaks" celebrate the first (and last) Human Be-In

1968 MAY 3 After police break up a student rally at the Sorbonne in Paris, a larger confrontation involving workers spreads throughout France. Strikes paralyze the country and threaten to bring down the government until De Gaulle rallies the army to his side.

1968 JUN 5 Jordanian immigrant Sirhan B. Sirhan kills Robert F. Kennedy on the night of his victory in the California presidential primary.

1968 AUG 20-21 After months of indecision during which the political freedoms of the Prague Spring expand, Soviet tanks invade Czechoslovakia and seize control of the government of Alexander Dubcek.

1968 Stanley Kubrick's *2001: A Space Odyssey* wins a special effects Oscar.

1969 APR 4 CBS cancels *The Smothers Brothers Comedy Hour* after the show's stars fail to submit their topical jokes to the network censors for review.

1968 AUG 26-29 At the Democratic National Convention in Chicago, the political struggle inside the convention hall between antiwar activists and party regulars is overwhelmed by a much more violent police riot outside the hall.

1969 SEP 24 The trial of the Chicago Eight opens. William Kunstler defends seven of those indicted for inciting riots at the 1968 Democratic convention. Black Panther Bobby Seale, whom Judge Julius Hoffman orders bound and gagged for contempt (OCT 29), defends himself.

1969 OCT 8-11 The Weathermen, a violent SDS splinter group named for a Dylan song, stage the Days of Rage in Chicago.

1969 AUG 15-17 Half a million hippies revel in the upstate New York mud at the generation-making Woodstock festival.

1969 NOV The Children's Television Workshop production of *Sesame Street* debuts on public television.

1968 Liberation theology develops out of the second Latin American Bishops' Conference in Medellín, Colombia. A statement issued by the bishops supports the rights of the poor and accuses the industrial West of enriching itself at the expense of the Third World.

Martin Luther King, Jr., and Coretta Scott King

dicted by Einstein's theory of relativity, but the failure of others to confirm his work invalidates Weber's claim.

1969 The U.S. bans cyclamates, citing experiments with mice linking the artificial sweeteners to cancer. However, when

at Golden Gate park in San Francisco, kicking off the Summer of Love.

1967 APR 28 Heavyweight champion Muhammad Ali refuses induction into the army because of the religious beliefs he holds as a member of the Nation of Islam.

further experimentation fails to confirm these findings, the ban is modified.

1969 JUL 20 Neil Armstrong, commanding the Apollo 11 mission, leaves the lunar module *Eagle* and becomes the first person to walk on the moon.

1968 OCT 18 Tommie Smith and John Carlos give the clenched-fist Black Power salute during the medal ceremony for the 200 meters at the Mexico City Olympics.

1968 OCT 19 Jacqueline Kennedy marries Greek shipping tycoon Aristotle Onassis.

1965-1969

The Body Politic

1970 SEP 6 The Popular Front for the Liberation of Palestine hijacks three planes from New York to Jordan, holding the crews and passengers hostage. Meanwhile, on the ground in Jordan, fighting between Palestine guerrillas and the Jordanian army creates a civil emergency that threatens to widen when Soviet ally Syria sends in troops to support the Palestinians. Fortunately, the Jordanian air force soon prevails, and Palestinian leader Yasir Arafat is compelled to order a cease-fire (SEP 24).

1972 FEB 21 Climaxing his greatest foreign policy success, President Nixon travels to Beijing to reopen direct communication with the Chinese Communist government of Mao Zedong for the first time since it came to power in 1949.

1972 MAY 26 Nixon and Soviet leader Leonid Brezhnev sign the Strategic Arms Limitation Treaty (known as SALT I) in Moscow, justifying Nixon's policy of détente with the Soviets. Nixon's trip is the first ever made by a U.S. president to the Soviet capital.

1972 SEP 5 Arabs belonging to the Black September terrorist group infiltrate the Israeli dormitory at the Munich Olympic Village, initially killing two members of the Israeli team. After 23 hours of tense negotiations in the international spotlight, the terrorists and nine hostages

Arts & Architecture

1970 Soviet dancer Natalia Makarova defects to join George Balanchine's American Ballet Theater in New York.

1970 Robert Smithson creates his *Spiral Jetty*, a bulldozed ridge arching into the Great Salt Lake. The Earth Art movement, existing outside galleries, ignores boundaries of time and space.

1971 With its fearless treatment of controversial political issues, Norman Lear's *All in the Family* begins a new era in television situation comedy.

Religion & Philosophy

1971 *A Theology of Liberation* by Gustavo Gutiérez endorses political mobilization of the faithful to remedy deep social divisions between the rich and the poor. Gutiérez is criticized, however, on the grounds that he essentially endorses Marxism.

Science & Technology

1970 NOV 18 Dr. Linus Pauling issues his controversial recommendation that high doses of vitamin C can prevent both the common cold and the flu.

1970 Har Gobind Khorana makes the first synthesized gene, following up the work of three Harvard researchers who first isolated a single gene in 1969 (NOV 22).

1971 Cyril Ponnamperuma's analysis of Australia's Murchison meteorite (found 1969) reveals five different amino acids, the chemical basis of life.

Daily Life

1970 APR 1 President Nixon signs a bill banning cigarette advertising on radio and television.

1970 APR 22 Millions across the nation celebrate the first Earth Day with antipollution rallies and urban cleanups.

1970 SEP 21 Howard Cosell, Don Meredith, and Keith Jackson broadcast the first Monday Night Football game.

1971 JAN 25 Charles Manson and members of his cult are convicted of the 1969 murders of Sharon Tate and six others.

are flown by helicopter to a nearby airport. A shoot-out there kills five of the eight terrorists and all the remaining hostages.

1973 FEB 28-MAY 8 Armed members of the American Indian Movement occupy Wounded Knee, South Dakota, to dramatize the plight of reservation Indians.

1973 OCT 6 Egypt (across the Suez Canal) and Syria (over the Golan Heights) launch a joint surprise attack against Israel on the Jewish holy day of Yom Kippur. Although Israeli troops suffer losses on both fronts in the early going, their counterattacks quickly push into Syrian territory in the north and

outflank the Egyptian army in the south. Israel eventually succeeds in reversing the Arab gains, although at a high cost in casualties. A cease-fire concludes the Yom Kippur War in November.

1973 OCT 19-21 In retaliation for American support of Israel during the Yom Kippur War, a group of Arab oil-producing nations imposes a ban on petroleum exports to the United States and raises prices to America's Western European allies by 70%. The oil embargo ends generations of cheap energy in America and leads to an international energy crisis marked by skyrocketing gasoline prices, gasoline shortages, and long lines at the pump.

Mao Zedong

1973 The soundtrack to George Lucas's *American Graffiti* begins a nostalgia craze for the 1950s.

1973 Upon its completion, Chicago's 1,454-foot Sears Tower becomes the world's tallest building.

1974 The Soviet Union exiles Nobel laureate Alexander Solzhenitsyn after charging him with treason following publication in the West of *The Gulag Archipelago*. A smuggled-out manuscript contained his literary-historical study of the Soviet prison and labor camp system.

1973 JAN 22 In *Roe v. Wade*, the Supreme Court rules, 7-2, that women have an unrestricted right to an abortion during the first trimester of pregnancy.

1973 DEC 15 Reversing a century-old position, the American Psychiatric

Association announces that homosexuality is not an illness.

1974 SEP 12 Busing protests disrupt the first day of school in Boston, where a federal judge soon intervenes to enforce a court-ordered desegregation plan.

1971 The introduction of the microprocessor makes available an essential component of modern electronic computers.

1972 Near Lake Rudolf in Kenya, Richard Leakey discovers skull fragments that he believes to be two million years old.

1974 MAR Chinese farmers digging a well discover the burial mound of Shi Huangdi, who died in 206 BC. Excavations soon uncover 6,000 full-size ceramic figures, each with an individual face, that were buried along with the emperor as substitutes for his royal retainers.

1971 SEP 13 New York state police storm Attica prison, ending a four-day siege during which 38 guards were held hostage.

1972 JUL 11-SEP 1 Bobby Fischer wins the world chess championship from Boris Spassky in Reykjavik, Iceland.

1974 FEB 5 The Symbionese Liberation Army kidnaps heiress Patricia Hearst from her Berkeley, California apartment. A ransom message (FEB 12) soon demands $70 in food for every needy person in the state, prompting the Hearsts to begin a $2,000,000 food giveaway (FEB 22).

1950 **May 1** President Truman approves aid for France in its colonial war against the Communist Viet Minh. The U.S. will soon pay 80% of France's costs.

1954 **March 13** General Vo Nguyen Giap and 40,000 Viet Minh besiege the isolated 15,000-man French garrison at Dien Bien Phu. French losses mount.

May 7 Dien Bien Phu falls, marking the end of French rule in Indochina.

July 20 The French and Viet Minh sign a cease-fire agreement in Geneva, establishing a temporary demilitarized zone (DMZ) along the 17th Parallel and partitioning the country pending reunification elections.

October 11 The Viet Minh occupy the North, making Hanoi their capital.

October 24 President Eisenhower advises Prime Minister Ngo Dinh Diem that the U.S. will provide military aid directly to South Vietnam.

1955 **October 26** Following an election held October 23 and rigged with CIA help, Diem declares himself the first president of an independent South Vietnam.

1956 **July 20** The deadline set in Geneva for reunification elections passes. Diem refuses to hold them because of the absence of freedom in the North.

1957 **October** The North Vietnamese decide to organize 37 companies of armed Communist insurgents in the Mekong Delta region of South Vietnam.

1959 **July** North Vietnam establishes the 559 Group to organize supply routes to the South along the Ho Chi Minh Trail.

July 8 In a VC attack on the American base at Bien Hoa, Major Dale Buis and Sergeant Chester Ovnand become the first Americans killed in the war.

1960 **January 1** There are now 760 American military personnel in Vietnam.

December 20 Hanoi announces the formation in the South of the National Liberation Front, a coalition of groups opposed to Diem.

1961   **November 3** General Maxwell Taylor recommends that 10,000 combat troops be sent to Vietnam. Instead, Kennedy sends more equipment and advisers.

1962   **January 12** The U.S. launches Operation Ranch Hand, the spraying of chemical defoliants (including Agent Orange) on trails used by the VC.

1963   **January 1** There are now 11,300 American military personnel in Vietnam.

January 2 Despite the presence of U.S. helicopters, 200 VC humiliate 2,000 South Vietnamese (ARVN) regulars at Ap Bac, revealing ARVN inadequacies.

June 11 As part of ongoing protests against the brutal Diem regime, Buddhist monk Thich Quang Duc commits suicide by setting himself on fire.

November 1-2 General Duong Van Minh leads a group of ARVN officers in a coup, undertaken with American knowledge and consent. Diem is murdered.

December Hanoi begins sending regular army (NVA) units to the South.

1964   **June 20** General William Westmoreland replaces General Paul Harkins as commander of the U.S. Miliary Assistance Command, Vietnam (MACV).

August 2 The American destroyer *Maddox* reports an attack by three North Vietnamese patrol boats in the international waters of the Tonkin Gulf.

August 5 U.S. warplanes bomb North Vietnam in retaliation for alleged attacks in the Tonkin Gulf.

August 7 The House unanimously approves the Tonkin Gulf Resolution. Only two Senators oppose the measure, which gives Johnson virtual carte blanche for the huge troop buildups that will follow his reelection.

September 30 The first major university demonstration against American involvement in Vietnam takes place at UC-Berkeley, but polls show that 85% of Americans still support President Johnson's policy.

October 30 Signaling a change in tactics, the Viet Cong attack the U.S. airfield at Bien Hoa, destroying six B-57 bombers and damaging eight more.

1 9 6 5   **January 1** There are now 23,300 American military personnel in Vietnam.

March 2 The U.S. begins Operation Rolling Thunder, the sustained bombing of North Vietnam, to pressure Hanoi into ceasing its support of the VC.

March 8 Two battalions of Marines, the first American combat troops in Vietnam, land at Danang to guard the American airbase there.

June 7 In an emergency cable, Westmoreland, already commanding ten battalions, asks for 25 more to prevent the "collapse" of South Vietnam.

July 28 Johnson announces that draft calls will be doubled as part of his plan to increase U.S. troop strength in Vietnam to 175,000 by November 1.

August 18-21 Marines conduct Operation Starlight, the first ground offensive fought only by U.S. troops.

November 14-16 The First Air Cavalry Division defeats three NVA regiments in the first major battle of the war, fought in the Ia Drang Valley.

1 9 6 6   **January 1** There are now 184,300 American military personnel in Vietnam.

March 1 The Senate approves $21 billion in emergency funds for the war.

1 9 6 7   **January 1** There are now 385,300 American military personnel in Vietnam. Since 1961, 6,644 have been killed, 5,008 of those in the last year.

January 8 A joint force of 30,000 U.S. and ARVN troops launch Operation Cedar Falls, the largest to date, against Communists in the Iron Triangle.

September 3 Nguyen Van Thieu is elected president of South Vietnam.

October 21 Antiwar activists stage protests in Washington, chronicled in Norman Mailer's *Armies of the Night*. Johnson's approval rating is at 28%.

1 9 6 8   **January 1** There are now 485,600 American military personnel in Vietnam.

January 21 About 20,000 NVA regulars besiege the forward Marine base at Khe Sanh. Johnson is determined to avoid an American Dien Bien Phu.

January 30-31 During a cease-fire for the Tet holiday, 84,000 NVA and VC launch a massive offensive in cities throughout South Vietnam. Although a military defeat, the Tet Offensive is a propaganda victory for the Communists, who prove that they can strike anywhere at any time. After Tet, Westmoreland can no longer credibly claim to be winning the war.

February 27 The Joint Chiefs forward a request for 206,000 more troops.

March 1 Clark Clifford replaces Robert McNamara as Secretary of Defense and convenes a high-level working group to review U.S. policy in Vietnam.

March 12 Running on an antiwar platform, Senator Eugene McCarthy nearly defeats Johnson in the New Hampshire primary, winning 42% of the vote.

March 16 U.S. troops under Lieutenant William Calley massacre 347 civilians at My Lai. The slaughter is kept secret for over a year.

March 31 In a televised speech offering peace talks, Johnson shocks the nation with the news that he will not seek a second term as president.

October 31 Attempting to break a deadlock in the Paris peace talks, Johnson orders a stop to the bombing, ending Operation Rolling Thunder.

1969 **January 1** There are now 536,100 American military personnel in Vietnam. During 1968, 14,589 were killed in action, and 92,818 were wounded.

March 18 President Nixon orders the secret bombing of bases in Cambodia.

March 19 Secretary of Defense Melvin Laird announces the new U.S. policy of "Vietnamization," whereby ARVN troops will gradually replace U.S. units.

May 20 After ten unsuccessful attempts, U.S. troops take Hill 937 in the A Shau Valley, called Hamburger Hill because of the high casualties there.

June 8 Nixon announces the first withdrawal of troops, 25,000 by August.

October 15 Antiwar groups organize the first nationwide Moratorium.

November 3 In a major speech, Nixon appeals to the "silent majority" that he believes supports his goal of "peace with honor."

1 9 6 9
(continued)

November 15 For the second Moratorium, more than 250,000 marchers descend on Washington, recalling the civil rights march six years earlier.

November 16 Journalist Seymour Hersh reveals the 1968 massacre of civilians at My Lai, further discrediting the U.S. presence in Vietnam.

December 1 Criticized as being unfair, the draft switches to a lottery.

1 9 7 0

February 21 Henry Kissinger begins secret talks in Paris with Le Duc Tho.

April 20 On television, Nixon promises to withdraw 150,000 more troops.

April 30 In another televised speech, Nixon reveals that U.S. troops have attacked Communist bases inside Cambodia following a U.S.-backed coup by Lon Nol on March 18. Nixon denies the invasion means a widening of the war.

May 4 Ohio National Guard troops kill four Kent State University students during demonstrations protesting the U.S. invasion of Cambodia.

1 9 7 1

January 1 There are now 334,600 American military personnel in Vietnam.

June 13 The *New York Times* begins publishing a top-secret Pentagon history of the war, leaked by Daniel Ellsberg. Nixon sues to stop publication of the documents and later organizes the Plumbers unit to "fix leaks."

June 30 The Supreme Court rules for the *New York Times* in the Pentagon Papers case.

1 9 7 2

March 30 The NVA launches an immense Easter Offensive across the DMZ.

May 8 Nixon announces that he will mine North Vietnamese harbors and step up bombing raids until Hanoi agrees to a cease-fire and the return of POWs.

August 12 The last U.S. ground troops leave Vietnam. The remaining 43,500 Americans are administrative personnel, plus helicopter and bomber crews.

October 8 In Paris, Le Duc Tho and Kissinger agree to a "breakthrough" peace plan, calling for a cease-fire and general elections in the South.

October 26 At a White House press conference, Kissinger announces that "peace is at hand," just two weeks before the presidential election.

December 13 With Nixon supporting Thieu in his objections to the October agreement, the Paris peace talks break down again.

December 18 Nixon orders the Christmas Bombing of Hanoi and Haiphong.

December 30 Nixon announces a bombing halt when the North Vietnamese indicate this will lead to a revival of peace talks.

1973 **January 1** There are now 24,200 American military personnel in Vietnam.

January 27 The U.S., South Vietnam, North Vietnam, and the Viet Cong formally sign a cease-fire agreement in Paris. Secretary of Defense Laird annouces the end of the draft, which had called 2.2 million American men.

March 29 The last American POWs are released on the same day the last U.S. troops leave Vietnam. About 8,500 civilian technicians remain in country.

1974 **January 4** "The war has restarted," Thieu announces. Nearly 14,000 ARVN and 45,000 NVA soldiers have been killed since the truce of January 27, 1973.

April 4 The House rejects Nixon's request for more aid to South Vietnam.

1975 **March 19** Communists take Quang Tri as an ARVN retreat becomes a rout.

April 8 The ARVN division at Xuan Loc, the last defensive line before Saigon, engages two NVA divisions in the last battle of the war.

April 17 Phnom Penh, the capital of Cambodia, falls to the Khmer Rouge.

April 18 Kissinger orders the evacuation of Americans from Saigon.

April 29-30 Frequent Wind, the largest helicopter evacuation in history, rescues the last Americans in Saigon as the NVA begins its final attack.

April 30 Duong Van Minh announces the surrender of South Vietnam.

1972   **June 17** At the Watergate office building in Washington, police arrest former FBI agent James McCord and four anti-Castro Cubans caught breaking into the offices of the Democratic National Committee. The purpose of the burglary is to fix electronic bugs planted during an earlier break-in. Documents and traceable $100 bills found on the men indicate they all work for the Committee to Reelect the President.

September 15 The burglars are indicted along with G. Gordon Liddy and E. Howard Hunt, who directed the operation for CREEP. Both are former Nixon aides, but the White House is not linked to the break-in by the grand jury.

October 10 Bob Woodward and Carl Bernstein write in the Washington *Post* that Watergate is part of a larger Nixon campaign of "dirty tricks."

November 7 After a Gallup poll in October shows that 48% of Americans have never heard of the Watergate break-in, President Nixon wins reelection overwhelmingly, receiving 60% of the popular vote.

1973   **February 7** The Senate establishes a select committee, chaired by Sam Ervin of North Carolina, to investigate "any illegal, improper, or unethical activities" that might have taken place during the 1972 campaign.

March 23 Federal district court judge John Sirica reveals a letter in which McCord, asking for leniency, admits for the first time that pressure has been brought to keep defendants silent, that witnesses have perjured themselves, and that others are involved. McCord soon names former attorney general John Mitchell, the chairman of CREEP, as "the overall boss."

April 30 Press secretary Ron Ziegler announces the resignations of chief of staff H.R. Haldeman, aide John Ehrlichman, and counsel John Dean, who is already talking to the prosecutors. Elliot Richardson replaces Richard Kleindienst as attorney general. On national television, Nixon promises to do everything he can "to ensure that the guilty are brought to justice."

May 17 The Senate Watergate committee begins its hearings. Howard Baker of Tennessee becomes famous for asking nearly every witness, "What did the president know, and when did he know it?"

May 18 Attorney General Richardson names Archibald Cox as Watergate special prosecutor in accordance with a Senate resolution passed May 1.

June 25 Implicating the president directly, Dean tells the Senate committee of a September 15, 1972, meeting during which Nixon gave the impression that he was "well aware of what had been going on."

July 16 During televised testimony before the Senate committee, deputy chief of staff Alexander Butterfield reveals that Nixon secretly recorded telephone calls and conversations held in the Oval Office.

July 23 Cox subpoenas nine specific tapes of conversations relating to the cover-up. The Senate committee also subpoenas tapes of conversations between Nixon and Dean. Nixon rejects these subpoenas three days later.

August 29 Upholding Cox's subpoena, Sirica orders that the tapes be turned over to the court so that Sirica can review them and delete any privileged portions before they are turned over to the grand jury. Nixon appeals.

October 10 Vice President Spiro Agnew resigns after pleading no contest to evading income tax on kickbacks he received while governor of Maryland. Two days later, Nixon nominates Congressman Gerald Ford to fill the vacancy.

October 12 Upholding Sirica, the Court of Appeals rules by a vote of 5-2 that Nixon must hand over the nine tapes sought by Cox.

October 20 The Saturday Night Massacre begins with a press conference during which Cox refuses to back down from his subpoena. An hour later, chief of staff Alexander Haig calls Richardson with instructions to fire Cox. Richardson and his deputy, William Ruckelshaus, resign in turn rather than carry out the order. Finally, Solicitor General Robert H. Bork agrees to fire Cox and abolish the office of the Watergate special prosecutor.

October 23 Appearing before Sirica, Nixon lawyer Charles Wright announces that the president will comply with the court order and release the nine tapes. Later, Chairman Peter Rodino makes his own announcement that the House Judiciary Committee will begin investigating Nixon's alleged abuses of power, with the end result possibly being impeachment.

October 31 J. Fred Buzhardt, special counsel to the president for the tapes, tells Sirica that two of the nine subpoenaed tapes do not exist.

November 1 Attempting to undo the damage caused by the Saturday Night Massacre, Nixon has Bork appoint a new special prosecutor, Leon Jaworski.

1 9 7 3
(continued)

November 4 In their Sunday editions, The *New York Times*, the Detroit *News*, the Denver *Post*, and the Atlanta *Journal* all call for Nixon's resignation.

November 17 "I am not a crook," Nixon tells the annual gathering of the Associated Press Managing Editors Association at Disney World.

November 21 Buzhardt tells Sirica that the tape of a crucial June 20, 1972, conversation between Nixon and Haldeman contains an 18½-minute gap.

November 26 The seven existing subpoenaed tapes, including the "gap" tape, are turned over to Sirica. Meanwhile, Nixon secretary Rose Mary Woods testifies that she created the gap on the tape by pressing the wrong button while transcribing it. A subsequent reenactment of the erasure suggests that only a contortionist could have performed the unlikely maneuver.

December 6 Gerald Ford is sworn in as vice president.

December 19 The Senate committee subpoenas 500 White House documents and tapes. Nixon refuses to comply with the subpoena.

1 9 7 4

March 1 The grand jury indicts Haldeman, Ehrlichman, Mitchell, and four other Nixon aides on 24 counts of conspiracy, lying, and obstruction of justice. President Nixon himself is named as an unindicted co-conspirator.

April 4 After waiting 38 days for a reply to its initial request, the House Judiciary Committee issues an ultimatum, giving the president just five more days to decide whether or not he will hand over the tapes. Hours before the deadline, Nixon lawyer James St. Clair asks for an extension.

April 11 The House Judiciary Committee votes to issue a formal subpoena giving the president until April 25 to produce the tapes (a deadline later extended to April 30 at St. Clair's request).

April 18 Federal marshals deliver to the White House a Jaworski subpoena for 64 tapes, including a particularly sensitive tape from June 23, 1972.

April 29 In a televised speech, Nixon announces that he will release transcripts of the subpoenaed tapes to the public. When the Judiciary Committee compares these edited transcripts to the few actual tapes in its possession, it finds many suspicious discrepancies and omissions.

May 1 The House Judiciary Committee votes 20-18 to reject the edited White House transcripts. The White House responds that it will release no further tapes and no more Watergate material.

May 15 The House committee issues two new subpoenas, one for White House diaries and another for 11 more tapes.

May 20 Sirica refuses Nixon's motion to quash Jaworski's April 18 subpoena and orders the 64 tapes turned over to the court. When the president takes the case to the Court of Appeals, Jaworski insists that the Supreme Court hear the case immediately because of its "imperative public importance."

May 22 Nixon refuses to comply with the two new subpoenas or "such further subpoenas as may hereafter be issued," citing presidential privacy.

May 30 The House Judiciary Committee responds by letter that the president's refusal is "a grave matter" that may constitute grounds for impeachment. The vote approving this letter is 28-10, reflecting a severe erosion of support for the president within the committee.

May 31 The Supreme Court agrees to hear *U.S. v. Nixon*.

July 24 In a decision read by Chief Justice Warren Burger, the Supreme Court unanimously rules that the 64 tapes subpoenaed by the special prosecutor must be turned over to Sirica "forthwith." That night, St. Clair announces live on network news programs that the president will comply.

July 27-29 The House Judiciary Committee, by a vote of 27-11, approves three articles of impeachment. Six Republicans vote against the president.

August 5 Nixon releases a transcript of three June 23, 1972, conversations with Haldeman that definitively prove his knowledge and direction of the cover-up, as well as his effort to block the FBI investigation into the break-in. It is the "smoking gun" Congress and the special prosecutor have been looking for. In an accompanying statement, Nixon admits that the transcripts are "at variance with certain of my previous statements."

August 8 In a nationally televised, prime-time speech, President Nixon announces that he will resign the presidency effective noon on August 9.

September 8 Nixon accepts the pardon granted him by Gerald Ford.

The Body Politic

1975 APR 17 The Communist Khmer Rouge topple Lon Nol's U.S.-backed regime in Cambodia, beginning the rule of Pol Pot, one of the most brutal in modern history. At least one million Cambodians will be killed by starvation, disease, or by Pol Pot's systematic executions.

1976 JUN 16 The worst race riots in South African history break out in Soweto when students protest a requirement that Afrikaans be the official language of the public schools.

1976 JUL 3 Israeli commandos stage a daring rescue of 103 hostages held by Palestine terrorists at the Entebbe airport in Uganda.

1977 FEB In an innovative foreign policy move, the Carter Administration announces a reduction in U.S. aid to those countries guilty of human rights abuses. Included are Argentina, Uruguay, and Ethiopia.

1977 SEP 7 The U.S. and Panama sign the Panama Canal Treaties, which provide for the gradual transfer of the canal from American to Panamanian control.

1977 NOV 19 Egyptian president Anwar Sadat makes a historic trip to Israel to promote peace in the Middle East. At the invitation of Prime Minister Menachem Begin, the Egyptian leader even delivers a speech to the Israeli Knesset.

Arts & Architecture

1975 *One Flew Over the Cuckoo's Nest,* adapted from Ken Kesey's countercultural novel (1962) about the relative sanity of inmates and patients at a mental hospital, becomes the first motion picture in 40 years to win each of the top four Academy Awards.

1976 Christo erects his *Running Fence* in northern California. The work is made up of 24 miles of nylon sheeting, which blow in the wind for two weeks. Christo's art is intentionally transient, lasting only as long as his materials do (or until he is forced to take them down).

Religion & Philosophy

1976 SEP 18 The controversial South Korean minister Sun Myung Moon organizes a "God Bless America" rally in Washington, attended by 50,000 members of his Unification Church, known as Moonies. Traditional churches attack Moon's faith as a perversion of Christianity, while par-

ents of Moon's young converts charge that he has brainwashed them.

1978 OCT 16 The College of Cardinals elects the first non-Italian pope in 456 years, Polish cardinal Karol Wojtyla, who takes the name John Paul II.

Science & Technology

1976 MAY 24 The Concorde, a supersonic jet developed jointly by the British and the French, begins regular commercial service between Europe and the United States. The flights are soon suspended, however, because of noise pollution and the possibility of environmental damage.

1976 JUL 21-24 A mysterious disease infects 182 members of the American Legion attending a convention in Philadelphia, killing 29 of them. Laboratory work traces the deaths to a bacterium that thrives in the stagnant water present in the hotel's air-conditioning system.

Daily Life

1975 JUL 31 The family of former Teamsters president Jimmy Hoffa reports him missing. His body is never found.

1975 AUG 10 In an interview, First Lady Betty Ford says she suspects all four of her children have tried marijuana.

1976 West Point and the other service academies admit women for the first time.

1976 APR 22 Signing a five-year, $5 million contract with ABC, Barbara Walters becomes the first anchorwoman of a network television news program.

1978 SEP 17 Private talks mediated by President Carter culminate in the signing of the Camp David accords between Israel and Egypt. Arab nations, however, denounce the separate Egyptian peace.

1979 JAN 16 As the Islamic revolution inspired by the exiled ayatollah Ruhollah Khomeini gathers force, Shah Mohammed Raza Pahlavi flees Iran. Crowds of more than one million people greet Khomeini's return to Tehran (FEB 1).

1979 MAY 3 In a decisive electoral victory, the Conservative party of Margaret Thatcher sweeps parliamentary elections in Great Britain, making Thatcher the first woman prime minister in that nation's history. Having campaigned on a platform of income tax cuts, scaled-down social services, and a reduced role for government in British life, she begins a conservative revolution that profoundly reshapes politics in Great Britain.

1979 NOV 4 Iranian revolutionaries seize control of the U.S. Embassy in Tehran, taking hostage 66 embassy personnel. Fourteen are soon released, but the fundamentalists hold the remaining 52, demanding that the shah (undergoing medical treatment in New York) be returned to Iran in exchange for the hostages' release. When the U.S. refuses, the hostage crisis begins.

John Paul II

1976 The Sex Pistols' first single, "Anarchy in the U.K.," introduces the violent, nihilistic punk-rock style.

1977 John Travolta's performance in *Saturday Night Fever* begins a disco craze in the United States.

1977 ABC broadcasts a miniseries based on Alex Haley's *Roots.*

1978-79 Hollywood's release of three films about the Vietnam War—*The Deer Hunter, Coming Home* and *Apocalypse Now*— reflects a national reassessment.

1978 NOV 18 After murdering California congressman Leo Ryan and his party, the messianic leader of the People's Temple cult, the Reverend Jim Jones, orders his followers to commit mass suicide by drinking a cyanide punch at their agricultural commune in Jonestown, Guyana.

1977 APR 30 Two thousand protesters occupy the site of a proposed nuclear power plant in Seabrook, New Hampshire.

1978 Health organizations announce the eradication of smallpox, but four labs keep viral specimens on hand for research.

1978 JUL 25 Lesley Brown gives birth to the world's first "test tube" baby at London's Oldham Hospital.

1979 MAR 28 The Three Mile Island nuclear accident forces the evacuation of 144,000 people near Harrisburg.

1977 MAY 4 In the first of five paid TV interviews with David Frost, Richard Nixon admits that his Watergate cover-up "let the American people down."

1978 JUN 6 California voters approve Proposition 13. This ballot initiative cuts property taxes by 57%, precipitating service cuts and a state budget crisis.

1978 JUN 15 The Supreme Court halts the $100 million Tellico Dam, ruling that the snail darter (found on the site) is protected by the Endangered Species Act.

1975-1979

The Body Politic

1980 JAN 4 President Carter orders an embargo on wheat exports to the U.S.S.R. in response to the Soviet invasion of Afghanistan (DEC). On April 22, the U.S. Olympic Committee votes to boycott the 1980 Summer Olympics in Moscow.

1980 FEB 2 The FBI releases details of its Abscam investigation into political corruption, during which an agent posed as an Arab sheik offering bribes in exchange for political influence.

1980 MAR 24 A sniper assassinates the respected Salvadoran archbishop Oscar Arnulfo Romero as he celebrates mass. No group claims responsibility, but many suspect the right-wing death squads.

1980 APR 24 When diplomatic initiatives fail, President Carter orders a military rescue of the hostages being held in Iran. The president calls off the mission at a staging area, however, because of equipment failure. Eight soldiers are killed during the pull-out when a helicopter collides with a transport plane.

1980 AUG 30 After two months of labor demonstrations that have crippled the nation, the Polish government grants striking workers at the Lenin Shipyards in Gdansk the right to unionize. With ten million members, Solidarity (led by electrician Lech Walesa) becomes the first independent trade union in a Warsaw Pact country.

Arts & Architecture

1980 DEC 8 Mark David Chapman kills former Beatle John Lennon outside his New York City apartment building.

1981 The Museum of Modern Art donates *Guernica* to the Prado in Madrid in accordance with Picasso's instructions that it be returned to Spain once democracy was restored there.

1981 JUN 6 Twenty-one-year-old Yale undergraduate Maya Lin wins a national competition to design the Vietnam War Memorial in Washington, D.C.

Religion & Philosophy

1980 APR The pervasive influence of Jean-Paul Sartre's existentialist philosophy is demonstrated by the crowd of 25,000 mourners who attend his Paris funeral. During his lifetime, Sartre insisted that man was doomed to bear the burden and responsibility of free will.

1981 MAY 13 Mehmet Ali Agca, a Turkish national, severely wounds Pope John Paul II during an assassination attempt. Investigators soon implicate three agents of the Bulgarian secret police (later acquitted for lack of evidence). Their findings prompt suspi-

Science & Technology

1980 JUN 16 The Supreme Court rules that genetically engineered organisms created in a laboratory can be patented.

1982 DEC 2 Sixty-one-year-old Barney Clark receives the first permanent artificial heart during an operation performed by Dr. Robert Jarvik at the University of Utah Medical Center. The polyurethane device, known as the Jarvik-7, keeps Clark alive for 112 days.

1984 APR 23 Researchers at the National Institutes of Health announce they have

Daily Life

1980 MAY 18 The long-dormant volcano Mount St. Helens erupts for the first time since 1857.

1981 JUL 29 Prince Charles marries Lady Diana Spencer in a televised ceremony viewed by more than 700 million people.

1981 AUG 1 MTV begins broadcasting over America's cable TV systems, furthering the trend away from the networks toward narrowcasting.

1981 AUG 3 The nation's air traffic controllers walk out despite a federal law pro-

1981 JAN 20 Minutes after Ronald Reagan's inauguration, Iran releases the 52 American hostages after 444 days of captivity.

1981 FEB 18 In his State of the Union message, President Reagan calls for cutting $41 billion from the Carter budget. He also proposes a 10% income tax cut in each of the next three years, an increase of $5 billion in defense spending, and more liberal tax rules for businesses. Congress passes Reagan's plan on August 4 with only slight modifications.

1981 MAR 31 John W. Hinckley, Jr., shoots and nearly kills President Reagan in order to impress actress Jodie Foster.

1982 Jenny Holzer displays selections from her *Truisms* on the color video display board in New York's Times Square.

1982 DEC 8 The Image Scavengers show, dominated by women photographers, establishes postmodern photography.

cion that the assassination plot may have been linked to the pope's active support of Catholic resistance in Soviet Bloc countries. John Paul II has been especially vocal in his support for the independent trade union Solidarity in his native Poland.

identified the virus thought to cause AIDS, but a court later decides that the French Pasteur Institute team was first.

1984 JUN 4 A team at the University of California successfully clones the DNA of an extinct species of horse.

hibiting the strike. President Reagan announces that strikers who have not returned to work by August 5 will be fired.

1982 JAN 8 AT&T agrees to divest itself of the 22 "baby Bells," which provide local telephone service in the U.S.

1983 AUG 21 The assassination of Philippines opposition leader Benigno Aquino begins a series of events leading to the ouster of Ferdinand Marcos in favor of Aquino's wife Corazon (1986, FEB 25).

1983 SEP 1 A heat-seeking missile downs Korean Air Lines Flight 007, which has strayed over Soviet air space.

1983 OCT 23 An explosives-filled truck blows up the Marine barracks in Beirut.

1984 DEC 3 Lethal gas leaking from a Union Carbide plant in Bhopal, India, kills 2,000 and injures 200,000. India's Supreme Court orders Union Carbide to pay $470 million in damages (FEB 1989).

1983 MAR 2 *M*A*S*H* airs its final episode to an unprecedented television audience of 125 million people.

1983 Michael Jackson's *Thriller* album dominates the charts with multi-platinum sales in excess of 20 million.

1982 JUN 29 The New York-based United Presbyterian Church and the Atlanta-based Presbyterian Church agree to a merger, ending a division along north-south lines dating back to the Civil War. The unified church will have approximately three million members.

1984 DEC 22 Bernhard Goetz shoots four youths trying to rob him on the New York City subway, and then disappears. Goetz surrenders after public opinion rallies behind the anonymous subway vigilante. Eventually convicted of carrying an illegal weapon, Goetz serves eight months.

Lech Walesa

1980-1984

The Body Politic

1985 MAR 1 President Reagan responds to the peace overtures of Sandinista leader Daniel Ortega Saavedra by declaring the U.S.-supported Nicaraguan contras to be "the moral equal of our Founding Fathers." Ortega then compares Reagan to Hitler.

1985 SEPT 16 Following years of intensifying trade deficits, the Commerce Department announces that the United States has, for the first time since 1914, become a debtor nation.

1985 DEC 12 Reagan signs the Gramm-Rudman-Hollings Act, which mandates congressional spending limits designed to eliminate the federal deficit by 1991.

1986 APR 15 U.S. warplanes stationed in Britain fly to Libya, where they bomb Muammar Qadaffi's headquarters during an 11-minute raid on Tripoli. Reagan orders the assault in retaliation for the bombing of a West Berlin discotheque.

1986 NOV 3 An obscure Beirut magazine reveals that the United States has sent arms to Iran, hoping that unnamed "moderates" there will help obtain the release of American hostages in Lebanon.

1987 JAN 27 Mikhail Gorbachev declares the need for systematic reform in the Soviet Union. His specific policies (announced JUN 25) come to be grouped under the general term *perestroika*.

Arts & Architecture

1985 JUL 13 The Live Aid concert in Philadelphia, organized by Bob Geldof, raises $70 million for famine victims in Africa.

1986 Andrew Wyeth's estate reveals the existence of 240 never-before-seen paintings of Wyeth's neighbor Helga.

1987 Vincent van Gogh's *Irises* sells for $49 million at auction, the highest price ever paid for a work of art.

1987 Tom Wolfe's *Bonfire of the Vanities* captures the popular imagination with its portrayal of 1980s greed.

Religion & Philosophy

1986 AUG 29 Three Lutheran denominations merge to form the Evangelical Lutheran Church with an estimated five million members. Although the new church represents only two-thirds of American Lutherans, it nevertheless becomes the third largest sect in the country.

1987 MAR 19 Television evangelist Jim Bakker resigns from the PTL ministry he founded after admitting to an adulterous relationship with church secretary Jessica Hahn, who has allegedly been blackmailing him. During 1986, PTL paid Bakker $1.6 million in salary and bonuses.

Science & Technology

1985 SEP 1 A joint American-French expedition discovers the wreck of the fabled luxury liner *Titanic* (sunk 1912, APR 14-15) about 500 miles south of Newfoundland. The wreck's exact location is kept secret, however, to discourage salvage attempts.

1986 JAN 28 All seven astronauts aboard the space shuttle *Challenger* die as their orbiter explodes 73 seconds after liftoff. A presidential commission later determines the cause to be failure of a solid rocket booster seal caused by low temperatures prior to launch.

Daily Life

1985 APR Coca-Cola announces that its 99-year-old formula will be replaced by a sweeter Coke for younger tastes.

1986 NOV 14 Ivan Boesky, who pleads guilty to insider trading, deducts half of his $100 million fine from his taxes.

1986 Nintendo introduces its line of video games into the American market. Sales top $3.4 billion by 1990.

1987 OCT 19 Computerized trading leads to a 508-point plunge in the Dow Jones, an even sharper drop than the 1929 crash.

1989 FEB 14 Iran's Ayatollah Khomeini offers a $3 million reward for the murder of Salman Rushdie, whose 1988 novel *The Satanic Verses* infuriated Muslim readers with its alleged blasphemies.

1989 APR 15 Chinese students gather in Beijing's Tiananmen Square ostensibly to mourn Hu Yaobang's death, but actually to demand greater democracy. They remain in the square night and day until June 6, when soldiers sent by Deng Xiaoping fire into the crowd.

1989 AUG 9 President Bush signs the Financial Institutions Rescue, Recovery, and Enforcement Act to "bail out" the nation's savings-and-loan associations.

1989 AUG 18 A newly elected cabinet supported by Lech Walesa and Jozef Cardinal Glemp takes over the Polish government, but the Communists retain the interior and defense ministries.

1989 NOV 9 East German authorities begin permitting citizens to exit the country without visas. Thousands cross into once-forbidden West Berlin the same evening, as the Berlin Wall begins to fall.

1989 DEC 10 The Velvet Revolution installs a new cabinet in which the Communists are in the minority. The new Czech parliament elects playwright Vaclav Havel president of the country's new Western-style democracy (DEC 29).

Mikhail Gorbachev

1988 JUN 12 The Corcoran Gallery cancels an exhibition of photographs by Robert Mapplethorpe, some of which features homoerotic imagery. The cancellation begins a censorship controversy, which culminates in congressional legislation (sponsored by Senator Jesse Helms) that excludes from federal arts funding all works which might be considered obscene.

1989 MAR 30 I.M. Pei's glass-and-metal pyramid, a cause of much controversy during its construction, opens as the new entrance to the Louvre in Paris.

1988 FEB 21 Flamboyant television minister Jimmy Swaggart confesses on the air to "moral failure" after being accused of committing indecent acts with a prostitute. The Assemblies of God church defrocks Swaggart (APR 8) when he refuses to forbear preaching for one year.

1986 APR 26 An explosion at the Soviet Union's Chernobyl nuclear power plant near Kiev sends clouds of radioactive fallout across much of Europe. Both plant and rescue workers die in the effort to prevent a catastrophic core meltdown.

1987 SEP An international conference meeting in Montreal drafts a treaty calling for a freeze and then a reduction in chlorofluorocarbon production, because these refrigerants damage the ozone layer. The Senate unanimously ratifies the treaty on March 14, 1988.

1987 OCT 23 The Senate rejects, by a vote of 58-42, the Supreme Court nomination of ultraconservative Robert H. Bork.

1989 MAR A grand jury indicts junk bond guru Michael Milken on 98 counts of stock manipulation and securities fraud.

1989 MAR 24 The *Exxon Valdez* runs up on a reef, releasing 240,000 barrels of oil into Prince William Sound. Exxon fires the captain for drinking while on duty.

1989 OCT 17 An earthquake measuring 7.1 on the Richter scale hits San Francisco.

1985-1989

The Body Politic

1990 FEB 7 Ending a stormy three-day meeting, the Central Committee of the Soviet Communist party endorses President Gorbachev's proposal that the party ends its 72-year stranglehold on the state. Boris Yeltsin becomes president of the new Russian Republic in May and quits the Communist party in June.

1990 FEB 11 South African resistance leader Nelson Mandela leaves Victor Verster Prison after more than 27 years of political imprisonment. President F.W. de Klerk has asked Mandela to help negotiate a settlement of the apartheid issue.

1990 JUN 26 Conceding that spending cuts will not be enough to balance the projected $160-billion federal budget, President Bush sets aside his 1988 campaign pledge "Read my lips: no new taxes" and agrees to discuss "tax revenue" increases with Congress.

1990 AUG 2 Iraq invades Kuwait after Kuwait refuses demands by Iraqi leader Saddam Hussein that it cede disputed oil wells on the Kuwait-Iraqi border.

1990 OCT 3 The reunification of Germany ends 43 years of division between East and West. The move follows an agreement between the United States and the Soviet Union to reduce troop strength in Central Europe to 195,000 soldiers for each nation.

Arts & Architecture

1990 Vincent van Gogh's *Portrait of Dr. Gachet* sells for $82.5 million, eclipsing the record set by his *Irises* (1987).

1990 *Vineland* is reclusive author Thomas Pynchon's first novel since *Gravity's Rainbow* (1973).

1990 Perry Farrell masterminds the fabulously successful Lollapalooza tour, featuring his band Jane's Addiction and six other "alternative" acts.

1991 Madonna's cinema verité *Truth or Dare* documentary records her "Blond

Religion & Philosophy

1991 FEB 3 A Presbyterian Church task force studying sexuality in the modern age issues a report condoning monogamous relationships outside wedlock and recommending that the prohibition against ordaining homosexuals be overturned. Strenuous objections from the rank-and-file members of the church cause the report to be rejected.

1991 SEP 22 The Huntington Library announces its decision to make available its collection of photographs of the Dead Sea Scrolls. The scrolls' clique of editors,

Science & Technology

1990 DEC The Food and Drug Administration approves Norplant, a new contraceptive implant with a failure rate significantly lower than other methods.

1991 Geneticists discover that genes may behave differently depending on the parent from whom the gene is inherited. In other genetic experimentation, researchers determine the location of a gene that appears to cause diabetes.

1992 JAN A Centers for Disease Control report states that the immune systems of

Daily Life

1991 OCT The issue of sexual harassment makes headlines during the confirmation hearings of Supreme Court nominee Clarence Thomas. Law school professor Anita Hill testifies that, eight years earlier, Thomas (then her boss) made indecent remarks to her.

1991 NOV 7 Basketball superstar Earvin (Magic) Johnson announces that he has contracted the virus that causes AIDS.

1991 DEC 4 A California jury convicts Charles Keating, chairman of the failed Lincoln Savings and Loan, on 17 counts of

1990 NOV 17 As the Soviet economy collapses, Gorbachev asks for special powers, which he is granted. On December 20, Foreign Minister Eduard Shevardnadze resigns, warning against "reactionaries."

1990 NOV 22 Margaret Thatcher resigns as prime minister of Great Britain after she fails to win a decisive victory in the Conservative party leadership contest.

1991 JAN 17 Operation Desert Storm begins at 3 AM as bombers and missiles attack targets within Iraq. Congress has already voted (JAN 12) to permit war on Iraq if Saddam Hussein's forces remain in Kuwait after the UN deadline (JAN 15). A ground invasion, commanded by Norman

Schwarzkopf, begins February 24 and ends 100 hours later with Kuwait's liberation.

1991 AUG 19 Communist hardliners stage a coup in Moscow after detaining Gorbachev at his vacation home. The coup fails when tank commanders support Boris Yeltsin's call for a general strike in resistance to the takeover.

1992 FEB 20 Ross Perot announces on Larry King's CNN talk show that he will run for president if supporters place him on the ballot in all 50 states.

1993 APR 4 President Clinton promises Boris Yeltsin $1.6 billion in aid to Russia during a summit meeting in Vancouver.

Vaclav Havel

Ambition" tour and confirms her status as a postfeminist icon.

1991 When Nirvana's *Nevermind* album makes "grunge" the most fashionable style in the country, record companies quickly sign up other Seattle-based bands,

as grunge makes the transition from underground to mainstream.

1992 MAY 22 Fifty-five million people watch Johnny Carson's last night as host of NBC's *Tonight* show. He took over the program from Jack Paar in 1962.

---

who have guarded access to the 800 manuscripts (discovered 1947-1956), protests, insisting that the Huntington's negatives are stolen property. But other scholars applaud the decision, claiming that the editors have intentionally mistranslated the few published scrolls.

---

over 200,000 people have been severely affected by AIDS. In February, the World Health Organization reports that more than 10 million people worldwide have contracted HIV, the AIDS-causing virus. WHO estimates that by the year 2000, up to 40 million people will be infected.

1992 JUN 14 At a United Nations environmental conference in Rio de Janeiro (known as the Earth Summit), delegates from 178 countries sign the Rio Declaration and Agenda 21, which outline cleanup strategies and encourage environmentally sound economic development.

---

securities fraud. Five senators who helped Keating deter bank examiners in exchange for campaign contributions face hearings before the Ethics Committee.

1992 JAN 27 Burdened by the heavy debt taken on during $1.1 billion leveraged

buy-outs of I. Magnin and Bullock's, R.H. Macy & Co. files for bankruptcy.

1992 APR 29 After a mostly white jury in suburban Simi Valley acquits four police officers charged in the Rodney King case, Los Angeles erupts in widespread riots.

1990-1993

The page number appears at left, followed by the illustration description.

Index

Antoninus Pius, 21
Antonius, Marcus, 17
Antony, Mark, 17
Anuradhapura, Council of, 39
Anzio, landing at, 215
Ap Bac, battle of, 239
Apaches, 170
apartheid, 186, 254
Apocalypse, 71
Apocalypse Now, 249
Apollo 1, 230
Apollo 8, 230
Apollo 11, 230, 235
Apollo 13, 230
Apollonius of Perga, 13, 25
Apollo-Soyuz Test Project, 230
Apologia pro Vita Sua, 157
Appert, Nicolas, 142-143
Appius Claudius Caecus, 11
Appomattox Court House, 161-162
Apprentices Act, Health and Morals of, 144
April Days, 197
April Theses, 197
Apuleius, 21
al-Aqaba, Pledges of, 47
aqualung, 208-209
aqueducts, 11, 17
Aquinas, Thomas, 61
Aquino, Benigno, 251
Aquino, Corazon, 251
Arabian Nights, 52
Arafat, Yasir, 236
Arameans, 33-34
Arbuthnot, John, 110
Arc de Triomphe, 145
Arch of Constantine, 25
Archestratus, 11
Archimedes, 12, 25, 176
Ardashir, 22
Arena chapel, 62
Areopagitica, 91
Ariana, 88
Arianism, 24, 43
Ariosto, Ludovico, 81
Aristaeus, 11
Aristarchus, 12
Aristophanes, 7
Aristotle, 9-11
Arithmetica, 22
ark of the Covenant, 4, 32-33
Arkwright, Richard, 121
d'Arlandes, marquis, 124
Armies of the Night, 240
armillary ring, 16
Armory show, 187
Armstrong, Edwin, 206

Armstrong, Neil, 230, 235
Army of Northern Virginia, 157
Army-McCarthy hearings, 221
Arnauld, Antoine, 99
Arnold, Benedict, 123, 129
Arnold, Matthew, 163
Arrangement in Grey and Black, 164
Arras, League of, 86
Ars amatoria, 18
Ars magna, 83
Arsacid Dynasty, 22
art nouveau, 175
Art of love, 18
Artabanus IV, 22
Artaxerxes I, 35
Arthur, 42
Arthur, Chester Alan, 132
Articles of Confederation, 124-125, 130
Aryans, 28
Arybhata, 42
Asclepiades, 16
Ashmun, Jehudi, 148
Ashoka, 12, 37-38
Asita, 36
Aspern, battle of, 145
aspirin, 175
Assassins, 57
Assemblies of God, 253
assembly line, 187
Assyrian Empire, 3-5
Assyrians, 33-34
Aston, Francis William , 189
astrolabe, 53
Astronomia nova, 88-89
Astronomical tables, 59
astronomy, radio, 204
Aswan Dam, 222
Atahualpa, 83
Atatürk, Kemal, 192, 200
Ataulf, 26
Athenodorus, 17
Atisha, 56
Atlanta *Journal*, 246
Atlantic Charter, 212
Atlantis, 231
atom, 187
atomic bomb, 207, 217-218, 220-221
Atomic Energy Commission, 220
atomists, 7, 9
Attica prison riots, 237
Attila the Hun, 26-27
Audubon, James, 149
Audubon Ballroom, 227
Auerstedt, battle of, 145
Augsburg, Diet of, 78-79
Augsburg, League of, 105

Index

Beatles, 233-234
beatniks, 219, 223
Beaumarchais, Pierre-Augustin Caron de, 122-123
Beaumont, Gustave de, 151
Beauregard, P.G.T., 160
Beauvoir, Simone de, 219
bebop, 208
Beccaria, Cesare, 121
Becker, Johann Joachim, 107
Becket, Thomas a, 58-59
Beckett, Samuel, 221
Becquerel, Henri, 174
Bede, Venerable, 51
Beer Hall Putsch, 201, 204
Beethoven, Ludwig van, 144, 147
Beggar's Opera, 113
Begin, Menachem, 248
Behaim, Martin, 71
beheadings, 57, 68, 82
Being and Nothingness, 208-209
Being and Time, 203
Beirut, bombing of Marine barracks in, 251
Belisarius, 42-43
Bell, Alexander Graham, 166, 178
Bell, John, 159
Bell Laboratories, 219, 222
bellows, 18
Bemis Heights, battle of, 129
Benedek, Laslo, 220
Benedictine order, 43-44
Bentham, Jeremy, 125
Benz, Karl, 170
Beowulf, 50
Berbers, 50, 58
Bergen-Belsen, 218-219
Bergerac, Cyrano de, 99
Bergman, Ingmar, 223
Bergson, Henri, 171
Bering, Vitus, 113, 116
Bering Strait, 113
Berkeley, George, 110
Berkeley, John, 100
Berlin, Congress of, 167
Berlin, University of, 146
Berlin airlift, 219
Berlin Wall, 232, 253
Bernard of Clairvaux, 58
Bernard of Saxe-Weimar, 95
Berno, 54
Bernoulli, Daniel, 113
Bernstein, Carl, 244
Bernstein, Eduard, 175
Berquem, Louis de, 70
Berryman, Clifford, 183
Bertholent, Claude, 125
Bessemer, Henry, 154, 163

Best, Charles, 200
Bethlen, Gabor, 93
Bethmann Hollweg, Theobald von, 193
Beukelszoon, William, 62
Beyle, Marie-Henri, 150
Bhagavad Gita, 14, 30
Bhagavata-Purana, 31
bhakti, 31
Bhopal disaster, 251
Bibars, 61
Bible, 18, 35, 77, 100, 103, 127, 185
Bible, King James version, 89
Bible of 42 Lines, 68
Bibliotheca, 52-53
Bibliothèque Ste.-Geneviève, 152
bicycle, 123
Bien Hoa, attacks on, 238-239
big bang theory, 203, 219
Bikini Atoll, 218
bikinis, 218
Bill of Rights, 130
Billboard, 222
Billy the Kid, 168
Biograph Theater, 205
biography, 142
Biologie, 144
biology, molecular, 221
Birds, 7
Birds of America, 149
Birdseye, Clarence, 202
bireme, 4
Birmingham, Alabama, bombings, 226
Birmingham, civil rights demonstrations in, 225-226
Biro, Lazlo, 207
birth control, 188, 254
Birth of a Nation, 188
Birth of Cool, 219
Birth of Tragedy, 165
Birth of Venus, 70
Bismarck, Otto von, 156-157, 164, 169-171
Bizet, George, 166
Black, Hugo, 225
Black Death, 63
Black Hills, 165
Black Hole of Calcutta, 119
Black September, 236-237
Black Shirts, 200
Black Sox scandal, 189
Black Tuesday, 203
Blackboard Jungle, 222
blacklists, 219
blackout, New York City, 234
Blackstone, William, 121
Blaiberg, Philip, 234
Blake, William, 125
Blanchard, Jean-Pierre, 142

Index

ABOUT THE AUTHOR

David Rubel is the president of
Agincourt Press, a book producer
in New York City. He specializes in
reference and children's books.
Works that he has written include
*The Scholastic Encyclopedia of the
Presidents and Their Times* (Scholastic,
1994), *How to Drive an Indy Race Car*
(John Muir, 1992), *Elvis Presley*
(Millbrook, 1991), and *Fannie Lou
Hamer* (Silver Burdett, 1990), which
was named one of the Best Books for
the Teen Age by the New York Public
Library.

ABOUT THE DESIGNER

Tilman Reitzle is the art director of
Agincourt Press. His book designs
include *America's War of Independence*
(Agincourt /Silver Moon, 1993),
the Isaac Asimov short stories *Robbie,
Sallie, Franchise,* and *All The Troubles
of The World* (Creative Education,
1989), as well as covers for *In My Taxi,
View:Parade Of The Avant Garde,* and
The Leroi Jones/Amiri Baraka Reader
(all Thunder's Mouth Press, 1992).
He lives in Hoboken, New Jersey.